The Prince of the City

The Prince of the City

Giuliani, New York and the
Genius of American Life

Fred Siegel

with Harry Siegel

ENCOUNTER BOOKS
SAN FRANCISCO

First edition published in 2005 by Encounter Books, an activity of Encounter for Culture and Education, Inc., a nonprofit, tax exempt corporation.

Encounter Books website address: www.encounterbooks.com
Manufactured in the United States and printed on acid-free paper.

The paper used in this publication meets the minimum requirements of ANSI/NISO Z39.48-1992 (R 1997)(*Permanence of Paper*).

FIRST EDITION

Library of Congress Cataloging-in-Publication Data

Siegel, Frederick F., 1945–
    The prince of the city : Giuliani, New York, and the genius of American life / Fred Siegel.
        p.   cm.
    ISBN 1-59403-084-7 (alk. paper)
    1. Giuliani, Rudolph W.   2. Mayors—New York (State)—New York—Biography.   3. Political culture—New York (State)—New York—History.   4. New York (N.Y.)—Politics and government—1951–
5. New York (N.Y.)—Biography.   I. Title.
F128.57.G58 S56 2005
974.7'1043'092—B22

                                                            2005040127

10 9 8 7 6 5 4 3 2 1

This book is dedicated to the memory of my brother Michael Siegel, a bounty hunter who never needed to draw his gun, and my wonderful friend, historian Jim Chapin who spread knowledge with the joy of an intellectual Johnny Appleseed.

Contents

Preface   ix

Part I ▲ New York before Giuliani

  1 Mayors and Mores in the Ungovernable City   1

  2 David Dinkins' Vision   15

  3 Failure and Ferment   35

  4 Rethinking   57

  5 Rematch   67

  6 The Changing of the Guard   85

Part II ▲ Giuliani Takes Charge

  7 Breaking the Mold   99

  8 The Democratic Rudy?   129

  9 Smart Policing   141

  10 Work Is the Best Social Policy   151

  11 Shakedown City   165

  12 Rudy on the Ropes   179

  13 Racial Racketeering   195

  14 The Mayoral Election: Ruth vs. Rudy   201

Part III ▲ The Second Term

  15 Lame Duck Term   215

  16 Impeach Rudy!   231

  17 CUNY and the Genius of American Life   241

  18 The Grand Guignol   249

  19 Rehearsal for Terror   257

  20 The Best of Times / The Worst of Times   265

  21 Bernard Kerik and Jason Turner: 279
       Round Two of Crime and Welfare Reform

  22 Running after Rudy—Part I   291

Part IV ▲ 9/11 and After

23 Terror from the Skies   301
24 Running after Rudy—Part II   309
25 City Hall after Rudy / Rudy after City Hall   323
Appendix: A Short History of Terror Attacks on New York   333
        (Real and Seriously Imagined)
Acknowledgments   341
Interview List   343
Notes   345
Index   369

Preface

This is a political drama that takes place on the stage of a once-great city. It's about the rivalry between those who hoped to restore the legendary Gotham to its former glory and those who lived well off its decline.

The leading characters are the Prince—Rudy Giuliani—and his small band of loyal followers on the one hand and a shifting cast of characters representing entrenched institutions on the other.

As in any good drama, some of the players switch sides at times. And unexpected twists and turns reveal the flaws of the pro-tagonist as well as those of his enemies.

It is sometimes said that history can be philosophy teaching by example. New York in the 1990s was one of those times. It was a period when dramatic differences in worldview were given the oppor-tunity to fight it out on the stage of America's most theatrical city.

Most Americans best know Rudy Giuliani from 9/11. The image of an undaunted mayor walking the streets of lower Manhattan comforting and inspiring his fellow citizens as the debris rained down around him has been stamped into the public consciousness. Yet his heroism that day doesn't even begin to describe his true accomplishments.

Giuliani first saved the city from its own, apparently intractable, political pathologies well before he saved the city and country from the panic that could have followed the 9/11 attacks. Time and again, from reducing crime and welfare, to driving the mob out of the garbage industry and reforming the City University, he achieved what the conventional wisdom had assumed was impossible. The third and by far the least known of his extraordinary accomplishments was to revive the idea of upward mobility for the poor in a city whose econ-omy had been organized around servicing poverty.

Rudy Giuliani, the immoderate centrist, is a contradictory

character who, like the city he came to embody to the nation, evokes clashing emotions. He is a self-promoting, self-absorbed man who made his own enormous ego serve the city's well-being. He ran his government with a Kennedy-like band-of-brothers assumption that those outside his circle couldn't be trusted. But he placed this tribal ethos in the service of universal ideals that transcended the traditional parochialism of New York's ethnic politics. He was the traditionalist who promoted the virtues of service, duty and hard work so evident on 9/11, though he was sometimes unable to honor those values in his personal life.

After 9/11, there were media attempts to discover a new, kinder, gentler Rudy. Such efforts missed the point. It was precisely his intransigent hostility to the city's reigning political pieties that made him so effective. It was his early determination to prepare for a terrorist attack, that, despite the mocking of his critics, served the city so well. You couldn't pick and choose from among his virtues and vices. You had to take him whole. For many, in the words of my father, Al Siegel, "Rudy was a beloved son-of-a bitch."

Giuliani's critics rightly saw him as a battering ram of a mayor. But they were so angered by the way he mocked the mores of New York's encrusted liberalism that they rarely grasped the depth and subtlety of his intelligence. His sometimes brilliant and often tactical use of his temper obscured the enormous preparation and planning that went into his policy reforms. Giuliani, who studied the city charter with the intensity and focus of Napoleon assaying battlefield topography, was almost always better informed and better prepared than the defenders of the old order.

With few exceptions, his critics never grasped the complexity of a man who could both hector his in-town adversaries and then speak to out-of-towners with grace and Clintonian eloquence. They couldn't see the man who spent a day talking intensely and sensitively with the individual residents of the Third Street Men's Shelter on the Bowery (a few blocks from my office at The Cooper Union).

Like Churchill, Giuliani's arrogance and sense of mission freed him from a narrow identification with a party. His tactical flexibility in pursuit of fixed ends kept his opponents off balance and served the city well. "It always appeared to me," noted Giuliani, "that the City of New York traditionally did better when the Mayor was somewhat unpredictable, when the Mayor was not a complete captive of one political party or the other.... To be locked into partisan politics doesn't permit you to think clearly."

▲ ▲ ▲

New Yorkers have long seen their city as a cosmopolitan dynamo in which the only constant is change. Philip Hone, the great pre-Civil War New York diarist and merchant, struck what would become a common chord in writing about New York when he complained that the local ethos was "overturn, overturn, overturn." Henry James picked up the same lament fifty years later when he wrote that New York is "crowned not only with no history, but with no credible possibility of time for history." New York is, always has been, and always will be a provisional city defined by what James termed a "dreadful chill of change." The famed 1940s journalist A.J. Liebling described the city as "renewing itself until the past is perennially forgotten."

The great exception to New York's dynamism is politics and government. There its deep-dyed ideological liberalism made it the most traditional of cities. Firmly anchored in the La Guardia years of the 1930s, which exert an almost mystical pull on the local imagination, New York turned the temporary emergency of the Great Depression into the permanent basis of its politics and government.

New York, notes urbanist Otis White, "was one of the last cities to give up elevator operators and trust people to push their own buttons." It was one of the last cities to adopt automated teller machines, and for more than thirty years it resisted automating entry to its subways. It is the only major city that still has in place the emergency housing regulations, known as rent control, passed during World War II. Gotham is still, as new arrivals quickly discover, the only major city that hasn't adopted multiple listings for real estate. The common thread is that in each case organized interests blocked innovation.

In 1961 Nathan Glazer, writing in *Commentary*, asked, "Is New York City Ungovernable?" That same question endured for the next thirty-five years. Glazer noted that since World War II the number of students in the city schools had declined by 7 percent while staff had grown by 22 percent, a pattern that repeated itself across city agencies. Rising government employment translated into declining city services, in part because the answer to all problems seemed to be to spend more money in the manner it had been spent since La Guardia.

The newly powerful reform Democratic clubs of the 1950s blamed these problems on a nearly moribund Tammany Hall. Glazer would have none of this. The problem, he argued, was that La Guardia's "rules and regulations—ironically set up in the first place to create a merit system to protect [the city and its] employees from unfair treatment and political manipulation—had taken on a life of their own and become the major obstacle in improving city services." In a union-driven social democratic city of civil servants, nonaccountability was built into the system. "Anything," Glazer explained, "which affects, even in the slightest, the interests and prerogatives of the employees runs into fantastic resistance, for the first aim of the rules and regulations is to defend the city employee against outsiders."

La Guardia's local version of FDR's New Deal generated an extraordinary array of organized interests, many of them offshoots of the city's vast public sector. Over time, New York developed a form of workers' control in which the public-sector unions effectively ran the schools, the subways, sanitation, and so forth largely on their own terms. In the Lindsay years, during the 1960s, advocates for various victim groups used the courts for similar purposes, so that over time mayors were hemmed in by an extraordinary array of political and legal constraints.

Glazer wrote before racial negotiations were imposed as an added layer of politicization on top of union and interest group collective bargaining. Faced with the pressing need to incorporate newcomers from the South into the life of the city, the Lindsay years in New York inspired, according to the late Daniel Patrick Moynihan, a new racialized political culture. Apocalyptic in tone, this culture "rewarded the articulation of moral purpose more than the achievement of practical good."

Befitting a city that was famously described in the 1930s as the only part of the Soviet Union where open debate was possible, attempts by interest groups to enhance their position were burnished with the magniloquence of great causes and world-historical struggles. The rhetoric of politics as a ceaseless "struggle" expressed itself in the belief, as one union official put it, that "our food bills are not a solely economic but also a political matter" subject to militant action. Everything from rents to admissions at the City University was seen as a matter of social or racial struggle. But there was a mock heroic quality to this rhetoric in which the city government was turned into the equivalent of a sweat shop boss and liberal administrators looking to expand opportunities for blacks were denounced as though they were Southern sheriffs.

Thirty years after Glazer asked the question, one of the city's best journalists, Sam Roberts of the *New York Times*, looked at the numerous problems faced by Mayor David Dinkins, Giuliani's predecessor at City Hall. Surveying all the constrictions on Dinkins' power to govern, Roberts' article, entitled "Given New York Today, Could Anyone Lead It?," asked: "Could anybody—anybody endowed with the ambition or illusions to want the job, that is—do any better?" Roberts' answer was that New York's troubles were basically institutional. Any mayor, he asserted, not just Dinkins, would be the captive of similar circumstances. It was taken as reasonable at the time to assume that New York was simply ungovernable. There were, notes urbanist Tony Proscio, who had worked for liberal Governor Mario Cuomo, a "long list of things from crime to transportation that we were told we couldn't do anything about."

Great as it was, Gotham was said to be the victim of vast structural changes in the organization of the national economy and society for which mayors could not be held responsible. New York was said to be unavoidably dependent on the generosity of Washington just as welfare clients had no choice but to depend on the beneficence of the city. Crime was similarly seen as an expression of the failure of American society to care enough to fully fund New York's social programs.

If Gotham was a victim of circumstances beyond its control, it wasn't fair to blame Dinkins for the city's failings. The widely accepted assumption of ungovernability meant mayors were largely unaccountable. And if the city was ungovernable through no fault of its own, there was no reason to challenge the suppositions behind New York's self-evidently virtuous political culture of compassionate liberalism. New York's problem, it seemed, was that it was too good, too compassionate for the rest of America, and the city could only hope that some day the rest of country would rise to its moral level.

The gap between the utopian rhetoric of New York politics and the dystopian reality of city life gave sway to a gestural radicalism exemplified by Al Sharpton. The Reverend carries on the tradition of militant protest though even his supporters and apologists have trouble pointing to anything specific he's accomplished. Sharpton "fights the power" and that alone is enough for traditional Democrats to enroll him on the side of the political angels.

The lawyer Ed Costikyan, one of the wise men of New York politics, summed up the situation when he said that "leadership was something that was seen as out of date, and probably in bad taste; you just had to accept things the way they were." By January 1992, midway through Dinkins' term, the city was overwhelmed by crime and job losses. The situation was so grim that even two-thirds of Dinkins' supporters, according to a *New York Times*/WCBS-TV news poll, thought that the city would get worse over the long term. Few assumed that, in Daniel Patrick Moynihan's formulation, "politics can change a culture and save it from itself."

▲ ▲ ▲

The title of this book—*The Prince of the City*—is meant as more than metaphor. The prince it refers to is the eponymous hero of Niccolò Machiavelli's classic book *The Prince*, published in Italy during the Renaissance. Machiavelli wrote it because he was tormented by the plight of his beloved Florence. Disdained by the papacy and the leaders of Italy's other city-states, Florence, he argued, could not be redeemed by a leader employing Christian means because "a man who wants to act virtuously in every way necessarily comes to grief among so many who are not virtuous." For such insights, Machiavelli was denounced by the religious establishment, which saw him as a devil of sorts. But the Founding Fathers of the American Republic found his realism bracing.

A good way to understand New York's recent rebirth is to think of Rudy Giuliani as a Renaissance Prince who revived his republic with more than a touch of Machiavelli's "corrupt wisdom." This is not merely a matter of Giuliani's characteristically Florentine looks, though his rectangular head and features seem as though they had been copied from a tapestry.

In *The Prince* Machiavelli sets out to resuscitate Florence, which had been laid low by feckless leadership, a cowed populace, and a military made up of mercenaries who—like the NYPD under Mayor Dinkins—were unwilling to act in the defense of the city's interests. For his solution, Machiavelli turned to the forgotten virtues of the classical world: discipline, courage, and fortitude in adversity. Giuliani was New York's Prince. He recalled the city to an older set of virtues-work, enterprise, individual obligation, and self-discipline-that had been lost since the 1960s mayoralty of John Lindsay. Even Giuliani's favorite aphorism, "I'd rather be respected than loved," is a play on Machiavelli's "It is better to be feared than loved."

Before Giuliani, New York politics had been mostly about striking caring poses in the course of paying off interest groups. Liberal mayors like Lindsay and Dinkins spoke endlessly of what the city owed the poor, but they delivered rising rates of crime and welfare. Theirs was the sovereignty of words over deeds. Dinkins carried himself with enormous dignity, but he was like the ruler, described by Machiavelli, who "never preaches anything except peace and good faith; and he is an enemy of both." While Dinkins dedicated his days to projecting his nobility at ceremonial events, the city was losing 330,000 jobs, and 60 percent of the population was looking to leave.

Crime didn't rise much in the Dinkins years, it just stayed unbearably high. It was accompanied by a pervasive sense of menace and decay. The late Lars-Erik Nelson, a *Daily News* columnist, explained that "when you take your children to a public playground and find that a mental patient has been using the sandbox as a toilet, it is normal to say, 'Enough! I'm leaving.'" When Marcia Kramer, a TV reporter, confronted Dinkins with the fact that aggressive panhandlers had driven her to the suburbs, Dinkins' response was, "Sorry you left us. Sorrier still that we can't raise your personal income tax."

Giuliani was never much of a politician. Defeated in his first run for the mayoralty, he took office in 1994 only because of emergency conditions like those that had faced Machiavelli's Florence. Like Machiavelli, he recognized that in public life virtues like generosity can turn into vices, while vices like anger and ambition can be used for virtuous ends. He told a hostile crowd demonstrating for pork barrel jobs that "the usual yelling and screaming...isn't going to stop me." Giuliani's words conformed to Machiavelli's advice that "above all a prince should live with his subjects in such a way that no development, either favorable or unfavorable, makes him vary his conduct."

As mayor, Giuliani was repeatedly and almost ritualistically accused of being hostile to minorities and indifferent to the poor. But he treated a murder in Harlem every bit as seriously as a murder on Fifth Avenue. Other mayors avoided racial animosity by looking the other way at inner-city crime. Giuliani did not. He was determined to restore hope to the inner city.

Giuliani's aim in trying to transform the political culture of the city was to make New York "more like the rest of America." He

self-consciously replaced Lindsay's and Dinkins' rhetoric of compassion, generosity and multi-culturalism—which in practice
translated into more social service jobs, higher taxes and ethnic
strife—with talk of work, self-sufficiency and a shared Americanism.
Giuliani spoke in the middle-class language of what the poor owe
to the rest of society, because, like other successful reformer mayors
such as Chicago's Richard Daley, he knew that if the cities were to
revive then they had to nurture and support the middle classes and
those who aspired to be middle class. Like Machiavelli, Giuliani
believed that "one judges by results." By that standard he was a
great success. He helped deliver more peaceful neighborhoods and a
rising quality of life to a wide range of New Yorkers.

The former union leader Victor Gotbaum, a Dinkins ally,
denounced those who were "enamored of middle-class, two-parent
families with children who don't have sex" because "middle-class
values" were "contrary to the environment and lives of [New York's]
students." The change under Giuliani was best encapsulated by a
large billboard along the Brooklyn-Queens Expressway. It read in
giant letters: "Citi: The Bank for the Upwardly Normal."

Under Giuliani, the ideal of upward mobility that Gotbaum
rejected once again became the defining credo of a city whose policies and politics had been based on the assumption that the
pathological was routine. A city that since La Guardia had been
organized around the presumption that the poor were caught in a
permanent Great Depression, so that the best we could do was to
make poverty comfortable, returned to the ideal of giving people a
chance to make better lives for themselves. As Giuliani himself said,
for many years "we blocked the genius of America for the poorest
people in New York." "I wanted," he explained, "poor people to
have the same kind of chance at a decent life my parents and grandparents had, I wanted them to have the same ladder of opportunity."

Giuliani's operatic personality obscured both his accomplishments and the limitations of what he achieved. I've written this book
largely to dispel the many misunderstandings about both his mayoralty and, given the likelihood that he will play a role in national
politics for some years to come, about his political personality as
well.

His critics have repeatedly said that whether it was on crime
and welfare or on 9/11 he wasn't so much good as lucky. This is
surely wrong. His success is reducing crime and welfare began while

the city was mired in one of its prolonged recessions. As for 9/11, he had been talking and thinking about the problem of terrorism— something about which most New Yorkers were oblivious—from literally his first day in office. The city's largely successful response to 9/11 was the product of years of preparation.

Some of his admirers, however, speak as if he did it all alone. He didn't. He had essential allies in City Council Speaker Peter Vallone and at times President Clinton and Governor Pataki. Critics and admirers alike sometimes spoke of how Giuliani defeated the interest-group liberalism that gnawed at the city's civic foundations. He didn't. He set one group of interests against another to buy time and some major reforms. But the power of the interest groups remains largely intact and so do the city's ongoing budget difficulties. No single mayor, not even an executive of Giuliani's abilities, can fully overcome an entrenched political tradition.

▲ ▲ ▲

I come to this story both as an historian and, at times, as a participant with first-hand knowledge. Giuliani declined to be interviewed for this book until it was already at the publisher when he called and offered to have a talk. But many members of the Dinkins and Giuliani administrations were generous with their time. Written a decade after Giuliani first came to office, this is the first book to draw on the Giuliani papers, which are not yet fully deposited at the Municipal Archives, as well as interviews with many of the major players in the story being told. (A list of interviewees can be found in the Notes and Acknowledgments.) When quotations are not footnoted, they are drawn either from these interviews or from occasions when the author was present. Some sections draw on transcripts of city council hearings. The public speeches referred to are available at the Municipal Archives or online.

PART I

New York before Giuliani

ONE

Mayors and Mores in the Ungovernable City

New York has a tradition of larger-than-life mayors who've become characters to conjure with in the national political imagination. Governing a center of money, media, and social movements gives Gotham's chief executives a disproportionate role in defining the country's assumptions about big cities.

The modern era in New York politics is usually associated with such theatrical figures as the dapper songwriter and Broadway Boulevardier, "Gentleman" Jimmy Walker, who symbolized the Jazz Age of the 1920s until he was driven from office by a corruption scandal. Subsequent mayors included the five-foot-two-inch titan Fiorello La Guardia, "the little Franklin Roosevelt," a raging reformer who could campaign (and curse) in five languages. Later there was 1960s matinee idol John Lindsay who made liberal hearts go atwitter even as his local version of the Great Society sent the city onto greased skids. In the 1980s there was Ed Koch, a Borscht-belt comedian who rescued the city from bankruptcy while playing the role of mayor. And of course there's America's mayor, 9/11 hero Rudy Giuliani, who saved the city from crime by playing the role of a Republican playing a Democrat playing a Republican.

▲ ▲ ▲

As a state senator in the 1920s, Jimmy Walker's approach to the city's tensions was to bring people together by legalizing Sunday baseball, boxing and movies. Walker, put in office by Tammany Hall, the city's legendary Irish Catholic political machine, would have liked to legalize Sunday drinking too, but in the Prohibition era it

1

was outlawed for the entire week. As mayor, Walker rarely allowed his job to interfere with his social life. He paid his personal bills with contributions from people who did business with the city and he paid the city's bills by borrowing. By 1932, explains historian Martin Shefter, "one-third of the entire city budget was devoted to debt service" and its total debt, conveniently financed by Wall Street just a few blocks from City Hall, "nearly equaled that of all the 48 states combined."[1]

The city, which had to borrow from the banks to meet its payroll, had been reduced to a ward of financier J.P. Morgan. When Walker and his gorgeous mistress left for Europe, walking away from the bribery and shakedown scandals he'd help create, his temporary successor as mayor was John P. O'Brien, a loyal Tammany guy. Asked who his police commissioner would be, O'Brien famously replied, "I don't know, they haven't told me yet."[2]

With the city suffering from a 25 percent unemployment rate, Fiorello La Guardia, who despised the bosses of both Tammany and big business, came in to clean up the mess. Elected in 1933 as a fusion candidate backed by both the Republicans and anti-Tammany reformers, he won with only 40 percent of the vote in a nasty three-way race by somewhat unfairly accusing an opponent of being an anti-Semite. "In exploiting racial and ethnic prejudice," wrote Robert Moses, "La Guardia could run circles around the bosses he despised and derided. When it came to raking ashes of Old World hates, warming ancient grudges, waving the bloody shirt, turning the ear to ancestral voices, he could easily out-demagogue the demagogues."

La Guardia, a tough campaigner who bragged, "I invented the low blow," carried the day with an unlikely coalition of Italian plebeians, WASP patricians and Jewish socialists. In the patronage-driven government he inherited, the surgeons hired for city hospitals by Tammany Hall had to be tipped if you expected them to operate.[3]

La Guardia was revered by left-wing New Dealers. They saw him as moving New York toward European style social democracy, if not outright socialism. But La Guardia was more paternalist than socialist. Tammany Hall served as a just-off-the-boat employment agency for new arrivals. La Guardia saw himself as a benign padrone who would similarly look after a population just a half-generation removed from peasantry by providing the same services honestly and efficiently.

In 1935 he issued an emergency proclamation temporarily banning the sale of baby artichokes in the city's public markets. The target was the Harlem racketeers shaking down grocers "who purchased, under force, this delicacy especially valued by the Italian community." Accompanied by bugle-blowing police officers, La Guardia shouted out the proclamation from a flatbed truck outside a wholesale market in the Bronx. "I want it clearly understood," La Guardia said in his ringing falsetto, "that no bunch of racketeers, thugs, and punks is going to intimidate you as long as I am mayor of the city of New York."[4]

In the early 1940s, while the U.S. and USSR were allies of convenience in the war against Hitler, a trade delegation from the Soviet Union dressed in its diplomatic finery came to visit La Guardia. La Guardia, the man of the people, looked at the Soviet diplomats and then at his own baggy paints and frayed shirt: "Gentleman," he said, "I represent the proletariat."[5]

He was beloved, explained Supreme Court Justice Felix Frankfurter, because he "translated the complicated conduct of the City's vast government into warm significance for every man, woman and child." But by transferring patron/client relationships from the immigrant neighborhoods to City Hall, La Guardia turned New York into an administered city of clients rather than citizens.[6]

In the short term, La Guardia screamed and bullied his way to better government. La Guardia, said New Dealer Rexford Tugwell, treated his own staff like "dogs." In one famed incident he called in a stenographer in order to humiliate a commissioner who was present. He shouted at her, "If you were any dumber, I'd make you a commissioner." La Guardia who rarely took a vacation, employed the technique of his hero, former New York City Police Commissioner Theodore Roosevelt, popping in to city offices unannounced to catch people goofing off. A mayor who gave a "prize" he called the "Order of the Shankbone" to the official who had made the biggest mistake since he last met with them was not to be trifled with. "It would be almost but not quite fair," wrote Tugwell, "to say that he was an instinctive dictator."[7]

La Guardia paid off the banks, promoted honest and efficient government by expanding civil service appointments and allied himself with Franklin Roosevelt, making New York into "the New Deal City." La Guardia, writes historian Thomas Kessner, became a master at milking money from the federal government. He was in Washington twice a week where he enjoyed extraordinary access to the president. Half joking, FDR said of La Guardia, "Our Mayor is probably the most appealing person I know. He comes to Washington and tells me a sad story. The tears run down my cheeks and the first thing I know, he has wangled another $50 million."[8]

La Guardia made good use of the money. He hated lawyers, calling them the "semi-colon boys." He loved architects and engineers who, with the help of federal grants, built the East River (now FDR) Drive, the Triboro Bridge, the Lincoln Tunnel, and the Queens Midtown Tunnel during his tenure as mayor. But not even the vast flow of federal money could keep up with the city's spending. La Guardia added an array of new taxes and his comptroller, who dismissed deficits as "entirely a bookkeeping transaction," adopted the old Tammany policy of rolling one year's expenses over into the next year's budget.[9]

The mayor didn't help matters with his relentless hostility to business. He pledged to make New York a "100 per cent union city," and when businesses threatened to leave, he threatened to blacklist them. "The forces of organized money," he argued, "are unanimous in their hate for me." When a 1944 report spoke of "the alarming flight of industry to younger cities," creating "ghost neighborhoods," he responded with plans for even more public works. Without massive city spending to absorb the returning veterans, he feared that, as in the worst days of 1930s, labor violence "hell will break loose."[10]

The glory years were indelible but brief. By the late 1930s, not even La Guardia's special relationship with FDR could keep the city on an even keel fiscally. When he came into office La Guardia used federal money to pay off the city's debts to J.P. Morgan and other banks. By the end of his three terms, the city was once again in hock to the bankers. New York, explained the Citizens Budget Commission, "faces a crisis in its fiscal affairs" because spending independent of relief was growing three times faster and debt five and a half times faster than the population. The mayor's ally, Comptroller Joseph McGoldrick, adopted the Tammany practice that La Guardia had once denounced of financing current expenditures with debt imposed on future generations. World War II temporarily rescued the city from its fiscal fate and the return of machine politics in the 1950s temporarily slowed the rate of increase of city spending, but except for boom times New York would never again be able to afford its government.[11]

La Guardia kept the budget in tenuous balance in part through substantial tax hikes. Levies such as the rent occupancy tax and the sales tax passed as 1930s emergency measures became permanent. The mayor added a utilities tax and raised the property tax to record levels. "High taxes and declining terminals and docks," writes Kessner, "were helping to drive the garment and printing industries out of the city." But when the New York Board of Trade told the mayor about the exodus he attacked them as "cowardly and despicable" for spreading "cheap propaganda" and a "deliberate lie."[12]

While Tammany's patronage hires could be fired, the vast civil service La Guardia created was expensive, untouchable and, after La Guardia left office, unaccountable. Every subsequent mayor would have to figure out how to work his way around them. Surveying the city's finances in 1944, Tugwell warned presciently that La Guardia's policies in buying off class strife had "made municipal bankruptcy inevitable."[13]

The passing glory of the Fiorello and Franklin friendship fueled an illusion that lives to this very day. Rudolph Giuliani notwithstanding, La Guardia remains in both persona and policy the standard against which all mayors are judged. The Tammany profligacy preceding La Guardia forced the city to beg the bankers for aid. The machine's excesses could be, as La Guardia showed, quickly cut by efficient administration. But while the Tammany hacks he displaced could be fired, the civil servants he put in their place were headless nails. Protected by civil service rules, they were insulated from the consequences of their own actions, let alone the actions of a future mayor trying to call them to account. "The Little Flower" left the city with uncontrollable costs. His heirs would end up begging both the bankers and the federal government for aid even as they taxed their own constituents to the hilt in order to support La Guardia's "reforms."

By the war's end, Tammany, despite the protests of some Catholics like former presidential candidate Al Smith, who had grown increasingly conservative, embraced the New Deal wholeheartedly. It regained City Hall by choosing the charming World War II veteran William O'Dwyer as its candidate. The eleventh consecutive Irishman to receive Tammany's nod for mayor, O'Dwyer led the city through a wave of post-war strikes at a time when both left-wing politics and mob influence were at their peak. Like the New Dealers who were both loyal Americans and sympathetic to the

Soviet Union, O'Dwyer was a good leftist supporter of civil rights and deeply entangled with the mob. And often there was little contradiction between the two.

In his classic essay "Crime as an American Way of Life," Daniel Bell notes that one reason that urban machines could take left-wing stances is that they sometimes allowed the mob to finance their campaigns rather than becoming beholden to "moneyed interests." Both the mobs and the unions took advantage of New York's geography. A fast-moving but congested city built on an island of narrow streets and tall buildings, each of Gotham's innumerable bottlenecks presented an opportunity for the unions to apply economic pressure and for the mob to engage in shakedowns. At the time it seemed not to matter all that much. New York with one million people employed in industry was the greatest manufacturing city in the world. The city barely shrugged when O'Dwyer's connections with Albert Anastasia of Murder Inc. forced him from office in 1951. Like Walker, O'Dwyer went off into political exile with a beautiful young actress on his arm.

Unfazed by O'Dwyer's disgrace, the city accepted mob-tainted Tammany's Robert Wagner, Jr., the cautious son of the New Deal senator famed for his pro-labor legislation. Wagner, who went on to serve three terms from 1953 to 1965, was as upright as O'Dwyer was crooked, but their New Deal liberalism was largely indistinguishable. Both men built hundreds of new schools, playgrounds, public housing projects and hospitals. The 1950s were the heyday of working-class politics. The achievements were impressive. New York pioneered the development of co-operative housing, group health coverage, and pre-paid medical plans. But the city also took the lead in policies that would prove problematic.

In most of the U.S. rent-control laws were a temporary response to World War II. In New York rent control became permanent and consequently so did the city's housing shortages. Tenant politics in New York, the big city with the lowest homeownership rate, became the new class struggle. In Gotham, candidates accused their opponents of being soft on landlords or weak on rent control with the same fervor and intelligence that accompanied accusations of Communism elsewhere.

La Guardia had tried to draw a sharp distinction between public- and private-sector workers, explaining that "I do not want any of the pinochle club atmosphere to take hold among city workers."

www.encounterbooks.com

Please add me to your mailing list.

Name

Company

Address

City, State, Zip

E-mail

Book Title

ENCOUNTER BOOKS
665 Third Street
Suite 330
San Francisco, CA 94107-1951

But it was an untenable distinction. In 1958 Wagner brought labor struggles into the halls of city government when he signed what was known as "the little Wagner act," which made New York the first city to give its municipal workers the right to unionize. The rise of public-sector workers as a political force entailed the decline of parties. City workers had been Tammany's key constituency; after Wagner they would become a powerful force in their own right. But where Tammany was always forced to consider a wide range of interests, public-sector unions were relentless advocates for their own narrow advantage.[14]

Between a unionized work force, rapidly expanding social services and the need for public works projects, the city was forced repeatedly to raise taxes and borrow. Wagner claimed that he had no choice since "human needs are greater than budgetary needs." It was a logic that would come back to haunt New York during the days of John Lindsay's mayoralty.[15]

Lindsay, a handsome man who cut a dashing political figure, was celebrated by the national press as the second coming of JFK. He ran for mayor in 1965 not only as a Republican but also, like La Guardia, as the fusion candidate of G.O.P. mavericks, the Democratic Party's upper-middle-class reform clubs, and the left-liberals of New York City's Liberal Party. In a Kennedyesque campaign, he promised to get the city moving again after the supposed stagnation of the Wagner mayoralty. In fact the city was in the midst of an economic boom.

The 1965 mayoral race was a three-way contest between Lindsay, Abe Beame, the Brooklyn candidate of the Democratic regulars who was almost as liberal as Lindsay but as short and drab as Lindsay was glamorous, and the conservative William F. Buckley, Jr.. Much of what Buckley campaigned on, such as workfare for welfare recipients and enterprise zones for poor neighborhoods, is now mainstream. But Lindsay and Beame took advantage of Buckley's rhetorical excesses and opposition to the 1964 civil rights act to paint him as a dangerous fascist who planned to set up concentration camps in New York. Asked what he would do if elected, Buckley quipped, "Demand a recount." He didn't need to; Lindsay won with 43 percent of the vote.[16]

Lindsay tried to remake the city in the image of his own political rectitude. Elected by Manhattanites, he treated New York's outer-boro Catholic neighborhoods as if they were an Up-South hotbed of right-wing racism. But well before the rest of the country, left-liberal New York had already experienced a civil rights revolution in the 1940s. Lindsay made every issue a matter of race. Whites fearful of rapidly rising murder rates or critical when the mayor intentionally doubled the welfare rolls in the midst of what was then the greatest economic boom in American history—at a time when the black male unemployment rate was 4 percent—were dismissed as racists. Worse yet, during the Lindsay years the anarchic energy which had always defined the city shifted away from economic pursuits into exhibitionism and violence.

Lindsay's greatest boast was that New York never suffered a riot on the level of Los Angeles or Detroit. That's true; instead there was, notes historian Vincent Cannato, a nearly continuous stream of smaller riots in East New York, East Harlem, the East Village, Flatbush, Brownsville and Bedford-Stuyvesant, not to mention those at City Hall by landlords, the police and the employees of the city's very own Neighborhood Youth Corps. As a mayoral aide noted: "We had some major problems. We always called them disturbances [not riots]. Molotov cocktails were always designated as unidentified objects...and the press would go along with it." This was the swampy ground on which Al Sharpton was initiated into city politics.[17]

In the famous phrase of writer Tom Wolfe, the administration's governing principle was "steam control." When Parks Commissioner and counter-cultural aristocrat August Heckscher was asked about meadows that had been torn up during demonstrations, he responded, "parks ought to be the safety valve for all this protest." "Vandalism," he explained, was "simply a way in which certain elements of my constituency used the parks. Some people liked to sit on the benches; others like to tear them up." When key Lindsay aide Barry Gottehrer put the Yippies' Abby Hoffman on the payroll as a community liaison, Hoffman and friends repaid him by writing giant "Fuck You"s on the walls of Grand Central Station. But the city kept paying him, and Hoffman used the money to subsidize his book *Fuck the System*. Gottehrer was pleased with the book, which he called "everything I expected and more," though he bemoaned the inclusion of information on panhandling and cheating the telephone company and transit authority. In the words of Robert Moses, "If you elect a matinee-idol Mayor, you're going to get a musical-comedy administration."[18]

The 1970 census found that in constant dollars the percentage of low-income families remained unchanged between 1959 and 1969 so that as of 1970 New York had the same percentage of poor people as the rest of the country. But in the 1970s Lindsay's policies caught up with the city. With more than a million people trapped on welfare, Gotham's non-white families suffered severely as poverty rates soared. Lindsay's policies produced the poverty they were supposed to alleviate.*

Every significant pressure group tried to shake down the mayor and most succeeded. "There is no question about it," boasted labor leader Victor Gotbaum, "we [the municipal labor leaders] have the ability to elect our own boss." Lindsay was forced to buy off the rapidly growing municipal unions with higher pay for less work which, along with the rapidly rising cost of welfare and the flight of business and talent, sent the city spiraling once again into near bankruptcy. The conventional wisdom of the day was that New York was ungovernable.[19]

Wagner had believed that "a good loan was better than a bad tax." Lindsay used both. The city's fiscal finagling moved into high gear during Lindsay's second term when Abe Beame was the city comptroller, and city spending outran Lindsay's imaginative array of job-eroding new taxes plus additional state and federal moneys. Beame, the diminutive clubhouse pol, cooperated with Lindsay, the stately aristocrat, in conjuring up imaginary revenue streams, deferring essential maintenance spending on the city's infrastructure, and generating arbitrary revenue estimates to borrow against eroded assets.[20]

Where the middle class had been previously drawn to the suburbs, by the mid-1960s they were fleeing the city. A 1966 ad that ran in the *New York Times* read: HAVE YOU EVER THOUGHT OF LIVING IN VERMONT? It went on: "Vermont has no really big cities with snarled transportation, strife, crime, bureaucratic waste, poor housing, air pollution, and all the seemingly hopeless problems of large metropolitan areas today."[21]

---

*In an earlier book, *The Future Once Happened Here*, I explain Lindsay's reasoning for expanding the welfare rolls. His policies created what can be described as "dependent individualism." People were entitled to welfare but the city was not entitled to ask for anything in return. This was the logical extension of the assumptions first cultivated by the left wing of the New Deal in which society demanded less and less from individuals and more and more from government institutions.

The city lost 600,000 jobs in Lindsay's wake and the banks refused to lend New York any more money. The roof fell in on his hapless successor Abe Beame, who was forced to allocate most of his first budget simply to paying off the short-term debt acquired to pay for the unprecedented social spending and union contracts of the Wagner and Lindsay years. In 1976, leading a delegation of mayors to Jerusalem's Wailing Wall, Beame pushed a one-word note between the stones. It read: HELP![22]

Beame didn't blame his predecessor; instead, like Lindsay, he declared that both he and the city were victims. Beame blamed, in order, "the banks, state Senate Republican Leader Anderson, President Ford, and finally the press." With Beame unable to act, no federal bailout forthcoming and the city on the verge of bankruptcy, the state government under the capable Governor Hugh Carey stepped in and imposed a Financial Control Board on the city. The FCB and its sister agency, the Municipal Assistance Corporation, allowed the city to re-enter the credit markets. Governor Carey took over the cost of paying for the city's courts and colleges, helping the city edge back toward fiscal health. But at the end of the day, while the city had avoided bankruptcy, the tax and spending problems that had produced the fiscal crisis were still in place.[23]

In 1977, Beame, who had been reduced to a spectator in his own administration as the FCB and MAC ran the show, tried to run for re-election. But a city-wide blackout that triggered widespread chaos and looting dogged his campaign. (When a similar blackout had occurred in 1965, the city had remained calm.) Beame was replaced after one term by Ed Koch, who had bested the future New York State Governor Mario Cuomo in the Democratic primary.

Once an outspoken liberal, the wisecracking Koch won the mayoralty in 1977 in part because he seemed the candidate most likely to face down the municipal unions. Koch, the first mayor in memory to say "no" to the interest groups, and the second Jewish mayor in succession, described himself as "a liberal with sanity," as opposed to the "wackos." He liked to walk around asking rhetorically "HowmIdoing?"

The city he inherited from Lindsay and Beame had lost 11 percent of its population in the 1970s. Thanks both to racial turmoil and a depth and breadth of government regulation unknown in any other American city, neither banks nor landlords had been investing in the city's aging housing stock, so existing building were losing their value. More and more landlords abandoned their property and the city government came to own wide swaths of Harlem and other poor neighborhoods. The city "had vast stretches…of derelict industrial sites; the shells of vacant apartment buildings, gas stations, and storefronts, and empty lots of all sizes, overgrown with weeds and strewn with garbage." Even worse was the widespread abandonment of sound housing in once tony neighborhoods like Brooklyn Heights and Park Slope. "The suddenness and scale of these phenomena," said Nathan Glazer, "left analysts dumbfounded."[24]*

Like La Guardia, Koch initially pruned the payroll and helped revive the city from its near bankruptcy. But Koch ran up against the underside of La Guardia's legacy when he tried to reform the civil service system. In 1978 New York City counted more than 39,000 civil service job titles in 243 occupational groups. (The federal government had only 22 occupational groups.) He fought for work rule changes in transit even to the point of being willing to take a subway strike, and he tried to clear the welfare rolls of the numerous cases of fraud, but in both cases he was defeated.

Koch was deservedly given credit for stabilizing the city's budget. Helped by the high inflation of the Carter years, he reduced the costs of the city's debts. When the inflation was followed by changes in federal tax law that produced first a Manhattan real estate boom and then a stock market boom, the city temporarily emerged from the fiscal woods.

Koch governed with wit and sarcasm. He didn't do much about crime, but when he was heckled for being too tough on criminals by a white liberal who had been mugged, he replied, "Mug him again." When asked critically about his attempt to lower the height requirements for the police department in order to encourage more Puerto Rican officers, the six-foot-two-inch Koch replied, "Did you ever see a five-foot-two-inch Puerto Rican with a gun?"

In his first term, Koch insisted, "the main job of city government is to create a climate in which private business can expand in the city and not to provide jobs on the public payroll." But then the

---

*The perversity of government policy was on display to the young Kathy Wylde, later of the New York City Housing Partnership. When she tried to rent an apartment in Park Slope and Sunset Park, she found she couldn't afford them because Lindsay's subsidies for welfare rents had priced her out of the market. She eventually settled in Bay Ridge because the absence of welfare families made the rents lower. The housing market, she explained, had "simply ceased to function."

economy began to benefit from the financial deregulation and economic boom of the Reagan years. From 1981 through 1986, Manhattan acquired approximately 45 million square feet of new commercial space, an area equal to the combined commercial space of Boston and San Francisco. With flush times, there was no longer any pressure to constrain spending. Koch the reformer, his funds overflowing, was replaced by Koch the conventional New York politician who made peace with "the New Tammany Hall": the collection of social service agencies, "community" activists, "civil libertarians," and public-sector trade unionists who lived off the city payroll.[25]

Koch's spending did pay off in one area. Worried about widespread middle-class abandonment of the city, Koch worked with David Rockefeller of the New York City Housing Partnership to pool private and government money into housing rehabilitation. At the same time, Koch in 1986 committed the city to spending $4.2 billion in private, city, state and federal dollars over ten years to rehabilitate city-owned abandoned housing. At about the same time, the economic boom of the 1980s led to the rediscovery of brownstone Brooklyn by young professionals. These two developments along with the church-built housing of the Nehemiah program helped lay the basis for neighborhood revivals during the Giuliani years.

In Koch's third term, though, street crime shot up and the roof fell in following a series of corruption scandals and racial incidents. Koch was personally honest, notes historian Chris McNickle, but his allies, the Bronx, Brooklyn and Queens Democratic Party leaders, were caught up in "bribery, extortion, thievery, and influence peddling." One of the malefactors, Stanley Friedman from the Bronx, had a sign in his office that read, "Crime does not pay...as well as politics."[26]

With the spending spigots reopened, liberals hated Koch far more for what he said than what he did. In his last six years in office, Koch governed, despite the occasional outburst of conservative rhetoric, as a conventional liberal. The mayor was a marvelous tummler, so when the stock market surge of the 1980s refilled the city's coffers few noticed that Koch in his last six years in office gave the city the worst of both worlds. Koch wrote that it's not that the poor "aren't deserving," it is that "our help doesn't do them much good and our energies might be better spent elsewhere." But his actions spoke louder: he made peace with the people he once mocked as "poverty pimps," using the new patronage of billions of dollars in social service contracts to buy off black, labor and Latino criticism. Under the supposedly conservative Koch, Gotham's spending on non-profit social service providers exceeded the total budget of other large cities.[27]

Koch hired 50,000 employees, more than half of whom were black and Puerto Rican, even as his rhetoric continued to inflame black leaders. City employment grew nearly three times faster than private sector jobs while city payroll costs rose at twice the rate of economic growth. When asked why he had added so many people without any clear improvement in the quality of city government, Koch answered, "I couldn't defend a situation where I had the money but couldn't hire people for needed services."

Beset by scandals and rapidly rising crime rates, the supremely self-confident Koch returned to his liberal roots without ever acknowledging that his policies had changed. In a 1987 speech before the liberal U.S. Conference of Mayors, Koch, who had been temperamentally tied to the Reagan administration, turned on the president with a blistering attack on the Republican's lack of urban financial aid. He blamed Reagan and the federal government for the South American drugs flooding the crack-scarred streets of New York's worst neighborhoods.

Koch, who even vacationed in New York and quipped "I get the bends when I leave the city," was less than an ideal spokesman for a La Guardia- or Lindsay-like national urban alliance. But nonetheless, trying to remake himself to avert electoral defeat, he embarked on a nationwide speaking tour to create a national urban coalition. He urged his fellow mayors to delay supporting any one candidate until all the contenders for the 1988 Democratic nomination had been forced to address urban issues. The mayor's standard speech now called for more help on AIDS, housing the homeless, and tracking people and businesses that evaded taxes. "I'm going to speak out about these things during the presidential campaign," he declared, "If the national Democratic Party wants to win, it just may want to pay attention." They didn't and perhaps it's just as well. During Koch's last six years as mayor, the city was spending at nearly three times the rate of inflation. But for all his efforts to buy off his enemies, the Koch mayoralty was, after the stock market crash of October 1987, on a downhill slope.[28]

TWO

David Dinkins' Vision

The knock on David Dinkins is that he was essentially aimless, a ceremonial mayor without direction or vision. Writing a defense of Dinkins' four years in office, Todd Purdum of the *New York Times* pointed to what was widely assumed to be his key weakness. The mayor, he insisted, "has never pretended to expansive vision or great ambition." Purdum wasn't alone. Many of Dinkins' friends and critics alike refer to his tenure with off-handed quips and more than a touch of condescension. An oft-repeated line referring to his well-known Edwardian devotion to impeccable dress and formal occasions suggests that "he served as the boro president for the city of New York." His policy perspective, they might go on, was reflected in his roundabout speaking style, as in Dinkins explaining that "One ought not be disinclined to venture...a consideration of what might be regarded..."[1]

This view of Dinkins, though it doesn't lack for anecdotal evidence, is most certainly wrong. It confuses style with substance. Dinkins was in fact a man with a vision, albeit a failed one.

Elected in the late 1980s resurgence of political liberalism, Dinkins was once a national figure. A man whose whole life had embodied the noble ideal of cross-racial coalitions, he was a major player in the post-Reagan resurgence of American liberalism. Nationally, the liberal revival fell short of victory when George Bush narrowly bested Michael Dukakis in the 1988 presidential election. But that defeat was ascribed to the many failings of the Dukakis campaign. By 1989, liberalism appeared to be back on track with Dinkins' triumph, along with the victories of Douglas Wilder and Norman Rice, the first African-Americans to be governor of Virginia

15

and mayor of Seattle respectively, and a number of lesser wins. Dinkins' election as New York's first black mayor was politically understood to "embody a new racial and political ascendancy."[2]

In his brief but stirring inaugural speech, Dinkins insisted that "As a descendant of slaves" his election represented "more than a transfer of power." It promised "to renew the quest for social justice." Noting that the walls of tyranny had come down in Eastern Europe with the collapse of Communism, so, he hoped, would the wall of racial injustice fall in New York. To that end, he called for a revival of 1960s-style community activism and promised that "this administration will redefine the relationship between City Hall and our local neighborhoods." In what would become his signature phrase, he envisioned New York not as a "melting pot" but as a "gorgeous mosaic" of ethnic, racial, and religious groups that maintained their distinct identity even as they worked together. New York Governor Mario Cuomo gave the inaugural speech high marks: "The best voice in America will be that of David Dinkins, the most credible voice...for the needs of people who have been left behind."*

Dinkins saw his march to success at home as passing through Washington. Presenting himself as a spokesman for a renewed urban liberalism, he organized a National Urban Summit in 1990 and a march on Washington two years later. He served as the spokesman for cities during the 1992 Democratic primaries and as the ubiquitous host of the 1992 Democratic National Convention held in Manhattan. He became a leading voice of American liberalism so that, by his own gauge, his stewardship of New York became the single most important barometer to measure the fate of the movement he represented.

Less than two months into office, buffeted by the ongoing fallout from both the personal financial issues that had dogged his campaign and the city's formidable fiscal woes, he gave an impassioned speech in Washington at the National Press Club in which he laid out a strong national agenda. Entitled "The Waning of Conser-

---

*In what was probably the most powerful passage in the speech, Dinkins told the city and the country: "I stand here before you today as the elected leader of the greatest city of a great nation, to which my ancestors were brought, chained and whipped, in the hold of a slave ship.... We have not finished the journey toward liberty and justice, but surely we have come a long way."

vatism and the Progressive Solutions of the 1990s," the speech declared that "the crest of the conservative flood has passed...it has lost its ability to intimidate so many into silence and despair...a decade of reaction and retrenchment has begun to yield a resurgence of progressive ideas." "For decades, he asserted, "the fear of communism abroad has blocked the path to progress at home." Describing the Soviet Union as a hologram, he denounced the Reagan years as a time of "cruelty masquerading as patriotism." With the Cold War over, now was the time for Gotham to benefit from a peace dividend that would redirect federal spending "from the Defense Department to American cities."

Dinkins acknowledged that the big cities were beset by crime, drugs and poverty but exulted that "If progressive ideas were a stock this would be the time to buy." And then giving the back of his hand to the Bush administration, he closed by asserting that if Washington ignored his pleas, "our urban centers will take the lead," so that "when the next national government takes office, it will have to come to us to find out what works and what needs to be done."

▲ ▲ ▲

Dinkins' victory in 1989 is, with justice, attributed to the success in New York City of Jesse Jackson's 1998 campaign for president. Jackson's presidential run was part of a now-forgotten liberal revival. In 1986, William Schneider, writing in the *National Journal*, saw that "Reagan's success in curbing inflation...had the unintended consequence of ending the revolt against government." Polls, he noted, showed rising support for spending on poverty, health and education. There was, said the *Wall Street Journal*, "a pent-up demand for spending programs" so that even Reagan, by then mired in the Iran Contra scandals, was calling for revamped job training and job search programs for displaced workers. An exultant editorial in the *New York Times* was given the emphatic title of "Look Liberalism!" "It's poking up everywhere like daffodils through the melting snows of the Reagan revolution"[3]

Liberal Democrats, demoralized by Reagan and Koch, were revitalized. "I've seen more people come back into politics this year than any time in the past twenty-five years," said Joel Blumenthal, the New York campaign manager for Arizona Governor Bruce Babbitt, one of the 1988 Democratic contenders.[4]

The liberal surge was made possible by insider trading scandals on Wall Street and the savings and loans scandals on Main Street that saw the public standing of big business plummet. Jesse Jackson tried to pick up the populist currents. Opening some of his speeches with George Wallace's old signature phrase, "send them a message," he talked of "economic violence" and "merger maniacs." "The barracudas," he said, "have little eyes and big mouths. They eat all the little fish, no matter what color."

Jackson's campaign was given a second more subtle push by the Sixties revival that accompanied the twentieth anniversary of the annus mirabilis of the Aquarian calendar, 1968. All the major magazines did features on the 1960s, leading *Newsweek* to ask in a cover story, "Will We Ever Get Over The 1960s?" To which the Jackson campaign, which was trying to rekindle the fervor of the civil rights movement, responded, "Why should we?"[5]

The underside of the Sixties revival, however, could be seen in the riots in Tompkins Square Park. The rioters, would-be lumpen-proletarians and self-proclaimed latter-day hippies fighting off the "yuppie scum" that were gentrifying the East Village, had largely taken over the park, shutting out local residents. When Mayor Koch ordered the police to clear the park out, a small riot followed.

Far more ominous, however, were the rumblings from the streets of the inner city that 1960s-level riots might be in store. "There is," said the Reverend Calvin Butts of Harlem's famed Abyssinian Baptist Church, "a revival of the kind of militancy we haven't seen in ten or fifteen years." In the spring of 1987, *Newsday* wrote that a series of racial incidents, most notably the Michael Griffith case, in which a young black man was killed by a car after being chased by a white gang in Queens' heavily Italian Howard Beach, had created "a growing feeling among blacks in New York that they are not getting a fair shake from the criminal justice system." "The day the Bernie Goetz case gets decided," noted Brooklyn Congressman Major Owens, referring to a famous 1984 incident on the subways in which an imbalanced white man shot three black teens who were about to rob him, "is going to be a critical day in the life of the city." Owens told the city to expect trouble if Goetz were acquitted.[6]

Koch's African-American police commissioner Ben Ward agreed, warning that "New York, 1987, shares some of the conditions that led to urban strife in the late 1960s." "Young blacks," he went on, "angry about conditions in their neighborhoods, will create a long, hot summer." Mayor Koch responded to the pressure with calls for a new Kerner Commission.[7]

Koch, vocally opposed to racial quotas, quietly changed the composition of the police department. He and Ben Ward increased the number of black officers by 17 percent, Hispanic officers by 60 percent and females by an astonishing 85 percent. But this did little to assuage the hostility to Koch expressed by black leaders like Congressman Charles Rangel and the Reverend Al Sharpton. That anger boiled over in the 1988 Democratic presidential primary when Koch, who was supporting Al Gore, referred to Jackson's apologetics for Yasser Arafat: "Jews and other supporters of Israel would be crazy to vote for Jesse Jackson, in the same way that blacks and other supporters of black causes would be crazy to vote for George Bush."[8]

Koch was stunned by the hostile reaction to his remarks. Koch hadn't changed, but the political mood had shifted out from under him. After nearly eleven years in office, remarks that had once been seen as "feisty" and "candid" were now taken as "divisive" and "mean-spirited." When Koch's generally ineffective but politically invaluable African-American police chief Ben Ward, a Jackson supporter, called on the mayor to apologize for his divisive remarks, Koch was forced to write a conciliatory letter in the *New York Times* expressing regret.

Jackson, carried by the liberal currents that he had helped create, went on to run second to Dukakis in New York State with Gore a distant third. But Jackson nearly doubled his 1984 vote. He beat Dukakis in New York City by winning 97 percent of the black vote and almost doubling the black turnout of 1980. Jackson's showing in the city sent the David Dinkins campaign for mayor into motion.

What was little noted at the time was the near record low turnout for the 1988 Democratic presidential primary. While left-of-center Democrats had been mobilized, moderate Democrats, demoralized by the social breakdown of the late Eighties, stayed away in droves. Two decades after the Sixties, unprecedented rates of divorce, drug use and violent crime suggested that the Aquarian experiment with moral deregulation had an increasingly costly underside. Crime was such a salient issues that Dukakis dropped four points in the New York State polls the day after Bush received the endorsement of the Police Benevolent Association.[9]

Moderate voters found that liberals and the ACLU—the two had become largely interchangeable—were at best indifferent to their

situation. "For all I know," wrote ACLU director Mel Wulf, tempting fate, "history may judge that the ACLU was responsible for the
disintegration of American society." It was a risk with other people's
lives he was prepared to take. When schools wanted to discipline dis-
ruptive students, the ACLU blocked them, insisting that students
must be "permitted to act in ways which are predictably unwise."
When the city tried to restrain aggressive panhandlers who frightened people, the ACLU said they couldn't and won in court arguing
that panhandling was a form of "free speech." When the city tried to
restrict the playing of loud and even deafening music in the subways,
a liberal judge upheld the ACLU's objections. "The Constitution, it
turns out," mocked one wag, "requires the NYC subway to resemble
Hell as closely as possible."[10]

Liberalism came to be reviled, even by people who were once
staunch Democrats, as part and parcel of the suffering imposed by
the breakdown of social institutions. In his speeches, Governor
Mario Cuomo had given the old liberal jalopy a fresh coat of rhetorical paint, but left its framework unchanged. Asked to define the
meaning of the word "liberal," residents of Brooklyn's lower-middle-
class Canarsie, many of them heirs of the socialist tradition of the
Jewish needle trades, associated the term with "profligacy," "spine-
lessness," "masochism," "elitism," "softness," "irresponsibility"
and "sanctimoniousness." The people of Canarsie were responding
to the growing disjunction between themselves and those George
Bush derided as "ACLU liberals."[11]

▲ ▲ ▲

Dinkins, who in the words of a close political ally, "loved his job" as
boro president, was slow to emerge as a politician. A cautious man, he
had risen so slowly through the ranks of his father-in-law's Carver
Democratic Club in Harlem as to "rattle few egos." Dinkins was well
liked but not always highly regarded. He had been nominated as a
deputy mayor in 1973 under Mayor Abe Beame, but Dinkins' tax
troubles—he hadn't at that time filed any income tax returns in four
years and owed $15,000 dollars—forced him to step aside. Thanks to
Beame, he later assumed the very minor position of City Clerk, whose
most visible responsibility was marrying people at City Hall. He ran
for boro president in 1977 but finished third. He ran again in 1981
only to be soundly defeated. He finally won on his third try in 1985.
The election was widely seen in political circles as "David's Turn."[12]

The phrase "David's Turn" referred, in part, to his junior membership in a sometimes tight-knit group of Harlem politicians know as the Harlem Machine. Its senior members were Congressman Charles Rangel, the high-powered labor lawyer Basil Paterson, and former Manhattan boro president and successful businessman Percy Sutton.*

As boro president, Dinkins had a seat on the city's powerful Board of Estimate where he made housing, the homeless and health care his hallmark issues. The Board of Estimate, which was abolished in 1989, was composed of the mayor, the comptroller, the city council president and all the boro presidents. The scene of political horse-trading, it had considerable power over both city contracts and the shape of the budget.

Dinkins, who fashioned himself in the words of one advisor as "the tribune of the underclass," took an extreme position on homelessness. He dismissed the evidence that drugs, alcohol and mental illness incapacitated most of the homeless as merely the "prevalent myth" pushed by people lacking compassion. The homeless, he insisted, were just "like other people in every respect except that they have no homes." This stance led to frequent clashes with Mayor Koch.

Dinkins was probably known less for the substance of his politics than for an administrative style that diffused authority so broadly across his staff that it was hard for his office to reach a decision. Notorious for his dithering style and billowing rhetoric, he was mocked for wasting people's time. His inability to reach a decision-he would sometimes delay coming to a conclusion for days-was so well known that when it came time for Dinkins to vote on a measure, other people waiting to do business at the Board of Estimate would leave for a leisurely lunch or dinner.

When the dynamic, hard-edged city councilwoman Ruth Messinger was preparing to run for mayor in 1989, she asked Dinkins if he had any intentions of entering the race. According to Messinger, who had been described by Michael Harrington, America's leading socialist, as his heir, she made it clear that she would step

---

*Anticipating Dinkins, in 1977 Sutton he used his position as Manhattan boro president to make the first serious African-American to run for mayor. But Sutton had numerous handicaps. A minority candidate in a still white majority city, he was in conflict with other minority pols including Herman Badillo, the Puerto Rican candidate.

aside if Dinkins wanted the job. But the boro president, a fellow member of the Democratic Socialists of America, enjoyed his new post enormously and expected to be there for a long time (this was before term limits), and replied that he had no interest in stepping up.

It was only when other members of the Harlem Machine declined to run for mayor that Dinkins, under enormous pressure, emerged as a vehicle for carrying on the liberal coalition created by the 1988 Jackson presidential campaign. As his close ally Ruth Messinger put it, "he was pushed by a juggernaut to run." The anti-Koch forces, noted then-City Council President Andrew Stein, "have anointed Dinkins as their champion. So he became not only the black candidate but also the so-called progressive liberal, left-wing candidate." Still, the ever-cautious Dinkins pondered, hesitated and delayed. It was only after he commissioned a poll that showed he could win that he took the first tentative steps toward a full-fledged campaign.[13]

Dinkins' greatest asset was his public persona. The *Times* referred to his "angry civility." Whatever the volcanoes inside him, he kept them firmly capped in a thick layer of decorum. His almost Victorian dignity and slow-to-judge empathy were inspiring for the black middle class. Listening to him speak, I once heard an African-American matron sigh, "He's such a good man."

Widely understood to have lived the most racially integrated life of any New York politician, Dinkins was at ease with the city's panoply of peoples. In the words of a white liberal supporter, "David Dinkins is not really a black politician. He's a coalition politician." The overlapping circles of white liberal elites, the lawyer/fixers of the city's permanent government, union leaders and black activists all looked upon him as a friend and ally. The city's problems, he insisted, were the fruits of institutionalized inequality and discrimination. His remedy was an even more aggressive pursuit of affirmative action.[14]

When Black Muslim Minister Louis Farrakhan unleashed one of his anti-Semitic diatribes, Dinkins was virtually alone among black leaders in condemning him. When racial demagogues, including the Reverend Al Sharpton, Alton Maddox and C. Vernon Mason, tried to claim that a black teenager, Tawana Brawley, had been raped by whites, Dinkins at first talked of a racially motivated conspiracy. But when it became clear that the supposed rape had been concocted by a frightened teenager fearful of her homicidal stepfather, he changed his tone. When Maddox, Mason and Sharpton claimed that Governor Mario Cuomo and Attorney General Robert Abrams were "racists" for not buying Brawley's story, he criticized them on television.

As the 1989 campaign progressed, things seemed to be going Dinkins' way. Mayor Koch's final State of the City address could have been given by the challenger. The speech, which set the stage for the campaign, opened with a brief nod to the sharp economic downturn and then rolled out a list of new or expanded social, housing and educational programs. In standard liberal mode, Koch called for more federal aid. "No City Can Do It Alone," he intoned. But if the feds didn't provide the dollars, Koch insisted on the need, even in the midst of an economic downturn, for new taxes to pay for these social programs.

With economic and social policy taken off the table, the candidates in the Democratic primary would have little to say about a rapidly deteriorating economy. Instead, the campaign was driven almost solely by racial politics and the personal animus that had built up against the incumbent during the nearly twelve years of the Koch mayoralty.*

Dinkins' campaign manager Bill Lynch, riding on the currents of the liberal revival and the Jackson for President campaign, reassembled the old coalition of blacks, white liberals, unions and social service organizations that had fallen apart in the wake of John Lindsay's disastrous mayoralty, while adding the growing bloc of Latino voters. The powerful United Federation of Teachers, which traditionally stays out of primaries, broke precedent and endorsed Dinkins. It was a formidable alliance united by the long list of grievances accumulated over the three terms of the Koch mayoralty.†

Dinkins, who had opened his campaign by telling the city, "I am running because our city has become sharply polarized," seemed certain to win the primary. But then Koch, pointing to the challenger's

---

*The campaign was nominally a four-way race with Dinkins, Comptroller Harrison Golden and builder Richard Ravitch, who had been an architect of both the city's financial recovery in the 1970s and its subway revival in the 1980s, as the challengers. But the highly competent Golden, who like Ravitch and Koch is Jewish, took a somewhat cerebral approach to politics that proved politically unappealing. Ravitch, a man of genuine accomplishments, who ran as the outsider, lacked the speaking skills and political instincts that are usually required for a mayor. Ravitch and Golden spent much of their time attacking each other so that the election turned into what was essentially a two-man race between Dinkins and Koch.
†The unions' election-day efforts to bring voters to the polls were particularly

lack of accomplishments, shifted the focus to Dinkins' competence. Koch's claim that "Dinkins just isn't up to the job" was echoed in the press. One journalist quipped, "No pol in the field could bring greater *gravitas* to an indecisive answer." Dinkins answered questions about his income tax problems by melding an apology for having been merely forgetful with being "hurt at the idea that anyone could doubt his sincerity regarding a minor lapse in his past." For a moment Dinkins' policy positions also seemed to catch up with him. He was unable to explain how he would pay for the new social programs he was proposing in the midst of a recession, and he said he was opposed in principle to asking a teen mother on welfare for the name of her child's father. Editorialists were aghast at his suggestion that the Taylor Law, which prohibited strikes by public-sector unions, should be repealed.[15]

But just when it looked as if Koch might fight off the challenge, a racial incident in which black youth Yusef Hawkins was killed by a largely white group of thugs in the Italian neighborhood of Bensonhurst turned the tide against the sitting mayor. The killing was quickly politicized. At the wake for Hawkins organized by Black Muslim leader Louis Farrakhan, Jesse Jackson gestured toward the coffin and remarked, "That boy lying in there could make David Dinkins the next mayor." Dinkins chastised Koch in words that would come back to haunt him when he insisted that Koch was at least partly guilty for the killing since "the tone and the climate of this city gets set at City Hall." Filmmaker Spike Lee went further by shouting that Koch's "finger was on the trigger." Emotions escalated, and at the funeral for Hawkins, Koch had to escape by the side door to evade a hostile crowd.[16]

The funeral was followed by demonstrations and marches organized by Sharpton and Sonny Carson. Sharpton was stabbed in a protest march through Bensonhurst marked by Italian toughs shouting about "niggers." A "day of outrage" march closed down Brooklyn's main artery, Flatbush Avenue. The demonstrators chanted "Whose streets? Our streets" and "What's coming? WAR." Skirting barricades, the marchers tried to take the Brooklyn Bridge, where they were met by a cordon of cops kept out of riot gear in

---

important in light of a new campaign finance law which limited individual contributions to $3,000 but allowed unlimited in-kind services such as phone banks, pulling operations and "educational" campaigns.

order to be less provocative; a barrage of bricks and bottles injured forty-four officers. (One cop complained, "Now I know what it's like to be a sacrificial lamb.") Columnist Jimmy Breslin seemed to sum up the political situation when he wrote, "as long as [Koch] is here, surely the city will have no peace."[17]

Dinkins' campaign slogan was "strong enough to hold the line," suggesting that only a black mayor could tamp down African-American anger. A final boost for Dinkins came shortly before election day when Governor Mario Cuomo "coyly hinted that whichever candidate could best bring a racially divided city together would win," which amounted to a coded endorsement of Dinkins. With many of the white moderates who would later be known as Rudycrats staying home, Dinkins went on to an easy win with 50 percent of the vote to Koch's 42.[18]

Dinkins, said Ruth Messinger, thought that "when he won the primary that the office was largely his." "There was a widespread assumption in my circles," Messinger went on, that "David would easily win" the general election. But in retrospect, Dinkins' primary victory was the last electoral gasp of the 1960s activism that had been revived in response to Reaganism.

▲ ▲ ▲

On January 11, 1989 the headline in the *Daily News* read GOOD NEWS FOR BAD GUYS: CRIMEBUSTER GIULIANI STEPS DOWN. There had been nobody in New York like Rudy Giuliani since Tom Dewey, the crusading Manhattan district attorney whose mob prosecutions made him governor and then twice the Republican nominee for president in the 1940s.[19]

Rudy Giuliani was a folk hero of sorts in New York. After stepping down from his post as federal attorney, he enjoyed 70 percent support in the polls and seemed likely to become mayor. The youngest Associate Attorney General in history, he had already been the model for the crusading anti-corruption lawyers depicted in two movies, *Serpico* and *The Prince of the City*. He was regularly described as the "incorruptible," "indefatigable" federal attorney who had successfully taken on both the Wall Streets swells and the corrupt clubhouse politicians connected to Koch. Brilliant and fearless, he hadn't hesitated in prosecuting powerful people like financiers Ivan Boesky and Michael Milken as well as E. Robert Wallach, well known as the best friend of President Reagan's Attorney General Ed Meese.

Over a decade and a half of prosecutions, Giuliani had rearranged New York's political landscape. In 1975 he took down corrupt congressman Bert Podell. In the course of the Podell trial, the ambitious prosecutor had humbled Podell's friend and character witness, then-Congressman Ed Koch. In the dramatic confrontation between future mayors, prosecutor Giuliani forced politician Koch to backtrack on his claims about Podell's character. The culmination of the Giuliani-driven political corruption cases came with the conviction of goateed, cigar-smoking Bronx boss and Koch ally Stanley Friedman. Looking back at the Friedman case, Giuliani told *Vanity Fair*, "I don't think there's anybody much worse than a public official who sells his office, except maybe for a murderer."[20]

Beloved by both the *Village Voice* and outer-boro ethnics, Giuliani was greeted as a hero when he entered Manhattan restaurants. Seeing him enter, people left their tables and flocked to him with promises of support should he run for office. But Giuliani's take-no-prisoners style made him an awkward politician, and he was undefined and untested as a candidate.

Giuliani's issues staff during his 1989 mayoral run was led by Democrat Jennifer Raab, a fellow attorney who kept a picture of Robert Kennedy over her desk. She was dismayed when the novice candidate "blurted instant opposition to Mayor Edward I. Koch's grant of bereavement leave to gays." Similarly, Raab worried that Giuliani's acknowledged opposition to abortion was sure to alienate the liberal Manhattanites who had once greeted him like a hero.

In a series of contorted demarches, Giuliani initially courted and then spurned the anti-abortion and largely Catholic Conservative Party. Instead, he consummated an alliance with the Liberal party in hopes of creating a La Guardia-like Republican-Liberal fusion ticket. Giuliani even announced his candidacy in the very room La Guardia had used fifty-six years earlier. New York, he said, borrowing a theme from his national Republican consultants who were soon to be fired, was known for "crime, crack and corruption. Now," he intoned, "is the time to take back our city from the violent criminals on our streets and the white-collar criminals in their office suites...from the drug dealers in abandoned buildings and the crooked politicians who have abandoned their oath of office."[21]

Well before he was attacked from the left, Giuliani came under fire from the right. His maneuverings had enraged the Conservative Party while the Republicans of the *New York Post* editorial page saw his alliance with the Liberal Party as more reminiscent of John Lindsay than of "the Little Flower." The *Post* went after his "tendency to flip-flop on issues ranging from abortion to commercial rent control." The *Wall Street Journal* editorial page was angry at the way he had flamboyantly arrested executives in their offices, carting them off in handcuffs like common criminals. They noted that Giuliani, a Democrat turned Republican, had voted for George McGovern. And they quoted his comment to a TV interviewer explaining that he didn't "look to see what the catechism of Conservatism says about how to solve a problem." Similarly, conservative Catholics like the *New York Post*'s Ray Kerrison found him unacceptable on social issues. "I can't figure out where he stands on abortion" or homosexuality, Kerrison complained.[22]

Giuliani had also earned the enmity of his fellow Republican and former ally United States Senator Alfonse D'Amato, a close confrere of Ed Koch. D'Amato had been angered by Giuliani's prosecution of one of his major campaign contributors, junk bond king Michael Milken. The senator, who was repeatedly the subject of ethics charges, seized on the opening produced by conservative criticism and Giuliani's missteps to recruit the wealthy cosmetic heir Ron Lauder to run against him in the Republican primary. And to make Lauder, a political novice, a credible candidate, D'Amato secured the Conservative Party nomination for his proxy.

Lauder, who was essentially a stalking horse for Koch, quickly began spending what would add up to $8 million of attack ads. He assailed Giuliani for taking the Liberal party line, voting for George McGovern and supposedly supporting tax hikes. Lauder's media guru Arthur Finkelstein even bought time for the attack ads on Channel 11's newscast, where Giuliani's wife Donna Hanover was the anchor. Lauder assailed his rival as a "shameless publicity seeker who handcuffed innocent stock brokers" and, in a theme that would be picked up by the Dinkins campaign, he asked, "Why are people afraid of Rudy Giuliani?" Lauder answered himself: "Because they should be." The Lauder campaign was so relentlessly negative that former Reagan media advisor Roger Ailes quit the operation because its aim seemed solely to "destroy" Giuliani.[23]

A debate on the local NBC affiliate quickly turned into a donnybrook as Lauder opened by thanking the moderator Gabe Pressman for the opportunity to "discuss my conservative ideas and Mr. Giuliani's liberal ideas." Later in the debate Giuliani mocked

Lauder on the subject of the homeless: "Ronnie doesn't really understand the suffering in this city. He has no idea what it's like.
Suffering to him is the butler taking the night off." Moving on in a
liberal vein at a time because he expected to be facing Koch in the
general election, Giuliani told Lauder, "Most of the people are
homeless because they cannot afford a place to live."[24]

The prosecutor went on to win the GOP primary with 67 percent of the vote. But under fire from Lauder and Koch
simultaneously, the political rookie faltered as a candidate. He was
further thrown off stride when he found that it was not D'Amato's
ally Koch, but Dinkins who emerged with the Democrat's nod.

Giuliani, who had once thought of going into the priesthood,
was deeply immersed in the Catholic tradition and enjoyed debating
ideas. He was driven by both personal ambition and a strong moral
compass, but his political affiliations were held far more lightly. He
began, like most New York Italian Catholics, as a Democrat, but like
many ethnics he moved away to become an independent in 1977 and
eventually a Republican at the start of the Reagan years. Still, noted
his 1989 issues director Jennifer Raab, "he was largely undefined
on the local political issues." "In New York," she said, "there are a
thousand interest groups with passionately held positions on issues
where Giuliani had no opinion" and "almost no staff" to give him
one.

He wrestled with his conscience on abortion, waffled—and
then under the influence of liberal Republicans like State Senator
Roy Goodman, the pro-abortion Liberal Party and Raab, who made
it clear that opposition to abortion would cost him dearly in votes
from Jewish women, Giuliani went pro-choice. On another litmus
test issue, gay rights, Giuliani, who had done some gay rights litiga-
tion and had ties to the gay Republicans of the Lincoln Club, was
generally supportive but balked on the issue of domestic partnership.
This was no small matter in the general election, where the Dinkins
campaign would make hay, at a time of rising deaths from AIDS, of
its support for the right of gays to inherit the rent-controlled apart-
ments of their partners.

Awash in Gotham's oceans of ideology, Giuliani had one great
advantage: an enormous capacity to learn. When he first went to
Washington in 1975 as a Deputy Attorney General, the graduate of
Manhattan College and NYU Law School talked of how "It was
a terrific opportunity. I thought it would be a seminar on how

government works." Raab was at first reluctant to talk to Rudy on the grounds that "I don't talk to Republicans." But when she went to see him, she was taken by the fact that he had "the trademark of a great litigator, the ability to quickly incorporate vast quantities of information." Aside from the issue of government corruption, Giuliani's positions on city issues were largely unformed. Raab and her small staff began to arm him with briefing books on topics ranging from transportation to housing and found that with a few exceptions such as needle exchanges—he was strongly opposed—he had an open and eager mind. When Raab brought in Ray Horton of the Citizens Budget Commission to show how Koch had used the Eighties boom to expand the city government's head count by 50,000 largely unneeded new hires, Giuliani began to develop a more sophisticated view of Gotham's fiscal plight. "Rudy," says Raab, "loved being a policy wonk."[25]

▲ ▲ ▲

Dinkins, sitting on a huge lead after the Democratic primary, seemed certain to be the next mayor. New York was a one-party town in which the only competition was between pro- and anti-Koch Democrats. In 1977, when Koch was first elected mayor, his general election opponent, Republican State Senator Roy Goodman, won less than 5 percent of the vote. By the early 1980s, Democrats held Gracie Mansion, every seat on the City Council, and every boro presidency. From 1983 until 1991 Democrats held every single municipal office except a single city council seat.

With a 5-1 Democratic advantage in voter registration, a 3-2 edge in fundraising, and the prestigious backing of investment banker Felix Rohatyn, an architect of the city's recovery from the 1975 fiscal crisis, Dinkins should have beaten Giuliani easily. Rohatyn sold Dinkins to Wall Street on the grounds that an African-American mayor had the best chance of forestalling widespread violence. But the candidate was vulnerable on both economic and ethical issues. Though it never came to the forefront of the media's coverage of the campaign, the issues of taxes and the economy were gaining public salience. Financial firms like Merrill Lynch, which had recently moved 2,500 jobs to New Jersey, were joining the factories that had fled New York in the wake of the Lindsay mayoralty. Just two week before the general election, Exxon announced that it was moving its headquarters to Dallas because it couldn't convince young execs to come and live in Gotham. Giuliani picked up the theme of decline to argue that "the city is right now at a crisis." If business flight and job losses continued, he warned, the "decline may be impossible to reverse."

Dinkins, focused on issues of redistribution, was slow to respond. He had been ambivalent about the economic boom of the 1980s, complaining that wealth from financial services "created new luxury towers in Manhattan even as one of four New Yorkers remained poor." He placed many of his economic hopes, Washington dollars aside, on the unlikely revival of manufacturing, which was declining in cities across the country. The Manhattan Boro President wanted to establish a regional economic-cooperation council with an unwilling New Jersey in order to staunch the flow of jobs to the lower cost environs across the Hudson. Derisive toward Dinkins, Giuliani quipped, "You cannot pass a law that requires people to live in New York City.... You can't put a wall around New York City."[26]

The prosecutor argued that Gotham had no choice but to make itself more competitive by reducing costs and crime while improving the efficiency of city government. Exempting police, fire and sanitation, he proposed an immediate freeze on city hiring. Referring to "the damage that a tax increase" would impose, he talked about improving the delivery of city services as an alternative means of balancing the budget. Giuliani even proposed reinstating the business tax cuts that Koch had shelved when the economy went South. Exxon, Giuliani noted, wasn't an anomaly. Between 1978 and 1988, New York State had lost thirty-seven of its eighty Fortune 500 headquarters. Giuliani, appealing to Democrats already dismayed by the liberal direction of their party, repeatedly described Dinkins as a tax-and-spend redistributionist whose policies were guaranteed to produce more flight. Dinkins, said the Republican, "totally misunderstands the economy of New York."[27]

Dinkins responded defensively by pointing to his blue chip advisors like Rohatyn and James Robinson, the CEO of American Express, and insisting that "I have no interest in higher taxes." Acknowledging that, given his proposals for new social initiatives, "it is difficult to spend less," he argued that more money for preventive social programs would save money in the long run. Instead of higher taxes, he looked for "partnerships" with Governor Mario Cuomo in Albany and, less plausibly, given the Bush presidency, Washington. "What I hope," he explained, "is to get further assistance out of Washington" for new programs to house the homeless and assist AIDS victims.[28]

The forty-five-year-old Giuliani responded to this rhetoric by dismissing Dinkins as an "incompetent" clubhouse pol who represented the "shadow government of influence peddlers." Dinkins, who as a member of the Board of Estimate had voted on a company in which he owned stock, was denounced as little more than a servant of the vested interests in the Democratic Party that had "brought the city to the edge of disaster." How, asked the Giuliani campaign, could Dinkins deal with the city budget when he was unable to manage his own finances? Not only had he failed to pay his taxes in the past, but during the campaign Dinkins was discovered to have sold his stock in Percy Sutton's Inner City Broadcasting Company, valued at one million dollars, to his son for the gift-tax-evading sum of $58,000. The boro president apologized, but a Giuliani commercial asked, "David Dinkins, Why does he always wait until he gets caught?"[29]

Faced with a barrage of questions about their candidate's competence, the Dinkins campaign took a variety of tacks. First, playing off Giuliani's very public education in trying to run New York's ideological and interest group gauntlet, they ran ads featuring his flip-flops on issues like abortion and gay rights. Then they played to Democratic loyalties by running ads that morphed Giuliani into Ronald Reagan while tying him to the Republican administration's policy of forcing poverty-stricken Haitian boat people to return to their native island.

Dinkins always maintained an above-the-fray pose consistent with his gentlemanly image, but those speaking in his name were anything but reticent in going after Giuliani personally. The campaign raised the question about the highly unusual 1982 annulment of the Catholic Republican's first marriage after fourteen years of matrimony. Giuliani's claim was that the marriage needed to be ended within the Church because Giuliani had married Regina Peruggi without knowing that she was his second cousin. In the closing days of the campaign as the contest tightened, Dinkins, an ex-marine, stood on the steps of City Hall surrounded by a raucous group of veterans, while his supporters shouted to the cameras about how Giuliani, who had received a Vietnam-era deferment, was a draft-dodger. When asked to speak directly to the issue Dinkins said that he would "leave such characterizations to others."[30]

Down the home stretch, the Dinkins campaign brought in Democratic stalwarts like Governor Mario Cuomo and Senator Edward Kennedy and union leaders to tug on swing voters' fraying partisan heartstrings. For his part, Dinkins declared, "I'm a John Kennedy Democrat. I'd certainly rather be a Democrat than a member of the party of Nixon, Reagan and Quayle."[31]

Dinkins frequently invoked the ideal of a "gorgeous mosaic" to describe his ideal for the future of race relations in New York. The media, obsessed by race, repeatedly noted that among America's largest cities, only New York and Houston had yet to elect an African-American mayor, yet it paid almost no attention to what Dinkins' "mosaic" and its accompanying identity politics might mean in practice. The press treated the election largely as if it were a civil rights story in which a black candidate was struggling against the declining, but still significant, forces of racism.

Both Dinkins and Giuliani were embarrassed by their supporters during the campaign. The Dinkins campaign suffered when Jesse Jackson compared Giuliani to the Southern segregationist Governor George Wallace and when adverse publicity forced Dinkins to fire the notorious anti-white thug Sonny Carson from his campaign. Carson, who been given $9,500 largely to stay quiet, protested his firing, replying to accusations that he was an anti-Semite by boasting, "I am anti-white. Don't limit my anti to just one group." For his part Giuliani was forced to distance himself from a celebrity backer, comic Jackie Mason, who had mocked the well-tailored Dinkins as an empty suit little better qualified to govern than a washroom attendant.[32]

Both candidates sought to downplay race even as they tried to take advantage of it in courting the key Jewish swing vote. The Giuliani campaign, for instance, frequently linked Dinkins, a supporter of Israel, with Jesse Jackson, whose support for Yasser Arafat made him anathema to most Jews. State assemblyman Alan Hevesi, a Dinkins ally in Queens, turned it around, telling his supporters, "If as a Jew you cannot vote for this man, you can never vote for a black." "Should Dinkins lose," wrote journalist Ken Auletta, "it is likely many blacks will whisper 'The Jews killed Dinkins.'" Auletta went on, "Reject Dinkins and we license haters like Sonny Carson.... Reject Dinkins and the racial polarization attributed to Mayor Koch will appear as a minor irritant." Auletta turned the "healing" theme on its head and revealed its underside, which could be described as "Let Dinkins heal or else!"[33]

Polls a week before the election had Dinkins winning by eleven percentage points but he ended up winning by 50,000 votes, or less than one point, making it one of the closest elections in the city's history. Dinkins won, according to a WNBC-*New York Newsday* exit poll, with 97 percent of the black vote, 71 percent of the Hispanic vote and a respectable 32 percent of the white vote. Giuliani's strongest support came from white Catholics who gave him 73 percent and a stunning 59 percent of the heavily Democratic Jewish vote.

"November 7, 1989, is a date that will live in history," Dinkins told a ballroom of exuberant supporters at the Sheraton Center Hotel. "We passed another milestone on Freedom's Road, a victory not for African-Americans alone but for all New Yorkers and for all Americans." Summing it up, Congressman Charlie Rangel described Dinkins' win as "the greatest thing that's happened to America in a long, long time."[34]

Dinkins was magnanimous in victory. The sixty-three-year-old grandfather offered his hand to Giuliani, whom he called "a decent man." When his supporters erupted in boos, Dinkins chided: "No, no, now hear me." The mayor-elect repeated himself: "Rudolph Giuliani is a decent man." Evoking the memory of his late father, he spoke to the historic nature of the occasion and promised to end divisiveness. "What can unite us," he told his supporters, "is far stronger than the forces that can keep us apart.... I intend to be the mayor of all of the people, not just of those who voted for me. I intend to be the mayor of those persons who voted for Rudy Giuliani as well."[35]

But Giuliani's core supporters had a hard time believing that promise. When the loser described his opponent as "Mayor-Elect Dinkins," the crowd erupted angrily. "Quiet, QUIET," Giuliani roared, to little immediate effect. Finally, he bellowed at the top of his lungs: "PLEASE BE QUIET AND LISTEN TO ME." He had to repeat similar pleas throughout his fifteen-minute speech. Even when he tried to lead his backers in pep-rally questions, they refused to cooperate. "We're going to unify behind the mayor of New York, aren't we?" "Yes," he yelled into the microphone. "No," many of his backers yelled at the same time. It was a harbinger of tensions to come.[36]

THREE

Failure and Ferment

When David Dinkins took office in January of 1990, he was potentially the most powerful mayor in the modern history of New York. The same political and civil rights currents that carried him to victory had also produced a new city charter giving the office of the mayor unprecedented sway.

Under the old charter, which was abolished at the same time that Dinkins was elected, the mayor shared his executive powers with the Board of Estimate on which he sat along with the comptroller, the city council president and the boro presidents. The Board "participated in the budget process, granted leases of city property, passed on land use development through its control of zoning, had the final say on all capital projects and on city contracts not awarded through competitive bid." In order to carry out his executive duties, a mayor had to engage in extensive horse-trading with the members of the Board who, if they banded together, could outvote him. In theory eliminating the board should have made it easier for Dinkins to bring the budget under control. Under the old system, you couldn't build a new school in overcrowded Queens without also building one in over-served Staten Island. To do something useful in one boro you had to bribe all the others in a log-rolling/vote-buying process that tended to guarantee overspending.*

---

*Two useful accounts of the background to the 1989 charter reform process can be found in Frank J. Mauro and Gerald Benjamin, eds., "Restructuring the New York City Government: The Reemergence of Municipal Reform," *Proceedings of the American Academy of Political Science* 37, no. 3, 1989. An essential source on

Each boro had one representative despite the vast differences in
population between largely white Staten Island at 230,000 people
and heavily minority Brooklyn at 2.5 million. This differential was
found to be in violation of the 1965 Voting Rights Act. Under pressure from the courts, the Board was abolished and its powers
distributed between the mayor's office and the hitherto insignificant
city council. But the way that the Board of Estimate's powers were
divided up left the mayor with the whip hand and the generally fractious fifty-one-member council in an enhanced but still relatively
weak position.[†]

Dinkins, who was in part a creature of the Board of Estimate,
was never able to seize the powers available to him. Far more interested in politics than policy, excessively deferential to "experts," he
was temperamentally ill-equipped to govern. Hampered from the
start by his ongoing personal financial scandals, which deprived him
of a much-needed political honeymoon, he was never able to master
either the city's interest group politics or its fiscal expression, an
ongoing budgetary crunch.[*]

His problem in part was not that he was a liberal per se but
that he was every kind of liberal. He sincerely believed in 1930s-era
labor liberalism and Lindsay-era ideals of community control though
members of the two movements had clashed bitterly over control of
the schools and would clash in his administration over whether senior centers should be run by the city with unionized workers or by

charter reform itself is Frederick A.O. Schwarz, Jr. and Eric Lane, "The Policy and
Politics of Charter Making: The Story of New York City's 1989 Charter," *New York
Law School Law Review* 92, nos. 3 & 4, 1998.

The 1989 charter reforms were the culmination of attempts to eliminate the
Board of Estimate begun in the early 1930s by Judge Samuel Seabury, the patrician
reformer who brought down Mayor Jimmy Walker and helped make La Guardia
mayor. When the city was unified in 1898, each boro retained its own separate political organizations. Seabury and La Guardia saw the Board as a pre-unification
atavism protecting the local ward bosses who operated out of boro-based bases.
Seabury proposed modernizing and centralizing city government by abolishing the
Board while upgrading the city council. The 1961 charter reforms were a step in
that direction, but Seabury's vision was achieved only with the 1989 charter
reforms. The history of the modern New York City charter can be found in Ross
Sandler, ed., *Forward: The One-Hundredth Anniversary of the Charter of the City
of New York: Past, Present and Future, 1898-1998 Reports of the Charter Commissions of 1936, 1961, 1975, 1983, 1988, 1988*, published privately by the New York
Law School Law Review.

†Koch's appointments to the Charter Commission were part of his re-election drive.
His appointees, led by Fritz Schwartz and Eric Lane, were given the chance to rein-

community-based organizations. He supported the social service liberalism of New York's extensive array of non-profit organizations, including homeless advocates whose plans to put more homeless shelters in outer-boro working-class neighborhoods clashed sharply with the new mayor's talk of community empowerment.

Dinkins, who spoke in a populist vein of wanting to help small business in his first inaugural address, was also an advocate of a corporate liberalism in which a partnership between big government and the big economic interests like Wall Street helped set policy that usually worked to the disadvantage of the little guy. Confronted by the tensions between his constituencies, Dinkins was paralyzed by indecision.[†]

Responding to the clamor of the pressure groups, Dinkins expanded the Office of the Mayor to unprecedented size. In 1959 Mayor Robert Wagner had a total mayoral staff of fifty-seven. When Dinkins entered office he had over a thousand employees and by the end of his term the total was more than 1,500.

In the absence of trust, Dinkins opened new mayoral offices to service each of the interest groups in his "gorgeous mosaic." There were the Mayor's Offices of European-American, African-American/Caribbean, Asian, Immigrant, Latino, and Lesbian and Gay Community affairs. He also created a Mayor's Office of Health Policy, a Mayor's Office for Children and Families, a Mayor's Office for Public-Private Partnerships, a Mayor's Office of Drug Abuse Policy, and the office of The Increase the Peace Corps that was supposed to reduce inner-city violence. Politically useful both symbolically and as a place for patronage employees to work between election campaigns, each office required its own staff, and produced a stream of paperwork largely duplicating the work of already existing agencies.

---

vent city government from a civil rights perspective. For one account of their activities see, "The City in Transition: Interim Succession and the Mayoralty: Report of 2002 NYC Charter Revision Commission": 25.

*Federal investigators probed his shady stock transfer deal; city investigators studied his Board of Estimate votes for conflicts of interest; and the mayor was forced to appoint an outside counsel to probe his own questionable activities as boro president. The probes petered out, but they made it even more difficult for the notoriously indecisive mayor to assemble a team to face the budget crisis he had inherited from Koch.

†When Dinkins abruptly changed his strategy on an issue, an aide complained to the mayor. Dinkins responded with "Well, I'm frustrated too." But, thought the aide, "Aren't you the mayor?" *Newsday* 11/3/93.

The incoherence of the Dinkins mayoralty came not from a lack of vision but from holding too many conflicting visions simultaneously. Dinkins achieved clarity of purpose, if not results, only in his approach to the federal government. He had a vision for a new national urban coalition, but he had no plan as to how to govern his fractious city. "This," commented one former staffer, "was an administration that didn't lack for talent, but these impressive people were never given marching orders that would allow them to reconcile the inevitable clashes of interest any mayoralty has to face."

Dinkins' supporters point to the terrible economy he inherited, in which Manhattan was suffering from a 16 percent office vacancy rate. But here too there was room for creativity. Between 1965 and 1990, New York City's expenditures, adjusted for inflation, more than doubled. Writing at the time, political scientist John Mollenkopf saw that Dinkins had a chance to create "a new post-industrial post-fiscal crisis liberalism." The city's budget, he argued, wasn't an insuperable obstacle. "The budget," Mollenkopf explained, "was $12 billion when Koch took over [in 1978]; January 15 [1990] it will be $30 billion. There's been some inflation, but also a real doubling of the public sector" within which "Dinkins could have maneuvered for better management and accountability."[1]

Required by law to balance his budget, Dinkins looked for help from the man he described as his "partner," fellow liberal and presidential aspirant Governor Mario Cuomo. But Cuomo, facing his own budget problems, offered scant help. Teamsters' chief Barry Feinstein, who had helped elect Dinkins, was unsympathetic. "Gloomers and doomers forecasting big deficits had almost always been wrong before. If there's money available," he said, "we're going to want it."[2]

Dinkins responded with small budget cuts and large tax hikes. Two days after taking office, Dinkins, despite his inaugural promise to be "the toughest mayor on crime the city had ever seen," responded to the fiscal crunch by suspending the upcoming police academy class of 1,848 cadets. While cutting cops, Dinkins and budget director Philip Michael managed to balance their first year budget with $859 million in new revenues derived from the largest tax increase in city history. But despite the hard times, the city's budget was a billion dollars larger than the last Koch budget. It included an additional $40 million in social programs and added 4,400 new workers to the city payroll.

The tax increases in the teeth of recession, along with the two billion dollars in new states levies from Governor Cuomo and the state legislature, were a severe blow to the city economy. The combination of rapidly rising state and local taxes was driving people out of the city.

In 1993 Lehman Brothers, a financial services company, moved 900 back office jobs to the same forty-two-story Jersey City office tower to which Merrill Lynch had moved 2,500 jobs a year earlier. Jersey City didn't need to offer any financial incentives. A spokesman for Mayor Bret Schundler explained, "We have no city payroll tax, no city income tax, no corporate tax, we don't even have an unincorporated business tax or tax on commercial leases."

Rather than eliminating unessential services and improving inefficient ones, the Dinkins administration looked outward to Washington and Albany for a solution to its problems. Dinkins, like his ally Congressman Charles Rangel, blamed the collapse of the cities on Washington's Cold War policies and military spending. In his first month in office, the mayor, who had long been associated with the Peace Dividend Network, a group of left-liberal critics of the Cold War, gave a speech in Washington. With the Cold War over, he saw an opportunity for military funding to be "redirected away from the Pentagon to the needs of the city." Dinkins looked forward to new funding for "infrastructure, housing, a universal and affordable health care program, a real war on drugs, Headstart programs, education, [and] pollution control." He told the Peace Dividend gathering that "the political power is there, I know. That power fueled by [our] campaign...must become the voice—not only of urban American, but of all America." This was the first of his wish lists and a theme to which he would return time and again.[3]

To implement his aims in Washington, Dinkins turned to his chief political aide, Bill Lynch, who felt that the established city lobbying organizations like the National League of Cities, founded in the 1920s, and the United States Conference of Mayors begun by La Guardia during the New Deal had become "social clubs." They were, Lynch said, "sleepwalking" through the urban crisis.[4]

Lynch, who had strong ties to both African-Americans and labor, wanted to organize the nation's mayors into an "action group." He thought that there was "a real opportunity...to rebuild the coalition that emerged in the 1960s," when the rising tide of minority empowerment promised to transform America. The lack of urban clout, Lynch insisted, could be overcome by energy and will. But for a quarter century the big cities had been gaining problems while losing jobs and voters. Chicago Mayor Richard Daley saw that he lacked his father's clout because "the machinery is gone." "In the past," he explained, "a congressional candidate who didn't have the mayor's benediction couldn't get elected." But by the 1980s candidates could run and win without the mayor's blessing. President Bush's urban policy, Daley went on, "has added insult to injury by funneling the declining money through the states rather than the cities."[5]

"Lynch's concept," noted Gail Brewer, who ran New York's much beefed-up and well-respected Washington office, "was that New York drives the country." After all, cities from around the U.S. came to Manhattan for their Wall Street bond ratings, and all the major politicians came to the city to raise funds. "We contribute so much to the U.S.," Brewer explained, that "we thought we might be able to reshuffle the [Washington] deck through cooperation with other cities with similar problems." Gotham's influence, it was assumed, "could be turned into political capital in Washington and support for changing the funding formulas."

But while the Dinkins administration was, with encouragement from Congressman Rangel, beginning its quixotic quest for more dollars from Washington, events unfolding in Brooklyn began to undermine its ideal of a "gorgeous mosaic." Sonny Carson, a well-known black nationalist, had been shaking down Korean grocers in the heavily Caribbean-American Flatbush section of Brooklyn. Then in September 1988 a nasty dispute broke out between Pong Ok Jang, the Korean owner of the Red Apple Grocery on Church Avenue, and Gieslaine Felissaint, a Haitian shopper who claimed to have been mildly injured in a scuffle with the merchant, who had accused her of shoplifting.

Carson, who fancied himself as "bad," accused the grocer of having "an attitude" and seized on the situation to impose a boycott. He charged that the Koreans' twenty-four-hour greengroceries were out to "destroy" the black community and culture. Carson demanded that the offending stores "be transferred to black ownership." Carson's thugs threatened anyone who entered the Red Apple Grocery while demonstrators shouted "we make you into chop suey" in mock Chinese accents (though the owner was Korean). For six months the New York Times studiously avoided the picketers screaming about "slant-eyed monkeys." But the New York Post gave the shakedown extensive coverage and made it into an issue that couldn't be avoided.[6]

Carson, who had first made a name for himself intimidating white teachers during the Ocean Hill-Brownsville school kultur kampf, bragged of that earlier conflict, "I transformed thousands of black kids into little Sonny Carsons." One of the kids he inspired was the young Al Sharpton, who saw Carson and his allies as "role models." The subject of a fawning 1974 Paramount movie, *The Education of Sonny Carson*, he was sentenced in 1975 to four to seven years in prison in connection with the killings of two men accused of robbing a Bedford-Stuyvesant hotel. In the wake of the trial, Carson, who would make famous the "no justice, no peace" slogan later adopted by Sharpton, told the press that "the only reason we were arrested in the first place is that we were trying to do the job of the New York City police."[7]

Carson, who declared "We're at war" and stood outside the Red Apple shouting "funerals not boycotts," was an enormous embarrassment for an administration elected to heal. But he had the backing of most of the city's black leadership. "Carson is a flamethrower," acknowledged State Senator David Paterson of Harlem, the son of Dinkins' close ally Basil Paterson, "and often that is what it takes to get attention."[8]

Dinkins, according to one of his friends, may have been immobilized by memories of the historic Montgomery bus boycott that had helped ignite the civil rights movement. By this account, Dinkins saw boycotts and pickets as unambiguously noble. Whatever his motivations, the mayor couldn't bring himself to intervene. When, after four months of tensions, Dinkins was asked if he would symbolically cross the picket line to visit the grocery, he replied, "What's the purpose of doing that?"[9]

Just as disturbing as the mayor's inability to distinguish between Sonny Carson and Rosa Parks was that the administration seemed to accept Carson's account of a situation in which there was no right or wrong but rather "two communities striving...for similar pieces of the pie." The mayor had repeatedly rejected the imagery of "the melting pot" for the multicultural ideal of a "gorgeous mosaic," but what was to hold the separate pieces together?[10]

After five months of the boycott, Justice Gerald Boyd, in a tacit rebuke of the mayor's passivity, issued an injunction requiring the protestors to desist from menacing customers. But Dinkins did nothing to enforce the decree on the grounds that such an order would increase resentment in the black community and that that the police were not a party to the lawsuit. Instead Dinkins convened a commission to study the matter and then he gave a speech billed as a "major, major appeal for calm and inter-racial understanding." Said Dinkins, "I oppose all bigotry against anyone, anywhere. I abhor it. I denounce it, I'll do anything—anything right and anything effective—to prevent it."

But no action followed and the courts were forced to step in. A unanimous decision by a four-judge appellate court upheld Judge Boyd's ruling. In pointed language it rejected both of the administration's contentions, noting that it was not up to the NYPD and the administration to decide whether or not to enforce a court order. The "boycott" finally ended after two years with the deli owner driven out of business and Carson declaring victory. Caught between constituencies, Dinkins "lost face," said Carson, who had pushed the mayor into a political cul de sac from which he was never to fully emerge.[11]

For a city already under siege from crime, it appeared that the mayor had abdicated one of his most basic responsibilities. But why?

Dinkins had come of age during the riots of the 1960s. His mayoral campaign had been implicitly based on the fear of future riots, and Dinkins proved eager to practice what Tom Wolfe called "steam control." He seemed to assume that it was better to let demagogues vent their anger than risk more violent confrontations.[12]

Dinkins' failure to enforce the law on Church Avenue was part of a broader social breakdown in New York. True to its Dutch and polyglot origins, Gotham has always been an open, tolerant city, invigorated by the chaos of commerce and imperiled by the disorder of what its first mayor, Peter Stuyvesant, called a "disobedient community." During the later Koch years the traditions of tolerance and lawlessness amplified each other to make New York increasingly unlivable. The public spaces that made New York special, its parks and plazas and sidewalks, had been taken over by homeless encampments, aggressive panhandlers and underclass toughs. "On the streets of Manhattan," explained one journalist, "psychotics talking to themselves or screaming at imaginary enemies mixed with a legion of beggars." Kent Barwick of the Municipal Arts Society complained, "You can no longer feel secure in any public space in New York.... Public space now belongs to no one, no one will defend it."[13]

Never clean, the city had become filthy. Trash collections were sharply reduced and the number of street sweepers cut by more than half; meanwhile, the streets had become public toilets with the right to urinate in public vigorously defended by the city's army of earnest civil liberties lawyers. Operating on the principle that no right was safe unless it was carried to an extreme, New York Civil Liberties Union attorneys protected the rights of stolen good merchants to take over city sidewalks, arguing that since these "merchants" sold stolen books (among other stolen items), they were thus entitled to vigorous First Amendment protections.

The subways, always somewhat frightening, had been made even less attractive by a new wave of tuberculosis often carried by deinstitutionalized mental patients whose right not to take their medicine had been secured by the same attorneys. Further, according to Judge Leonard Sand's decision, endorsed by the civil libertarians, subway riders could expect to be hassled by panhandlers exercising their free speech rights. "What's at issue here," explained a lawyer for the panhandlers, "is an effort to make the subways a sterile environment devoid of protected expression." "It is the very unsettling appearance and message conveyed by the beggars," Sand concurred, "that gives their conduct its expressive quality."[14]

As a practical matter there was little expectation that those same panhandlers would be expected to pay for their ride as 155,000 riders a day either jumped the turnstiles or "paid" with coins literally sucked out of the turnstiles. The police responded to such misdemeanors with summonses that had little effect. About half of the so-called "desk-appearance tickets" issued for misdemeanors such as turnstile jumping, public drunkenness or urination were simply ignored by recipients who didn't bother to show up in court.

The breakdown of civility and authority was pervasive. The schools, noted Emily Sachar, who was then teaching the lower grades in Brooklyn, were, "first and foremost, a place to act out, to explode, to play and shout and rant, to vent." Neither the teachers, whose contractual rights allowed them to dress as casually as the students, nor the administration, which lived in constant fear of lawsuits, saw themselves as authorities responsible for creating an atmosphere of learning. One principal went so far as to wear a dashiki and shades to suggest that he too was "fighting the man."[15]

At the same time, as recompense for past racist practices, the NYPD effectively ceased policing all but the most serious crimes in the inner city. The result was that young men growing up in father-less families experienced neither the cop on the beat nor the personalized authority of strong teachers in the schools. Early viola-tions of the law were treated with indifference; "minor crimes" such as stealing car radios and low-level burglaries were effectively decriminalized. The upshot was that violent crime quadrupled between 1966 and 1990, reaching its peak with the crack epidemic of the late 1980s and early 1990s.

In the summer of 1990 "wolf packs" of young teen toughs armed with easily accessible guns roamed the city. In one eight-day period, four children were killed by stray gunshots as they played on the sidewalks, toddled in their grandmothers' kitchens or slept soundly in their own beds. Overall, in the first six months of 1990 more than forty children were killed by random gunfire.

1990 set the record for the number of murders. On one espe-cially gruesome but not atypical August day alone, a Bronx prosecutor was cut down in a hail of gunfire while shopping and a Brooklyn politician was gunned down in his campaign headquarters. Then there was the case of twenty-two-year-old tourist Brian Watkins, in Gotham with his family for a visit to the U.S. Open Ten-nis tournament. A wolf pack of eight black and Hispanic youths, who were not from impoverished backgrounds, set upon the family at a subway station. When Brian came to his mother's defense, he was stabbed to death. The attack was part of an initiation ritual for a gang that required a mugging for membership.[16]

"Crime is tearing at the vitals of this city and has completely altered ordinary life," declared Thomas Reppetto, president of the Citizens Crime Commission, a private watchdog group. "Worst of all, it is destroying the morale of our citizens." Liberal columnist Sid-ney Schanberg spoke of a "combat emergency" so severe that "we might have to suspend some civil liberties." But instead of acknowl-edging the crisis, Dinkins' tried to shift responsibility to Washington: "If the problems of drugs and crime were only in New York, then you could ask, What is it that you folks are doing wrong? But all of our urban centers are afflicted similarly. The fact that it's happening somewhere else doesn't mean that I don't have a problem to address. But the fact that the problem is regional or nationwide does say that the Federal Government should assist in addressing it." When this statement failed to quell the outcry, Mayor Dinkins gave a second statement that left observers baffled. "I say that if two nations are in dispute and one diplomat says to the representative of another government, 'Her Majesty's government is exceedingly distressed,' everybody knows that we're mad as hell. Now however, I'm prepared to say that I'm mad as hell, not simply, 'We're exceedingly distressed.'"[17]

In the wake of the Watkins killing and Dinkins' non-response, the mood in the city was summed up in a *New York Post* front-page headline: DAVE DO SOMETHING. But even then Dinkins hesitated. It was left to City Council Speaker Peter Vallone to take the lead in beefing up the police force. More cops, Vallone insisted, had to be hired even if the city was faced with the prospect of vast deficits and huge budget cuts. When Dinkins responded, "What about social services?," Vallone replied, "we're wasting a lot of money" on welfare and insisted that without safety the city's future was in peril. Vallone and the council then designed a Safe Streets/Safe City plan that raised $1.8 billion for the police largely through an income tax surcharge. But even when the legislation passed, Dinkins refused to commit himself to any specific number of new police so as to ensure the maximum possible dollars for funding social programs.[18]

▲ ▲ ▲

Even when Dinkins was preparing to assume office, one of his advisors warned that he "had all this unexamined liberal rhetoric that assumes unlimited ability to pay for services. Rather than saying here are five new initiatives and here's how you can deliver services better to the poor, you had this open-ended prattle." The "prattle" continued into his administration. Dinkins saw increased spending as the glue that held his electoral coalition of constituencies together, and he was unable to choose amongst them. With the economy continuing to sag, Dinkins' dithering produced what financier Felix Rohatyn, chairman of the Municipal Assistance Corporation, described as a "social, political and economic crisis far more serious than the fiscal crisis of the 1970s."[19]

Rohatyn, the Robert Moses of municipal finance and a key administration supporter among the financial elites, insisted that "the city will have to make fundamental changes in the way it goes about its business.... We need to question the city's overall wage and personnel policy." And surely there was room to cut personnel, beginning with just a fraction of the 50,000 workers Koch had added to the city payroll. Dinkins promised Rohatyn that he would curb labor costs, which represented nearly 40 percent of the budget. "Don't worry," he reassured the MAC chair, referring to his union political allies, "they'll take it [the cuts] from me." But Dinkins never took a clear stand with labor or any other prominent group of backers.[20]

In mid-August 1990, the corrections officers, who policed the city's violence-ridden nine-jail complex on the East River's Rikers Island, went on strike. The union blockaded the roads connecting the island to Queens, producing massive traffic jams, while bloody fights broke out between guards and inmates. Dinkins could have invoked the state's Taylor Law that makes strikes by public employees illegal and provides for prohibitive penalties for striking state workers. Instead, he said he was "sure in blazes" angry with the guards, but he quickly caved in and agreed to most of what the union had demanded.[21]

The sheer incoherence of the Dinkins administration was put on full public display in October 1990 during two days of extraordinary policy pirouettes. First the city agreed to a 5.8 percent increase in teacher's salaries it couldn't afford. Forty-eight hours later, Dinkins announced that he was laying off as many as 15,000 city workers while freezing wages and hiring. The public saw an administration in disarray. Smelling blood in the water, political rivals like Public Advocate Andrew Stein were already talking of a run for mayor against the incumbent in 1993. Less than a year into his term, Dinkins was forced to announce that he was not a first-year lame duck, that he would be a candidate for re-election three years hence.

Dinkins made some cuts but new taxes outweighed the budget reductions by a ratio of four to one even at time when, as Rohatyn put it, "virtually all human activities [in New York city] are taxed to the hilt." Vallone, who saw himself as a representative of the city's middle class, warned, "The reality is that we have an extremely small tax base and we can't drive out those who pay the freight."[22]

Frustrated by the mayor's lack of leadership, Vallone went public with his complaints and told *Newsday*, "There seems to be no one who can make a final decision on the other side except for the mayor himself-who has a good many things on his mind, obviously. There is an inability to delegate power." Rohatyn agreed. Noting that the credit markets were growing increasingly skittish about the city's fiscal stability, he called for a set of pain-sharing agreements to be worked out by big government, big business and big labor, the same partners that produced the 1975 rescue of the city's finances. It seemed an unlikely prospect.

In the spring of 1991, with Gotham sinking deeper into recession, the Wall Street bond-rating agencies threatened to downgrade the city's credit rating. That would make it more expensive for the city to borrow money to close its yawning budget deficit. Dinkins and his budget director Philip Michael told one of the credit agencies, Moody's Investors Services, that they were negotiating with the unions to defer some of their newly won, but clearly unaffordable, 3.5 percent wage increase. But there were no such negotiations, and when the unions realized what was going on they bridled. At a news conference, Dinkins insisted that the unions "understand the situation that we find ourselves in." But they didn't. Teamsters' president Barry Feinstein, and Stanley Hill, the executive director of AFSCME District Council 37, fumed about how the administration "stinks from the head."[23]

In 1991 and 1992, with the city tottering on the edge of fiscal disaster, Dinkins did everything he could to win concessions from the unions. He threatened them with a "Doomsday budget" replete with massive layoffs. When Rohatyn pressured Dinkins to ask for more from labor, union leaders responded with anger. "We predict major warfare over those issues of privatization—taking away the work from the city workers and giving it to community groups or whomever," said Barry Feinstein of the Teamsters. Never willing to make clear choices, Dinkins walked a fiscal tightrope, telling the city, "We must never, never abandon the compassion, the concern and the caring which are the hallmarks of our government. Bond ratings are important, but our bond with the people is every bit as important."[24]

"Before you get structural reform out of the liberal-labor axis," quipped *Newsday* columnist Gail Collins, "you will see polar bears [from the Central Park Zoo Dinkins threatened to shut down] sleeping in the subway." Failing serious reform, Rohatyn hoped to see the state Financial Control Board play a larger role in the budget. Faced with a possible loss of control at home, Dinkins intensified his efforts to gain more leverage in Washington.[25]

▲ ▲ ▲

When it came to organizing a national urban coalition to "demand" more money from Washington, Dinkins was as dedicated, energetic and implacable as he was tentative and timorous in governing New York. In the tradition of La Guardia, Lindsay and the later Koch, Dinkins moved quickly and energetically to promote a 1990 National Urban Summit. The aim was to generate publicity for a plan to pressure Congress into spending more on New York and other big cities.[26] *

Chicago Mayor Richard Daley and an impressive list of chief executives from Milwaukee, San Antonio, Boston, Detroit, Philadelphia, Los Angeles and twenty-seven other cities attended Dinkins' Urban Summit in New York. At the summit's opening press conference on November 12 1990, and in the short book that emerged from the meeting, the attending mayors spoke in the 1960s language of "consciousness raising" and non-negotiable "demands." We "demand the attention and resources that are long overdue...we are not here begging for a damn thing.... We have a right to demand what our people deserve," said Atlanta's Maynard Jackson while Cleveland's Mike White, stealing a line from the 1976 film *Network*, declared, "We're mad as hell and we're not going to take it any more."[27]

The rhetoric at the conference, which was funded by major American corporations such as American Express, First Boston, Merrill Lynch Capital Markets, Paine Webber, Time Warner, and IBM, was alternatively threatening and pleading. Dinkins spoke of the cities as though they were battered children suffering from Father Washington's shameless neglect. With others, he threatened to take revenge by compiling an annual "urban scorecard" for members of Congress, the president and state officials and then campaigning against those who rated poorly.

But the mayors had been sounding the alarm for so long that their cries had become politically inaudible. Power had flowed out of the cities to the suburbs and even fast-growing exurbs where the new high tech economy was taking shape.

---

*In 1961, New York had received just $110 million, or 4.5 percent of its budget, in federal aid. By 1975, after inner-city riots, President Lyndon Johnson's Great Society and President Richard Nixon's revenue sharing, federal aid to New York rose to $2.47 billion, or 20.6 percent of the city's budget. Between 1975 and 1990, the city's budget more than doubled from $12 to $27 billion while federal aid grew only slightly. By 1990 the federally funded share of the budget declined to 9.3 percent of the city budget. The 1980s explosion in spending was paid for by the city's booming

Two months after the summit, in January 1991, Dinkins continued its themes in his second State of the City speech where he enthused that "we are working" with a new coalition of mayors "to revive our partnership with the federal government." But what followed was in a very different key. Four years into the recession with no new federal aid in sight, he spoke of "the bitter disappointment" of "abandonment" and difficult adjustments. "We will be happy to share with Washington the solutions we have developed to the problems of the 1990s," he insisted in a line from his early days in office when he presented himself as the harbinger of a new political order. But then he went on, "We will be happy to take care of...problems on our own -if the federal government will desist in the practice of draining away our tax dollars without returning services." New York, he noted, picking up on a theme borrowed from Senator Daniel Patrick Moynihan, gets back 74 cents for every dollar it sends to the capitol. There was, Dinkins sighed, a "$24 billion balance of payments deficit with our own government."[28]

But having chastised Washington, Dinkins, like a chronically beaten wife returning to her abusive husband, again placed his faith in the federal government. "I envision," he pronounced, "a wave of angry, determined Americans...grandmothers and emergency room doctors, collecting hundreds of thousands of illegal guns seized by police departments...depositing them on the steps of the Capitol, I see them camped on the Mall demanding a new kind of Civil Rights bill...guaranteeing freedom from fear.... The Lord can not grant us this peace, it can only come from Washington."

▲ ▲ ▲

In a stroke of good luck for Dinkins, three weeks before the April 7, 1992 New York State presidential primary, former California Governor Jerry Brown, long belittled as Governor "Moonbeam," upset front-runner Arkansas Governor Bill Clinton in the Connecticut Democratic primary. And that in turn made both the mayoral

---

finance sector, which had profited from President Reagan's deregulation of financial markets and by a marked increase in aid from New York State, which also benefited from the boom. But in Dinkins' off-kilter calculations, the 1970s were a fine time for the city, or at least for city government, because it was the period in which federal aid peaked. By contrast, the 1980s, when African-American incomes rose sharply in New York, were deemed a disaster because federal aid, though it continued to go up, declined as a percentage of the city's budget.

conference Bill Lynch and Dinkins had planned and the New York primary a week later all the more important.

After a week in which Dinkins had been embarrassed by the shootings of two students shortly before he spoke at their high school, Lynch worked with Jesse Jackson to bring Clinton, Brown and thirteen mayors to Gracie Mansion for what was dubbed a mini-urban summit. In a race in which the cities had largely been ignored, the mini-summit, said Boston Mayor Ray Flynn, was "our first and maybe our only opportunity to put urban issues on the table." Michael Kharfen, the Dinkins community affairs commissioner, explained that the event "helps in articulating to communities that a lot of what we're able to do is tied to Washington."[29]

Jerry Brown, who has been described as having more positions than the Kama Sutra, answered the mayors' questions with a populist attack on the elitism and corruption of American politics. Clinton, anticipating his presidency, spoke knowledgeably about well-tailored programs addressing specific urban problems, mostly welfare reform, small business aid and community policing. But he also made it clear that he intended to be fiscally prudent. Clinton went on to win the New York primary.[30]

After the primary Dinkins turned his attention to a planned May 2, March on Washington on behalf of America's cities. On April 30, shortly before the planned march, South Central Los Angeles erupted in bloody riots. The riot was triggered by acquittals of police officers who had been videotaped beating drugged-up motorist Rodney King. The verdicts produced the second major LA riots in 27 years.*

The 1965 Watts violence had been a cataclysmic event that was widely described as more rebellion than riot and was instrumental in generating Great Society funding for the big cities. But while in the 1960s the violence was understood to reflect the failures of society, the 1992 riot was broadly taken as a pathological expression of South Central LA's gangster culture.

Despite the hopes for the march raised by the new LA rioting,

---

*South Central was depicted in most press reports as a vast wasteland devoid of business, but in fact it was the home to almost 330,000 jobs, most of them in the immigrant economy of small manufacturing and food processing. The contrast between the non-white immigrants who were slowly rising up the economic ladder and the rioters was all the more vivid because the rioters made a point of targeting the Korean businesses that drove the local economy.

the event didn't live up to expectations. Even with the support of 150 mayors and 220 organizations and predictions of 100,000 marchers, the Washington park police estimated that only 35,000 attended. They were mostly New York City public employees as no other city—not even Washington—contributed sizeable numbers.

Ben Hooks of the NAACP told the marchers that American cities were the site of the "homeless, jobless, hopeless and helpless," and like other speakers, including Mario Cuomo, Hooks called (despite the recent Gulf War) for reduced military spending in order to make it easier to pay for social programs. As a group, the speakers played up the threat of further rioting, with Dinkins warning that "We knew how close we were to the fire, and we must stop the anger and the pain before it is too late." He was seconded by Baltimore Mayor Kurt Schmoke, who threatened, "We don't want to have to burn down our cities." These comments drew a tart response from Milwaukee Mayor John Norquist, who asked why anyone would want to invest in desperate places that might soon go up in smoke. Mocking the strategy of "rattling the tin cup" in Washington, he cautioned, "You can't build a city on pity."[31]

But in the time between the march in early May and the Democratic National Convention in mid-July, Dinkins, rather than highlighting New York's virtues, continued to paint a scene of unremitting woe. He spoke voluminously about the plagues besetting the city, from AIDS and tuberculosis, to homelessness, unemployment and the danger of riots, all of which he attributed to the Republicans.

Dinkins and his Police Chief Lee Brown had basked in the approval of the city's newspapers and civic elites when New York stayed calm despite the explosion in Los Angeles. But a week before the convention, in a case of bad timing, one of Dinkins' warnings came true when rioting broke out among the drug runners of heavily Dominican Washington Heights.

The spark for the explosion was a confrontation in an apartment vestibule between a decorated undercover cop, Michael O'Keefe, and a drug dealer named Kiko Garcia. The apartment was on a block where there had been fifteen narcotics and seven felony arrests in the two weeks prior to the confrontation. With 122 murders in 1991, the 34th Precinct of Washington Heights led the city in killings, many of them drug-related.

O'Keefe stopped Garcia, an illegal immigrant, because he

appeared to be carrying a gun. A struggle ensued; when Garcia pulled his weapon, a banged-up O'Keefe shot and killed him. But when news of his death spread in the neighborhood, it was accompanied by wild rumors, some spread by Garcia's associates, about how he had either been executed at point-blank range or had been beaten to death with a police radio. Al Sharpton was there to rev up the volatile crowds, claiming that O'Keefe had executed Garcia with a shot in the back, something "they didn't even do in the Wild West."[32]

Garcia, who had bragged in a videotape taken from the supposed "witnesses" to the "execution" that drug dealing "is legal here on these blocks, it's LIBERATED," was found in the autopsy to have cocaine in his blood. The District Attorney's report completely vindicated O'Keefe. But both the press and Dinkins immediately depicted the event as a case of police brutality.[33]

The *New York Daily News* carried a screaming headline, "He Begged for Life." Its story was picked up by credulous television reporters who failed to note that the only basis for the accusation came from "witnesses" who were relatives of Garcia's boss in the drug trade. Police Commissioner Lee Brown was out of town, but Dinkins, who had once lived in Washington Heights and had to know that it was the cocaine capital of the Northeast, didn't just express sympathy to the dead man's family; he treated the incident as a matter of police malevolence and quickly invited the Garcia family to Gracie Mansion and arranged for the city to pay for the funeral. Egged on by the press and the mayor, the drug runners rioted for three days, trashing Korean-owned stores. There were twenty-three injuries and millions of dollars worth of damage but fortunately only one death.

The riot may have been small potatoes by LA standards, but still it left many ordinary New Yorkers shaken and the police demoralized. As calm returned, anxieties shifted to the logistical nightmare of the Democratic convention. But thanks to the efforts of Deputy Mayor Bill Lynch and Director of Operations Harvey Robbins, it went off without a hitch.

The convention was the political and personal highlight of Dinkins' four years in office. For a week, beginning with his fifteen-minute address to open the convention, he fulfilled the role that had led his supporters to push him into running for mayor in the first place. Energized as he had rarely been in governing, he became THE national spokesman for urban liberalism. Alan Finder of the *New York Times* captured the scene:

> At one point, within a span of 48 hours, the Mayor delivered a welcoming speech from the podium at Madison Square Garden; addressed tens of thousands of people crammed into Times Square for an AIDS rally and, the next morning, a salute to Broadway; took Nelson Mandela, the head of the African National Congress, to meet with Gov. Bill Clinton at the Democratic nominee's hotel; was host to mayors from around the country at Gracie Mansion, and kicked off a glitzy fashion show featuring top New York designers under a huge air-conditioned tent in Central Park. Amid the swirl of events, Mr. Dinkins also managed at least a half-dozen television interviews and countless appearances at breakfasts, luncheons and receptions for convention delegates. And he was greeted with standing ovations and compliments, about both his city and his performance as host to the Democratic National Convention.[34]

Dinkins was center stage for the televised concluding ceremonies as he, presidential nominee Bill Clinton and vice-presidential nominee Al Gore raised their clasped hands in a promise of victory. Dinkins, said *Newsday* columnist Jimmy Breslin, "was insane with joy because he had his face right out there while the people cheered and the cameras, the cameras, focused on him." There was a sense, recalls Lynch that "the city was back."[35]

Dinkins was at the top of his game. New York State was not in play for the presidential election, but Dinkins' efforts couldn't help but boost black turnout nationally. And given his prominence at the convention, he had reason to hope that, should Clinton win, a financial rescue package might be his reward.

A great deal was riding on a Clinton victory. The claim that twelve years of Reagan-Bush were responsible for everything from poverty and unemployment to AIDS and intolerance was repeated so often by Governor Cuomo, Mayor Dinkins and the members of the city's Congressional delegation that it took on an almost liturgical quality. In the topsy-turvy world of New York City politics, the 1970s, when the Bronx burned and the city almost went bankrupt, were remembered fondly by many liberal politicians as an era of federal support. By contrast, the boom of the 1980s, when minority families made major gains in income, was decried by Manhattan Boro President Ruth Messinger and Public Advocate Mark Green as the decade of greed because Reagan-era federal subsidies failed to keep pace with the city's exploding budget.

New York's liberal politicians reacted to Bill Clinton's election with chords of FDR's theme song, "Happy Days Are Here Again." One headline read, OFFICIALS COUNTING THE DAYS TILL THEY COUNT CLINTON AID. So sure was *Newsday* of the imminent arrival of federal manna that under the headline WHAT'S IN IT FOR US it ran a collection of wish lists compiled by urban experts.[36]

An ecstatic Dinkins aide announced that the mayor wanted to follow in La Guardia's footsteps and "set the urban agenda." La Guardia had gone to FDR's Washington with a wish list sixty years earlier; David Dinkins could do no less. A jubilant Dinkins, his own re-election possibilities seemingly enhanced by Clinton's victory, waited less than a half a day after the election before sending off twenty pages to the president-elect asking for help with everything from infrastructure to the arts.

But a great deal had changed since La Guardia formed a political partnership with FDR. New York no longer had the clout to call the shots in Washington. In 1933 when La Guardia was first elected mayor, New York had a population greater than the fourteen smallest states combined and twenty-two representatives in Congress. By 1992 as population and power shifted South and West, it had only twelve congressional districts wholly within city limits. In the 1992 congressional elections, New York State lost all three of its seats on the powerful House Appropriations Committee and two of its three seats on the Ways and Means Committee. "We are a hurting state," said Gail Brewer.

Nonetheless, Dinkins was optimistic. He told New Yorkers that he was the man who could deliver dollars for the city because "I'm in and out of the White House all the time." But with national polls running better than two to one against increased local aid, Clinton, faced with a reluctant Congress, was never able to give New York much help. The president's proposed $19.5 billion Stimulus Program, based largely on the U.S. Conference of Mayors "ready-to-go" construction and infrastructure projects, was soundly defeated even though the Democrats controlled both houses of Congress. Clinton, however, was able to take a great deal away from New York. A Marine Midland bank study found that half the families hit by his tax increase lived within ninety miles of the Empire State Building. Because of New York's density of high incomes, made necessary in part by the high cost of living, $19 billion in taxes were extracted from the region, explains economist Leslie Hunt of HSBC Holdings.[37]

▲ ▲ ▲

New York was a city that believed in Washington more than Washington believed in itself. That meant that time and again sophisticated New Yorkers would cooperate in their own fleecing. "New York," explained Senator Daniel Patrick Moynihan, "is a liberal state and . . . can't break out of the notion that anything you get from the federal government is free. But the formulas are the other way around." After twelve years of blaming Republicans for New York's problems, a senior aide to a high-ranking Democratic official commented that Clinton had "continued in the bi-partisan tradition of transferring money from New York to the Sunbelt." This was no surprise to Senator Moynihan, who, referring to Gotham's Congressional delegation, which voted for the Clinton tax hikes while opposing a capital-gains cut that would have helped the city, noted bitterly that they "can be depended on to vote for legislation that will transfer resources out of New York."[38]

FOUR

Rethinking

By the end of Dinkins' first year New York had hit a wall. A national recession put almost all state and local governments under pressure, but the problems in New York were particularly severe. Like Britain in its famous 1979 "Winter of Discontent," or the stagflation of the Carter years, the private sector engine for welfare state spending had seized up while the interest groups that drove the spending refused to relent in their demands. The Dinkins and Cuomo tax increases weren't bringing in the expected revenues as business and people exited. Surveys showed that more than half the city's population wanted to leave.

But outside of Dinkins' liberal orbit, the policy pot was beginning to stir. "We know," noted new Milwaukee Mayor John Norquist, "that at the end of World War II, Detroit, the Arsenal of Democracy was thriving, while Berlin was in ruins. But if you were to visit those cities in 1990, you'd assume it was Detroit that had been destroyed by warfare. How can we explain this?" Norquist's predecessor, the venerable Henry Maier, had been president of the United State Conference of Mayors. Maier, who held office from 1960 to 1988 was, says historian Richard Bernard, "a genius at federal grantsmanship and a master at blaming others for Milwaukee's problems." Maier raised taxes twenty-four times in twenty-eight years, leaving his city far worse off than he found it, but when he finally exited office still insisted that only the federal government could save Milwaukee from its own failings.[1]

Norquist would have none of this. Cities, he explained, are the only natural units of government. They emerge organically as centers of trade and culture. Left to their own devices cities flourish. But reviewing federal policies on transportation, housing, welfare and shipping that subsidized suburbanization and subverted the cities, the Milwaukee mayor concluded passionately that on a bipartisan basis "the federal government has been busy destroying its own cities, both by design and by accident for the past fifty years." His alternative, laid out in an article entitled "No More Tin Cups," called for the cities to break free of their dependency on Washington's handouts while reasserting themselves as natural marketplaces and producers of wealth.[2]

Norquist wasn't alone in trying to rethink urban policy. In the wake of three consecutive Democratic presidential defeats and talk of a Republican realignment, a ginger group calling itself the Democratic Leadership Council was pressing its party to rethink its assumptions and break free of New Deal and 1960s Liberal orthodoxy. Founded in 1986, the centrist "New Democrats," as they called themselves, were led by Al From, a former congressional aide with a vision for remaking his party, and Will Marshall, a policy polymath. They were determined to escape the political gravity of the New Deal and the Great Society and pull their party into the information age. But first the Democrat Leadership Council had to fight to establish itself.

To win media attention, From and Marshall invited Jesse Jackson to speak at their 1990 convention in New Orleans. Jackson proved a difficult guest, stealing the show with a speech that went out of its way to bait the centrists. When he left the podium, half the crowd of a thousand and virtually the entire press corps left the anteroom with him and moved into the ballroom where Jackson continued to hold court.

Left behind was a panel featuring David Osborne, a little-known writer on local affairs whose reputation rested on his book Laboratories of Democracy, a study of innovation on the state level. Osborne, who like Norquist came out of a left-wing anti-Vietnam background, had in the course of studying the specifics of state innovations tapped into a lost Brandeisian strain in American Liberalism.

Once revered as a liberal prophet, Louis Brandeis, the driving intellectual force behind Woodrow Wilson's 1912 presidential victory over Bull Mooser Theodore Roosevelt and an advocate of strong centralized power, had long been eclipsed by the big government politics of the Depression and the New Deal created by his nephew Franklin. But in his day Brandeis had been a relentless critic of outsized institutions, whether they be industrial monopolies or the bureaucratic state that dwarfed the individual and demeaned the citizen. A strong advocate of federalism, Brandeis wrote, "It is one of the happy incidents of the federal system that a single courageous state may...try novel social and economic experiments without risk to the rest of the country."[3]

Osborne, speaking in this tradition, laid out the argument that formed the basis of his enormously influential book *Reinventing Government*. Barely able to be heard above the din created by Jackson and the press in the adjoining room, Osborne intrigued those who remained to listen to him. They included Virginia Governor Chuck Robb (son-in-law of Lyndon Johnson, the last New Dealer to win the White House), Louisiana Senator John Breaux, former senator Lawton Chiles, who would soon use Osborne's ideas to win the Florida gubernatorial race, and Arkansas governor Bill Clinton who would do likewise with the presidency.[4]

They were taken by Osborne's argument—accompanied by examples—about how governors could do more with less by scrapping rule- and input-driven bureaucracies in favor of stressing outcomes and accountability. Osborne insisted that what he was advocating was neither liberal nor conservative in the conventional sense. "Our fundamental problem," he wrote in *Reinventing Government*, "is that we have the wrong kind of government.... We do not need more government or less government, we need better government."

In the early 1990s, New Democrats and Republican thinkers gathered regularly as part of the New Paradigm Society organized by Jim Pinkerton, a libertarian policy thinker in the Bush White House, and New Democrat Elaine Kamarck. Policy intellectuals, explained Pinkerton, were turning away from partisan warfare to the question of how to make government work. "It felt like the start of the space program," wrote journalist Joe Klein, "Everything started to come together. It was a refounding."[5]

Both sides of the aisle embraced Peter Cove and Lee Bowes of America Works, a for-profit job agency that had a remarkable record of placing welfare recipients in long-term jobs. America Works had first been "discovered" in the early 1980s by left-liberal economic journalist Bob Kuttner but forgotten about during the 1980s boom. In the late 1980s and early 1990s the organization was rediscovered, and its two highly personable leaders became key players in tying together a network of reformers who saw the chance to break out of the old ideological straitjackets and make progress on American social problems

It took another year and half until Osborne caught on publicly in New York, but in the interim the Manhattan Institute for Policy Research began to establish itself as an intellectual force in Gotham. The Institute's founding director was Bill Hammett, an intense thirty-four-year-old Wall Street financial analyst turned policy entrepreneur. Housed in a run-down building on West 40th Street and operating on a shoestring, the Institute made its initial reputation sponsoring two works published by Basic Books that struck at the heart of welfare state assumptions and helped set the public policy agenda for the next two decades. George Gilder's 1980 *Wealth and Poverty* showed how steeply progressive taxation slowed economic growth and thus served as an impediment to upward mobility for the poor. Charles Murray's 1984 *Losing Ground* set the stage for welfare reform by arguing that public assistance as it had metastasized in the 1960s under Lyndon Johnson and John Lindsay had trapped the poor in socially dysfunctional settings that helped produce a semi-permanent underclass. In September 1988, Murray, in a bleak article for *Commentary* called "The Coming of Custodial Democracy," argued that, barring a dramatic shift in policy, the underclass was going to become a permanent fixture of New York life. Short of simply eliminating welfare, the best we could do, he insisted, was simply to learn to live with the crime and the fear the underclass generated even as we continued to provide custodial care for the dysfunctional poor.

In the early 1990s, the restless Hammett, who had an extraordinary talent for seizing opportunities, turned his attention to the dire state of New York under Dinkins by founding a new magazine, *City Journal*. Hammett, caustic, difficult, often seemingly at odds with himself, grasped what conventional conservatives had missed: In a city that prided itself on its role in intellectual life, there was a conceptual vacuum at the heart of city politics. He saw that New York politics, its rhetorical ideals aside, had become primarily a matter of patronage. He was disdainful of the city's leading Republicans whom he saw "as just a bunch of rich brain-dead assholes who liked to complain about things." Later, speaking to the *New York Times,* he put a more dignified face on the same sentiment, explaining, "The commitment of New Yorkers to ideas does not, to say the least, run very deep. What New York is about is amassing money, acquiring influence and power. Whose law firm is up and whose is down. Which developer is in, which is out. That's how this city runs. But when the new people come in, without fresh ideas they'll be dead."[6]

To succeed, Hammett explained in a memo, we must "tear down the present intellectual and institutional edifices that support the old regime, while at the same time providing a positive vision of what we want to replace it with. Either approach without the other will fail." And the way to reach people who didn't spend their time reading policy articles or books was through the Manhattan Institute lunches. Hammett gathered people from the press, Wall Street, real estate, academia and the foundations, people you "didn't see at the musty establishment get-togethers held by the Association for a Better New York or the New York City Partnership." These were the people who were devoted to New York but alienated from the Dinkins mayoralty. The effect, explained NYU Professor Mitchell Moss, who was close to the Dinkins administration, was that "the Manhattan Institute filled the intellectual vacuum created by the loss of brain power in the Republican Party, by the abandonment of New York by the Ford and Rockefeller Foundations and the dismal level of political discourse at the universities in the city."[7]

"Hammett," noted his colleague Larry Mone, "wanted to bring in writers and intellectuals, not pols. He thought that if they could shake up the debate the pols would come along." Hammet argued that "liberals," or more precisely ex-liberals on the rebound from the failures of liberalism, were the sharpest people around because they had been forced to examine their assumptions. He thought that unlike the city's tiny coterie of conservatives, the ex-liberals were personally attuned to the sensibilities of the city. He set out to recruit them.

The irascible Hammett was one of the few people who took the decline of the city seriously. Hammett argued that categories like "Liberal" and "Conservative" were inadequate to describe the city. "We're in favor of radical decentralization of government, of radical welfare reform.... We're in favor of the assimilation of immigrants.... We're shaking things up." This was an approach that recommended itself to skeptical liberals who didn't consider themselves conservative. "The Manhattan Institute became a kind of Alcoholics Anonymous for many liberals," explained Sol Stern, a former top aide to Andrew Stein and the executive director of Governer Mario M. Cuomo's Commission on Juvenile Justice Reform.

"We can go there and confess that we, too, think something is fundamentally wrong with the way the city works." Among the other prominent liberals drawn to the Institute were Bobby Wagner, son of the three-term mayor of the 1950s and 1960s, former Schools Chancellor and Cardozo Law School Dean Frank Macchiarola, and educational reformers Sy Fliegel, who had turned around a school district in East Harlem, and Colman Genn, "the Serpico of the schools," who had taken down a ring of corrupt Republicans in Queens who had been selling principalships. "The liberals have become enamored with the status quo," explained Genn. They had become "the bureaucrats, the unions, the runners of the current system.... Strangely enough, the right wing is now pushing for change. There's a terrific switching of roles."

Beginning in 1991 under its first editor Richard Vigilante and then under his successors Roger Starr and Fred Siegel, *City Journal* began to publish articles laying out the basis for a new urban agenda. George Kelling, co-author with James Q. Wilson of the seminal 1982 Atlantic article on "broken windows" policing, a former social worker whose life's mission was to improve policing, was given a policy megaphone by the Institute, which he put to effective use. In a Winter 1991 *City Journal* article, "Reclaiming the Subways," Kelling described how Bill Bratton, head of the transit police, had followed the "broken windows" approach of policing small crimes like fare jumping to sharply reduce major offenses. Here in précis was the policy that would produce a dramatic decline in crime under a new mayor.

The Summer 1991 issue had an article by Larry Mead, an NYU professor and one of the intellectual architects of welfare reform, explaining how putting welfare clients to work cleaning the streets and parks through what he called "workfare" could benefit both them and the city. Here too was a peek into the future.

In the fall of 1991, *City Journal* ran "Where the Money Goes" by economist Stephen Craig. He showed that while New York City spent 75 percent more per capita than other big cities, it spent a smaller proportion than the others on basic services. New York ran its own welfare state, spending far more on social services, health and housing without achieving a healthier or more upwardly mobile poverty population.

A Spring 1991 roundtable called "Can Neighborhoods Save the Day?" represented the road not taken. The panel, which included famed sociologist Nathan Glazer, Charles Murray, George Kelling, Fred Siegel and Ed Costikyan, a prominent New York attorney, discussed political decentralization as the path to reform. Decentralization, explained Costikyan, was a means to accountability, an alternative to bureaucracy with its stultifying overlays of overlapping audits designed not to produce effective government but merely to avoid obvious scandals. The ongoing scandal of city government, said the decentralizers in parallel with Osborne, was the vast sums expended to produce little in the way of outcome.

By the summer of 1991 the city's policy world was abuzz. Speaker Vallone, City Council President Andrew Stein and a variety of committees, commissions and think tanks were weighing in with plans to rescue the city. But what most caught the Dinkins administration's attention were the hearings held by the well-heeled and well-connected Stein, who had twice defeated Dinkins in contests for the Manhattan boro presidency. Looking at a run for mayor in 1993, Stein was clearly using the occasion to help launch his campaign.

The star of the Stein hearings was Ed Rendell, the newly elected mayor of Philadelphia, who had already taken on his city's unions in a bid to pull Philly back from the brink of bankruptcy. Rendell had gone so far as to hire a private company, Colin Service System, from the New York suburb of White Plains to provide janitorial services at Philly's beautiful but massive city hall at a saving of $750,000 a year.[8]

The administration was forced to join the debate. Dinkins announced a major speech on reform. Asked why he was giving the talk, the mayor responded, "We're on top of things, and that's important because some people have the impression that that's not the case."[9]

At the end of July 1991, just two days before the state Financial Control Board, which had the power to take over the city's finances, was to meet, a solemn Dinkins, hands folded, delivered a live eighteen-minute television address. The "Reform and Renaissance" speech contained the usual Bush-bashing and a few of the standard liberal nostrums like a residency requirement for all city workers, a practice which had helped grease the skids for Philadelphia's decline. And where else but in New York, the New Deal city intellectually frozen in the 1930s, would a mayor in the 1990s speak of how "the legacy of La Guardia and Roosevelt threatens to become a sad remembrance of the past"? But more importantly, this was a sober speech in which Dinkins acknowledged that "this is the most critical time in the history of our city.... The price to be paid for failure," he warned, "is the existence of our city itself."

Then, seeming to borrow his arguments from his critics at the Manhattan Institute, Dinkins spoke of city government as "a system that is inherently defective and outdated. In good times, the government expands in size without any improvement in the way our services are delivered. In bad times, the government merely reacts from crisis to crisis.... I will not allow the size of government to increase," he went on, "while the range and quality of services declines. My goal is.... to deliver more services with less revenue." To those ends he proposed:

▲ downsizing the city work force from 246,000 to 236,000 workers;

▲ changing the stifling work rules that inhibited productivity, reducing the salaries of starting workers and reducing the high ratio of supervisors to line workers, all of which required union cooperation;

▲ studying the possibility of contracting out some jobs such as towing and parking tickets to private companies;

▲ giving the mayor control over the Board of Education and reforming special education; and

▲ issuing monthly updates of productivity gains and calling for a revival of labor-management productivity councils.

Conceptually, at least, Dinkins had broken new ground. But the editorial response was overwhelmingly negative. "The trouble with his agenda," noted the *New York Times* editorialists, is that "this is not the first time he has promised reform." The speech, they said, "sounds like that of a brand-new mayor, not one in office for eighteen months." Further, they complained, "skepticism is in order because he hasn't been able to win significant concession from the unions." Other comments described the speech as a "re-hash" of "warmed-over" versions of old ideas.

Denouncing what they saw as more symbolism than substance, a sarcastic *Newsday* quipped, "You'd think that the mayor who embraced structural balance as his mantra in March would have one concrete plan to announce by the end of July. Sadly, he didn't."[10]

▲ ▲ ▲

The timing for the publication of *Reinventing Government* in January 1992 couldn't have been better. Nationally, Osborne had been linked to Arkansas Governor Bill Clinton's rising presidential campaign.

Locally, a December 1991 *Times* poll reported that 60 percent of adult New Yorkers would like to leave the city and 51 percent actually planned to leave. Seizing the moment, Sol Stern, City Council President Andrew Stein's ideas man, was in touch with Osborne even before the book's publication and Elaine Kamarck was writing about Osborne's ideas for *Newsday*.[11]

Osborne remembers it as a "wild time." There was a palpable sense of anticipation in the room when Osborne took to the podium in mid-February at a Manhattan Institute forum. Andrew Stein was present, as were numerous members of Giuliani's staff and a host of reformers. Osborne argued that the bureaucratic and centralized structures of city government, once a creative response to the problems of nineteenty-century industrialization, were obsolete in the information age. His master metaphor for describing the changes he proposed derived from the distinction between what he called "rowing" (directly providing government services) and "steering" (overseeing the delivery of those services by nonprofit agencies and private companies as well as by government).

Osborne told his audience that he favored not the privatization of city services per se, but rather competition between public and private providers to introduce a measure of accountability into government services. Merely contracting out, as in the case of the Koch administration's Parking Violations Bureau scandal, opened up new opportunities for kickbacks. The most serious corruption, he insisted, "was not the petty payoffs so common in building inspections, but the ongoing scandal of a municipality so straitjacketed by formal rules and regulations that it failed to perform no matter how much money was poured into its coffers."

The Manhattan Institute event was followed two weeks later by a morning colloquium on *Reinventing Government* organized by Andrew Stein and an evening book party for Osborne at Mortimer's, a chic Manhattan restaurant. Stein opened up the morning discussion, held just around the corner from City Hall, by asserting that "New York City government today is simply not working." Barry Feinstein, president of Local 237 of the International Brotherhood of Teamsters and a Dinkins supporter, concurred. "City management," he asserted, "is a failure." The Governor's son, Andrew Cuomo, who was the head of Dinkins' own commission on the homeless, similarly sounded an Osborne-like note by insisting that when it came to government programs "results rather than process should be rewarded." He pointed to his own programs for the homeless that provided housing and services at two-thirds what the city paid to house a homeless family in a welfare hotel. When it was his turn, Osborne spoke of making government more responsive to the needs of citizens, or "customers" as he described them. His calls for "de-massifying" bureaucracies to make them more responsive and "incentivizing" employees by rewarding performance generally fell on receptive ears

Even before Osborne's talk had ended, the Mayor's office had issued a twenty-eight-page response tweaking Mr. Stein for admitting he had touted the book before reading all of it. The Dinkins document also claimed that the city was already undertaking many of the reforms Osborne had called for and was even considering the possibility of privatizing some city services.

Questioned about whether he was supporting Stein for mayor, Osborne replied, "I will talk to anybody.... I'm spending three hours with Rudy Giuliani this afternoon." In that meeting Osborne told Giuliani and his chief policy aide Richard Schwartz about Peter Cove and Lee Bowes and America Works. Overall Osborne described his conversation with Giuliani as "the most interesting conversation I've ever had with a politician." Osborne saw Giuliani as a student of government who knew how to ask the right questions.[12]

Cove and Bowes would go on to brief Giuliani on welfare reform, and a few months later they in turn held another party for Osborne, whose wonkish book had by then become a fixture on the *New York Times* bestseller list. Giuliani, who had not yet announced his second run for mayor, was there, as were Manhattan Boro President Ruth Messinger, Dinkins' Deputy Mayor Stanley Brezenoff and Columbia public policy professor Bill Eimicke. Cove remembers that "everyone left to right was excited by the book, there was a sense that something significant was happening. Something that might bridge the left-right divide." Giuliani, who had read the book carefully by then, held court, asking Osborne questions. Giuliani, said Cove, was "fabulous" as he conducted a dialogue with Osborne as Messinger and others listened on attentively.

FIVE

Rematch

By 1993 Manhattan liberalism had lost some of its formerly effortless sense of superiority. A stunned *Village Voice* reporter described the scene at a town meeting held after Jeffrey Rose, a psychotic homeless man, had grabbed a baby away from its mother on the tony Upper East Side of Manhattan and began stabbing the baby in the face with a pen. When angry residents asked why Rose, who had been arrested eight weeks earlier for pushing a man through a glass deli counter, was back on the streets, Ettie Shapiro, director of a local neighborhood center for the homeless where Rose was a sometime client, responded: "The fact is as human beings we have very little control. And people don't want to face it." This produced boos and hisses. When a representative from the state office of mental health told the meeting that Rose had had a hard life, a local resident replied, "Don't give us this liberal crap."

At a meeting on the Upper West Side called in response to similar incidents along Broadway where the tree-lined median had been turned into an open-air insane asylum, Joe Brown, a computer programmer and community activist announced, "Something died recently.... We are today announcing the passing of brain-dead liberalism." Village resident Michael Gross, writing in *New York* magazine, saw that the city's tradition of tolerance, pushed too hard, had produced the intolerable. "The very things that made the Village what it is have now made it nearly unlivable," he complained. "After decades spent trying to fix the rest of the world, Villagers," he went on, "have been forced to recognize that now it is their world that needs help."[1]

For people caught up in the ferment of the early 1990s in New York, the Dinkins administration's failures were so manifest—the conditions of day-to-day life so intolerable, the disparity between New York's recession and the national economic recovery so obvious—that it seemed clear that Dinkins would have a very hard time winning a second term. The question, said Karen Rothmyer of *Newsday*, who saw the upcoming 1993 mayoral election as a rhetorical rematch of the 1992 presidential race, was "Can Giuliani successfully sell himself as a Republican version of Bill Clinton?"

Policy-minded reformers saw an obvious opportunity for renewal, but most of the public saw the situation as hopeless. Andrew Stein and Rudy Giuliani, the two major challengers, discovered that most voters, including many of their core supporters, were hostile to Dinkins but so gloomy about the city's prospects that they dismissed the possibility of reform.[2]

Whenever the contenders presented their ideas to the citizenry-at-large, including presumably well-educated upper-middle-class voters, they were met with three recurring phrases that captured the public's underlying sense of resignation. They were: "It could be worse," "What else can Dinkins do?" and, referring to the city's underclass, "Don't make 'em madder." Giuliani tried, with little success, to turn the "it could be worse" argument to his advantage. Comparing Dinkins to Churchill during the Battle of Britain, Giuliani noted "there was not much Churchill could do to stop the bombs from falling, but...he didn't just say that things were worse in Czechoslovakia."[3]

In the early 1990s over a million New Yorkers, many of them potential Stein or Giuliani voters, had simply given up on New York and moved elsewhere. Many of those who remained found the "it could be worse" argument highly plausible in a city widely assumed to be ungovernable. Besides, it was pointless to attempt reform, argued those remaining, given the impermeable nature of New York's vast and impenetrable maze of self-serving government bureaucracies. And besides, if you voiced too much discontent with an African-American mayor, might that not stir up the underclass whose violence was assumed to be a fact of life one just had to live with? The defeatism was clear in the answer to the poll question of whether Dinkins or Giuliani would do a better job with race relations. Forty-one percent picked Dinkins and 34 percent Giuliani despite the fact that by 54 to 24 those same people agreed that race relations had worsened under Dinkins.[4]

The sheer cynicism of New York's politics was exemplified by the case of City Councilman Rafael Colon. A man of deep consistency, he began his council career by defending people who assaulted meter maids and he ended by being indicted on 706 counts of larceny and fraud in a scheme to steal $800,000 by hiring phantom workers. Along the way he was accused of beating his ex-lover, owing child support for his eight children by four different women, putting a dead cousin on his payroll and, like many Bronx council members, living outside the city. His political passing produced barely a murmur. The city, Dinkins' challengers would discover, was blanketed in a permafrost of pessimism.[5]

▲ ▲ ▲

After his narrow loss to Dinkins in 1989, Giuliani seemed like a sure shot for the 1993 Republican nomination for mayor. But memories lingered of his flamboyant and sometimes overturned prosecutions of Wall Street brokers as well as the aftertaste of the bitter 1989 primary race he had run against cosmetics heir Ron Lauder. There was a truce of sorts between the candidate and Al D'Amato after Giuliani endorsed the Senator for re-election in 1992, but relations were cool at best. Giuliani did receive the support of the Manhattan and Staten Island Republicans led by Roy Goodman and Guy Molinari respectively. But the Queens County Republicans were skeptical about Giuliani. Their skepticism paled, however, before the open hostility of Brooklyn Republican leader Robert DiCarlo. A senior vice president at the financial firm of Kidder Peabody, DiCarlo's arbitrageur Richard Wigton had been ostentatiously arrested and humiliated by Giuliani on the trading floor in front of his colleagues, but never convicted.

The Republicans were sufficiently antagonistic to flirt with the possibility of backing the city council president, Democrat Andrew Stein, for mayor. Stein tried, with some success, to capitalize on both the "astonishing" level of "discontent" with the former prosecutor among the Republican leadership and on his wealthy father's close relationship with D'Amato. Stein's audacious plan was to win the nomination of both major parties.[6]

Stein, who held a hearing on how gun-toting marshals were conducting Rambo-like raids in order to collect fines from small business owners during the city's ongoing ticket blitz, depicted a bureaucracy that was literally feeding off its citizens. Small business owners, liable for any trash in front of their stores, were enraged by sanitation inspectors waiting for pedestrians to litter so that the store could be ticketed. The issue resonated broadly because the fines collected by the city on what were cynically described as "slow moving targets" had grown nearly 40 percent under Dinkins. Stein deftly rode the resentment generated by the disjuncture between a city capable of besieging its citizens with tickets but incapable of doing anything about crime to pull nearly even with Dinkins in the polls.

Stein sometimes needled Dinkins, as when, referring to the Washington Heights riot, he told a cheering audience at a police conclave, "The police should be invited to Gracie Mansion, not the families of drug dealers." Stein had a reputation as a policy lightweight, but thanks to a highly capable staff led by Sol Stern, he also wooed dissident Democrats, as well as Republicans and independents by laying out a vision of reform.[7]

The City Council President regularly laid Gotham's massive jobs losses at Dinkins' doorstep. While the mayor was placing his faith in a Clinton bailout, Stein noted that the new president would face innumerable demands on the federal budget. Further, noted Stein, the president was on record as saying that he wanted to reward cost-effective "entrepreneurial governments" that emphasized competition and consumer choice, hardly a description of New York. Stein also criticized Dinkins' key assumption that the city was the victim of Washington's policies. Dinkins, he noted, liked to complain that federal aid had shrunk from 20 to 11 percent of the city budget since 1980, but failed to note that in those same years the city budget had "skyrocketed from $12 to 30 billion.... It's hard to imagine," Stein noted caustically, that Washington will feel "obligated to underwrite New York's profligacy by supplying a fixed percentage of the ballooning annual budget." And if Gotham's problem was money, why, asked Stein, had the city's homeless bureaucracy been unable to spend $70 million in health care dollars that lay unused?

Stein's strategy was to make himself into the inevitable Democratic nominee and then offer himself to the numerous anti-Giuliani Republicans as their best hope as well. In May 1993 he issued a policy book rich in suggestions on how to save money and revive the economy by streamlining the city's bureaucracies. But Stein had a hard time winning support from the activists and insiders who drove the Democratic primaries. Faltering, Stein was the first of the 1993 candidates to go on the air with a commercial built on the widespread assumption that Dinkins was a weak leader. "Life in the city's tough enough," the ad asserted. "Without a mayor strong enough to fight back for people, it's even tougher." But despite running an expensive campaign that circumvented the city's campaign finance laws, Stein's call for civil service reform and good government never caught on.[8]

Part of Stein's problem was his political persona. "If you knew him," quipped a Giuliani operative, "you weren't that worried." Stein, who had made his reputation crusading against nursing home abuses, had an affinity for celebrity glitz that made him an easy target for the press. The son of a wealthy publisher of local newspapers, Stein didn't help his campaign when he held a garish fundraiser featuring his friends Frank Sinatra and Shirley MacLaine. And when Queens Democratic leader Tom Manton abandoned him, Stein was forced to drop out of the race.[9]

His failings aside, Stein had followed a flawed strategy. Overlooking the deep malaise that had overtaken the city, he assumed that the self-evident failures of the Dinkins administration, the loss of hundreds of thousands of private-sector jobs, and record crime levels were enough to guarantee him the Democratic Party nomination. He was mistaken. The interest groups most dependent on the city and whose votes and get-out-the-vote operations were crucial to winning the Democratic primary much preferred slow decline under Dinkins to the risks of reform.

Giuliani, who was proposing policies similar to Stein, also found it difficult to get his ideas taken seriously. But the former prosecutor had the advantage of a far more formidable political persona.

Study had been the leitmotif of Giuliani's career. When his mentor, Judge Lloyd MacMahon, handed him the receivership of a bituminous coal mine in Kentucky, Giuliani faced hostile miners who introduced themselves to him by asking, "Are you a Jew?" But Giuliani, like all great trial lawyers, was a quick study, and he used his knowledge of mining acquired for the occasion to win them over. "A leader," insisted Giuliani, "should have independently acquired understanding of the areas he oversees. Anybody who's going to take on a large organization must put time aside for deep study." He also contended that leaders have to know enough to fit all the specialized advice they receive into a coherent whole.[10]

After his narrow defeat in the 1989 mayoral election, Giuliani spent four years studying city government in preparation for taking office. Building on the base of knowledge he had acquired with Jennifer

Raab in the 1989 campaign, he and his staff analyzed and debated the articles appearing in the *City Journal*. After the *City Journal* ran a special issue on the salience of quality-of-life concerns, Giuliani picked up the quality-of-life flag and made it his own. Beginning in January 1992 with a long presentation on New York City government by Robert Wagner, Jr., his aides organized an extended set of seminars on key topics. George Kelling, the co-conceptualizer of "broken windows" policing, public space guru William H. Whyte and Reaganite economist Lawrence Kudlow were among the presenters. Giuliani generally listened attentively and asked pointed questions, but at times he engaged in hard-edged debate. He was strongly supportive of tax cuts. But when Kudlow insistently asserted that the new mayor's number one priority, the city's looming budget deficit notwithstanding, had to be quick and massive tax cuts, Giuliani made it clear that public order was his priority. On another occasion, when some of the guest attendees set an hysterical tone in discussing racial issues and told him to "stop pussyfooting around" on the relationship between race and crime, he told them to calm down and back off. "Crime," he insisted, "was not a racial issue."

But what was an issue for the electorate? Dinkins, wrote Sam Roberts, entered "office with only modest performance expectations according to the polls" yet "seemed even to some supporters to frequently perform below them." Still, two years into his term, a two-to-one majority of Dinkins supporters continued to back him despite many of them assuming that things would get worse rather than better over the long term.[11]

Dinkins' core support was unwavering even in the face of a stream of scandals involving his supporters. For instance, while their members in the Parks Department were facing layoffs and the union was raising dues, District Council 37 of AFSCME (American Federation of State, County and Municipal Employees) booked one hundred rooms at the Princess Resort and Casino in the Bahamas at the members' expense. AFSCME wasn't alone; three Dinkins appointees—the President of OTB (the Off-Track Betting Corporation), the only money-losing bookie in town; the head of the HHC (Health and Hospitals Corporation), which was raining red ink; and the Commissioner of the Human Resources Administration—traveled to the Virgin Islands for a conference on "the urban agenda." This produced some newspaper headlines but little in the way of public outrage.[12]

Similarly, another skein of scandals involving plumbing, sanitation and taxi inspectors was barely noticed. Corruption at the Parking Violations Bureau, where a scandal had been central to Koch's fall from grace, was shrugged off. The mood was summed up in a *Times* headline that read, "Amid a Heritage of Graft, a Taxi Bribery Scandal Seems Shocking to Few." Surveying Dinkins' core supporters, pollster Lou Harris found that Dinkins' white deputies and not the mayor were blamed for the scandal.[13]

Even the Laura Blackburne case didn't make ripples. In the midst of a recession in which New York City and State had lost more than a third of all the jobs eliminated nationally and the layoff of city employees was an ongoing possibility, Blackburne, Dinkins' appointee to head up the New York Housing Authority, had added fifty-three new administrative positions at a cost of more than $3 million a year. In an agency that, according to HUD estimates, needed 2,400 workers, there were already 4,200 employed. That's because the Housing Authority was running its own mini-HRA with its own offices of Minority Women Business Enterprise, Education and Alternative Resources, Youth, Action and Social and Community Services.

Blackburne, who was double-dipping as both head of the Housing Authority and as a member of the state-run Metropolitan Transportation Authority, was also in the news for spending $1,700 to have herself helicoptered from a ceremonial occasion to a speech she was giving in Atlantic City. Then, in February 1993 it was revealed that she had spent $32,000 to redecorate an already reasonably well-appointed office, including $3,000 on a pink leather sofa. Amidst more stifled yawns than embarrassment, she was forced to leave office.[14]

The Blackburne case was of little interest to New York's newcomers. In the years since 1980 the city had received 854,000 immigrants, the greatest influx of newcomers since Ellis Island had been closed in 1924. Of Gotham's 7.3 million people, 2.1 million were foreign born and 40 percent of the households spoke a language other than English.

Many of the natives were almost as anxious to leave as the immigrants were desperate to arrive. A *New York Times* poll found that 62 percent of the adult population said that life had worsened over the past four years. Only 9 percent said it had improved. And there was no expectation that things could be improved by a new mayor. As one respondent put it, "It's a bigger job than anyone can handle." Of those who had recently left the city, a Lou Harris survey found that 49 percent said that they or someone living with them had been mugged or attacked in the three years before they departed. And even among the new arrivals, both citizen and immigrant, two-thirds planned to leave within three years, and half said they doubted that the city had a decent future. If the middle classes left, warned City Council Speaker Peter Vallone, the city's tax base, already resting on a "precariously small number of people," was sure to crumble.[15]

Senator Moynihan shared Vallone's pessimism. In the early 1990s, as the percentage of welfare recipients in New York who were working actually went down despite the intentions of Moynihan's 1988 welfare reform legislation, the senator laid out a bleak vision in his *American Scholar* article "Defining Deviancy Down." Moynihan decried the cynical use that had been made of urban pathology. The breakdown of the black family, he noted, was extraordinary by historical standards, "yet there is little evidence that these facts are regarded as a calamity in municipal government," in part because such a collapse supports a vast network of social workers for whom "breakdown is a job opportunity."

Speaking to developers and businessmen of the Association for a Better New York in April of 1993, an acidulous Moynihan invited the audience to ask itself "what in the last fifty years in New York City is now better than it was." In 1943, he noted, there were 44 homicides by gunfire, 73,000 people on welfare and the illegitimacy rate was 3 percent. In 1992 those numbers were 1,499, 1.1 million and 45 percent. And while the New York of the late twentieth century had been unable to build Westway or any other major project, the George Washington Bridge had been built in the corrupt old days of Mayor Jimmy Walker in forty-nine months and well ahead of schedule. The violence that accompanied family breakdown, he went on, had numbed New Yorkers who had withdrawn into a protective shell, a "narcoleptic state of acceptance," similar to that of "combat infantrymen." The theft of car radios had effectively been decriminalized and people put up "no radio" and even "already robbed" signs in their car windows that the Senator described as "flags of urban surrender."

An angry Dinkins, who had been in the audience and heard the speech as a racial attack on his administration, responded that in Moynihan's "good old days, I wore the uniform of a U.S. Marine and I had to sit in the back of the bus."

Thoroughly marinated in a social science Calvinism, Moynihan largely dismissed the ferment around "reinventing government." "We're too brittle for that," he explained. Similarly, the press—with the exception of Joe Klein at *New York* magazine—either treated reinvention with a mixture of skepticism and scorn or followed Dinkins' lead in treating the new ideas as a Republican plot aimed at undermining liberal achievements. But, as one Dinkins advisor acknowledged, "there's nothing that Giuliani is talking about that isn't already on the backroom agendas within the administration."

In an article entitled "Mayoral Race in 'Toontown'," *Newsday*'s Michael Powell described the reaction to Giuliani's plan to save money on the Health and Hospitals Corporation. It's worth quoting at length:

> Rudolph Giuliani's proposal seemed customized for a city facing a billion dollar deficit—not even adventuresome by the standards of those who would reinvent government...
>
> Take a few money-losing hospitals, set up not-for-profit boards, and steer them into the private sector. Poor people would still flock to the clinic, employees would remain unionized and the pitiful quality of care just might improve....
>
> Now run this modest proposal through the Looney-Toons lens of negative ads and New York City's truncated mayoral dialogue and it comes out this way: Reaganite ex-prosecutor plots to throw poor patients out on the sidewalk while laying off thousands of black, white and Latino workers....

In this campaign, Powell concluded sorrowfully, "any hint of a new idea has often been dispatched with the force of a city dweller squashing a cockroach in the dish drain."

▲ ▲ ▲

In early September, Giuliani gave what was billed as his "Quality of Life" speech. The speech, which tied concerns about public space to the economy, crime and homelessness, was a conceptually coherent anticipation of much of Giuliani's unorthodox but highly successful first year as mayor. There were numerous reporters in attendance, but the arguments, which later were widely taken as common sense, were so unassimilable by the press that it went virtually uncovered by the city's dailies.

The logic of the speech derived from the assumption that what makes cities attractive and gives them much of their competitive edge over the suburbs was public spaces where, as Walt Whitman had poeticized, the life of democracy and commerce was leavened. The loss of public space, and with it public life, asserted Giuliani, had been a grievous, potentially fatal blow to the greatness of Gotham. "What unnerves most city dwellers is not crime per se," explained the candidate, "but rather the sense of menace and disorder which pervades day to day life." Giuliani then described the litany of day-to-day dysfunctions:

> It's the 'street tax' paid to drunk and drug ridden panhandlers.
> It's the 'squeegee' men shaking down the motorist waiting at a light.
> It's the 'trash storms,' the swirling mass of garbage left by peddlers and panhandlers and open-air drug bazaars on unclean streets.

These were, he said, signs of social and political breakdown in a city unable to protect either its space or its children. Giuliani went on to assert that the social breakdown threatened the city's economic viability in a competitive economy where "talented people...choose where they live based on quality of life." Then he asked the audience a question, "Is there anything you can do about it? Or do the rights of so few who are doing this have to take precedence over the rights of the rest of the people?"*

After linking Dinkins to the Church Avenue, Crown Heights and Washington Heights troubles, Giuliani referred to Moynihan's "Defining Deviancy Down" essay. The challenger insisted that in our attempt to be overly sensitive to the needs of the few, we destroy the rights of the many. The antidote, he insisted, was to use "broken windows" policing to restore the city's neighborhoods.

The city, he agreed with Dinkins, "owes the homeless help in achieving a second chance." But there had to be reciprocity. Rights couldn't simply be a one-way street; they had to be matched with obligations so that "in return, the homeless owe the city cooperation in reaching for that second chance."

---

*An example of what Giuliani was talking about came late in the campaign. Thirty-year-old Andrew Eristoff had been campaigning for city council with a pledge to get bicycles off the crowded sidewalks of Manhattan's East Side where a number of elderly pedestrians had been run down. When a cyclist approached Eristoff on 20th Street and 1st Avenue while he was campaigning, Eristoff asked the rider to stop because it was dangerous and illegal. The rider, Elie Granger, 31, replied, "I could hit you, and that would be illegal too and nobody would do anything about that either." He then punched the councilman, producing a pool of blood from a gash that resulted in twenty-two stitches. Granger was wrestled to the ground by Eristoff's aides and passers-by. It could have been worse; handed over to the police, he was also found to have been carrying a knife.

As the contest developed, the Giuliani camp found that their policy proposals, like limiting the homeless to ninety days in short-term shelters, were denounced as heartless "municipal Reaganism." Dinkins mocked Giuliani's talk about quality-of-life problems. He stuck with the 1960s concept of "victimless crime." The incumbent insisted that "killers and rapists are the city's real public enemies—not squeegee pests and homeless mothers."[16]

The Dinkins re-election team, building on the theme of "other people aren't so perfect either," continued to insist that New York was a city victimized by Washington just as Dinkins himself had been victimized by events and Republicans. Their first campaign ad began, "Along with the oath of office, they gave him massive deficits, a hostile administration in Washington and a city at the boiling point." Mike Tomasky of the *Village Voice* asked, "Who are 'THEY?'" The ad, noted Tomasky, pushed a "not so subtle polarization" and an attempt to make people feel sorry for the mayor. The upshot was that as the campaign moved past the pro-forma September party primaries, policy issues were either soft-pedaled or ignored while the campaign was increasingly fought out over the subtext of race and crime.[17]

▲ ▲ ▲

David Dinkins probably would have preferred to run a positive campaign for re-election. He tried at one point to float the idea that City Hall should expand its purview into the investment banking business. New York, his advisors suggested, could have its own industrial policy with the city-funding emerging industries like biotech and software while shoring up old-line industries like jewelry and apparel. Like Dinkins' hopes for a federal rescue, the idea went nowhere. This still left the possibility of a traditional campaign based on using the public treasury to buy votes. But the man Dinkins called his "partner," fellow liberal and New York Governor Mario Cuomo, didn't cooperate.[18]*

Before he would provide Dinkins with new dollars, Cuomo,

---

*Tensions between a New York governor and a New York City mayor are par for the course regardless of their respective party affiliations or ideology. That's because New York City, whose budget is larger than all but eight states, has to go hat in hand to the state government for many minor matters generally left in the hands of local jurisdictions. Everything from the closing time for bars to speed limits to the retirement age for public employees is in the hands of the governor and the state legislature.

backed by Municipal Assistance Corporation Chair Felix Rohatyn, demanded substantial cost-savings from the municipal labor force. Cuomo threatened the unions with a Financial Control Board takeover of the city's budget if they refused to play ball, but labor wouldn't budge.

Dinkins, feeling betrayed by Albany, responded angrily, "If the FCB tries to take over, the Korean boycott would be nothing compared to that." Dinkins threatened to "bring in Jesse Jackson and make this a real black-white thing."[19]

Tensions between the governor and the mayor intensified five months before the mayoral election. This issue for the governor was that more state money for Dinkins to buy votes meant fewer dollars for Cuomo to expend on disaffected upstaters and suburbanites for his own 1994 re-election campaign. With Dinkins threatening a doomsday budget unless the city received an additional $280 million in state aid, the three private members of the Financial Control Board, all Cuomo appointees, did what no Board had done in a decade. They publicly criticized what they called Dinkins' "permanent deficit." With two billion dollar shortfalls looming in the not too distant future, Heather Ruth, one of the private members of the Financial Control Board, told Dinkins that rather than look to Albany and Washington, "The process of identifying priorities, initiating changes and eliminating the permanent deficit is the city's responsibility." In an interview, Ruth, speaking for the other two private members, said, "We believe that it is unlikely, even if you get the best possible productivity and efficiency, that the city will be able to afford its current array of services. They have got to set priorities, do those services which they place a high priority on as efficiently as possible and be prepared to eliminate low-priority services." But in the year and a half leading up to the 1993 election, Dinkins actually added 8000 jobs at the Health and Hospitals Corporation and the Board of Education.[20]

Unable to run on his record, failed by his "partners" in Albany, and Washington, the Dinkins re-election strategy was summed up by two *Daily News* columnists. Jim Sleeper, a Dinkins critic, saw that the mayor's re-election strategy could be described with the slogan "vote your fears, not your hopes." The appeal to fear was highlighted by a Dinkins leaflet depicting a Latino father and mother on a mattress in a vacant lot. The caption read, "Rudolph Giuliani wants to bring you back to the old days." It drew an angry response from Latinos who said it was demeaning to depict a hard-working community as homeless dependents. Columnist Earl Caldwell, who was close to the Dinkins campaign, came to the same conclusion as Sleeper in a column headlined DAVE'S GOTTA PAINT RUDY AS DANGEROUS.

But how to do it? Dinkins' ace in the hole was Giuliani's behavior at a police rally held a year earlier in September 1992. The rally, which drew 10,000 cops to the steps of City Hall, was ostensibly a response to Dinkins' call to eliminate police representatives on the Civilian Complaint Review Board that reviewed cases of alleged officer misconduct. But the anger in the air was a reaction to the incident that had touched off the Washington Heights riots five weeks earlier, when Dinkins aggressively sided with a drug dealer who had been killed in a deadly confrontation with undercover cop Michael O'Keefe. The riled-up cops began chanting "no justice, no police," a play on "no justice, no peace." With some bearing racist signs such as "Dinkins we know your true color—yellow bellied" and "Dump the washroom attendant," the cops broke through police barriers and blocked traffic from the Brooklyn Bridge for half an hour. It was an ugly scene that had largely but not entirely died down when Giuliani, unaware of what had taken place earlier, arrived to speak. The candidate mounted a flatbed truck and twice in the course of his speech described Dinkins' police policies as "bullshit." The Dinkins campaign waited till the final days of the mayoral race to air TV ads featuring Giuliani fulminating before the out-of-control cops.

The ads were the capstone of a racially polarizing campaign that had remarkably little effect in moving voters. While Democrats regularly hinted that the Giuliani campaign would try to use racial issues to win, it was the Dinkins camp, aware that it lacked the ability to broaden his appeal, that first played the race card in an attempt to bring out the base. The race-baiting began when Eric Adams of 100 Black Men in Law Enforcement attacked Democrat Herman Badillo, a Puerto Rican who was backing Giuliani, as a race traitor for being married to a white woman. Soon after, Dinkins stood by silently as a group of black ministers denounced Giuliani as a fascist. Congressman Charles Rangel, a bitter opponent of whites being allowed to adopt black children, chimed in by insisting that Giuliani was so unqualified that if he wasn't white he couldn't have been a candidate. "The campaign," noted an insider, "was plagued by the sense that we're the good guys so anything we do is OK."

The Dinkins message was echoed and amplified by the *New York Times*, which looked at past record levels of crime and welfare and the loss of 330,000 jobs to assert that the only reason Dinkins wasn't a sure shot for re-election was white racism. "In 1989," wrote *Times*man Todd Purdum, "Mr. Dinkins...brought New York politics in line with its demographics: It was the last of the country's ten largest cities to elect a black, Hispanic or female mayor. Now he's a wounded incumbent.... What happened?" "The short answer," said Purdum, "is not much."[21]

In the course of the campaign, a flock of politicians and celebrities sang from the same script. Mario Cuomo argued that "it's not his record people are against, it's his race, just as in 1989 when he should have won easily.... The real question is why were they against Dinkins in '89?" President Clinton pulled out all stops when he came to town. Dinkins, he said, was facing a tough campaign only because "too many of us are unwilling to vote for people who are different than we are." "*This is not as simple as overt racism....* It's this deep-seated reluctance we have, against all our better judgment, to reach out across the lines.... This is not just New York, this is LA, this is the rural South."

Jesse Jackson is reported to have "leapt with joy" at Clinton's statement, but a Dinkins aide saw it differently. "Clinton," he said, "opened the door in a nuanced way, but in New York you never know who comes marching in the door next." It was only after the president's statement, noted Andy Logan in the *New Yorker*, that Dinkins' campaign manager said that "Giuliani reminded him of David Duke." Former light heavyweight champ Jose Torres, who campaigned arm-in-arm with Dinkins, said that Giuliani appealed to "anti-Semites and Ku Klux Klanners." The charges had scant effect on the electorate, but they helped poison the waters for whoever won the election.[22]

Giuliani, backed fulsomely by the *New York Post*, was relatively restrained. His slogan—One Standard, One City—was a subtle counterpoint to Dinkins' discredited "Gorgeous Mosaic." His media advisor David Garth, who had run winning campaigns all the way back to John Lindsay, went out of his way to present a kinder, gentler Rudy, running ads featuring the candidate's wife and mother.

Garth did a good job of encouraging the idea that there were wholesale Democratic defections to the challenger. In fact the switches were largely confined to high-level figures like Ed Koch; Bobby Wagner, son of the former Mayor and grandson of Senator Wagner, the architect of the New Deal's labor legislation; and Herman Badillo, the city's first Puerto Rican Congressman. The latter two had been caught up in the ferment and rethinking of the early 1990s.

Giuliani criticized supporters at his rallies when they referred to "those people." But many of his supporters continued to speak—and think—in such terms, as when state senate candidate Richard DiCarlo told an almost all-white Bay Ridge audience that "it's time to take back our city." Later, he told an elderly white audience that if Dinkins won, everyone "might as well move out of the city."[23]

But all the back and forth vituperation, reminiscent of the 1989 campaign, changed few minds. The same top/bottom alliance that elected Dinkins in 1989 stood with him in 1993: wealthy Manhattan liberals, real-estate developers, Wall Street executives, and the black business leaders who bankrolled both of Dinkins' mayoral campaigns. Giuliani could claim that like his fellow maverick Republican La Guardia he was running as a fusion candidate with the backing of the Liberal Party. In fact it had been reduced to little more than a patronage machine, but it offered Giuliani a second ticket line for those New Yorkers who feared their arms might fall off if they pulled the Republican lever. Giuliani's base remained the "Rudy-crats," an alliance of Republicans and middle-class white ethnics at odds with those above and below them on the financial scales.

One indication of the immobility of the opposing political camps was the reaction to the Girgenti Report on the Crown Heights riot. In 1991 a black mob rampaged for three days in the heavily black and Jewish Brooklyn neighborhood with minimal police interference after an accident in which a black child was killed by a Hasidic motorist. Wild rumors spread quickly after the accident and in the ensuing violence a mob shouting "get the Jew" pounced on a young Hasidic scholar who was murdered.

In the report commissioned by Governor Cuomo, attorney Richard Girgenti demonstrated that although Dinkins was well informed about the situation, he refused to take action. Eighty Jews and a hundred police were injured. Still the mayor chose, in classic John Lindsay style, to let the mob "vent."*

The damning Girgenti Report might have seemed to be concus-

---

*Sharpton had done his best to stoke up the anger. At the funeral for Gavin Cato, the young boy whose death in the traffic accident set off the rampage, Sharpton eulogized in full Farrakhan mode about Jewish "diamond merchants" and warned that there would be "no compromise, no meetings no *kaffe klatsches*." "You [whites]," he warned, will have to "pay for your deeds" because "we are the royal family on the planet" that created philosophy and mathematics, "we are the alpha and omega of creation.... God is on our side." Nonetheless, Sharpton summed up the assumption of much of the city when he said that with another mayor "it could have been much worse." Philip Gourevitch, "The Crown Heights Riot and Its Aftermath," *Commentary*, January 1993.

sive. When asked, 58 percent of those questioned said they didn't believe Dinkins when he insisted that he didn't know that the violence was out of control. The rioting came to an end after three days only when deputy police Commissioner Ray Kelly took it upon himself to end it. But a post-Girgenti report poll by the *Daily News* found that the findings had a negligible effect on the public's opinions of the candidates.

Giuliani, still a less than effective campaigner, was also unable to exploit the issue of the city's massive job losses. A *Crain's New York Business* poll rated the candidates equally likely to revive the economy even though 68 percent of those surveyed thought that the mayor had some (45 percent) or a great deal (23 percent) of responsibility for the weak economy. Part of the problem for Giuliani was that while even minimal layoffs at City Hall became a major political issue with extensive news coverage, not even massive private-sector job loss received much news coverage. The effect of the skewed reporting was that 40 percent of the presumably well-informed businessmen polled thought that New York had lost no more than 100,000 jobs in the last four years, well less than a third of the actual total.

The closing weeks of the campaign were taken up with a debate about debates. Dinkins' campaign advisor Harold Ickes didn't want a one-on-one debate. If there was a debate, Ickes wanted a three-way with the Conservative candidate, six-foot-six-inch banker and G.K. Chesterton scholar George Marlin, so Marlin and Dinkins could crush Giuliani in a sandwich attack.

Marlin and Giuliani were largely in agreement on fiscal issues but the well-spoken banker was sharply critical of the prosecutor's stance in support of abortion and gay rights. Much of the energy for Marlin's campaign came from a fight over the Rainbow Curriculum, an attempt to introduce a gay-friendly course plan, into the elementary grades. Giuliani refused to be subject to the erudite Marlin's William Buckley-like debating skills.

The only debates that took place were between Marlin and Dinkins. Dinkins and Giuliani never met in the course of the campaign. Marlin remembers, "We agreed to disagree about everything except Rudolph Giuliani." He says he was surprised how unprepared Dinkins was for the debate. The mayor had a sheaf of 5-by-7 cards to read from, and "Dinkins answered questions by reading directly from the cards, sometimes the wrong card."[24]

Shortly after the election, while driving in relatively conservative Bay Ridge, Marlin tells the story of a lady with a station wagon full of children stopping him and announcing, "You were the person I should have voted for, but I voted for Giuliani because I wanted to stop Dinkins." Giuliani himself played on that sentiment with campaign handouts in Catholic outer-boro neighborhoods that read: "A vote for the Conservative Party candidate is a vote for Dinkins." The message took hold—when the votes were counted Marlin received less than 1 percent of the total.

Giuliani's anti-Dinkins message took hold on Staten Island. The smallest boro was still smarting over the 1989 charter changes, which eliminated the Board of Estimate and with it most of the island's influence over city politics. The charter change engendered a vigorous Staten Island secession movement supported by 60 percent of the island's adult population. Staten Islanders were accustomed to being condescended to by Manhattanites. When the New York Bar Association (located on 43rd Street) held a debate on secession, they didn't even think to invite anyone from the boro considering it. But on election day Staten Island got a measure of revenge.*

The 1993 election numbers bore a striking resemblance to the tally of four years earlier. But while Dinkins won by 47,000 votes in 1989, he lost by 50,000 in 1993. With the teachers' union remaining neutral, Giuliani picked up the votes of some moderate liberals who had become swing voters after four years of continued decline, but they were more than matched by the 1989 Giuliani voters who had chosen to exit the city. The biggest change—the difference the drove the outcome—noted Bill Lynch of the Dinkins' campaign, was the size of the Staten Island turnout, where the secession issue had produced a 3,500 vote swing from the 1989 election. For all the ferment and angry exchanges, Dinkins was defeated largely by charter changes that had been designed to further empower African-American politicians.

Dinkins' defeat was atypical for New York mayors or black

---

*An editorial in *The Staten Island Advance* on 10/8/93 spoke to the secessionist sentiment. It read: "It takes hours to get someone to answer the phone in some agencies, days to get an intelligible answer to a simple question, months to transact straightforward business, years to get the proper permits to open a business or build an addition. Try to get a birth certificate, let alone a building permit."

incumbents nationally. He was the first New York mayor in the twentieth century to lose a bid for re-election. Nationally, on average, white support for the same black mayoral candidate increased by 25 percent when they became an incumbent. Even in white-majority cities, black incumbents running against white challengers were re-elected 74 percent of the time. Having a black mayor also seemed to change white attitudes on racial issues over time. In Chicago, where Harold Washington, the city's black mayor, fought hand-to-hand for four years with racially hostile members of the city council, he was able after his first term to make substantial gains among white liberals. In New York it went the other way, with Giuliani making gains among Upper West Side Liberal women defecting from Dinkins on the crime issue.[25]

Dinkins was defeated, in part, by a rigid adherence to his "vision." The incumbent might have won over just enough jittery, crime-weary, undecided white moderate Democrats and independents to squeak by to re-election if he had flooded the streets with police in the run-up to the election. With an additional $5 hundred million in tax revenue, Safe Streets/Safe City had enabled him to hire 6,000 additional police officers. But he had hired only 2,000 in order to spend more money on social services. Dinkins lost because he was never able, unlike first-time black mayors in other cities, to win over white swing voters.

Michael Tomasky, writing in *The Nation,* surveyed the reasons for Dinkins' failure. "Progressive New York," he wrote, "speaks only in the coded language of identity politics and entreaties to oppressed subgroups. It's a language that sounds noble when talking of black or Latino 'empowerment,' cloaking itself in the rhetoric of civil rights, and comity...but in the end it is the same old interest group palm-greasing, just like the Irish pols used to play it, dressed up in a multicultural tuxedo." "Above all," Tomasky concluded, "there has to be a single standard for civil behavior." By a slim margin, the voters agreed. They had, in their wisdom, not so much chosen Giuliani as rejected Dinkins. The outcome, a narrow victory for uncertainty over fear, was not a mandate for fundamental change. But then again the same was true of La Guardia's victory in 1933.

The Changing of the Guard

I n the months after the election, City Hall veterans talked of how Giuliani, the first mayor in sixty years to ascend to the position without ever having held elective office, might not be able to govern. Speaking to that possibility, three days before Christmas, the outgoing mayor came before the council to give an unprecedented farewell address to the city's near-permanent political class. Seeking to defend his own legacy and define the limits of his successor's power, Dinkins reminded the council, which had often bucked him, of their own power under the new charter. "There was," he commented bitterly, "no overwhelming mandate, of defeat or of victory" in the recent election. "New York City," he went on, "has elected a mayor with a very different ideology and philosophy than we have seen in City Hall in recent decades." The incoming mayor's narrow victory and alien philosophy, Dinkins suggested, meant that it was up to the council to use its muscle to keep Giuliani in line. "It's up to you," he told council members, "to make sure that New York's working people—the union members who bailed us out of fiscal crisis—do not become scapegoats for a city's ills." "Now more than ever," here he raised his voice, "New Yorkers will look to their Council to protect the MOST PROUDLY PROGRESSIVE GOVERNMENT ON GOD'S EARTH." The council applauded the mayor fifteen times during his twenty-four-minute speech and then gave him a framed proclamation praising him for creating "a kinder, gentler city."[1]

Mark Green, who had been Dinkins' Commissioner of Consumer Affairs, heeded the call of the farewell address. Sworn into the largely powerless position of Public Advocate, Green, who had his eyes on the mayoralty, delivered the lengthy inaugural speech of a man who expected to take over in four years. Like many high-ranking Democrats, Green assumed that Giuliani, shut out by the political class, would prove himself incapable of running the city. Like Dinkins, Green spoke of a rescue from Washington. If the federal government "invested billions of dollars in the nineties in a Gulf War, isn't it time now we invest in an Operation Domestic Storm here at home?" he asked rhetorically. Neither Green nor Dinkins understood that they were speaking a political language that was being overtaken by the election results from around the country.[2]

▲ ▲ ▲

The big city elections of the early 1990s were a referendum on urban decline. In Los Angeles, Republican businessman Richard Riordan, a white centrist, won on the slogan "Tough enough to turn the city around." In the wake of the Los Angeles riots, he defeated Asian-American Mike Woo, who had promised to carry on the policies of outgoing liberal mayor Tom Bradley, an African-American, who had dominated the city's politics for two decades. In both LA and New York, moderates who talked about jobs and crime defeated "rainbow coalition candidates" who had tried to portray their opponents as rabid right-wingers.

The same set of centrist Democratic Leadership Council issues dominated the black-on-black elections in Detroit and Cleveland. In Detroit, where the angry left-liberal Coleman Young had dominated politics since the early 1970s, Young's handpicked successor Sharon McPhail, a self-described "homegirl," was defeated by former Judge Dennis Archer, who ran as a moderate. But it was a measure of the changes afoot that even McPhail spoke of cutting taxes and increasing the number of police, while Archer, in an affront to the Young legacy of racial separatism, promised to reach out to the surrounding white suburbs in order to bring jobs to the dying city. McPhail tried to paint Archer as "selling out" to whites, but the old appeal to racial solidarity backfired. When Archer was asked what he would do about jobs, he made the increasingly accepted argument that anti-crime efforts were the path to economic renewal.

In Cleveland, incumbent Mike White won re-election against council president George Forbes, who ran as the candidate of black power and the public sector unions. Angering the unions by eliminating some of the city's exotic work rules, White presented himself as pro-business, pro-police and an effective manager above all, arguing that "jobs were the cure for the 'addiction to the mailbox,'" referring to welfare checks.[3]

The change wasn't confined to the big cities. Across the Hudson from Manhattan, former Wall Streeter Bret Schundler had brought business savvy and a push for lower crime and taxes to Jersey City, which had long been dominated by a machine best known for the number of felons it had produced. In Hartford, Carry Saxon Perry, the first black female mayor of a sizeable city, was defeated for re-election after three two-year terms characterized by business flight and gang wars. Perry, a former social worker, described herself, as Dinkins did, as a "healer." She lost to Mike Peters, a former fireman, who became the first white mayor in twelve years by capitalizing on the anger of alienated homeowners.

In Boston, liberal Mayor Ray Flynn, Dinkins' ally on the national stage, was replaced by Thomas Menino, the city's first Italian chief executive, and one whose focus was entirely local. The issues in Boston were captured in a *Globe* headline that read "CANDIDATES FACE A TYPE OF 'EXIT' POLL: Fleeing Families Fear Boston Can't Be Fixed." Menino scored points whenever he stood up to the powerful teachers' union, which along with rising water and tax costs was seen as driving families with school-aged children to the suburbs.[4]

Like John Norquist in Milwaukee and Steve Goldsmith in Indianapolis, Menino was dedicated to keeping and attracting middle-class families. The new wave of mayors was exemplified by Richard Daley of Chicago who was accused of "thinking more like a businessman than a politician." "The whole idea," of his administration, Daley explained, was "to get the middle-class back into the city." That was the approach the Giuliani team brought to New York City government.[5]

▲ ▲ ▲

Giuliani's transition process took place in the looming shadow of massive budget deficits and a sick economy weakened by a slew of tax hikes. The outgoing comptroller, Democrat Elizabeth Holtzman, had earlier warned that the Dinkins tax hikes would deepen and prolong the recession in New York. The warning, she noted, had come to pass. New York's economic recovery lagged far behind the country, producing a $2 billion budget gap for the next fiscal year, projected to grow to $3.2 billion by fiscal 1997. A slow recovery was beginning, she acknowledged, but Holtzman expected a growth of only "19,000 jobs a year over the next three years. At that rate, it will take about twenty years to recover the 361,000 jobs lost in the recession." The city, she concluded, could expect budget deficits as far as the eye could see.*

Giuliani took Holtzman's point. In order to balance the budget as required by state law, "we have to increase the number of private-sector jobs," the mayor-elect asserted. And the only way to do that was "to reduce the size and cost of city government."

The formal transition led by Giuliani's close confidante, Dennison Young, organized 800 people into forty committees and subcommittees. The key staff members leading the committees were intensely aware of what reform mayors had done elsewhere and were in contact with those mayors' policy advisors. The various committees on procurement, transportation, health, social services and so on tossed around ideas for agency consolidations and possible privatizations.

Some of the most significant testimony before the transition committees came from Harvey Robbins, director of the Office of Operations in the Dinkins administration. Robbins laid out the case for consolidating a number of minor agencies and reducing the number of deputy mayors. He talked about the absence of clear lines of authority that had forced his Office of Operations to serve as an arbitrator between the budget office and the line agencies. He was listened to carefully as was Koch's former Commissioner of Transportation Ross Sandler who took up a similar line of argument.

A key transition document was the draft of a paper by Sandler later published in the *City Journal* in which he explained how the powerful Office of Management and Budget created in the wake of the 1970s fiscal crisis confused management and budget, subordinating the latter to the former. Prior mayors, he argued, had been cut off from the operation of the line agencies directly delivering public

---

*In a December 1993 Comptroller's Report to the City Council on "The State of the City Economy," written for Holtzman by economist Steven Kagann, he pointed out that the tax burden on New Yorkers is nearly twice the national average. He warned that if the mayor went ahead with a proposed additional $580 million in new taxes on top of earlier massive tax increase, the city could lose 265,000 private sector jobs by 1994 even as the rest of the country had recovered from the recession. The city did even worse than predicted, losing about 345,000 jobs.

services by the proliferation of innumerable "layers of staff between the mayors and the agency heads." "The result," Sandler went on, "was a disadvantageous paradox in which power had been simultaneously overly centralized in City Hall and overly diffused between mayoral agencies so that no one commissioner had the power to discharge his or her responsibility to manage, and neither they nor the mayor could be held responsible for their failings."

Giuliani gave careful consideration to decentralizing city services as a response to the dilemma Sandler had described. In extended discussions with his staff, Giuliani had debated the virtues of giving more authority to local officials who could then be held clearly accountable for a particular service. There was also a political dimension to his interest in decentralization. Two of his key supporters—Staten Island's Republican Boro President Guy Molinari and Queens' Democrat Boro President Claire Schulman—were the leaders of the two boros where secessionist sentiment had been the strongest. They were eager to restore some of the power that had been taken away from their offices by the 1989 charter revision. Giuliani told the press that decentralization "might allow us to define the mayoralty more sensibly.... It may be that you really should have less than all that power because you can't do all of that well."[6]

But in the debates about decentralization, time and again Giuliani in questioning its advocates found that their answers about ways the budget deficit could be curbed by dispersing power came up short. Besides, to control the budget he needed the cooperation of the city council and its powerful speaker, Peter Vallone. The council, newly empowered by both the charter changes that eliminated the Board of Estimate and the failings of the Dinkins administration, would respond ferociously to any change that enhanced the powers of the boro presidents at their expense. Over time, Giuliani chose to centralize power in the mayor's office, but the ideas associated with greater local autonomy never completely died away. And as a practical matter, consolidating executive authority could be entirely consistent with decentralizing the delivery of city services.

The centralized approach made the loyal band-of-brother prosecutors around Giuliani all the more important. A natural leader, he gathered a group of loyalists around him wherever he went. (Andrew McCarthy, who later successfully prosecuted the Blind Sheik responsible for the 1993 World Trade Center Bombing, described Giuliani as "the most inspiring man I ever worked for.") During his time at the law firm of Patterson, Belknap and Webb, Giuliani's independent ways drew in a group of men who in a double entendre become known as "Rudy and the Rudettes." During his days at the Justice Department, where future key mayoral staffer Denny Young and Deputy Mayor Randy Levine worked under him, his followers were known unflatteringly as the "Yesrudys." Bright, dedicated, capable like Giuliani of working nearly round the clock and largely in agreement on the central issues, the men Giuliani had led as a lawyer became the core of the administration.

▲ ▲ ▲

Tensions between Dinkins, a lame duck angry about having lost, and Giuliani, a mayor-elect anxious to get to work, came to the surface ten days after the election. Giuliani complained about Dinkins' ongoing attempts to negotiate a last-minute settlement with the sanitation workers since garbage collection was going to be considered for privatization. He accused the outgoing mayor of a "cheap political trick" in planning the resignation of Victor Gotbaum, Dinkins' appointee on the Board of Education, so that Gotbaum's replacement would have to be left in office for at least six months. Both of these disputes played out in a gray zone. What was clearly unfair on Giuliani's part were his repeated attacks on the contract Dinkins negotiated for the U.S. Tennis Center in Queens, home of the U.S. Open, one of the four premier tennis events in the world. Giuliani repeatedly described the well-wrought contract as a "boondoggle." But in marked contrast with the city's arrangements for Yankee Stadium, the tennis center has proven to be of lasting benefit to the city; it is the most profitable of the city's stadiums for New York's treasury.*

The tensions over last-minute appointments were summer storms. More enduring was the clash between Giuliani and the liberal political establishment represented by the *New York Times* over the findings of the Kummerfeld Report, "On Eliminating the Structural Budget Imbalance." The report, commissioned by Dinkins in May 1993, after the Financial Control Board issued a tongue-lash-

---

*Giuliani was so angered by Dinkins' literally last-minute appointments on December 30th 1993 that he personally wrote to some of the appointees urging them to decline. One such letter written on 1/5/04 went to Thomas Schwartz of the law firm Skadden, Arps, Slate, Meagher & Flom who had been appointed Chairman of the Campaign Finance Board replacing Father Joseph O'Hare. In this case the appointee took Giuliani's advice. Municipal Archives.

ing, originated as "part of an effort to quash criticism about his handling of the city's finances."[7]

Kummerfeld's report, which appeared after the election, warned that the city was rapidly approaching a "fiscal collision point" because "spending is growing faster than revenues." The core problem, it explained, was that "the base of recurring spending is significantly larger than the recurring tax base." Faced with a choice between funding the city's basic services and the "overwhelming human needs of the deprived population, ...the quality of life functions get starved or deferred, at best." The report's solution was a set of dedicated funds to pay for basic functions. "Otherwise," he predicted, New York "will become another Detroit."[8]

The thirty-page report had its share of conventional bromides such as asking for more money from Albany and calling for a state takeover of Medicaid, a perennial wish of mayors that is always rejected by governors. But, less conventionally, it also called for a phased end to rent control and the elimination of the state's Wicks law, which, among other things, prohibited the hiring of general contractors on government-funded projects, which inevitably leads to inflated construction costs. Some of the Kummerfeld proposals designed to allow the city to manage its cycle of booms and busts were later picked up by the Giuliani administration as part of a package of proposed charter reforms.

The press played up certain section of Kummerfeld's report. On the savings side, the report insisted that there was little to be gained in reducing or eliminating social programs since virtually all were necessary; it called for reducing costs through 35,000 layoffs and asking the next mayor to cancel the new police class. On the revenues side, it asked for tolls on the East River bridges; an increased property tax on single family homeowners; and extending the sales tax to long distance calls, newspapers and periodicals, personal services and cable TV and movie theaters.

The report's political core, which called for higher taxes and layoffs while preserving all of the city's welfare and social spending, was supported by the *New York Times*, *Newsday*, the Citizens Budget Commission (a business-funded budget watchdog group), the New York City Partnership (which represented the city's largest and politically best connected companies), and Standard & Poor's, a bond-rating agency. Richard Larkin of Standard & Poor's, "whose utterances on the city's fiscal health have been studied by city officials like tea leaves," said Giuliani's aim of reviving the economy was laudatory but "largely beyond the control" of a mayor.[9]

But in a sign of an unexpected alliance to come, the Kummerfeld Report was denounced by both the unions and Giuliani, who described it as uncreative "old thinking." Giuliani, the first mayor in the century to win without carrying Manhattan, was, like Koch in his early years, the candidate of the outer-boro home-owning middle class. In a speech to Women for Giuliani, he described Kummerfeld's call for bridge tolls as the equivalent of "giving people a one-way ticket" out of the city.[10]

Giuliani's "old thinking" comments offended the *Times*, which delivered an editorial lecture to the mayor on how "for his own good and the city's he needed to read every line" of the report. But Giuliani wasn't about to be lectured by the editors of the *Times*, who were players in city politics as much as observers. Giuliani held them partly accountable for the failed social and economic policies of the 1960s, when the paper's editorial board, effectively part of the Lindsay cabinet, had pushed for a massive increase in the welfare rolls. The *Times* editorial board, he also noted, had been enthusiastic about Dinkins' ill-advised tax hikes. He shot back, in a letter mimicking the tone of the *Times*: "I would commend to your reading list *A Ship Without a Captain*," a recent, detailed report of the Dinkins administration's Procurement Policy Board, which sank from sight under the old-thinking regime. Over time, the new administration would largely ignore the self-described "paper of record." But within the administration the term "Kummerfeld" became a synonym, even a gag-line, for something that was obviously wrong-headed.*

▲ ▲ ▲

Two of Giuliani's key appointments, Deborah Wright at Housing Preservation and Development and Bill Bratton at the Police Department, almost didn't happen. Back in 1961, famed sociologist Nathan Glazer writing in *Commentary* worried about the city's administrative osteoporosis: "Our need," he wrote, "is for disruption of the organizations [by people] who can batter the bureaucracies and

---

* Giuliani's respect for the *Times* wasn't enhanced when, according to some of those present, at a meeting with the editorial board the paper argued for more cops for Times Square, the site of their office, and police cuts across most of the rest of the city.

make them respond to real problems." Wright and Bratton fit that bill. Both were fearless risk-takers who broke with what was expected. Both proved wildly successful.

Wright, a graduate of both Harvard Law and Harvard Business School, came from a long line of preachers. Wright's father was a powerful and well-respected pastor in Brooklyn and her aunt, Marian Wright Edelman of the Children's Defense Fund, was one of Washington's leading liberal anti-poverty warriors. Wright, then in her early thirties, had played a role in the Dinkins administration by helping to straighten out the scandal-ridden New York City Housing Authority at a time when the federal government was threatening to withhold monies from the city.

When Dinkins was defeated, Wright expected to go to work in the private sector for Richard Parsons, the new chair of The Dime Savings Banks. But the very persuasive Parsons was also the chair of the Giuliani transition committee. As Wright tells it, Parsons sat her down on his couch and began, "I know you don't want to stay in government, but Giuliani doesn't have a coterie of black advisors and it would be important for the city if you could meet him." She was hesitant, but Parsons placed her possible role in the context of both the city's racial tensions and what he saw as "the historic opportunity" presented by a Giuliani administration. When she finally agreed to at least meet the mayor-elect, Parsons counseled her not to mention Marian Wright Edelman.

When they met, a reluctant Wright, to her great surprise, was "disarmed by the self-deprecating" Giuliani. The first thing he said was, "I'm not just interviewing you, you're interviewing me as well. Let's talk about David Dinkins." She was charmed by his intelligence and by his open acknowledgment that he needed her because, as he explained, "I don't know about housing." Giuliani was unconcerned about her connection to Dinkins; the one thing he wanted to know about her was where she stood on the city's vast holdings of *in rem* housing. *In rem* is Latin for "against the thing." In this context it refers to the vast stock of abandoned housing the city owned because the landlords, strapped in part by the city's rent-control regulations, had walked away from their properties. While other cities auctioned off such buildings, New York started taking possession of them in the early 1970s on the premise that the housing bureaucracy could rehabilitate such properties and then turn them over to non-profits or tenants' groups as a source of affordable housing. But as Malcolm

Gladwell explained in an insightful *Washington Post* dispatch, the result was instead that "New York has become the largest slumlord in the country, with 33,000 units of some of the worst housing in the city on its hands. None of the buildings pays taxes. By one recent survey, 58 percent had rat problems and 30 percent had holes in the floor. Unable to manage or protect its inventory of buildings properly, New York loses about $3,500 per apartment per year."[11]

In rem housing was costing the nearly bankrupt city a small fortune to maintain, and it undermined neighborhoods to boot as it was taken over by drug dealers and junkies. "Shaking hands," as Wright put it, "on a conceptual level," Giuliani and Wright agreed on the need to move abandoned and run-down housing into private hands as quickly as possible.*

The last and most significant personnel choice for the new administration was the appointment of Bill Bratton, chief of the Boston police department, as New York Police Commissioner. Between 1983 and 1986 Bratton had reduced crime on "the T," Boston's decrepit trolley line system, by 27 percent. In New York, he achieved even more impressive results. When he took over as the top transit cop in April of 1990, the infrastructure of the subways had been considerably improved during the Koch years through the efforts of Robert Kiley and David Gunn who rebuilt tracks, switches and signals, and reduced the graffiti. But the subway's stations and cars were still overrun with hustlers, hoodlums and the homeless. More than one "customer" in twenty jumped the turnstiles and passengers were subject to long lines at the token windows and aggressive panhandlers trolling the subway cars.

Bratton inherited a thoroughly demoralized transit force. Schooled in the innovative use of statistics, the Boston native was a natural leader who could inspire by example. In one famed case, he had walked on to a Boston overpass alone and convinced an armed gunman to surrender. Working with George Kelling, the co-conceiver of "broken windows policing," Bratton first revived morale by spending time underground with his troops. Then he instituted a new set of polices that drove crime down dramatically.

Dinkins had been dismissive of the idea that you can police disorder. Like most mayors and even police chiefs, he thought that

---

*The Koch administration was the first to tackle the *in rem* situation. With the help of the Community Preservation Corporation, Koch made a big dent in rehabilitating the housing units that had been defaulted into the city's hands.

police responding to 911 calls should react to major crimes and criminals. This idea had taken hold in the 1970s, replacing earlier concepts of beat-walking and neighborhood policing, both as a response to improved telecom technology and a reaction to corruption scandals. By contrast, Kelling and Bratton saw crime as a seamless web. They said that if you took care of the small things like broken windows or subway fare-beating, you'd affect major crime as well. That's because the people breaking the small rules were often the same ones committing the major felonies. In a 1992 *City Journal* interview, Bratton explained that there was an inextricable interconnection between fare-beating and other crimes. Roughly two of thirteen fare-beaters, he noted, had outstanding felony warrants. Catch the fare-beaters and you also capture the felons carrying weapons. Bratton got his force to buy into "broken windows policing." It worked. Subway felonies dropped 75 percent, and robberies 64 percent between 1990 and 1994. Transit police sweeps of fare-hoppers found that one out of every seven people arrested either possessed a weapon or was the subject of a felony warrant. This had the added bonus of dramatically cutting down on fare-beating and increasing paid ridership. All of which sent a signal that the subways were once again under the purview of the police.

But Bratton's success in the early 1990s was largely invisible to Dinkins. Bratton returned to Boston where he briefly served as chief of police.

Initially the front-runner for the Police Commissionership in the Giuliani administration, Bratton was ambivalent about the possibility because he had only been at his new job as Boston's police chief for a year. Torn, Bratton temporarily withdrew. In his absence, the capable Ray Kelly, Dinkins' last police commissioner, became the front-runner. But when Bratton, who was touted by the Grand Council of the Guardians, a black police officers' organization, threw his hat back into the ring, he received the nod. Making the announcement at his transition headquarters, Giuliani explained, "This is a difficult choice because I have great respect for Commissioner Kelly, great respect for what he's done with the Police Department throughout his career." But, he continued, he felt it was important to bring in a new chief who could take a fresh look at policing.

Announcing his return to New York with a burst of Churchillian rhetoric, Bratton told the city "I did not come here to lose. We will fight for every house in the city. We will fight for every street. We will fight for every borough. And we will win." [12]

PART II

Giuliani Takes Charge

SEVEN

Breaking the Mold

Giuliani's January 1994 inauguration did little to shake the city's pessimism. While the national economy was recovering robustly, Gotham's unemployment rate was 11 percent. The city had been losing an average of 235 jobs a day for four years, its economy sinking under the weight of a government that employed one of every five New Yorkers directly and another one in five indirectly not to mention the one of out six (a total of 1.2 million) residents on the dole. In addition to the city's ownership of nearly 5,000 abandoned buildings and 30,000 apartment units and its responsibility for managing some 3,000 buildings of public housing for some 600,00 residents, it also owned 500 gas stations, seventeen hospitals, radio and television stations, a hotel and eighty off-track betting parlors. The weight of this burden placed a $2.8 billion budget deficit—a sum larger than the budget of four states—on the shoulders of the new mayor.[1]

It wasn't clear that Giuliani could rise to the challenge. He delivered an ineffectual inaugural speech. With his seven-year-old son Andrew tugging his leg, the new mayor proclaimed, "The era of fear is over." New York, he insisted, was "governable." But with Gotham averaging five murders a day, most people took a wait-and-see attitude. Still, the speech struck some of themes that would define his mayoralty. Giuliani talked with pride of his immigrant grandfather Rodolfo "who came here with twenty dollars in his pocket" but achieved a better life for his family. And he insisted that in a city where "diversity" was rightly respected "as a source of our strength," it was imperative to apply a single "standard of fairness" that transcended racial and ethnic lines.*

Pride of place in the inaugural speech went not to crime or the economy but to the February 1993 attack on the World Trade Center that took six lives and commanded seven paragraphs. The attack could have been far more costly. Had the 1,500 pounds of explosives carried in the terrorists' van been parked just a few feet closer to a wall that sealed the foundation off from the Hudson River, there would have been far more death and damage.

Dinkins, mayor at the time, had been on an overseas trade mission when the bombing took place and was little effected by the attack. But Giuliani, who quickly recognized the link between the bombing and the 1990 assassination of the anti-Arab extremist Meir Kahane by Islamists, saw the attack as a momentous event with enormous implications for the future. New Jersey Governor Jim Florio similarly talked of "a new chapter in American history" in which "as a society, we're going to have to start thinking about things like access to weapons and explosives."[2†]

The newly installed mayor praised the police, fire, and nursing rescuers, and described the city's response to the terror attack as a model for what he hoped would be Gotham's self-reliant future. It was a moment, said Giuliani, when "50,000 New Yorkers took charge of themselves and each other, showing on their own even before any city worker could help them...the New York spirit." The response, said Giuliani, was "a demonstration of the courage and ingenuity we must apply to restoring public safety, saving our schools, creating jobs, controlling our budget deficit and improving the quality of our lives."

Only after these comments did he turn briefly to another emergency, crime. He mentioned the city's fiscal and economic problems only in a passing phrase. The speech was a lost opportunity to educate the public on how crime and the economy were connected.

Giuliani took pains in his inaugural speech to talk of how, in a break with recent years, he had put together a highly "bipartisan"

*In a campaign speech before Women for Giuliani, he began similarly by saying he would speak not to women's issues but on what was "important for all New Yorkers."
†On the Kahane killing, see the appendix "A Short History of Terror Attacks on New York." There were suspicions in the wake of the 1991 Gulf War of Iraqi involvement in the 1993 attack. The lead bomber, Ramzi Youssef, whose nom de guerre was "Rasheed the Iraqi, came into the U.S. from Iraq. The bombers, who had

government. This was true insofar as two of his four deputy mayors, John Dyson in charge of economic development, and Ninfa Segara, who had the education portfolio, were Democrats. But neither of them had any City Hall experience. With one exception, none of the top Giuliani staff had ever worked in the office of the mayor. This led Sam Roberts of the *Times*, voicing a common concern, to write that "the fledgling administration is long on earnestness and independence—some say arrogance—and short on experience. Arguably, it owes little, but knows less." Or as a former official told Roberts, "You don't populate a whorehouse with virgins."[3]

Roberts' doubts about whether Giuliani's novice crew could govern were shared by the city council, which viewed the new mayor as a usurper. They couldn't imagine how a Republican could lead an overwhelmingly Democratic Gotham. The city's legislative body, its powers enhanced by the new charter, had already flexed its muscles by frustrating fellow Democrat David Dinkins. What would they do to a Republican? Egged on from Albany by Assembly Speaker Sheldon Silver, a fellow Democrat, the council rank and file, which represented the city's interest groups more than its neighborhoods, assumed that it would be able to block Giuliani's initiatives.

The members of the Financial Control Board were backed by both Robert Kiley of the New York City Partnership, which represented the city's most powerful firms, and the influential Richard Larkin of Standard & Poor's, the bond-rating agency. The Board saw no reason to give Giuliani the benefit of the doubt and instead wanted to take over the city's finances themselves.

In the first week of the new administration, the private members of the Board, at the urging of Eugene Keilin, the new chairman of the Municipal Assistance Corporation, came to pay the new mayor an extraordinary visit. They told him that the $2 billion plus budget gaps were far too large to close in one year without layoffs so severe as to rend the social fabric. The implication was that there was a danger of civil disorder under a new mayor deemed illegitimate by some black leaders.

It appears that the outspoken and thoughtful Larkin, who had

---

lived in Brooklyn and Jersey City, had made hundreds of phone calls to Iraq in the weeks leading up to the attack. Another bomber, Abdul Yassin, fled to Iraq where he was given sanctuary and put on Saddam's payroll. In Dinkins' absence, Deputy Mayor Norman Steisel and Police Commissioner Ray Kelly took charge of the city's very effective response to the terror attack.

turned himself into a de facto fiscal monitor, decided, in retrospect, that he had been far too easy on Dinkins. Dinkins had, he argued with the 1975 fiscal crisis in mind, done far more short-term borrowing than was prudent. Putting the new mayor on notice, Larkin made Giuliani explain in considerable detail how he would handle the city's short-term borrowing differently. Larkin made it clear that he would be watching closely and that Standard & Poor's was more than willing to give a vote of no confidence in the new administration by downgrading New York's bonds.

Three days after taking office Giuliani responded to the fiscal woes by announcing—and enforcing—a hiring freeze. Any exemption had to be approved by him personally. Dinkins, noted Allen Proctor of the Financial Control Board, had technically had such a freeze in effect for the past two years, during which time the city nonetheless added thousands to the payroll. In another exercise of control, Giuliani, breaking with traditional practice, required deputy mayors to clear their top appointments with him.*

The mayor also moved quickly to change the tone of the streets. For many motorists, the first sign that they'd entered New York were the nearly ubiquitous "squeegee pests" who would approach at a red light and offer to "clean" your car with a dirty rag in exchange for a few quarters. In the past the squeegees just ignored the tickets that they had been given for blocking traffic. Building on an initiative begun by Police Commissioner Ray Kelly in the waning days of the Dinkins' administration, Giuliani and Bratton intensified the police focus on the "squeegees." Under Giuliani, they began to make arrests. Forty percent quickly disappeared; the other 60 percent were arrested, and of these half were found to have previous arrests for serious felonies and almost all had drug-related arrests.

Norman Siegel of the New York Civil Liberties Union had claimed that the squeegee men were just "down on their luck" homeless people. But three-fourths of those arrested turned out to have legitimate addresses, 30 percent had previous arrests for serious felonies, and almost all had drug-related arrests. Although they had

---

*Municipal Archives. A Giuliani memo of January 5 addressed to all Commissioners and Heads of Covered Organizations called for a 1 percent cut in the current agency operating budgets and 10 percent for 1995. The memo also announced, "To ensure that spending is controlled, I am instituting a strict monitoring system" subject to personal review by the mayor

seemed to be ubiquitous, it turned out that there only seventy-five squeegees. In a month they were gone, and Giuliani began to build credibility.

A "Gateway Initiative" to clean up the garbage-infested arterial roads leading to and from the highways was also launched in the first week. That took longer to bear fruit, but when it did it led *Washington Post* columnist Richard Cohen to exclaim in July 1994, "Something astonishing is happening in New York. Could its name be Rudolph Giuliani?"[4]

But despite his energy and his quick start, prominent voices still doubted that Giuliani could make much of a difference. George Will, like many conservatives, thought that New York was so far gone that the November election had been "irrelevant." Senator Moynihan concurred. Shortly after the new mayor took office, Moynihan told a hearing on juvenile violence conducted by New York's former Public Advocate Andrew Stein: "the out of wedlock ratio in New York City today is 43 percent and there are districts where it is 94 percent. If you know that number today, you know what the situation of teenagers in high school will be in sixteen years' time. This tells you that the next two decades are spoken for.... There is nothing you'll do of any consequence, except start the process of change. Don't expect it to take less than thirty years."[*]

The pessimism seemed entirely justified. The welfare rolls seemed certain to grow; in 1993, for the first time ever more than half the births in New York were to out-of-wedlock mothers.

To make matters worse, the city was about to run out of cash reserves to cover its payroll. New York was so short of money that for more than a year it quietly but deliberately stalled on paying vendors. But because the administration was tight with information the press never caught on and the city avoided a panic.

A substantial portion of the city thought the danger came not from inaction, but from measures that might stir the underclass into riots. A poll taken during the election campaign by the local all-news cable TV station NY1 found that one-third of those surveyed

---

[*]Caught up in a social scientific version of Calvinism, Moynihan's comments took on an increasingly bitter tone. In the summer of 1994 at Senate hearings on the failure of the 1988 welfare reform, the senator expressed his pessimism in apparently off-the-cuff remarks. He talked about the fourfold increase in teenage pregnancy from 1960 to 1991 as "an unbelievable national tragedy for every segment of society." And then he suggested that a biologist who looked at the recent surge in

expected riots if Dinkins was defeated. Speaking on television, African-American police leader Eric Adams had threatened, "We're going to have to consider arming ourselves with bullets" if Giuliani's "forces of evil" win.[5]

Giuliani's first visit as mayor-elect was to Harlem and Salem Baptist Church where the pastor, John Brandon, a supporter, greeted him. The newly elected mayor told the congregation, "You're all the same." Then, as Eric Pooley of *New York* magazine described it, a young man with his hair in cornrows looked startled, then puzzled, and then offended. Giuliani went on: "The people of this city—it doesn't matter what their race, age, ethnic background, gender or sexual orientationt—they're basically the same in what they worry about." Now the young guy in cornrows grinned; he got the point. Rudy went on, insisting with some exaggeration, "the people of Staten Island and the people of the South Bronx look at the world in exactly the same way." But it turned out the guy in the cornrows was the exception. Brandon was soon driven from his congregation for the sin of backing Giuliani.[6]

No matter what his accomplishments, Giuliani would never be forgiven for displacing Gotham's first African-American mayor. On election night, one of Dinkins' supporters described the defeat as "like a death in the family." More ominously, the Reverend James Forbes of Riverside Church said that Dinkins' defeat felt to him like the assassination of Martin Luther King all over again. *Newsday* editor Les Payne said that Giuliani was "rabid" and described Ed Koch as a "zany bigot" for having backed him. In Washington, Dinkins' close ally, Congressman Charles Rangel, no sooner met privately with Giuliani than he began publicly sniping at the mayor-elect.[7]

Anyone predisposed to hate Giuliani probably had their sentiments reinforced on January 9, 1994, a little more than a week into the administration, when a hoax involving a Harlem mosque threatened to explode into rioting. This was the administration's first real test.

The trouble began while Bill Bratton was in flight from Boston

---

teenage pregnancy might wind up "talking about 'speciation,'" implying that the multi-generational offspring of inner-city female-headed households were becoming a people almost entirely apart from the rest of society. In other words, urban pathology was intractable and the costs and casualties it imposed on the cities were simply going to have to be accepted as a normal part of doing business. *Newsday* 8/2/94.

ready to begin work as Police Commissioner. On 4 o'clock on a Sunday afternoon, an anonymous caller to 911 told the dispatcher, "He's sticking up the Muhammad's Mosque" at Fifth Avenue and 125th Street. The caller continued, the robber "has a gun too." The dispatcher's call for assistance mentioned only the address but didn't point out that the mosque was a "sensitive location" and that there is no sign in front identifying the third floor of the building as a Nation of Islam mosque.

The call was a set-up. When the first two officers responding ran up the stair to the third-floor mosque, they were met by a dozen members of the Fruits of Islam security force. They threw the cops down a flight of stairs after taking a police gun and radio. A nasty brawl then ensued on the sidewalk.

As the incident began to unfold, Giuliani was well aware of a similar, deadly fracas that had occurred in April 1972. That year two cops responding to an "officer down" dispatch ran into a building on East 116th Street that—again, there was no sign—turned out to be a Nation of Islam mosque where Malcolm X had preached. The officers didn't know the report of an officer down was a hoax. They were forced down the stairs, pummeled, and one of the officers, Philip Cardillo, was executed at point blank range. During the tensions that followed, Nation of Islam leader Louis Farrakhan and Congressman Charles Rangel used the threat of riot to force the police to back off and release the prisoners who had been taken into custody for Cardillo's murder. The police department, under Commissioner Patrick Murphy and Deputy Commissioner Ben Ward, later the top cop under Ed Koch, tried to sweep the killing under the carpet. No one was ever tried for the execution and Mayor John Lindsay and Commissioner Murphy effectively blamed the police for the incident. Neither man attended the murdered officer's funeral and the whole affair had a devastating effect on police morale.[8]

With the 1972 Harlem mosque and the 1992 Washington Heights incident in mind, Giuliani was determined to produce a different outcome. With eight officers hurt, he pressed Bratton to take action: "You have officers injured. You have stolen police property. Why aren't you going in?" But Joe Leake, the boro commander on the scene, was worried about the threat of a riot. A deal was worked out in which police were allowed to search the mosque where they found the radio and gun. The Muslims promised to surrender the people they knew had been involved shortly. As with a similar promise in 1972, they quickly reneged. But the 1994 incident, Bratton notes, had already sent out two messages from the new mayor: "To the cops: I'll support you with the benefit of the doubt." To the city: "There's a new sheriff in town, and we're not going to tolerate disrespect for the police."[9]

When the incident died down, the curtain went up on the next installment of New York's ongoing racial theater, still featuring the usual cast of characters. Congressman Rangel denounced Giuliani on television and warned that the new mayor would be unable to govern if he continued on his current path. The Reverend Wyatt T. Walker called Giuliani a "fascist" in a radio broadcast. C. Vernon Mason, of Tawana Brawley fame, a "lawyer specializing in grassy knoll defenses of crooks of color," denounced the police for an "attack" and a "siege" on a place of worship, arguing that the police would never have entered a white church. (The police had, however, done just that a few months earlier when they went into St. Patrick's Cathedral after a killer.)[*]

Liberal opinion was aghast. Giuliani, it seemed was, as the Dinkins campaign had warned, threatening to produce a racial conflagration. One reporter confided that he was "never so afraid of the city going up in flames." But Giuliani, who had expected some sort of racial challenge to his fledgling mayorality, refused to back off. A mayoral aide explained, "You can't just let community pressure change the facts. Once you do that" you don't have the rule of law.

After the election, Sharpton had engaged in some back-channel meetings with Rudy Washington, the new Commissioner of Business Services. But when Sharpton (described by the *Village Voice*'s Wayne Barrett as the "portly prince of provocation") attempted to join a meeting between Bratton and the Nation of Islam leaders, he was turned away. Sharpton bellowed, "This is an insult and affront to our community." He threatened to have Giuliani "impeached by the early spring." In the wake of the incident, Sharpton became an even more frequent presence on the local cable news station NY1, where he was given a nearly nightly platform to denounce the mayor

---

[*]The grassy knoll quotation comes from Richard Brookhiser. The police were attacked no matter what they did. Two years earlier, the police didn't move quickly after a rap concert at City College in Harlem had been wildly oversold. When nine people were crushed to death, the police were accused of racist inaction.

and assert contrary to the evidence that "the police had entered the mosque with their guns drawn."[10]

Giuliani aides met privately with Harlem leaders. But he was dismayed to find that, in what he saw as a breach of trust, the same political leaders who spoke reasonably in private turned around and spewed vitriol in public. Angered by these attacks, which implied that the new mayor could be rolled by public pressure, Giuliani said of Congressman Rangel, the most notorious offender, and his allies, that their relationship would have "to be a two-way street." Then he added imprudently, "They are going to have to learn to discipline themselves." Reporters repeatedly peppered the mayor with questions about how it was that he could refuse to meet with an important black leader like Sharpton. Giuliani responded, "I think you're making too much of Al Sharpton. I always thought you [reporters] made too much of Al Sharpton." Round one went decisively to Giuliani. But at a cost. Already demonized, he was disinvited to speak at a Harlem church and he was loudly booed a month later when he spoke in Brooklyn for Martin Luther King's birthday.[11]

▲ ▲ ▲

"If you want to understand how Rudy thinks about management," a long-time Giuliani associate once explained to me with a grin on his face, "you have to remember that at Yankee games he's the guy who's keeping score, writing down how each out, how each run scored, took place." Another aide put it this way: "He's not just watching the Yankees, he's thinking about how he would manage them." Giuliani loves baseball "because it brings together three things that he loves, statistics, teamwork and individual effort." Baseball spoke to Giuliani's mathematical and military cast of mind, or what former Deputy Mayor John Dyson described as his "Tinkers to Evers to Chance mentality," referring to the famous double-play combination renowned for precision teamwork.

"When Rudy read *The Godfather*," noted former Deputy Mayor Joe Lhota, "he studied it from the point of view of how to communicate effectively down to the lowest ranks of an organization, so that every foot soldier understood his marching orders." Lhota, who himself once diagrammed the organizational structure of *The Godfather* for a Harvard Business School seminar, says admiringly, "You could draw a clear line on an organization chart for almost everything the Rudy administration did." That allowed the city government to speak clearly and with one voice. To make sure that the one voice reached down within the administration, the new mayor invited the leaders of every city agency to a weekend seminar at Gracie Mansion on the topic of "Reinventing Government." The speakers included Philadelphia Mayor Ed Rendell, who had rescued his city from the brink of bankruptcy; David Osborne of *Reinventing Government* fame; and Linda Wachner of Warnaco and Richard Parsons of the Dime Savings Bank who both talked about how they had turned around troubled companies with a particular focus on labor relations.

"Fascinated" by the way "the structure of an organization affects its performance," Giuliani quickly recognized the problem of a city government in which power was both too centralized and too diffused. His solution, in part, was to build on the lessons of his mentor, Judge Lloyd MacMahon, who "ran his office like a boot camp." Giuliani began each work day since 1981 when he had been at the Justice Department with an 8 a.m. meeting, an almost military-style briefing with his top staff in which the position of the enemy was evaluated and short- and long-term strategies for combat were considered. The importance of the "8 a.m. morning meeting," he wrote in his book *Leadership*, "cannot be overstated.... I consider it the cornerstone to efficient functioning."[12]

The 8 a.m. meeting, explained Deputy Mayor John Dyson, allowed the administration to cut through the bureaucratic process to get a great deal done fairly quickly. It gave all the deputy mayors and key staff daily access to Giuliani. With all the major players at the table, it allowed a proposed innovation to get a timely response and, if approved, it expedited its enactment. The morning meetings satisfied Giuliani's executive appetite for the details of a problem and his desire to follow through quickly with the resources needed to get the problem resolved.

The morning meeting was also a place for open and lively discussion. Abe Lackman, Giuliani's first budget director, remembers the mayor as "open-minded." Receptive to exploring ideas, "he was anything but dictatorial before a decision was made." When Giuliani wanted to add money to the Fire Department for new safety equipment and Lackman disagreed, the mayor didn't order the budget director to add the dollars. Instead he took him to visit a fireman who had been badly burned.

Bruce Bender, the right-hand man for the Council Speaker,

Democrat Peter Vallone, says that during their weekly meetings, "Rudy was a good listener. He would ask tough, to-the-point questions. But if you challenged him, if you made a strong argument backed up with evidence, he would change his mind even if that went against what his staff had recommended." One example came when Deputy Mayor Fran Reiter, the representative of Ray Harding's Liberal Party in Giuliani's cabinet, convinced the mayor not to save money by eliminating the city's Division of AIDS Services. Reiter argued cogently at a late-night dinner—Giuliani was always at work—that while the agency had its failings it was essential to help AIDS patients make their way through the maze of city offices. The mayor agreed and, though it was after midnight, called Lackman at home and told him, "Take it off the table."[13]

"Rudy," Lackman observed, "had a fascinating mind, he never took anything for granted, he always asked good questions." A junior aide was struck, sitting in on the meetings from the sidelines, on "how little" Giuliani was affected by political calculations: "The city really is his top priority." The identification of the man and the city was so complete, he explained, that Giuliani poured himself in to the city's problems "as if his own life depended on it." Giuliani kept a two-word plaque on his desk, in silent reproach to his predecessor: "I'm Responsible."

The meetings could be "fun," a chance, as one staffer put it, "to keep track of all the fights that had been picked with vested interests." But being held in a crisis atmosphere seven days a week could also be "brutal" for anyone hoping for a semi-normal life. This was of little concern to Giuliani, who could function at full speed on just a few hours of sleep. One staffer, desperate for time off, told the mayor that he was an orthodox Jew so he could skip the Saturday session.

Giuliani had tried persuading his friend Richard Parsons, who had headed his transition, to become Deputy Mayor for Economic Development. Parsons would have become the highest-ranking African-American in the administration. But Parsons, who had just become the CEO of Dime Savings bank, declined the job and took a less demanding post as chair of the city's Economic Development Corporation. Instead the Deputy Mayor slot went to John Dyson, a well-to-do Democratic businessman and former senatorial candidate from Dutchess County.

Dyson, trained as an economist, had served as Chairman of the New York State Power Authority under Cuomo; earlier he had been the state's Agriculture and then Commerce Commissioner under the fiscally tightfisted Hugh Carey, a Democrat who had been the only genuinely successful New York governor since the spendthrift reign of Governor Nelson Rockefeller. Upon his appointment to the Giuliani administration, Dyson promised to "unfurl a new banner over our skyline that says, 'New York is open for business,'" and, he added, "not just big, politically well-connected business." He promised to cut taxes and red tape while bringing "an entrepreneurial spirit to government."[14]

Dyson saw strong similarities between Carey and Giuliani. Both men were willing to ignore the polls and take the heat for tough decisions based on what was good for the city or the state as a whole. Crucially, Carey and Giuliani, said Dyson, both understood that in New York "bloated, self-serving government is the problem not the solution."

The deputy mayor rankled many by describing the city through the eyes of a businessman who has a product that's not selling: "In New York City, we raised the price of our product, which is the taxes, the red tape, the regulations, very high. And at the same time, we lowered the quality. We've got to switch this around. We've got to lower the price, which is why we [have to] cut taxes. And we are bringing up the quality." "When we produce a better product at a lower price," he concluded, "people will be interested in buying New York again."[15]

▲ ▲ ▲

February 1994 was an extraordinary time in the political history of New York City. It began with the new mayor's unprecedented testimony in Albany, followed a day later with his first budget address. After this came his first State of the City speech and then a statement on the budget. Taken together, the four statements were a both a rallying cry and a battle plan to seize control of the sinking ship.

Giuliani's call in Albany for a state takeover of the city's Medicaid burden was unremarkable. New York is the only state in the country in which localities pay for a portion of Medicaid. But every mayor makes a forlorn plea for a takeover that is thoughtfully considered and rejected by whoever is sitting in the governor's chair.

But Giuliani's testimony before the Assembly Education Committee signaled a frontal challenge to the old order. Sheldon Silver of Manhattan's Lower East Side, the acting Assembly Speaker, asked the virtually scripted question of whether additional state money

would benefit New York's schoolchildren. In the standard performance, the mayor responds with a yes and then goes on to say that of
course the problems are so intractable, the needs so great, that vastly
more than the additional money offered will be needed. The ques-
tioner then gets to make a seemingly statesman-like gesture that
allows him to support both more money and fiscal prudence.

But Giuliani responded by telling Silver: "The fact is the system
is so disorganized, so disoriented toward administrative overhead
and fat, that to give me enough money to really help children, you
wouldn't have enough money to do that. The real thing that has to
be done, and the way in which we can be honest with the people of
New York, is to cut the living daylights out of the overhead in the
system." Giuliani spoke of unleashing a "relentless campaign" to
"literally crush the cost of bureaucracy in the school system." The
stunned Silver was clearly unhappy since the teachers' union, which
was counting on more money for the school system, was one of his
principal backers.*

Giuliani was genuinely repulsed by the self-serving and impenetrable bureaucracy at the Board of Education. But his immediate
problem was run-away educational costs. If the city budget were to
be balanced, then the bloat at the Board of Education would have
to be lanced. Budget director Abe Lackman later explained that the
"threat of a Financial Control Board takeover was a constant source
of creativity."

Unlike any mayor since before La Guardia (with the partial
exception of Ed Koch), Giuliani personally mastered the budget.
With Lackman and Finance Commissioner Marc Shaw as his tutors,
he spent long days studying the fine points of the city's finances.
When he came to the podium at City Hall the day after his testimony
in Albany, he was ready to speak without notes or teleprompters on
a subject he had internalized.

---

*The Board of Education Special Circular No. 12 regarding the teacher-mentoring
program described part of the bureaucracy that Giuliani was challenging. The teacher-
mentoring program was "a worthwhile $11 million, three-person effort to have
experienced teachers guide neophytes." The fourteen-page special circular was
addressed to the following: "Community school board presidents, superintendents,
UFT and CSA district representatives, principals, UFT chapter leaders, district business
managers, directors of personnel, district directors of instruction and professional
development, MTIP liaisons, SBM/SDM district liaisons and facilitators, deputy chan-
cellors, executive directors, head of office." *Newsday* 2/2/94, 2/18/94.

The new mayor decided to protect the capital budget and the police. New York, largely a collection of islands, had once been the engineers' city. Woven together by bridges and tunnels, the city's interest in infrastructure had been displaced in the 1960s by the rise of social services spending and the fall of master urban planner Robert Moses. As welfare spending displaced infrastructure mainte-nance, let alone new construction for badly needed cross-harbor tunnels, the city engaged in "deferred maintenance," allowing bridges to corrode only to be forced to spend even more in the long run to repair the damage.

"Simply put," Giuliani told the TV and radio audience listen-ing to his State of the City speech, "the crisis is this: as of July 1 New York City doesn't have enough money to meet its expenses. Our expense budget is short by $2.3 billion, arguably the biggest deficit any administration has ever inherited. Without decisive action now, that gap will grow to $3.4 billion by 1998, which would be a calamity for the people of New York City. I don't intend to let this happen." And then he laid out four propositions:

▲ First, we're going to cut the size of government so we live within our means. For the first time since the 1970s we'll pro-pose an expense budget that actually decreases spending in real dollars.

▲ Second, we're going to cut taxes to attract jobs so our people can work.

▲ Third, we're going to consolidate or eliminate city departments and introduce competition with the delivery of services as part of our program to reinvent city government.

▲ And finally fourth, we're going to work with Governor Cuomo and the State Legislature to assure that the city gets a fair share of state revenue.

In the past, he noted sharply, "We have budgeted on the the-ory that we were unique." But the city, he insisted, could not—as the Lindsay, Beame, Koch and Dinkins mayoralties had unsuccessfully attemped—"tax its way out of recession." It couldn't once again hold the public sector harmless at the price of laying an even greater burden on the private sector, driving people and businesses out of New York. He said he would break that downward cycle by reduc-ing the cost of government.

With one eye on competition from across the river where New Jersey Governor Christine Whitman had announced plans for a 30 percent income tax reduction over three years, Giuliani called for cuts in the commercial rent tax, a levy unique to Gotham, and the unincorporated business tax. In both cases, his aim was to meet the regional competition by helping to jump-start small businesses in the outer boros. To aid the Manhattan tourist industry, he promised to cooperate with Governor Cuomo to reduce the city's 21.5 percent tax on hotel rooms and to encourage new entry-level jobs; he also called for a reduction of the city's sales tax on clothes under $100. Finally, Giuliani vowed not to use the future growth of revenue to increase city spending down the road. This was a promise he would prove unable to keep.

To reduce the cost of government, he said he would, on a competitive basis, bid out services formerly delivered only by government and sell off city assets the government should never have acquired in the first place. "Would you believe," he asked incredulously, his voice rising, his eyes looking straight into the television camera, "that the city now owns and operates more than 500 gasoline stations, only a portion of which are used to fuel emergency vehicles? To start with, we're going to close at least 85 of them."

Aside from the dismay expressed by the public-sector unions, the biggest reaction came from three elements in his plan. First, he proposed to cut $291 million and 2,500 administrative positions at the Board of Education. He also planned to privatize two of the city Health and Hospitals Corporation's eleven public hospitals even as he guaranteed to continue providing health care for the poor. And finally, he proposed to fingerprint welfare recipients to eliminate fraud.

The mayor had offended virtually every interest group in town. The Citizens Budget Commission and other welfare advocates were opposed to fingerprinting welfare recipients. School Chancellor Cortines found the proposed education cuts "unrealistic." Councilwoman C. Virginia Fields, angry about the hospital cuts, went to the heart of the old order when she said, "It's not just a service issue; there is a jobs issue." The City Council's twenty-two-member Black and Latino Minority Caucus (out of a total of fifty-one councilmen) issued the mayor a 1960s-style list of non-negotiable demands. They threatened to block any budget Giuliani proposed unless he rolled back the cuts. Una Clarke, a prominent member of the Minority Caucus, said the budget plan was aimed at harming the poor and would create not "a leaner but a meaner city." Asked by the author (who was one of her constituents) what should be cut, Clarke replied emphatically with one word: "POLICE."[16]

A day after the budget presentation, a small but revealing incident took place at City Hall. In the ongoing circus of continuous protests, this was a relatively quiet moment. Bella Abzug, the colorful and lively left-wing former congresswomen and senatorial candidate from Manhattan, was standing on the long wide steps of City Hall announcing her resignation from her unpaid position as chair of the Mayoral Committee on the Status of Women (not to be confused with the Mayor's Commission on Women). Her action, she said, was to protest the new administration's rude and "shocking treatment of her staff." When Giuliani began ascending the steps, she tried to hand her resignation to the new mayor who, barely taking notice of her, replied, "Why don't you send it in?" A few steps on he added, "I have a feeling when I get it I'll accept it." Watching the pas de deux, a bystander quipped, "in one era and out the other."[17]

Giuliani paid little attention to the daily demonstrations against his budget that created a carnival-like atmosphere on the steps of City Hall. But sniping from the schools chancellor was another matter. Ramon Cortines had become Chancellor in September 1993 after a long and bitter search to replace Joe Fernandez, who had been pushed out during the Dinkins years. Fernandez had lost the confidence of the public by supporting the so-called Rainbow Curriculum, a set of gay-friendly instructional materials aimed at the primary grades.

Cortines, who had been chosen by Board of Education members allied with Giuliani, had as the manager of the San Francisco schools earned a reputation as a low-key and competent but administratively limited leader. The school system he inherited, however, would have been ungovernable even had he been a great manager. The Bureau of Supplies was known as the Bureau of Surprise, and contract bid-rigging was a common practice. Local school boards operating with considerable autonomy had control over not only the hiring of everyone from principals to cafeteria workers but also millions of dollars in contracts as well. For the local boards operating mini-political machines, education was secondary to the patronage and contract possibilities offered by the schools. Politicians saw the local school boards as a source of cash and campaign workers. (Turnout in school board elections rarely exceeded 5 percent, so that people with a financial stake in the school boards dominated the voting.) In some cases, school board jobs and even principalships were offered for sale.

The school chancellor didn't have to answer to the mayor, but rather to the Board of Education. The district superintendents put in place by local boards didn't have to answer to the chancellor. And the school principals, who were tenured, didn't have to answer to the superintendents. Teachers, were who also largely tenured and protected by an extremely favorable contract, didn't have to answer to the principals—and of course students were rarely held accountable for their behavior.*

The trouble between Giuliani and Cortines began early in the new administration when few thought the new mayor would be able to gain even minimal control over city bureaucracies long staffed by Democrats. The mayor and chancellor had an extended meeting in which the administration laid out the depth of the city's budget woes and the need to cut back the Board's byzantine bureaucracy. Cortines, according to Giuliani aides, said he understood the problem and raised no serious objections to the upcoming cuts. Then Cortines left the meeting and savaged Giuliani before the awaiting press. It was a breach of trust that was never healed.

Giuliani's anger was animated by the Board of Education's extraordinary indifference to its impact on the city's overall budget. The Board, knowing that it would always be funded, had been cavalier about filing reimbursement requests for money it was owed by Albany. City Hall was simply expected to pick up the slack. Subsequent to the nasty exchange between mayor and chancellor, Budget Director Lackman unleashed a numerical barrage. He noted that of the Board's 85,000 employees only 53,000 were teachers. Further, in the past twelve years school spending had risen 50 percent but 65

---

*The best account of school corruption can be found in Lydia Segal's *Battling Corruption in America's Public Schools*. East New York was an impoverished, mostly black neighborhood, with a long history of failing schools and political intrigue. It was also a Wooten family fiefdom. Priscilla A. Wooten, then the local City Councilwoman, was chair of the Council's Education Committee, and two of her sisters held posts in District 19. One sister, Gloria B. Corley, had been a school board member since 1983, much of that time as president. As a member, she had a strong hand in selecting principals in the district—and complained bitterly after a 1996 state law forbade school boards to hire and fire principals. Another sister, Queenie Wooten, worked in the district office, in charge of facilities and intergovernmental relations. *New York Times* 12/5/02.

percent of the new dollars went to administration and only 18 percent to teachers.[18]

Giuliani responded to Cortines with a withering blast at the
schools in his State of the City address. He attacked "the disgrace-
ful elevation of the bureaucracy over the children." He noted that
from 1980 to 1992 spending on administration grew twice as fast
as overall school spending. To what end?, he asked. "The Board of
Education has countless thousands of administrators.... There are so
many that the chancellor has formed a search committee to find and
count them," he jibed to laughter and applause. Then, trying to prepare parents for what was to come, he suggested, "Let's be honest.
Money has become the biggest dodge for explaining the failure of
our school system.... It's almost become a mantra: If we only had
more money."

He drew the most applause when he praised Arlene Beckles, a
heroic African-American police officer who, bedecked in curlers, had
captured a gun-toting bandit who tried to rob her beauty parlor.
But most of the speech was somber. Looking back with undisguised
criticism at his predecessor, he talked of inheriting "a city filled with
fear of crime," despair with public education, and even "helplessness" produced by policies that "taxed thoughtlessly and spent
lavishly." He warned that this "state of the city has to end, because
if it doesn't end, it will end our city.... Unless we correct what is
wrong, we're facing disaster." To repair Gotham, he echoed the rhetoric of La Guardia and called for "non-partisan" government,
praising the cooperation his "fusion" administration had received
from Speaker Peter Vallone and the rest of the City Council. Returning to Beckles, he emphasized the importance of "merit," which, he
said, means "fresh approaches, fresh ideas, because no party, no
race, no religion has a corner" on virtue and intelligence.

Giuliani challenged the federal formulas that gave President
Clinton's Arkansas 75 cents of every Medicaid dollar while New
York got only 50 cents. But locally, he insisted, the solutions had to
come through "reinventing government." To that end he announced
that he had signed a contract with America Works, the successful
for-profit job-placement agency, to find private-sector employment
for welfare recipients. A watchful Stanley Hill, President of District
Council 37 of the American Federation of State, County and Municipal workers, cautioned, "If you are reinventing government...you
are talking about city workers." But Hill had undercut himself by

taking his top staff out of town to a Florida Disney World retreat where he said everyone was working very hard to figure out how to counter a Republican mayor.[19]

The day following his State of the City address, Giuliani again pounded away at his core themes when he presented the outlines of his four-year budget plan. In order to pay for a workforce far larger than most other cities, "New Yorkers," he reminded the listeners, "have to live with the burden of three of the four largest budgets in the nation [that is, the federal, New York State and New York City budgets]. Most American have to live with only one." He decried the fact that "Our government dominates the local economy" and promised to reduce 15,000 jobs permanently. Then, speaking directly to Eugene Keilin, he laid out part of his strategy for the reductions: "By committing to not rehire four of every five employees who leave the payroll, I will urge the MAC to make available $200 million in MAC funds to cover the costs associated with severance.... If these funds are not available...then these reductions will be accomplished through attrition and layoffs." The implication was that if Keilin and MAC didn't cooperate, the firings would be on their head. And to make sure that the boom and bust cycle of the past didn't repeat itself, he promised to shrink the ability of government to overspend by keeping government expenditures on a short leash through "tax cuts in every year."

In the wake of his second budget presentation, Giuliani seemed to have won a major victory when Chancellor Cortines said he had "discovered" a lost continent of more than 3,500 Board of Education employees that had long been hidden within the city's infamous school bureaucracy. It turned out the Board had twice as many employees as had been claimed by Cortines.

On the same day as Cortines' "discovery," City Council Education Chair Herb Berman revealed that in the midst of the fiscal crisis, the city's thirty-two local school boards had spent $2.2 million on conferences in Hawaii, Las Vegas and Puerto Rico. Marcia Kramer of the local CBS affiliate picked up the issue. Using a hidden camera, she recorded a municipal employee bragging that she went gambling in Vegas on city time. But the Cortines and Berman revelations did little to stem the interest groups' outcry against the mayor. These only intensified when, on the same day as the chancellor's revelation, the mayor pressed forward on the reform of the Health and Hospitals Corporation and its failed Kings County Hospital project.[20]

The city hospital system was breaking down. In October 1993, in the midst of the mayoral election campaign, the chair of the City Council's health committee predicted the "collapse of the entire city's [public] hospital system in two years."[21]

Most large cities have one public hospital. Many big cities have no public hospital, having closed them when the federal government stepped into health care in 1965 with the passage of Medicaid to help the poor and Medicare to aid the elderly. New York, however, never adapted to that change. Gotham's Health and Hospital Corporation (HHC) managed eleven acute care hospitals, five health-care facilities, and many neighborhood clinics in the five boros.

Riddled with political patronage, hamstrung by union inflexibility, and unable to bill their patients effectively, five of the eleven hospitals had either lost or nearly lost their accreditation since 1989. While the hospitals' quality declined, their employment rolls rose. In the last two years of Dinkins' term the number of managers had risen by 600 while the total hospital work force grew by 3,200. Management jobs were treated as sinecures. Managers who failed at one post were shifted to another, and then another.[22]

Facing a $160 million deficit and amidst talk of layoffs, the HHC President Billy Jones, a Dinkins appointee, backed by the HHC Board, demanded an additional $60 million subsidy from the city. "We have been led to believe that they will pay for it," Jones said. "I don't see this as a big problem." But Giuliani did. Referring to both the HHC and its board, he warned, "It was constituted by the city government; it could be reconstituted." Abe Lackman, Giuliani's budget director, wrote back to Jones telling him, "The city cannot afford to be a deep pocket for HHC." He ordered a halt to any new spending, including a proposed $300,000 golden parachute for Jones himself. When the HHC balked at complying, the number two man in city government, Deputy Mayor for Operations Peter Powers, the mayor's boyhood friend, strode into a HHC meeting to block the severance package. Jones left with one-eighth of the severance payment he'd asked for and the Giuliani administration began a sweeping overhaul of the HHC's financial practices.[23]

Kings County Hospital in Brooklyn, the city's oldest acute care facility, exemplified the system. Giuliani described the hospital, built in the 1920s, as a "medical museum." With more than 1,200 beds organized in antiquated open wards, Kings County's 6,000 jobs made it the largest employer in Brooklyn. One billion dollars had been allocated to rebuilding the antique hospital in a city already suffering financially from an overcapacity of hospital beds. But Louis Miranda, the new Giuliani appointee as chair of the Health and Hospitals Corporation Board, noted that after "six [HHC] chairmen, nine [HHC] presidents, twelve years and $119 million in expenditures," there was only a huge hole in the ground to show for all the money expended. Miranda temporarily suspended construction.[24]

In reaction, angry demonstrations, hovering on the edge of violence, broke out in front of the HHC headquarters near City Hall. Marchers shouted, "JOBS NOT JAILS." Jesse Jackson came to town and compared Giuliani to George Wallace, the Alabama segregationist. Brooklyn political leaders led by Assemblyman Clarence Norman, chair of the Kings County Democratic Party, accused the new administration of racism. But Norman's law partner had been given a $1.2 million contract to facilitate minority hiring even as the first $119 million spent on the project had produced nothing more than four acres of excavated dirt, a parking lot and unusable architectural plans.

Speaking at the City Club, the new mayor rebutted Norman et al., insisting, "We have to have the courage to face down those who disguise patronage and power as 'health care for the poor.'" Turning the tables, he argued, "I'm the one fighting for the poor by improving education, safety and jobs. A city that shows it can create private jobs is going to turn around."[25]

▲ ▲ ▲

A mid-February poll in *Newsday* found that, after a month on the job, Giuliani was more popular than his policies. The city liked his take-charge style even if it cringed at the specifics of his "reinvention" and "restructuring." Giuliani would from time to time bash the bureaucracies in the language of the American victory in the Cold War. Speaking of the schools, he quipped, "If you give the Board of Education more money you end up with something like the old Soviet Union. If we were not in this addiction to more money, we'd acknowledge it's how government works that's the problem."[26]

For their part, his liberal rivals regularly attacked his "Reaganism," a virtual swear word in many New York circles. Public Advocate Mark Green said, "his bureaucracy-bashing is Reaganism revisited." Sheldon Silver and Albany's minority caucus, led by the ethically challenged Assemblyman Larry Seabrook, boycotted a meeting with Giuliani as "a show of force" against what they described as Giuliani's "trickle-down Reaganite agenda." A host of columnists chimed in on cue talking about "Reaganomics redux," as well as "Rudynomics," while one academic accused Giuliani of turning the public sector into his "evil empire." (Privately, the Giuliani people noted that as a result of Reagan's deregulation of the financial markets, New York had boomed in the 1980s, allowing minority families to make major gains.)[27]

Giuliani was undeterred. When the sanitation union refused to cooperate on cost savings, the administration deployed "the nuclear bomb threat" of giving garbage collection over to private firms. When sanitation responded as if the threat was merely a bluff, Deputy Mayor Dyson responded, "If you don't work with me, you'll deal with guys who left a million a year law practices for the fun, as prosecutors, of putting guys in jail." But there were carrots as well. The unions were pleased to see that the Giuliani administration— while talking about both layoffs and, even more threatening, privatization—was also proposing some creative options.

Abe Lackman, who had been the budget expert of the Republican majority State Senate, was the second person hired by Giuliani. The son of Holocaust survivors, Lackman, who had been a Sixties radical, retained some of the against-the-current impulses of his youth. When he came on board, Giuliani had assumed that 12,000 to 20,000 layoffs were unavoidable. But Lackman laid out an alternative to massive layoffs. He proposed using MAC (Municipal Assistance Corporation) money derived from the city's sales tax to finance severance agreements with city workers. But he found MAC chair Eugene Keilin, a backer of the Kummerfeld Report, cool, at best, to the idea.

Lackman reasoned that the city needed to do more than just cut workers; it needed union cooperation to change some of the work and staffing rules to make city government more flexible. In the back of Lackman's mind was a case from the state's highest court known as the Triboro Decision. It said that if the city can't negotiate a new contract, all the terms and rules of the prior contract hold. Practically, that meant that if you wanted to change the city's rigid work rules you needed union cooperation. And to get union cooperation you needed to give something in return. That something would develop into severance packages rather than outright layoffs even as the threat of privatization loomed in the background.

Here was the germ of what would become one of Giuliani's key policy choices. But it needed other players to push it through. One of them was labor negotiator Randy Levine. A native of East Flatbush and a graduate of Hofstra Law School, Levine was, like his long-time friend and Justice Department colleague Rudy Giuliani, a Yankee fan from Brooklyn.

Levine, who tends to focus relentlessly on the issue at hand, insisted on being "professional" in negotiations. "It's important," Levine explained, "to listen to what the other side has to say." "I never in my fourteen years [as a management lawyer] tried to break a union," he explained. When Stanley Hill, leader of the 130,000 workers in District Council 37 of AFSCME, checked Levine out, he found that Levine had a reputation for being "tough but fair." "I got a call from someone who told me, 'You can work with him,'" Hill said. "He works to solve problems and not to confront or undermine you."[28]

In *The Prince*, Machiavelli advises the new ruler to inflict whatever damage is required quickly both as an assertion of strength and as way of allowing the anger time to cool. In that vein, the new administration wanted to reduce the headcount quickly to maximize the budgetary savings and avoid further fights over job cuts. Levine, who had experience with the widespread private-sector labor force reductions during the 1991-1992 national recession, saw how he could make Lackman's alternative to layoffs work.

Rather than outright layoffs, those who agreed to the severance package would get both a lump-sum payment based on years of service and continued health benefits for a year. In return, the unions agreed to relax the civil service rules and allow the administration to move people to where they were needed in city government. Traditionally, for example, a redundant secretary working for the Department of Transportation couldn't be moved to, say, the Fire Department, where there was an opening. Instead, the city would have to go through an entire hiring procedure to bring a new secretary into the Fire Department. Now, in a process known as "broad banding," the unions allowed the city to move a secretary at Transportation to fill a hole at Fire without the cost of a new hire.

The unions were intrigued by the possibility of reducing the headcount by 9,500 workers through the severance package since the rest of Giuliani's goal of a reduction of 15,000 in the city's head-count could be achieved by attrition. But Eugene Keilin, Governor Cuomo's choice to replace Felix Rohatyn as the head of the Munici-pal Assistance Corporation, balked. Keilin, an anti-racism activist in the 1960s whose father was a civil rights attorney, was a strong sup-porter of government social services. Keilin, who had made his money working with Felix Rohatyn in deals to restructure failing private-sec-tor companies such as Weirton Steel and United Airlines, had his own strong ideas about how city government should be reorganized.

A highly partisan Democrat, Keilin was said to loathe Giuliani In late March, he took to the pages of the *New York Times* to deliver a message to the mayor. Giuliani had protected police, firefighter and teachers from cuts. But Keilin argued that "a sense of rough justice requires that there be no sanctuaries" from the budget ax. In practi-cal terms, Keilin thought that there were substantial savings to be had from both police cuts and the "civilianization" of police work that could be done by clerks rather than uniformed officers. Two days later, the *Times* weighed in with an editorial backing Keilin. He also received strong support from the minority caucus on the city council who saw Giuliani as supporting the heavily white police force at the expense of the social service jobs held by black and Puerto Rican city employees.[29]

Lackman offered the administration's initial public reply, arguing that the proposed merger of the city's three police forces (Transit, Housing, and the NYPD) would guarantee considerable savings. This was met with considerable skepticism since other may-ors had tried to merge the police forces and failed. But privately the Giuliani people were making a different case. Sergeants, they insisted, found that when they barked out an order to civilian employee, very little followed. Cops, they noted, had a far higher level of efficiency than run-of-the-mill city workers. Accustomed to working in a paramilitary organization, cops responded more quickly and effectively to what needed to be done.[30]

Giuliani wouldn't take Keilin's "no" for an answer. He told the press, "It's our [the city's] money. It's not his [Keilin's] money.... It isn't his role to be suggesting the budget priorities or the political pri-orities of the city." Giuliani threatened to make Keilin, and by extension Cuomo, the fall guy for any layoffs he might have to impose if MAC refused to allow the city to use its own money to finance the severance packages. Keilin caved.[31]

▲ ▲ ▲

As Giuliani approached his first hundred days in office during the second week of April 1994, he seemed to be doing reasonably well. Challenged by one of the worst winters in memory, one with more than a dozen extra-heavy snows including an all-out blizzard, Sanitation Commissioner Emily Lloyd efficiently cleared the streets, and the Arab man who killed a Hasidic boy on the approach to the Brooklyn Bridge was captured by Bratton's cops within twenty-four hours. The mayor, sensitive to the city's ethnic dynamics and aware that, as in the wake of the 1993 bombing of the World Trade Center, other terror plots might be underway, made a point of distinguishing the city's Arab population from the gunman's vicious deed.

There had been some significant mistakes. Giuliani's first Buildings Commissioner quit abruptly after news reports of dubious business practices. A riot in the Rikers Island prison complex made it clear that Anthony Schembri, his Corrections Commissioner (and the model for the TV show the "The Commish"), wasn't on top of his job. And sometimes Giuliani let his personal pique get the best of him. His disdain for Public Advocate Mark Green became clear when he summarily dismissed a reasoned proposal by Green for "managed competition" in the repair of police cars as "idiotic."

Giuliani's take-charge, in-your-face style drew hostility while his attacks on budget-busting bureaucrats and their programs drew a nearly endless round of protests. An average day might draw hospital workers holding a mock funeral to protest the possible privatization of public hospitals; parent groups angry about school funding cuts; and AIDS activists including the actress Rosie Perez shouting, "Wake up, baby! OK? Because if you cut this [AIDS funding], you're going to cut yourself."

Giuliani's poll numbers were twelve points below Dinkins at the same point. Still, he was gaining ground among some Democrats. When a reform Democratic leader took some shots at the mayor at his local clubhouse, he was, much to his surprise, shouted down by his members. And Speaker Vallone, the most powerful Democratic office holder in the city, introduced Giuliani to a Queens Civic Association, declaring, "I think we have the right person at the right time to lead us into the next century."

But Giuliani made only very limited headway among minority voters. Still angry over Dinkins' defeat, they had fresh reasons to dislike him. On top of the budget cuts in agencies with heavy minority employment, he refused to build a new police academy in the heavily Latino South Bronx; eliminated Dinkins' offices of racial and ethnic affairs; and ended the city's 10 percent bonus for minority contractors. The press, accustomed to counting by race, picked up on these themes and repeatedly complained that Giuliani lacked the requisite number of minority hires

Giuliani saw his most important early accomplishment as having begun to change the tone and assumptions of city government. But the budget pressures cast a deepening shadow over the administration. Facing up to the fiscal situation, Giuliani had continued to pressure the Board of Education to make additional staff cuts. He called on the prominent lawyer Edward Costikyan to devise a plan to decentralize the Board of Education into five smaller and more accountable boro boards. Then, dissatisfied with the limited cuts Cortines had been willing to make, Giuliani appointed Herman Badillo as a fiscal monitor to investigate the board's finances. He said a monitor was essential to provide him with "accurate information" on the Board of Education's finances and bureaucracy.

The mayor was particularly angry with the Board's long-time budget director Leonard Hellenbrand who was the keeper of the Board's byzantine bookkeeping secrets. Hellenbrand, described by a political pro as "brilliant at hiding funds," was a master of moving money between the Board's thousands upon thousands of different ledger accounts to obscure just how much was being spent for what. For his part, Cortines denied that he knowingly misled the mayor. He later said he wanted to consolidate the Board's five different computer systems into one. But seeing the Badillo appointment as a vote of no-confidence, the decent but ineffectual Cortines threatened to resign, saying, "My integrity is not for sale." Giuliani heard the news of the threatened resignation while he was taping a very upbeat WCBS-Radio show on his first hundred days. Clearly annoyed, he described the threat on live radio as "peevish."[32]

The political establishment that had been shaken by Giuliani saw an opportunity to strike back by rallying around the chancellor's ire. In the words of one experienced Democrat, "Anyone with a hard-on for Giuliani got in their whacks." The mayor's "bullying style," his budget cuts and even the way he looked became the object of opprobrium. Parents' organizations and the press turned on Giuliani with a fury; he had few defenders. His critics assumed that they had Giuliani cornered; he couldn't, they reasoned, begin a politically harrowing search for a new chancellor so soon after the bitter fight required to select Cortines only half a year earlier.

But Giuliani was more interested in bringing the deficits under control than calming the press. He characterized Cortines as having been "captured by the bureaucracy of the system," while Deputy Mayor Peter Powers made it clear that they were more than willing to begin the search for a new chancellor. Governor Cuomo and Speaker Vallone stepped in to mediate and eventually negotiated a compromise that left Badillo in place to oversee the Board of Education's finances and Cortines rescinding his resignation for the time being.[33]

The image of an implacable mayor immune to the ordinary rules of politics began to take hold. Journalist Andrew Kirtzman captured the popular sense of the scene: "Thousands of protestors, union members, politicians were fighting one man, who stood alone each day at the podium inside City Hall's Blue Room, a solitary figure facing a sea of skeptical reporters. He was an army of one."[34]

The imagery served the mayor well. But no mayor facing a budget crisis—not even a Rudy Giuliani or a Fiorello La Guardia— could bring the city's problems under control without the help of allies. Peter Vallone would prove to be the mayor's invaluable ally.

▲ ▲ ▲

On January 2, 1994, Vallone, having already attended early Mass, was in office working as usual at 8 a.m. when the new mayor, postponing his customary 8 a.m. meeting, walked into his office. Vallone was stunned. It was the first time a mayor had come over to the speaker's side of City Hall; other mayors expected the council leader to come to them. The two men, both Italian Catholics with an outerboro mentality, had never really spoken. Giuliani asked Vallone why the speaker's side of the building was so clean and his own so dirty. Vallone explained who the new mayor had to talk to on the cleaning staff.

Vallone, a temperamental moderate even as Giuliani was an immoderate centrist, had been at work trying to draft compromise legislation that would allow horses to continue to be used for Central Park carriage rides while insuring a more humane treatment of the animals. The men quickly connected on a personal and a professional basis. "Rudy pitched in to help work on the legislative language," said Vallone, "and together we drafted the first piece of

legislation passed under the new mayor." It was the start of a relationship that pulled the city out of its fiscal morass by transcending
partisanship.

Herb Berman of Brooklyn, a Vallone ally and the chair of the
council's crucial finance committee, was afraid that the arrival of a
Republican mayor would, notwithstanding his talk of non-partisan-
ship, bring "Albany-style party bickering and gridlock to city
government." Berman, who had been influenced by the intellectual
ferment of the Dinkins years, saw politics in Albany as "an endlessly
petty contest to embarrass the other party which should have no
place in New York City where Republicans were so few that the primary divisions were between boros." Besides, he explained, given
its fiscal woes, the city needed bipartisanship to survive. But he was
afraid that Giuliani, who saw the council members as first cousins to
the corrupt hacks he had put into jail as a prosecutor, would trigger
a self-defeating partisan battle. The council could, if it were
sufficiently angry with the new mayor, undermine the mayor's efforts
to balance the budget as was required by law.

Vallone recognized the problem. The speaker, an enormously
decent man, represented the heavily Greek and home-owning urban
village of Astoria, Queens, which had gone heavily for Giuliani in
the 1993 election. Vallone, who pushed for more cops and the constraints on property taxes that were strangling the neighborhoods,
had been at almost constant odds with Dinkins. In his 1993 State of
the City speech, Vallone anticipated some of the themes of the Giuliani years. He called for breaking up the Board of Education and the
Metropolitan Transportation Authority, two of the area's most dysfunctional fiefdoms. "We will continue to demand help from
Washington and Albany," he told the crowd gathered at City Hall,
"but we will do what we can to help ourselves.... The city has not
done a good job of encouraging business investment."

He saw that "Giuliani didn't know the members of the council
from Adam." Similarly, he thought the "wild hostility" of some of
the council could be tempered by meeting the mayor. So, Vallone
brought each council member one-by-one to Gracie Mansion to talk
with Giuliani. Each meeting began with the council member laying
out his or her concerns for ten minutes; then Giuliani would
respond. This at least partly "humanized the council members to the
mayor and bridged some of the mutual hostility."

For his part, Giuliani went out of his way to keep Vallone and

his chief political aide Kevin McCabe in the loop. "They made a con-
vivial group," noted journalist Andrew Kirtzman, "these four
Catholic school guys from the boroughs. Giuliani, Powers and
McCabe had all attended Bishop Loughlin High School in Queens
while Vallone had gone to its Manhattan rival, Power Memorial."
Giuliani extended himself to the council at large by holding an
annual reception at Gracie Mansion, and he even showed up, briefly,
for the council's annual outing.[35]

Vallone, who jealously guarded the council's newly found powers under the 1989 charter, was, like Giuliani, almost violently
opposed to a Financial Control Board takeover of the city's finances.
"I banged on the table in opposition during one meeting" out of four
or five early meetings with the FCB. "My staff, he explained, referring in part to "brilliant" but largely unknown Bruce Bender, "was
far stronger than the FCB crew." Still, Vallone recognized that the
"FCB threat" was crucial in selling difficult budget decisions to a
reluctant council.

Vallone depended heavily on the judgment of his staff to build
a consensus. This was the way he worked: "First" he "had to be convinced of a policy by the staff," because he knew that "if the staff
could convince me, I could convince the council." Then Vallone
would sit down and reason with his key council allies such as Archie
Spigner who represented the African-American homeowners of
Jamaica, Queens, and Victor Robles, a Brooklyn Latino moderate.
Then he "widened his circle" and asked his chief critics on the council, Ronnie Eldridge of Manhattan and Sal Albanese of Brooklyn, to
weigh in. Finally he moved to secure support from every boro before
he and Bender went to the mayor with the council's proposals.

The process didn't always work. There were tough institutional
battles pitting the prerogatives of the council against the claims of
the executive. At one point during the 1994 budget battle, for
instance, Lackman cut off council computer access to the financial
numbers. But remarkably for New York, the mayor and the speaker
generally worked well together to face down the looming disaster.

But even with this team in place, there was rough financial
sledding ahead. Trying to be upbeat, the mayor, referring to the severance agreements, pointed out that "we have achieved the part" of
the fiscal plan that people said "could not be done." City Council
Finance Chairman Herbert Berman agreed. He called the agreement
a "major accomplishment." But Berman, aware of the dismal num-

bers that were largely hidden from the public, warned that "the budget itself has a long way to go.... People do not realize what a horrendous job it is going to be to close this budget gap."

Berman was right. It wasn't until the second quarter of the 1996 fiscal year that the city would be able to see light at the end of the budgetary tunnel.

EIGHT

The Democratic Rudy?

I n his first year in office, at the same time he was storming the citadels of New York City's Democratic Party establishment, Giuliani took pains to build a good working relationship with Governor Mario Cuomo and President Bill Clinton, both Democrats. In August 1994, Mayor "Rudy Dinkins," or so he was described, took to the op-ed page of the *Washington Post* to argue on behalf of President Clinton's crime bill then being held hostage in the House to a mesalliance of anti-police liberals and anti-social program conservatives. Sounding like a conservative, Giuliani insisted, "The grim reality of crime in America requires a clear emphasis on stronger enforcement and more severe punishment." But then, switching into a Dinkins-like mode, Giuliani praised the bill's programs including Midnight Basketball, an object of considerable derision. He claimed that Midnight Basketball offered "hope that in the future we can reduce the need for so many police and so many jails by funding proven prevention programs for young people, including sports programs, school programs and counseling." As proof he mentioned the Beacon Schools, one of the few Dinkins initiatives he had continued, in which "thirty-seven schools are now kept open in the evening, offering programs for kids.... This bill would allow us to expand the program to help many more children."

Giuliani's relationship with President Clinton was driven, like his links with Governor Mario Cuomo, by the relentless pressure of the city's massive budget gap. From the very first time that Giuliani met the president as mayor-elect in December 1993, fiscal issues had been paramount. Accompanied into the Oval Office by a very friendly Senator Moynihan, the mayor and the president spent forty

minutes discussing crime, welfare, and an issue near and dear to
Moynihan—the federal aid formula for Medicaid that systematically
shortchanged New York. Arkansas, the senator noted, got three federal dollars for every dollar it contributed to Medicaid; in New York
it was one to one. Giuliani also expressed doubts about the president's plan to fund local police forces with federal aid, and he joined
with Mayors Ed Rendell, Steve Goldsmith and Robert Lanier to criticize the terms of Washington's aid.[1]

Clinton's first budget cut did little for the cities but substan-
tially sliced federal support for New York's subways. Giuliani made
his displeasure known when he snubbed a presidential visit to
Brooklyn College organized to promote the crime bill. "We haven't
seen a lot from Washington," explained a mayoral aide, "they've got
to work with us if they want us to cooperate." But when the two
men met privately afterwards, Giuliani explained, "We need to get
more specific on the amount of aid being given, how long that aid is
going to last." This was the beginning of extended negotiations
between the two men with Congressman Schumer serving as the go-
between.[2]

From the mayor's point of view, the new version of the $30 bil-
lion bill that was introduced in early August was a huge
improvement. With Cuomo gearing up for his re-election campaign,
Clinton's new version also met the Governor's request for federal
funds to pay for the jailing of illegal immigrants convicted of crimes.
But even more importantly, the money to hire more cops, build more
jails and pay for social programs was to be distributed, unlike Medicaid or welfare, on the basis of funding formulas based on
population and crime rates that favored New York City. Further,
thanks to Schumer, the White House agreed to allow the city, which
had already hired new police, considerable flexibility in deciding
how its dollars would be spent.

But to win liberal support, the crime bill had become a congressional grab bag filled with money for programs open to
conservative criticism. Opponents, like Pennsylvania Republican Bill
Goodling, pointed out that seventeen separate federal agencies were
already administering 260 federal crime prevention programs
designed to serve delinquent and at-risk youth, few of which had a
record of success. The crime bill went down to narrow defeat. At
that point Giuliani, his standing already enhanced by signs that
Gotham was getting a grip on crime, offered the president help in
lobbying Republican House members.

New York Republicans were outraged when the Republican mayor joined the Democratic president to lobby for the new version of the crime bill. Giuliani told his critics, "I'm the Mayor of America's largest city, and my city comes first. Political parties come second." To his rural and suburban critics in the GOP who were angered by the bill's ban on assault rifles, he noted, "Republicans now run the two largest cities in America," so that "part of the Republican program should be to show that we can help to solve urban problems as effectively, if not more effectively, than Democrats."[3]

Lobbying by Giuliani, Riordan, Rendell and a host of other mayors got the new version of the Crime Bill passed, giving both Clinton and Giuliani a political boost. It helped generate Giuliani's reputation as a politician who put the good of the city before partisanship, and it sent Giuliani over 50 percent in the polls for the first time since he had been elected. New York Republicans winced when Giuliani and Cuomo posed together for TV ads supporting the crime bill. But their complaints were constrained by the upcoming New York Governor's race. They were hoping that Giuliani, whose star was clearly rising, would endorse Republican challenger George Pataki in his bid to deny Cuomo a fourth term.

▲ ▲ ▲

Governor Cuomo and Mayor Rudy Giuliani needed each other. Cuomo, campaigning for a fourth term during an extended recession, needed Giuliani's support to shore up his support in the moderate-to-conservative swing neighborhoods of metropolitan New York City where the mayor was very popular. Guiliani needed Cuomo to balance his budget.

As late as 1988, when he was prominently mentioned as a possible Democratic Party presidential candidate, 85 percent of New Yorkers polled described Cuomo as "a good leader" for the state." Cuomo, who had mounted an eloquent critique of the death penalty, was spoken of as "the nation's most gifted philosopher-politician," "the philosopher-king of the Democrat Party" and its "humble conscience."

But by 1990 and the national recession, the future had arrived for Cuomo and it wasn't appealing. New York went into the recession earlier and was far harder hit than the rest of the country with the exception of California, which was suffering from the sharp drop in military spending at the end of the Cold War. The state was being forced to pay a heavy price for the "New York Idea."

The New Deal, which took root more deeply in New York than almost anywhere else, generated an interest group politics that was kept in check in the 1930s, 1940s and 1950s by the great solidaristic efforts at combating Depression and war. But by the 1960s and the governorship of Nelson Rockefeller, the tendency of powerful organized interests to raid the treasury at the expense of the unorganized sent the economy aground. Cuomo explained:

> There are many special interests and that doesn't make them bad. Advocates for the elderly are a special interest, children's advocates are a special interest, banking advocates are a special interest. People who own yachts and don't want a tax on luxury yachts, people who are homeless and want shelter are all special interests. My message to them is the same: You are a special interest. That's fine. I am in charge of the whole.

But he wasn't. Cuomo has been mistakenly accused of being just another knee-jerk liberal trying to redistribute money either downward into failed social programs or laterally into declining trade unions. In fact, like Rockefeller before him, Cuomo had been willing to bestow benefits on any effectively organized bloc of votes.

In a state where the largest lobbyists were almost all from the public sector, broadly defined, the legislature used the taxpayer's money to insulate the key interest groups associated with each legislative chamber from the effects of the recession. It didn't matter that the pie was shrinking so long as the interest groups were able to grab a larger piece of what was left.

Cuomo complained bitterly and sometimes with justice that New York was being shortchanged by Washington. But Federal aid to New York State and its local governments actually increased by 15.4 percent after inflation between 1983 and 1988. It just couldn't keep up with Cuomo's spending. To be fair to the former governor, the state legislature left to its own devices would have spent even more.

What did all of the expenditures buy? The world was well aware of New York City's underclass, but the poverty rate in the upstate cities, including Buffalo and Syracuse, was 22 percent compared to 19 percent for the Big Apple and 13 percent for the country as a whole. But these numbers underestimated the real level of poverty since the cost of living in New York City was more than double the national average. When the cost of living was taken into account, New York State had a poverty level only four points below Mississippi's. New York State's high school graduation rate was 45th in the country, and its adult illiteracy rate tied with Mississippi and Alabama in scraping the bottom.*

In 1990 Cuomo should have been in serious trouble. The Empire State, which had lagged far behind the national average in job growth during the boom years, faced massive budget deficits created by state spending that grew nearly twice as fast as the economy. Worse yet, even Cuomo's supporters had a hard time pinning down his practical accomplishments. Said Cuomo ally Meyer "Sandy" Frucher: "I'm a big supporter of the governor, but I have to tell you that I think almost nobody has any idea of what he's been doing up there for all these years." His sentiments were echoed by a hard-nosed New York liberal. "I have nothing but bad words to say for him. I don't care how many beautiful words you speak, to pay so little attention to how your government works is a kind of betrayal of the ethic of public service. The state government is mind-bogglingly screwed up, and everybody knows it."[4]

In Connecticut, Massachusetts and Vermont, lesser problems sent incumbents into retirement. But New York State's politics were so sclerotic, its media so overwhelmingly liberal, that Cuomo's vulnerability was barely noticed. In 1990 the nearly moribund Republican Party nominated an obscure, inarticulate and somewhat dotty investment banker named Pierre Rinfret for Governor. Among the few voters who were aware of Rinfret's Republican candidacy, most thought he was a French painter; others suspected he might be a hockey goalie or a fashion designer. Rinfret became better known when in answer to a question about crime, he told New York City's WOR-TV, "What I really want is a vigilante system with people carrying guns." Yet Cuomo barely won 50 percent of the vote. Rinfret finished a distant second, only narrowly edging out NYU Professor Herb London who ran as the Conservative Party candidate. The articulate London captured some of the discontent ignored by the legislature where incumbents were more likely to be indicted than defeated.[5]

By the summer of 1994, Cuomo's star had faded further, along

---

*Part of the low literacy rate can be explained by immigration. The point here is that Cuomo's doubling of educational expenditures yielded no return.

with New York's economy, which suffered the worst job losses since the Great Depression. Not even the formidable powers of the governorship, which had made three terms the norm for any incumbent who wanted them, looked like enough to win Cuomo a fourth term.

He was increasingly seen as out of touch. When Cuomo was told that Texas had overtaken New York as the second most populous state, he responded, "I don't know what difference it makes, frankly." But the difference, as a growing chorus of critics pointed out was measured, in part, by a declining ability to influence Washington. "We are a hurting state," said Brad Johnson, former director of New York State's Washington lobbying office.[6]

In 1994 Cuomo was ripe for the taking; as in the prior race, however, a weak GOP had no major candidate to challenge the governor. Senator Alphonse D'Amato, on the advice of political consultant Arthur Finkelstein, stepped into the breach and proposed a little-known political ally, State Senator George Pataki from the Hudson Valley town of Peekskill. Finkelstein, a secretive figure rarely seen in public, thought the amiable six-foot-six-inch Pataki's soft-spoken Jimmy Stewart style and scant voting record made him a hard-to-hit target. Pataki's newly found support for abortion and his pro-death penalty/anti-tax voting record made him the ideal candidate to defeat the incumbent. D'Amato and Finkelstein planned to turn the campaign into a referendum on Cuomo's stewardship.

The competition between Cuomo and D'Amato's protégé put not only Giuliani but also Al Sharpton in a strong bargaining position. Cuomo, who needed a strong black turnout, had been cultivating Sharpton since the 1992 senatorial election in which he had, much to the annoyance of Senator Moynihan, bent the rules to help Sharpton qualify for the primary ballot. Once Sharpton was in the primary, the major candidates were careful not to offend him. *

In 1994 when Sharpton again ran in the Democratic senatorial

---

*The 1992 Democratic Senatorial primary had been a veritable festival of identity politics. Though the state was in the midst of a major recession—New York State had lost jobs at three times the national rate—the contenders, former Congresswoman Liz Holtzman, Mondale's former vice-presidential candidate Geraldine Ferraro, and New York Attorney General Robert Abrams competed with Sharpton over who was the most egregiously victimized. Abrams won the bitterly contested primary, but Sharpton established himself as a force by garnering 90 percent of New York's African-American vote. In total, he won 166,000 votes out of the roughly 656,000 votes cast in New York City.

primary, this time against Moynihan, Cuomo, although he had formally endorsed the incumbent, went out of his way to cozy up to Sharpton. In June 1994, when Cuomo appeared at a Sharpton campaign event organized by Buffalo's African-American clergy, the front page of the *Buffalo News* depicted the two men as the best of friends. Each expected to boost the other's turnout.*

Giuliani played the situation for all it was worth. While Giuliani and Cuomo were in negotiations for a second severance package, Pataki came a-callin' to City Hall, and was left waiting. Still, one part of the negotiations was repeated-Giuliani's feints in the direction of endorsing Pataki. In late September, he hinted that he was closer to Pataki than Cuomo on a number of issues and perhaps even getting ready to endorse the Republican nominee. Cuomo responded by noting, "The Mayor's in a bind.... If he wants to help this city then it would be very good for him to help me."[7]

Each move was matched by a countermove as Giuliani continued to bargain with Cuomo over the near-immediate help he needed with the budget. Giuliani was trapped in a fiscal vise that couldn't be opened without state aid. Barely three months into the new fiscal year, falling tax revenues had opened an $800 gap in Giuliani's budget.

For his part, Cuomo was finding the soft-spoken Pataki a difficult opponent, so he tried his hand at painting the challenger as a right-wing radical. Cuomo told the upstate *Middletown Times Herald-Record* that his re-election was necessary to prevent the "harshness and cynicism" of union and immigrant-bashing and racism that he said were on the rise. He warned that the state would cease to be a haven of "humanism" and "civility" if he were to lose. His wife, Matilda, chimed in by painting Pataki as an acolyte of the right-wing preacher/politician Pat Robertson. If Pataki won, she warned, "We could have race riots." But the theme failed to take hold. The breach between Cuomo's grandiloquent verbalizing about New York as "the tabernacle of democracy" and the reality of upstate's sharp decline was far too wide to be overcome.[8]

There was a similar disparity between Cuomo's rhetoric of mutuality and the vote-buying that drove the campaign once the

---

*The author got an angry 6:30 a.m. phone call from Cuomo after he wrote a column discussing the governor's chummy relationship with Sharpton. Cuomo assured me that he wasn't courting Sharpton because "what you see as cause is merely correlation."

scare tactics had failed. "Cuomo," noted *Newsday*, "Courts the Voters One Interest Group at a Time." The governor traveled around the state handing out $5 and $10 million "grants" to ethnic and interest groups, especially in the New York metro area. Cuomo and the upstate voters had largely given up on each other. His campaign became so metro-focused that people joked that he was running to be "the governor of New York City."[9]

Cuomo badly needed a shot in the arm from Giuliani. Reporters who traveled with Cuomo joked about him as "the ghost of liberalism past" and noted the increasingly nostalgic tone of his musings. But as late as October 23, Giuliani was still giving hints that if he didn't endorse Pataki he would at least stay neutral. Then, two days later, the two front-page headlines in the *New York Times* told the story. In the upper right in bold caps: GIULIANI, DEFYING HIS PARTY, BACKS CUOMO FOR 4TH TERM; just to the left in the center column, the smaller headline read: NEW YORK UNIONS AND MAYOR AGREE ON 7,600 JOB CUTS: SEVERANCE NOT LAYOFFS.[10]

The basis for the Cuomo endorsement was buried in the union story. The Cuomo-controlled Municipal Assistance Corporation was, despite the objections of its chair Eugene Keilin, providing a $110 million severance package to reduce the city payroll and the budget gap along with it. When the buyouts were completed, the city payroll, which had stood at 244,000 when Giuliani entered office, would be reduced to 230,000, the lowest total since 1985 when Ed Koch was beginning his hiring binge.

Buffeted by considerable debate within his own camp where some of his top advisors, who were partisan Republicans, argued forcefully for no endorsement, a nervous Giuliani, sweating visibly, stepped to the microphones to make his announcement. He delivered a tortured statement in which he never acknowledged the real basis for his choice but instead tried to square his "Republican principles" with his support for Cuomo.[11]

"Originally," he began, "I was going to use this time to explain the budget actions we are taking to continue the restructuring of city government." Then, invoking La Guardia and adopting a Clintonian tone, he spoke of how the "voters want the gridlock and the partisan politics to come to an end...to step beyond partisan stereotypes...to look at and do what has to be done—for people.... I have often said I would not be the Republican Mayor or the Democratic mayor but just the mayor of New York City." In that context, the key question, he asserted, was "which candidate would do the best job in redressing New York's balance of payments deficits with Albany and Washington." His answer was Mario Cuomo because "he has already reduced some of the deficit" and "is committed to doing so." These words would later be thrown back at Giuliani and Cuomo as evidence of "the dirty deal" between the two.[12]

In a shot at Pataki's relationship with New York's Republican senator, Giuliani charged that if the challenger won it would produce the corrupt "government of D'Amato for D'Amato and by D'Amato." The mayor said that while he and Cuomo had some "strong disagreements," "Mario Cuomo is his own man" and could be trusted to keep his word. Near the end of his brief endorsement announcement, Giuliani, straining the credulity of all but the most partisan Democrats, said, "I've come to the conclusion that it is George Pataki who best personifies the status quo of New York politics....it is Mario Cuomo who offers us the best opportunity for change."[13]

Joel Benenson, a Cuomo campaign spokesman watched. When he heard the endorsement, he burst out with a joyous "I can't fucking believe it." "When news of Rudy's endorsement reached DC 37 it erupted in cheers.... Clinton on Air Force One raised his arms in celebration." An ecstatic *New York Times* compared Giuliani to La Guardia as Democrats and liberals rejoiced while Staten Island's Republican boro president Guy Molinari, a key figure in the mayor's 1993 victory, spoke for many Republicans: "the only thing that makes sense is that he become a Democrat." And for a while columnists with space to fill speculated about whether the mayor described as "Benedict Rudy" by Republicans might switch parties. But Giuliani, thinking he had brought down D'Amato's man, talked about "realignment" in the Republican Party. As Pataki went into a free-fall, his seven-point lead turning into a thirteen-point deficit, Giuliani went on the campaign trail stumping for "Mario."[14]

A few days after he announced his support for Cuomo, Giuliani's updated budget showed $100 million in new state aid. Barnstorming upstate, Pataki pointed to the new money for the city as part of an insidious "deal." "Mario Cuomo," he argued, "has been using taxpayer money to save his job and buy votes." The idea of an "insidious deal" quickly caught on upstate where Cuomo was cordially despised. In the Lake Placid region, small-business people placed dartboards with pictures of Cuomo on them in their offices.

One gas station owner with a Cuomo dartboard told customers that they should feel free to take a throw. While selling me some oil, he summarized the situation: "The Governor I hate has cut a deal to win reelection by giving my money to the city I hate." The challenger, whose campaign as a stealth candidate had been running out of steam before the Giuliani endorsement, surged upstate where a backlash drove people to Pataki.

Giuliani's upstate swing on the governor's behalf only made matters worse by trying to make D'Amato the issue. On the day before the election, he warned, "If the D'Amato-Pataki crew ever gets control, ethics will be trashed." But D'Amato wasn't on the ballot—Cuomo was. Pataki scored by describing the governor in Finkelstein's slogan: "too liberal, too long."[15]

Before the vote Cuomo estimated that he needed a 500,000-vote margin out of New York City. He won the city by 600,000 votes but lost by 700,000 votes upstate and by 100,000 in the suburbs. Turnout was as high as 80 percent in some anti-Cuomo counties. Voters, energized by the ads run only upstate in the last seventy-two hours about "THE DEAL" between Cuomo and Giuliani, flocked to the polls.

For the first time in seventy years an upstater was elected governor. Pataki won with the lowest Manhattan vote total of any twentieth-century gubernatorial victor. Cuomo won among the wealthiest and the poorest, replicating the liberal Lindsay's and Dinkins' coalitions that had come to define the core of the Democratic Party. But as with Giuliani, the bulk of middle class went for Pataki.

There was a bitter reaction in the city. Giuliani's Deputy Mayor Fran Reiter of the Liberal Party, which had backed Cuomo, spoke of "an ongoing national war between those who support urban America and those who don't." Brooklyn councilman Herb Berman, usually a moderate, said "It's time to unwrap the movement for the 51st state." A Manhattan lawyer who backed Cuomo blamed the defeat on people who "aren't informed. It's the stupidity of the voters and the irresponsibility of the press."[16]

Curiously Giuliani was largely unscathed. Governor-elect Pataki refused to take his calls for three weeks. But events outside New York soon drew the men into what was at least a working if not a cordial relationship. In the city, a *New York Magazine* headline dubbed Giuliani a "Glorious Loser." When the mayor attended a Broadway Association luncheon, 500 business and real estate executives rose spontaneously from their seats to give him an ovation. The Sunday after the election, Giuliani went to a Baptist Church in African-American Bedford-Stuyvesant. Greeted with warmth, he expressed no regret for backing Cuomo.[17]

NINE

Smart Policing

Three months into office, Giuliani participated in a panel discussion on crime sponsored by the *New York Post* along with Mayors Thomas Menino of Boston and Sharon Pratt Kelly of the District of Columbia as well as Arthur Teele, Jr., Chair of the Miami Metro-Dade County Board of Commissioners. When asked by the moderator what they would do if they were offered a pot of money with no strings attached, Kelly warned against the "simplistic" assumption that law enforcement could do very much about crime, since wrongdoing was a matter of economic distress. Menino seconded her, saying that he would reduce crime "through job training and education" and mocked those who thought "$4.75 an hour jobs at McDonald's" might be a path out of poverty. Teele argued that children who grow up in single-parent families and drug-infested homes "are just as much a victim as the people they pull a gun on and rob." All three argued that government social programs were the key to crime reduction. Their comments represented the conventional wisdom of the day, which had been summed up by Mount Holyoke Professor Richard Moran: "there is no law enforcement solution to the crime problem."[1]

When Giuliani stepped to the podium, he took exception to all the others' arguments. He said he would use much of the money for law enforcement. In a direct challenge not only to liberal but also to policing orthodoxy, he pointed out that "a lack of jobs per se can't explain" wrongdoing since crime in the twentieth century was at its lowest in the 1930s during the years of the Great Depression. "The economy," Giuliani noted, "has been weak and the economy has been strong and it bears no relationship to the crime rate." He was right—crime exploded during the economic boom of the 1960s and 1980s. Criminals, like all individuals, even those designated as victims, Giuliani asserted, have to be held individually accountable.

In a city whose political culture had been defined since the 1960s by the intersection of big government and personal license, or what might be described as "dependent individualism," the mayor insisted that "we're fooling people if we suggest" that the solutions to our "very deep-seated problems are going to be found in government social programs. We constantly present the false impression that government can solve problems that government in America was designed not to solve." Government, he said, couldn't serve as a substitute for the family in instilling the values of citizenship. He lamented the loss of civic education in the schools which he saw as part of a larger pattern in which the institutions that socialized the young had lost their authority. "Families," he explained "are significantly less important.... Religion has less influence.... Communities don't mean what they meant thirty or forty years ago."

Cautious, even pessimistic, he suggested that it could take up to a decade before churches and communities could reduce crime by reasserting their moral authority. In the interim, making an analogy with Reagan's military buildup that helped win the Cold War, he argued, "We need more protection, we need more police, we need more jails and prisons, in order to offer a reasonable degree of safety to people so we can get through the period of time we're in now."

"At the core," he insisted, "the struggle to rebuild the city is philosophical," a matter of common beliefs. He lamented the loss of the shared values he saw as essential for a lawful society. "It's shared values that hold us together.... It's all about, ultimately, individual responsibility."

His voice rising, his arms punching the air for emphasis, he went on: "People are wrongly taught that there is something wrong with 'authority.'...We see only the oppressive side of authority." But proper authority, he insisted, protects freedom while freedom in the absence of responsible individuals descends into anarchy. What was needed, he argued, was a balance between rights and responsibilities, between what we want to do and our obligations to others.

The mayor's remarks drew grimaces from his fellow panel members and applause from most of the audience. Norman Siegel of the New York Civil Liberties Union said it was "frightening... radical...scary stuff.... This is the real Rudy Giuliani. I'm not sure people knew who they were electing."[2]

Confident though he was in his own abilities, Giuliani saw many more years of a rising prison population before crime could even begin to be controlled. But he was wrong on both counts. In the course of the next two years, the New York Police Department under Bill Bratton, a man with a strikingly similar managerial style, brought crime under control without resorting, as did much of the U.S., to rising rates of incarceration.

The Police Department Bratton inherited was, thanks to earlier reforms, already in many respects the finest in the country. But it was not a crime-fighting organization. Bratton benefited from studying the careers of his predecessors starting with Lindsay's last police commissioner, Patrick Murphy. Commissioner Murphy downgraded the policing of what were then described as "victimless crimes" such as gambling, prostitution, public drinking and urination. But that tactic didn't constrain more serious crimes as Murphy had forecast. The number of murders in New York grew four-fold between 1961 and 1972, a rate of increase second only to Detroit. Crime metastasized during the economic boom of the 1960s when the black male unemployment rate in New York City was but 4 percent. Murphy and many other police chiefs had promoted the claim that crime was largely an involuntary expression of poverty, poor housing and racism. If that were true, there was little reason to hold the police accountable for the growing mayhem.

But the police could be held accountable for corruption. Reviled by the rank and file for his role in the Harlem mosque incident and rocked by the Serpico scandals, Murphy pushed data-gathering and statistics with an eye to constraining corruption by holding precinct commanders liable for misdeeds on their watch. The message conveyed to the average cop was keep clean and you'll be all right even if you don't do very much about crime. The unofficial motto of the NYPD became "don't get involved."[3]

Ben Ward, appointed by Mayor Koch as the city's first African-American police commissioner, wanted to fight crime. After taking office in 1983, he quickly reversed the Murphy approach and began arresting people for "quality of life crimes" such as drug-dealing, gambling and prostitution. But in the absence of access to information on an arrestee's criminal record, the police had no idea if the person arraigned for a minor crime was the same individual wanted for a major crime. Ward's campaign had only a limited effect. Even as the economy boomed in the mid-1980s, major crime, driven in part by the crack epidemic, grew to record levels. One incident in particular—the murder of rookie patrolman Edward Byrne while he was standing guard at the home of a witness who had agreed to testify against a drug gang—symbolized the city's loss of control over its own streets.

Ward had tried to take the initiative. In 1984 Ward and Giuliani, then a U.S. Attorney, cooperated to launch Operation Pressure Point. They flooded high-crime neighborhoods like Washington Heights, the East Village and the Lower East Side with officers. Ward placed cops on almost every corner and kept them there round the clock. Operation Pressure Point arrested a massive number of offenders, but it had a scant overall effect. The courts were too overwhelmed to process most of the cases and the dealers moved just far enough away from the sweeps not to be bothered.*

Dinkins' first police commissioner, Lee Brown, was an innovator who wanted to break with the failed command-and-control model of reactive "911 policing" in which law enforcement was called into motion only after a crime had occurred. A clear failure, it cut off the cops patrolling in air-conditioned cars from the citizenry that needed to be protected and it led to an arrest in only 3 percent of calls. Under 911 policing, the rate of violent crime quadrupled between 1966 and 1990.

Brown, who had a Ph.D. in criminology, proposed a new set of strategies. First, he wanted to decentralize the police bureaucracy by creating mini-chiefs with clear areas of geographic responsibility. Secondly, working with Deputy Commissioner Jeremy Travis, he strengthened civil enforcement so that the District Attorney worked with the NYPD to shut down properties used as crack houses. Finally, where Ben Ward had made some tentative stabs at community policing, Brown sharply increased the number of police walking neighborhood beats. Brown, who was mocked as "out of town Brown" for his many speaking trips—he was away during both the Washington Heights and Crown Heights riots—was far more effective as a thinker and a promoter than as a manager. The department produced a 114-page booklet on community policing and radio ads announcing, "The beat cop is back." While the *New York Times*

---

*In the words of a conversation I overheard between two lowlifes near my Cooper Union office in the East Village, "Man, this is fuckinincredible. Avenue A is crawling with cops, but ain't shit bothernus here."

wrote adoring articles on community policing, in practice there was very little in the way of implementation. In the precincts, officers joked about "the community policing show." And when an annual award for community policing went to a CPOP (community police) officer who had saved twenty-five wedding dresses from a fire, it became a standing joke in the department, where the CPOPs were known alternatively as "scarecrows" or "social workers." Morale was terrible. The authority of leadership was so low that one cop felt emboldened to sue Dinkins and Brown for forcing him to patrol in drug-ridden Tompkins Square Park because he claimed it was a health hazard.[5]

Brown's successor for the final year of the Dinkins administration was Ray Kelly, the officer who had seized the initiative from the dithering Dinkins and brought the Crown Heights' riots to an end. Kelly's report on community policing was scathing. The CPOP officers tended to work bankers' hours, rarely shared information with the rest of the department, and in general had little effect. Kelly's assessment was later seconded by Bratton who noted that the implicit assumption behind community policing, that more cops on the streets meant less crime, was wrong. There were, Bratton explained, "no concrete means by which they [the CPOPs] were supposed to address crime.... They were simply supposed to go out on their beats and somehow improve their communities." In Chicago, the city that had invested the most in community policing, there had been no effect on crime; in fact, a few years later, Chicago, with one third of the population of New York, surpassed Gotham in the number of murders.[5]

Kelly, a far better administrator than Brown, never had much of chance to drive the department although he did make a start in curbing the squeegees. Just before he took command, the newspapers had been filled with the case of Michael Dowd, a crooked cop caught up in the drug trade. A commission headed by Dinkins' Deputy Mayor for Criminal Justice Milton Mollen was appointed to deal with corruption, and crime fighting again had to play second fiddle.

Bratton's philosophy was shaped in part by absorbing the lessons of why prior innovations had failed. He told the citizens, "My number one priority is fear reduction." He told the aggressive panhandlers, "Get off drugs, get off the booze, get off your ass and get a job." He told cops that their job would no longer be defined by what they shouldn't be doing. As one of his closest aides, Jack Maple, lamented, active cops who made a lot of collars were considered a problem by the brass who then had to process the paperwork. "Nobody ever got in trouble," groused Maple, "because crime numbers on their watch went up."[6]

In 1993 the average cop made less than dozen arrests during the year. That was about to change. Bratton tapped into the latent energy of the department's "crime fighters." He announced that for the first time since the Lindsay/Murphy years uniformed cops could make drug arrests.

Under the old regime, "when night fell the NYPD went home, shootings peaked between 8 p.m. and 4 a.m. but the narcotics division closed up at 7 p.m.; the warrant squad didn't begin work until 8 a.m. and never worked weekends." That all changed under Bratton.[7]

The new commissioner communicated a revolutionary goal: "winning the war on crime." A ramrod of a leader, he was offering the rank and file a new deal. If they wanted to be crime fighters, he'd back them up to the hilt—as long as they were clean. At the same time as he used the Mollen report on police corruption to clean house, he also encouraged the time-servers and "empty-suits" to depart by promoting young risk-takers, like forty-five-year-old John Timoney, to the top leadership positions. Timoney, like Bratton, was a well-read, college-educated, thinking man's cop. Born in Ireland, Timoney captured the new spirit when he talked of how "we didn't do any police work for twenty-five years.... We spent the last twenty-five years doing nothing but worrying about corruption." Bratton gave cops the chance "to smoke out the phonies who claimed the department does not let us do our job while they were using this as curtain for inaction."[8]

This was all part of what Bratton, borrowing his terminology from management reformers, called "reengineering" the police department. Reengineering was a break from the military model of 911 policing. The NYPD, Bratton observed "was divided into little fiefdoms.... The organization was very military-oriented, with a strict chain of command, and information didn't flow easily from one bureau to another." That had to change. "What I was trying to do," said Bratton, "was similar to what Lee Iacocca had done with Chrysler."[9]

Just as Giuliani made sure his staff read David Osborne's *Rein-*

venting Government, Bratton, dubbed "the CEO Cop," made Michael Hammer and James Champy's book *Reengineering the Corporation* required reading. With the success of American corporations in remaking themselves during the 1980s in mind, he created a dozen "reengineering teams" to reconsider all the major operational assumptions that had gone into the organization of the department. But even before the reports were in, he committed himself, corporate style, to what public-sector managers were loathe to do—setting a target of 10 percent crime reduction for 1994.

In corporate jargon, Bratton flattened the hierarchies and created what is known as a loose/tight organization in which subordinates are given autonomy within a shared framework but then have no excuses if they fail to produce. He streamlined the outsized command and control mechanism of One Police Plaza, the massive paper-processing headquarters run on a civil service mentality. He eliminated many of the intermediate layers of authority and pushed resources and responsibility down to the precinct commanders. They in turn were given a great deal more discretion on how to operate with the understanding that their careers depended on reducing crime without relying on rough stuff.

Behind this new framework was an increased access to information. Traditionally the department was not only hierarchical but also sharply segmented. "The biggest lie in law enforcement," noted Jack Maple, "is we work closely together." Every specialized bureau guarded its secrets—robbery, auto crime, homicide each had their own cache of information that it treated as scarce capital it wasn't willing to share. But, said Maple, "the McDaddy of all blue walls of silence is the one that normally separates the Narcotics Division from the Detective Bureau." Almost no one had access to all of the department's nineteen separate data systems, partly on the grounds that corrupt cops might sell the information back to the criminals, but mostly because catching crooks was not the department's top priority. Bratton began to change that. Information, instead of moving up and down the hierarchy, began to move "laterally across bureau and division boundaries."[10]

The precinct commanders, armed with better intelligence, in turn conveyed Bratton's messages to the rank and file about active "broken windows" policing which took seriously neighborhood complaints about the disorder created by so-called victimless crimes. The regular cop too was given greater discretion to police disor-

derly situations by diffusing them with cajolery or bluff if possible
before they escalated to the point where arrests had to made. This
greatly increased interaction between cops and would-be criminals
produced extraordinary results. In one case a young Midtown cop
earned the moniker of "Strategy Man" because he took down a
whole ring of criminals by following up on an open-beer violation.
In another, the search of a van used for prostitution turned up
twenty-seven pipe bombs and other weapons.[11]

Within a few months the department was better at sharing
information, but then the problem was the information once gathered was often out of date. Collecting crime data was considered a
menial clerical task. "As far as the department had been concerned,"
Bratton explained, "statistics were not for use in combating crime,
they were only for keeping score at the end of the year. Even then,
the only statistics they paid attention to were the robberies. But even
that was smoke and mirrors.... Nobody used them for anything."[12]

Jack Maple, like Bratton the son of a working-class civil-serv-
ice family, wanted to change that. He was an incredible character.
While working with the Transit Police, he began to sport a bow tie,
homburg and spectator shoes. He claims that he got the idea for up-
to-the-minute data-gathering in early 1994 while soaking up a few at
Elaine's, a tony East Side watering hole.

Maple asked for all the stats for East New York, the crime-
ridden 75th Precinct, to be mapped with pins, gradually moving to
computerized map projections on which various kinds of info could
be superimposed on top of each other. "For the first time," noted
police historian Eli Silverman, "all the crime and arrest data that
were floating in the vast NYPD universe were brought together."
Here was the basis of what became CompStat. Together with broken
windows policing, CompStat's daily computerized mapping of criminal incidents worked "a revolutionary change in policing."[13]

CompStat became the means to solve problem first by sharing
information and then by searching for patterns. At the 8 a.m.
CompStat meeting, which took place at the same time as the Giuliani
morning meeting, the previous day's crime statistics were made visible to the department's leadership. For the first time the precinct
commanders could plan their daily operations on the basis of up-to-
the-minute crime information mapped out geographically by
category. This gave the NYPD a means to overcome the problem of
"displacement." When Ben Ward and Rudy Giuliani went on their

TNT (Tactical Narcotics Teams) raids, the crime just moved a few blocks over. With up-to-the-minute mapping, the open-air drug markets were disrupted time and again until they either dried up or were driven indoors where they did less damage.*

CompStat gave precinct commanders direct access to the brass and broke through the traditionally rigid layers of authority. It had the effect, as one Brooklyn precinct commander said, of putting the department leadership "more and more on the same wavelength." But it also put the precinct commanders in a tough spot. If there had been a surge of muggings or burglaries on a particular block, they were expected to analyze the problem and explain what they intended to do about it with the understanding that if it wasn't resolved, they would be called on the carpet. CompStat and "reengineering," says Eli Silverman, "acted like a booster cable to the NYPD's battery, providing the cranking power need to activate decentralization and command accountability."[14]

The results were extraordinary. In Dinkins' last year, crime dropped by 7 percent without any general reduction in fear since most of the decline was concentrated in midtown and areas where Business Improvement Districts had begun to restore order. In 1994 crime dropped 12 percent followed by 16 percent declines in 1995 and 1996. The biggest declines came in crime-ridden outer-boro neighborhoods. Overall, New York's decline in crime accounted for more than 60 percent of the national decline.

As fear declined even more rapidly than crime, the effect on daily life was palpable. A virtuous cycle was set in motion in which people spent more time in public places, and, as good uses of public space drove out bad, more people were drawn back into the public life of the city.

Time magazine, whose 1990 cover story THE ROTTING OF THE BIG APPLE had produced enormous dismay, trumpeted the change by placing Bratton on its cover. As murder rates plunged to a twenty-five-year low in the first half of 1995, *New York* magazine got carried away with a cover story on THE END OF CRIME AS WE KNOW IT, but the improvement was palpable.

---

*Police Strategy Paper No. 3 issued in April 1994 looked back on the TNT raids and concluded that the areas targeted were "too large" and so "never could be secured, [meaning] crack activity was only displaced," rather than eliminated. It also noted that the raids "became predictable to criminals." Municipal Archives.

By 1995, noted the *Boston Globe*'s Fred Kaplan, on 105th Street and Amsterdam Avenue in Harlem, where there had been a funeral a week, people were sitting out on the stoops once again. And eighteen-year-old Presley Navarete noticed, "I hardly hear gunshots anymore.... It's all because of the cops, the cops are everywhere." The director of the neighborhood youth center, reported Kaplan, saw a new day in Harlem in which "the sun even seemed brighter; the air seemed lighter."[15]

Bratton explained what had happened: "we changed behavior." That meant 163,428 fewer felonies between the start of 1994 and the end of 1996, a year that saw the city's lowest number of crime complaints in more than a quarter century. The big crime, murder, dropped 16 percent in 1996 and has fallen nearly half since 1993. Senator Moynihan's fears of the seemingly inexorable impact of the underclass turned out to be unfounded.*

---

*What was good for the city was bad for root-cause criminologists, conservatives who had predicted the coming a new generation of fatherless "superpredators," and die-hard Dinkins supporters. Jack Maple had fun with the criminologists invested in root-cause arguments. "They're all going to be up there with their wizard hats on, you know, the ones with the half-moons." Many of the Rudy-haters argued that it was all a mirage or a matter of national trends or...Criminologist with professional reputations began a still ongoing effort to explain away the success.

Here are their favorites explanations, and what's wrong with them, in descending order of significance:

1) *The economy:* But crime dropped before the economy rose. The economic recovery, which began in 1992 nationally, didn't arrive in New York until the last quarter of 1995. The unemployment rate of 8.5%, which was well above the national average of 5.4%, continued to grow until 1997. Nationally, crime dropped just 5% between 1993 and 1996 while falling 35% in Gotham. The city accounted for one-third of the national decline even though it was only 2.5% of the population.

2) *Imprisonment:* While the prison population grew 43% nationally from 1993-1998, the New York State prison population increased by just 8.5%, the third slowest rate in the country.

3) *The big brother effect:* The claim: Younger brothers watching their older siblings suffer from crack addiction and the violence of the crack trade turned away from drugs and gangs. There's some truth to this, but this was both a limited explanation and, to the extent it applied, not confined to New York. If this was a major cause of the crime collapse, crime rates should have been collapsing across the U.S., where mostly they were going down just slightly.

4) *It's true, BUT...*Michael Massing, often a thoughtful writer on criminal justice matters, predicted a vast crime surge because New York wasn't spending enough on social services. The drug trade, said Massing, is on the rebound. He approvingly quoted a middle-aged black man who saw that "Crime is going to go up .... They're hounding people off welfare. These people are not going to starve. They'll steal." The reality was simpler. The effect of a more active police force stopping and frisking suspects meant that fewer people were willing to carry guns. Fewer people carrying guns meant fewer murders and so on.

TEN

Work Is the
Best Social Policy

Most New Yorkers learned about the mayor's plans for welfare reform in an appropriately Gotham-like manner. In October 1994 police were in the process of booking a man named Herbert Steed on charges of bilking 225 African tourists out of $800,000 when they discovered that he had a welfare ID card in his pocket. Steed, it turned out, was living in a $4,000-a-month apartment in the Trump Tower, owned a bevy of luxury cars and was negotiating for the purchase of an English manor house on Long Island Sound. He was also receiving $352 a month in welfare relief benefit on the grounds that he had no income and no assets while living in a tiny Queens flat.

Steed was by no means the biggest offender. The previous year, a woman who collected welfare under fifteen different names and for seventy-three fictitious children pleaded guilty to collecting $450,000 in welfare payments from 1987 to 1994. But Steed was the most notorious and most egregious offender. Giuliani seized on Steed's case to prepare the public for the coming welfare reforms he would outline at the onset of his second year in office.

▲ ▲ ▲

While Giuliani was preparing Gotham for welfare reform, in Washington, the Republicans, led by the mercurial Newt Gingrich of Georgia had captured the House of Representatives for the first time in forty-two years. Gingrich and his supporters had run on a proposed "Contract with America," in which individual accountability would replace welfare-state paternalism as the guiding philosophy of government. In Albany Mario Cuomo, the leading spokesman for

151

American liberalism, had been replaced by Republican George Pataki, who won on a platform that called for tax reductions.[1]

Giuliani, who had governed in his first year by cooperating with Cuomo and Clinton, was intellectually well prepared for the shift to the right. He quickly redirected his administration to take advantage of the new political landscape. His ambitious 1995 State of the City address laid out two closely connected propositions. He called for both a radical restructuring of New York's relationship with Washington and Albany and a radical restructuring of welfare. Speaking before the National Press Club in Washington on behalf of America's cities, Giuliani called on Washington to "set us free, free to solve our own problems, free to spend our own money in our own way." Giuliani saw that it was not only the poor but city government itself that was caught in the trap of dependency. New York, he argued, needed to become independent of Washington and its subsidies for welfare programs just as welfare recipients need to become independent of government subsidies.[2]

At the outset of his career, Giuliani had been weak on oratorical skills. An admiring colleague in the federal attorney's office remembers that the staff felt like "they need to take a few stiff drinks" before they listened to his "robotic" performances. But after two runs at the mayor's office, he finally found his voice with his second State of the City speech. Speaking in whole paragraphs, without notes, and in the voice of the self-sufficient middle-class, he delivered a commanding performance.

"The old agenda," said Giuliani, "was based on looking to others for solutions to our problems. The new urban agenda should declare that we can solve our own problems." "We are," he went on, "the experts on urban life...on its problems...and its promise." For too long, he explained, cities were "defined by their problems." Instead, cities "should be defined by their assets."

The city, he explained, picking up Senator Moynihan's theme, was trapped in a losing game in which year after year it transferred far more in taxes to Washington than it ever received in benefits. This worked for the liberal interest groups since the money from Washington was sent to the social service industry and government workers who dominated local politics even as it gave some of the very wealthy a chance to bask in the glow of their generous willingness to pay the highest taxes in the U.S. The losers in this game, however, were the aspiring poor, would-be entrepreneurs and the middle class who could afford neither the gestures of the rich nor the cost of the public sector.

New York's vast alternative economy, organized around social service and non-profit jobs directly and indirectly subsidized by the city and its taxpayers, was dedicated to maintaining this political and social status quo. Giuliani looked back to an older and more elevated view of the city's economy that saw it as an engine of opportunity. Cities, he explained, don't "generate poverty; they generate wealth, which attracts poor people seeking to ascend into the middle class.... It's our goal to increase that number. Let's seize this opportunity," he concluded, "to show Albany, Washington, and the world how a modern American city operates: independently, without constraint or overbearing direction from state and federal authorities."

Turning to the city's fiscal problem, he laid the budget crunch at the door of social spending. If New York, he stressed, didn't spend "ten times as much [per capita] on welfare, and four-and-a-half times as much on health care, if our expenditures were in line with the average" of the ten largest cities, "we would enjoy a $6 billion surplus, instead of a structural deficit of more than $2 billion."

Welfare, he noted, drained the city of not only money but also social capital. It robbed people of "dignity and hope, all of which can be found in a job." Instead of welfare as an entitlement, he spoke of organizing the city's aid to the poor around the idea of reciprocity. "For every benefit," he said, "there is an obligation, for every right, a duty." In practice that meant that able-bodied people on welfare would be expected to work for the city in return for their benefits. Tying the major strands of the speech together, he said: "We are asking of New York City precisely what we are asking of those on welfare—self-reliance."

In February, Giuliani went to Albany to make his case before the state legislature and the newly elected governor, fellow Republican George Pataki, who was still smarting over Giuliani's support for Mario Cuomo.

Pataki had his own woes. During Cuomo's last five years in office the state had lost 550,000 jobs while the welfare rolls had grown by 435,000, or nearly a third, to reach 1.65 million. Cuomo, like Dinkins, had exacerbated the recession with tax increases, arguing that "taxes do not matter for business location decisions." But they did. And the problem of New York's tax burden could only grow as the incoming Republican governors in New Jersey and Connecticut, Christie Whitman and John Rowland respectively, beckoned to New York's businesses with planned tax cuts. Pataki proposed substantial cuts in the income tax, and he proposed to pay for them by reducing New York's Medicaid spending (the highest in the nation) as well as welfare reforms including fingerprinting some beneficiaries to reduce fraud. Councilwoman Una Clarke referred to the finger-imaging as "Branding the Slaves"—a characterization that carried some weight in local newspapers until it was pointed out that city mangers and commissioners were already fingerprinted as part of their contract with the city.[3]

Giuliani disconcerted the state legislators by breaking with the tradition of mayors coming to Albany to beg for help. The mayor described the Pataki cuts as "an excellent opportunity...to manage government more efficiently." As if this weren't enough, he told the legislators, most of whom were recipients of campaign funds from the powerful teachers' unions, that "it would be a waste" to give city schools more aid. New funds would only be squandered. His priority, he said, was mayoral control over the schools so that they could be better managed. Franz Leichter, a liberal legislator from Manhattan was "frankly flabberghasted.... In all my years here, it's the first time I've ever heard a mayor come up here and not plead for more financial aid."[4]

Back in Gotham, Giuliani's proposed city budget called for spending 2.3 percent ($1.4 billion) less in the coming fiscal year as well as small tax cuts on clothing, condos and co-ops. By comparison, the biggest cut during the 1970s fiscal crisis had been a mere half a percent. Trimming taxes was meant to suggest a better future ahead. But for the politicians representing the public sector—that is, virtually the entire political class of New York—it was salt in the wounds of the largest spending cut since 1933 when the city was in the midst of the Depression and Mayor Jimmy Walker and his mistress were about to flee rather than risk jail. If enacted, Giuliani's budget would be the first time in the modern history of New York that spending was cut two years in row.

Giuliani made it clear: "We must choose between pulling ourselves into the late twentieth century or remaining mired in the tired and abandoned policies of the Great Society" of the 1960s. Still, the mayor was quick to point out that even after this "slashing" Gotham "would still be providing more money in each of these [social, health and education] programs than any other city in America." The future, he insisted, was in private-sector jobs.

Chancellor Cortines, facing a 7 percent cut, unloaded on Giuliani: "Kiss the ring and we'll give you another buck, but if you complain you may not get the money you need." Kenneth Raske, spokesman for the city's hospital industry, argued against cutting one of New York's growth industries. (In the previous fifteen years, health care, which was growing twice as fast as Wall Street, had added more than 100,000 jobs, most of them publically subsidized through a massive expansion of the state's Medicare program.) Columnist Jack Newfield took up Raske's cry, claiming, "This is like the government of Texas attacking the oil industry in the name of economic growth."[5]

What Raske and Newfield were defending was described by Richard Schwartz, a senior Giuliani advisor, as "leaky bucket economics." The city hospitals were overstaffed; they employed about three times as many workers per patient than the city's private hospitals. They were, Schwartz said, "the most inefficient job creation programs in America."

> You take someone's dollar from a paycheck, you send it to Washington, Washington sends it to Albany, Albany sends it to New York City, the city matches it with 50 cents, Albany matches it with 50 cents, then New York transfers that money to the corporate headquarters of the HHC [Health and Hospitals Corporation], which then transfers the money to the HHC hospital, then finally that money translates...into a [make work] job."[6]

But even this was a success compared to the city's welfare and social services industry. With less than 3 percent of the national population, New York spent more than one-fifth of all local social service dollars in the country and six times the per capita local government average on Medicaid, welfare, homeless services and foster care. What did it get in return? Adjusted for the cost of living, Gotham, despite its vast expenditures, suffered from a poverty rate almost as high as benighted Mississippi.

Senator Moynihan was puzzled by the fact that record levels of family breakdown were not regarded as a calamity for municipal government. But family breakdowns supported a vast network of job opportunities. New York was spending about two and half times as much on administering welfare as other high benefit states like Connecticut, Massachusetts and California.*

---

*Welfare administration supported a wide array of job titles. John McKnight of Northwestern University listed the new cadre of social service jobs. They included but were not limited to:
  job trainers, street gang workers, land clearance experts, urban education specialists, environmental aides, urban environmental specialists, legal assistance

For the new alternative economy New York had created to replaced departing private-sector jobs, the more dysfunctional the family, the better. Broken families served as Keynesian multipliers by generating immediate social spending. Welfare and Medicaid were seen as something akin to free money, since city monies spent on them generated matching state and federal funds, pumping up the local economy. Leave aside the cost in local and state taxes—let alone despair and desperation. In mining for Washington's fool's gold, New York had created a vast alternative economy.

Social services had become big business and the key to a politics that revolved around serving and expanding what counted as poverty. In 1993 alone, New York City awarded 30,000 social service contracts worth nearly $3 billion. State and federal contracts brought in another $4 billion to the social service industry. The District of Columbia aside, New York had the highest proportion of government workers to the total work force of any U.S. city. While the city's private-sector job base shrunk by 10 percent between 1984 and 1994, social service jobs increased by 60 percent to 150,000, a growth of 55,000 jobs. Overall, publicly funded jobs in government, health care and private social services accounted for a third of all employment in Brooklyn and just under half in the Bronx. More than one million people in the city—one-third of all employment—worked in government, health and social services.

The social services industry, along with aligned public-sector unions and non-profits, dominated the permanent Democratic majorities in the city council, the state assembly, and the day-to-day politics of the city. And when it was challenged politically, "the new Tammany," as *Crain's* described it, could count on its allies on the courts who had been chosen by those same politicians.

The difference between the old and the new Tammany was that the old party bosses were openly self-interested and even somewhat accountable. Before La Guardia's reforms, Tammany's patronage

---

lawyers, library consultants, job locators, public health physicians, parole consultants, nurses, public housing officials, teachers aides, civil rights watchdogs, employment counselors, prevention specialists, police trainers, urban housing specialists, rat abatement experts, vocational counselors, literacy specialists, drug counselors, defensible space architects, and the administrators, auditors, lawyers and consultants to support them all.

Fred Siegel, *The Future Once Happened Here*, New York: Free Press, 1997: 205-206.

operation was accountable to the election results. When their failures were sufficiently egregious, Tammany was thrown out of office. It was subject to regular attacks from crusading newspapers and reformers. The new Tammany, by contrast, was wrapped in a cloth of sanctimony. It professed to represent the interests of the poor. Protected in part by civil service and union power, it was immune to elections, and rather than being subject to scrutiny by the press it was mostly treated as a sacred cow. The most basic form of political accountability, the ability to "throw the bums out," was lost to an interest group political monopoly more suffocating than Tammany at its worst.

The defenders of what Giuliani derisively described as "the compassion industry" reacted ferociously to his budget plans. *Newsday* columnist Jimmy Breslin thought the mayor was consumed with a "mad desire to get at the poor because he is a prosecutor and being poor is a felony." The Reverend Calvin Butts said the poor would "be forced into the streets, they'll be forced into crime, they'll get sick and die." Public Advocate Mark Green compared Giuliani to Herbert Hoover and then quoted FDR: "Better the occasional faults of a government that lives in a spirit of charity than the constant omission of government frozen in its own indifference." [7]

But for all the angry ranting, some liberals like then-Congressman Charles Schumer saw that "we Democrats ran out of philosophical steam."

Moynihan concurred: "Liberalism faltered when it turned out it could not cope with truth." Rather than face up to the failings of the social programs they had championed, Democrats, he said, had "rewarded the articulation of moral purpose more than the achievement of practical good." [8]

▲ ▲ ▲

No place in America had resisted welfare reform more ferociously than New York. No place needed it more. Between 1989 and 1995, more than 270,000 New Yorkers had been added to the welfare roles, creating a total greater than in all but the two worst years of the Great Depression. That left Gotham with an unsustainable ratio of one adult welfare recipient for every seven workers, at a time when the national ratio was one to twenty-eight.

The 1988 Federal Family Support Act authored by Senator Moynihan tried to push the states into either more job placement, or failing that, into more job training. Other states, like Wisconsin, which took the lead in welfare reform, assumed that there was no substitute for work itself. In New York City and State the number of welfare recipients actually placed in jobs went down as the social service industry ginned up a vast job-raining apparatus which succeeding in creating jobs for the job trainers but little else.

But then again, no place in America has been so strongly resistant to the importance of work. Other than Philadelphia, the city whose liberal traditions are most like New York's, the Big Apple has had the lowest male labor force participation rate in the United States. African-Americans and Puerto Ricans were actively discouraged from entering the work force by a system of income, food and housing subsidies that often paid more than entry-level jobs. The concept of "dead-end jobs," so crucial to the growth of welfare in the first place, had a death grip on the minds of the city's social activists.

Placing welfare clients in low-wage jobs, complained Megan McLaughlin of the Federation of Protestant Welfare Agencies, "merely shifts people to the ranks of the working poor, trapping them in dead-end jobs." The city's training programs for welfare had to be extensive and elaborate if they were to prepare welfare recipients for jobs that were, as was their due, financially and personally satisfying from the beginning. Dedicated to ending not welfare but welfare reform, activists like Maureen Lane had contempt for low-end labor. "Work," she argued, "is not a substitute for welfare because it either pays too little or takes jobs from union members."[9]

But many of the new immigrants who poured into the city during the 1970s and 1980s were more than willing to take entry-level jobs. New York in the 1980s received 854,000 newcomers to America, the largest influx of immigrants since the imposition of immigration restrictions in 1924. Of the city's 7.3 million people in 1995, 2.1 were foreign-born. Forty per cent of the city households spoke a language other than English at home.

Many of the new immigrants, white and non-white, were moving up. In 1994 the ethnic group with the highest median household income in the city was Filipinos with $46,754. American-born whites were a distant second with $38,382, followed by Indians. In 1990, median family income for American-born blacks, more than a third of whom worked in government, was $21,548, compared to $30,000 for African-born blacks and more still for blacks born in

Jamaica. American-born blacks had a higher poverty rate than any largely black immigrant group except Dominicans.[10]

The new immigrants were succeeding not because the low-end jobs they often occupied were growing but because between 1970 and 1990 New York lost unskilled white workers faster than it lost unskilled jobs. African-Americans, however, never competed for those jobs. Black labor force participation rates plummeted while the opportunities were taken by the new arrivals, including African immigrants, instead. There was a growing black middle-class as native-born black workers moved up into better paying public-sector jobs. But another, smaller segment of black workers dropped out of the labor force altogether. The so-called "dead-end jobs"—taxi, restaurant, hotel, garment and cleaning work—which were once major sources of black employment, were increasingly filled by immigrants.[11]

"The problem," explained Senator Moynihan, the principal author of the 1988 legislation, "was that hugely influential voices were invariably raised against [reform] efforts, calling them puni-tive coercive, mean." In practice, this meant that the same anti-poverty lawyers who had done so much to create the welfare explosion of the 1960s and their heirs fought along with their many friends in the courts and the legislature to limit work requirements for welfare recipients. By 1993, New York ranked forty-third in the percentage of adult welfare recipients with jobs, thirty-second in paternity established, but second in the percentage of participants in vocational training/skills training programs.[12]

Until the mid-1990s, the Democratic majority in the New York State Assembly, dominated by representatives of the social services industry, blocked any welfare reform. As one disgruntled member put it, "people up here just don't think there's a problem." They had good company in Governor Cuomo, who resolutely insisted that female-headed teenage families just weren't a problem: "if you took a fifteen-year-old with a child, but put her in a clean apartment, got her a diploma, gave her the hope of a job…that would change every-thing." If we did all this, concluded Cuomo, "the fact that she had a baby at fifteen wouldn't produce *any* disorientation at all, and the hope that comes from new context would solve the problem."[13]

▲ ▲ ▲

Machiavelli, steeped in the classic Greek and Roman writings on cit-

izenship, spoke of "pious cruelty" and "the bad use of compassion."
An effective Prince will, he noted, "by making an example or
two...prove more compassionate than those who being too compassionate allow disorders which lead to murder and rapine." Looking
to make "an example or two," Giuliani made it clear that New York
couldn't "sustain a million people on welfare. You can't do it from
the point of view of the amount of misery and hopelessness that it
causes."[14]

Unlike other localities looking at welfare reform, Giuliani did-
n't request permission from the Federal government to break with
the provisions of Senator Moynihan's 1988 Family Support Act.
What Giuliani changed, explained Baruch College professor Tom
Main, "was not welfare law but welfare administration." Giuliani
advisors such as Anthony Coles were armed with both the knowledge of an earlier, though largely forgotten, welfare reform that had
shown signs of success and by the vast new powers afforded the
mayor by the 1989 charter changes.

In the late 1970s, Mayor Koch, with the city still struggling to
escape from its 1975 fiscal implosion and well aware of widespread
fraud, allowed his welfare commissioner Blanche Bernstein to
tighten the requirements for receiving aid. She found that every
minor hurdle—such as requiring people to pick up their checks in
person—produced major reductions in the caseload. And when in a
test Bernstein required a group of able-bodied people receiving
benefits to show up for workfare jobs, as many as 40 percent never
appeared.

Bernstein's reforms generated an outpouring of vitriol. She was
regularly picketed by protesters accusing of her of racism and worse.
Congressman Charles Rangel charged the Koch administration of
"planned genocide." Koch caved in and fired Bernstein. He replaced
her with Stanley Brezenoff, a self-described "unabashed liberal" who
saw welfare as a success. Asked later about his view of the world,
Brezenoff responded, "I'm not going to say people aren't responsible
for their actions, but..."[15]

Koch had to deal with a Board of Estimate; Giuliani didn't.
Freed from the Board by the 1989 charter reform, Giuliani had only
to face a council with quite limited budget powers. And in dealing
with the council in his second year, Giuliani discovered a powerful
weapon. The mayor and the mayor alone had the power to set the
revenue estimate, the framework in which all discussions of spending

had to take place. By lowballing the expected revenue for the coming year, the mayor was able to keep the council, strong supporters of social services industry spending, on the defensive.

Finally, Giuliani, with the help of Randy Levine, split the labor/liberal coalition that could have thwarted welfare reform. His chief weapon was not, as generally assumed, the threat to lay off union workers. (Dismissed workers can no longer vote in the union election, but they can vote against the mayor.) The unions in general—and the largest single bargaining agent for city workers, District Council 37 of the American Federation of State Count and Municipal Employees (AFSCME)—were thrown off balance by Giuliani's plan to privatize city services. By the end of his first year in office, the Giuliani administration was well on its way to replacing city workers for repaving work in Queens and maintaining Parks Department buildings in Manhattan. There were also plans to privatize the city's warehouse and leasing operation as well as two of its thirteen hospitals.[16]

Faced with the threat of privatization, District Council 37, led by Stanley Hill, agreed to allow the city to use welfare recipients to work off their benefits by helping to clean the parks. In return Hill got a no-layoff promise for all but his hospital workers as well as no pay hike for two years, but then a 13 percent pay hike over the final three years of the five-year contract. Workfare (or WEP, the Work Experience Program) would double the Parks Department's labor force by the end of 1995, making the parks cleaner while saving the city about $600 million even as it gave welfare recipients a way to earn their benefits.

Richard Schwartz, who ran the city's workfare program, organized it around the idea of "job readiness," a concept he borrowed from America Works, which makes sure people who had never developed regular habits learned to get to work on time and dressed properly. At America Works, a for-profit company, if a client couldn't consistently come on time to learn "job readiness," they couldn't be in the program. Peter Cove and his partner Lee Bowes taught their welfare clients the sort of things that are passed along routinely in the course of a less isolated existence. They showed their clients how to dress for work, adapt to a routine and how to respond when given instructions by a supervisor. The actual jobs skills were left to the companies that did the hiring. What companies wanted were people who were reliably ready for work.

Workfare had been tried in New York on a small scale in the mid-1980s without success. But the program had been isolated from larger social trends.

In the early 1990s, a far larger program was accompanied by not only a new resolve born of fiscal necessity but a new set of public assumptions that couldn't be dismissed as merely reactionary Republicanism.

It was President Clinton who appealed to the country's core values of work, self-sufficiency, responsibility, and reciprocity. Clinton, a Democrat, spoke of "a hand up, not a hand out" as he appealed to the Congress to "end welfare as we know it." Giuliani, operating in the space that Clinton had opened, spoke of replacing "entitlement" with "enablement" by "return[ing] work to the center of city life." Intentionally inverting New York's standard rhetoric, Giuliani insisted that "moving people from welfare to work is both progressive in political philosophy…and demonstrates true faith and belief in people's abilities."[17]

Workfare in New York served to reduce the welfare rolls at both the front and back end. It encouraged people to find work on their own rather than clean the parks. At the same time workfare laborers contributed markedly to the improvement of the parks and the cash-strapped city's overall well-being. Still, for those who used welfare in the old-fashioned way as low-end unemployment insurance, cleaning the parks chafed.

"There is no reason," Blanche Bernstein had explained a decade earlier, "to believe that the poor are less adept at manipulating welfare than the rich are at manipulating the income tax system." Giuliani took that insight to heart. Well aware of the fact that a random check of welfare recipients in nearby Newark, New Jersey found that 23 percent were also receiving New York City benefits, the administration began to make home visits to some would-be clients while fingerprinting everyone in the program. Just these changes doubled the rate of those ruled ineligible to receive welfare. The upshot of workfare and the eligibility reviews was that by the end of 1996, with the city still in recession, the welfare rolls had declined by 18 percent from 1.16 million to 950,000. But that was only the beginning. The revision of the rules also began to change the way people thought about work versus welfare.[18]

When *New York Times* columnist Joyce Purnick visited workfare mothers on the job, she was taken by their generally optimistic mood. Elizabeth Elder, a twenty-nine-year-old mother of four, at her job cleaning a Bronx park, told Purnick, "They should have done this a long time ago. If they had there wouldn't be children having children." If the rules had been stricter when she was younger, Elder went on, she might have "thought twice" about some of the choices she had made.[19]

ELEVEN

Shakedown City

A vast city squeezed into spaces that were laid out two centuries ago, a fast-moving but dense and dirty metropolis built on an island of narrow streets and tall buildings, Gotham was made up of innumerable bottlenecks, chokepoints, and cheek-by-jowl living that generated nearly endless opportunities for the mob and its unions to exact tribute. The New York minute is no cliché when you're trying to unload fish and every second that passes depreciates the value of your cargo.

New Yorkers are all too familiar with reform that paradoxically takes the form of new regulations, which in turn, provide new opportunities for corruption. In order to enforce the maze of often contradictory regulations, the city gives discretionary power to inspectors who can almost always find something "illegal." Faced with new vulnerabilities, even legitimate shopkeepers are forced to pay protection in the form of new bribes. "The crooks come in through the back door," a merchant complained to Giuliani, "the inspectors come in the front door, and it's all the same to me. I get robbed at both ends." The same could be said of the city's economy as a whole. The mob and extortionate taxes both raise the cost of living, reduce city revenues, and make economic life even more precarious than it has to be.[1]

If that sounds harsh, consider the words of Lieutenant Rayman Rahim, the commander of the Sanitation Department's enforcement police. He was one of ten members of the sanitation police indicted in the fall of 1993 by Manhattan District Attorney Robert Morgenthau for extorting up to $10,000 a year from restaurants, shopkeepers and street vendors. Lieutenant Rahim explained, "I used my summons book like a gun to get money."[2]

Rahim had plenty of company. Morgenthau found that "every major plumbing contract in Manhattan and the Bronx in the last decade involved kickbacks to union officials and mobsters." But then again almost every aspect of life was subject to a shakedown. In the parks, city employees were requiring "hard cash for softball permits" to play on the public diamonds.[3]

As mayor, Giuliani found that three-quarters of the city's elevator inspectors were shaking down building contractors with threats of citing minor violations, while taking bribes to overlook major violations. They were joined by the more than half of taxi safety inspectors who were taking bribes to overlook defective cabs. About the same time, Morgenthau had found that, in the private sector, a third of Manhattan apartment managers were taking tens of thousands of dollars in kickbacks from building contractors.[4]

Time as well as money could be extracted. It took sixty-four bureaucratic steps to obtain the necessary permits to build a house. You could do it yourself and spend weeks. Instead builders, and even ordinary citizens looking to do upgrades, hired one of the city's 1,600 expediters (or "code consultants," as they liked to call themselves) to wait on the lines and serve as fixers who knew how to cut through the red tape. Once construction began on a project, contractors sometimes found it prudent to pay off hustlers threatening to disrupt the work site in the name of minority rights.[5]

The schools were a cesspool unto themselves. At Brooklyn's once-celebrated Erasmus High, the head custodian, who in 1993 enjoyed a base salary of $65,467 plus numerous perks, could rarely be found at the school. He had "wheeled his private 30-foot boat on to the school's athletic field and ordered three custodians to repair it during school hours. The boat stayed there for three months." The same custodian was later filmed by *60 Minutes* sailing his repaired 35-foot yacht off Sheepshead Bay.

The New York custodians were obligated to do very little. They were independent contractors who could hire friends and relatives to work for them. They could even use Board of Education money to buy themselves jeeps, and the civil service protected them. While they earned considerably more than teachers or cops, custodians were required to sweep the cafeteria floor only once a week. By comparison, the common room at Rikers Island jail was by court order required to be mopped two times a day. A neighborhood or civic group wanting to use school facilities, which were closed down daily at 3 o'clock and on weekends, had to pay the custodian directly. Even school teams had to pay for the use of a pool, gym or field. This was worker's control with a vengeance.

While liberals, with the support of the public, were constantly calling for more school funding—the city was spending a quarter of its budget, $8 billion a year, on education—scam artists were carting away the loot. Rancid food, sinking buildings, sweetheart leases, slush fund supplier kickbacks, phantom purchases, warehouse theft, phony trips, mob-connected bus drivers with the highest pay in the U.S.—these were the order of the day.

The mayor's disdain for the Board of Education was regularly confirmed by the inquiries of Ed Stancik, the relentless Special Investigator for Schools who exposed everything from coke-sniffing custodians to principals who faked their attendance numbers to teachers who helped their students cheat on standardized tests. In one notorious case, Virginia Noville, a Brooklyn principal known as the "the cookie monster" because she sold junk food at high prices to her inner-city students, was caught in a sting. Noville met with Community School Board member Edward Cain in his Cadillac parked near Katz's Delicatessen on the Lower East Side. Noville took $2,000 from her purse and as she handed it to Cain laughed about how the wad was "the resume for the job." Cain, who was wired, responded, "You just bought yourself a principalship."[6]

But although individual miscreants were periodically carted off to jail, the organizational structures that had given rise to their crimes were never changed. That's because, while the mayor had the obligation to fund the schools, the responsibility for running them was left in the hands of a Board of Education whose members were part of the political culture that produced the corruption in the first place.

▲ ▲ ▲

Giuliani the mayor wanted to finish what Giuliani the prosecutor had begun: reduce the mob tax to help revive the economy. But he was constantly running into entrenched arrangements, institutional roadblocks and cynicism masked as superior wisdom. Murray Kempton of *Newsday* spoke for the city's world-weary insiders when he worried aloud that "to be in business is generally to find out that reformers cost you more than extortioners."[7]

The first major anti-corruption effort was the fight in 1995 and

1996 to take the Fulton Fish Market back from the mob. You didn't have to be a cynic to doubt the chances for success. The lower Manhattan fish market, where famed Democratic Party politician Al Smith had worked as a young man, had been controlled by a branch of the Genovese crime family since the 1920s. The career lawyers in the Corporation Counsel's Office noted that not even the great La Guardia, a heroic racket-buster, had tried to tackle the problems at the market. And while some mayors such as Ed Koch made noises about the market, most, like David Dinkins, chose to ignore it. For their part, prosecutors, particularly Manhattan District Attorney Robert Morgenthau, had initiated a number of successful cases, but when one set of wise guys was hauled off, another quickly replaced them.

The combination of a highly perishable commodity whose value declines literally with each tick of the clock and a limited number of loading docks made the Fulton Fish Market an ideal location for mob influence. The numerous chokepoints at the market created a long chain of shakedowns. The first came when the truckers who arrived at 3 a.m. from points ranging from Maine to Louisiana paid off to make sure they got their rigs loaded. The last was the tribute paid to the crews who promised to "protect" the retailers' vans and purchases while they went about acquiring fish for their stores. One Brooklyn restaurant owner who failed to grasp the rules was beaten and his car destroyed for parking in the wrong spot. When in 1993 Councilman Ken Fisher brought the restaurateur before the council, the Fulton fish thugs were there to glower at the witness. In a memorable hearing, with the FBI quietly standing watch, he had to testify with a bag over his head.[8]

Money for the mob meant higher prices for consumers and lost revenues for the city. The fish market, which employed 1,000 workers, was losing market share to other cities. Councilman Ken Fisher noted during city council hearings in 1995 that, although it was still the largest market in the U.S., it was doing only $800 million in sales compared to nearly twice that fifteen years earlier. A North Carolina seafood supplier explained that he stopped using the market after the mob-connected wholesalers pulled a gun on him on one occasion and stole $40,000 on another. The lost business was costing the city $3 million a year in rent and taxes.[9]

In March 1995 Giuliani, working with his chief of staff Randy Mastro, who had tackled the fish market as a prosecutor, unveiled a plan to regulate the market in order to free it. The city would issue market licenses only to firms free of mob influence. Prospective merchants and their employees would have to be fingerprinted and subjected to background checks by the Department of Investigation.

When Giuliani brought his plan before the city council, he received strong support from Ken Fisher and Peter Vallone, but there was opposition on several fronts. The Committee to Preserve the Fulton Fish Market, a mob front group, warned that reform would destroy the wholesale fish business. At the same time, Giuliani critics Ronnie Eldridge of the Upper West Side and Steve DiBrienza of Brooklyn loudly objected to fingerprinting as a violation of civil liberties. DiBrienza, the tribune of entrenched interests, also took up the accusation peddled by the Fulton insiders that the Giuliani-Vallone reform efforts were anti-Italian.

Some of the tenants at the market tried to work with the reforms. The buying cooperative in the Old Market Building wanted out from under the mob. Two days after the council hearings, arsonists turned off the sprinkler system, poured gasoline in the hallways and torched their building. That turned the tide in the council, which passed the reforms by an overwhelming majority.

Randy Mastro, who like the mayor was capable of working effectively for eighteen hours a day, was subject to a series of credible mob threats and had to be placed under police protection. But the man who faced even greater danger was the Commissioner of Business Services, Rudy Washington. While Mastro was directing the strategy, the low-key Washington, who has been described by another member of the Giuliani team as "probably the gutsiest guy in an administration of very tough guys," was on the ground at the market directly facing the wrath of the Genovese crime family's friends and employees.

At the Fulton Fish Market, Washington, accompanied by Deputy Chief Wilbur Chapman of the NYPD and about sixty young, mostly rookie cops, and a few lawyers arrived to arrest twenty-three mob-connected members of the United Seafood Workers, Smoked Fisher and Cannery Union. Washington, anticipating some trouble, arrived wearing a bulletproof vest, but even so he was unprepared for what followed. They were greeted by an eruption as the loaders, their fish hooks in hand, surrounded him and his contingent chanting, "We're going to get you niggers," referring to Washington and Chapman.

Rudy Washington contacted Randy Mastro by cell phone and told him "I'm afraid someone is going to die here tonight." The handlers smashed truck windows, shut down the loaders, and for the moment took control of the situation. Literally backed up against pillars, Washington and Chapman, a veteran of the 1977 blackout and Crown Heights riots, unholstered their guns. But when the fish handlers saw "the fear in the eyes of the young cops, and the guns in the hands of Washington and Chapman, they opened a path to allow the trapped cops to leave."

At 8 a.m. the following morning, Washington and Mastro, fresh from a night of turmoil, went to City Hall for a press conference with the mayor. An angry Giuliani threatened "to shut the market down altogether," and then "reconstitute the whole operation" with a new crew of people. "I was never prouder of the mayor that than at that moment," said Mastro.[10]

That night Police Commissioner Bratton gave Chapman the men he needed to take back the market and arrest the twenty-three men wanted on outstanding criminal warrants. For the next month, Washington, accompanied by rotating shifts of two hundred cops, spent sixteen hours a day in the hostile market dealing with a series of hit-and-run work stoppages, job actions and minor acts of sabotage. He received death threats and his house had to be guarded round the clock. It was only when Washington promised to make good on the mayor's threat to shut the market down that owners and union leaders stepped forward at a dramatic 3 a.m. meeting on the wharves of the Staten Island Ferry Terminal to broker a peace.

It wasn't the end of the trouble. But it was the beginning of the end of Cosa Nostra control over the market. The administration and its allies had achieved a "decisive breakthrough." With Giuliani, said an admirer, "the intractable was no longer the impossible." By 1998 the cost of fish had declined by 13 percent and the volume of trade had grown by 14 percent. The licensing arrangement used at the Fulton Fish Market then became the model to reform the city's other markets.[11]

▲ ▲ ▲

With the Fulton Fish cleanup accomplished, Giuliani brought together some of the city's real estate magnates to talk about breaking mob control of trash hauling. Giuliani got a cool reception. They told him that it was a great idea in principle but that it couldn't be done. The major property owners represented by the Real Estate Board of New York argued that any attempt to change the old arrangements would, as with race relations, only make matters worse. Rhetoric aside, they had cut their own deals with the carters so that they thought it would be best to leave things as they were. But the modus vivendi they had achieved with the mob left smaller businesses out in the cold.

The city picked up residential trash. But for businesses, retail shops, colleges and hospitals, trash hauling was controlled by a cartel created by the Lucchese and Gambino crime families. The cost of the mob tax was considerable, on average inflating the cost of garbage collection by 40 percent. New York was the only major city in which none of the major national trash hauling companies such as Brown & Ferris Industries were allowed to operate. The mob cartel divided up the territory among its members and set the rates. If a customer wanted to change carters he had to come before a "court" presided over by Mattie "The Horse" Ianello, who might grant a "waiver" but only at the price of an exorbitant payoff.

The U.S. Attorney for the Eastern District of New York, Andrew Maloney, had brought a successful RICO (racketeering suit) against the cartel in 1989. But while Maloney's actions wounded the cartel, thew didn't take it down. In the early 1990s, Dinkins' Consumer Affairs Commissioner Mark Green (a future mayoral candidate) and his close aide Rich Schrader had tried to break the cartel by bringing Brown & Ferris into New York. When they agreed to come a company spokesman said, "We're sending a message to Cosa Nostra." The mob, through its front organization, the Council of Trade Waste Associations, responded with lawsuits and TV ads mocking Brown & Ferris as out-of-towners. The cartel also sent a note to Brown & Ferris tucked inside the severed head of a German shepherd. When a gutsy local firm, Chambers Paper Fibres, tried to take customers away from the cartel, their drivers were beaten and one of their trucks was destroyed. That left Brown & Ferris without customers.*

As with the Fulton Fish Market, taking down the garbage cartel was a team effort. While federal prosecutors and District Attorney Morgenthau continued to apply pressure with new RICO

---

* "What Mark and I wanted to do," explained Schrader, "was more than civil and criminal enforcement." Those were essential, he said, but "we wanted to do something more fundamental, we wanted to change the rules of the game, we wanted to reduce costs by creating a competitive market for trash hauling."

cases, the Giuliani team picked up where Green and Schrader had left off.

Unlike Dinkins, Giuliani used the power given to the mayor by the city charter. He came before the city council to propose a licensing arrangement similar to the one that had been set up at the Fulton Fish Market. The powerful Real Estate Board was opposed, and the carters argued through their well-connected lobbyists that the reforms would drive mom and pop trash haulers out of business. The acrimony became so intense that council member Fisher, who with foresight argued that honest carters had nothing to worry about, had to be afforded police protection for his home and office.

Nonetheless, the administration won council support for the creation of what came to be called the Trade Waste Commission (TWC). Deputy Mayor Randy Mastro was made the chair. It was given the power to establish a free market for trash hauling. The TWC gave 10,000 New York businesses the right to cancel their exist garbage contracts and negotiate with any firm willing to compete. The mob, noted Schrader, responded with "arguments that could have come from a command and control Soviet economist." The cartel talked about "the danger of chaos" if it weren't kept in control and warned that "profit making" would destroy the industry.

Mastro soon set out a flyer bearing the seal of the City of New York that began, NOTICE FROM MAYOR RUDY GIULIANI AND THE NEW YORK CITY TRADE WASTE COMMISSION. "THIS MAY BE YOUR INDEPENDENCE DAY.... You will now have freedom of choice and the right to a fair and honest price. EXERCISE YOUR RIGHTS." They did. By June 1996, big companies were abandoning the cartel. Garbage-hauling costs for smaller businesses dropped by 25 percent and the price for large buildings dropped by as much as 40 percent. The $1.5 billion paid for hauling trash was reduced to $900 million. "For business," exulted Mastro, "it was the biggest tax cut in the history of the city."[12]

▲ ▲ ▲

As long as Cuomo was governor, Giuliani said little about the state-run but mobbed-up Jacob Javits Convention Center, located south of Madison Square Garden on the city's far west side. The Center, quipped a high-ranking tourist official who insisted on anonymity, "doesn't have a future in the convention business. It's never been in the convention business."[13]

Built with its back to the water, inaccessible by subway, far off the route of most cabs, the Javits Center was problematic from the start. Constructed two years behind schedule after a bid-rigging scandal and $111 million over budget, it was created and run as a jobs program for bond underwriters, consultants, vendors, and mob-connected unions. The Javits Center, named after the former senator, came into operation under Governor Cuomo who gave it a marvelously perverse organizational framework. The business side of the operation was run by civil servants hemmed in by onerous rules and with no incentive to compete for business. The actual work of the center was given over to private unions, unrestrained either by the state Taylor Law forbidding strikes by public-sector unions or by state ethics laws.

Even in the city of scams, the Javits Center work rules, which required three workers for the job of one, stood out. Worse yet, the three under-worked guys often insisted on being further overpaid by shaking down the exhibitors for bribes at every point since the rules required that even the simplest tasks had to be done by the Javits Center's mob-connected unions.

Rob Rosenfeld, who sold technical support services, came from Chicago for a computer show. He was stunned when he wasn't allowed to plug in his own computers; that required a licensed electrician who in turn required a bribe. He was further taken aback to find that even after he paid off to get simple work done, like setting up his tables, he'd often have to pay again. Facing tough competition in the computer field, and angered by one shakedown too many, he refused to pay yet another bribe and was threatened. When Rosenfeld in turn threatened to punch out the next guy who tried to extract a payoff, Javits officials stepped in and gave him a little peace. But he never returned to the Javits Center. "In Chicago," he explained, "you give the guy an extra twenty bucks and they leave you alone."[14]

Giuliani and Mastro initially led the rhetorical charge to reform the Javits Center, which was running a $1.6 million deficit in 1995. Structurally, the problems were similar to those of the Fulton Fish Market. "We convict and convict," said James Kallstrom of the FBI, "but previous officials never changed the rules and regulations...that allow these rackets to continue."[15]

But Giuliani didn't have to take up these cudgels himself. Pataki stepped in and appointed a new manager, Robert Boyle, to overhaul the Center. Operating along reform lines similar to those imposed at the Fulton Fish Market, Boyle took over licensing who was allowed to work at the Center, and cleared out most of the mob in the process. He was fought by Norman Siegel of the New York Civil Liberties Union who saw the licensing as a violation of "freedom of association," and by Assembly Speaker Sheldon Silver, who had political ties to the mob-connected Carpenters' Union. But Boyle and Pataki prevailed and exhibition costs dropped from 10 to 40 percent. By 1998, the Center was actually turning a $4 million profit. Looking back on the conflict, Bruce Bender, Speaker Vallone's chief of staff, summed it up: "You have to give Rudy credit, he took on the people you don't take on and he won."[16]

▲ ▲ ▲

The biggest scams in New York are entirely legal. The Port Authority of New York and New Jersey and the Metropolitan Transportation Authority, established in 1921 and 1968 respectively, were both intended to take the politics out of administration by turning over important government functions to impartial professionals who were given considerable autonomy and political insulation. But over time they produced the worst of both worlds, becoming thoroughly politicized and largely unaccountable.

Giuliani's predecessors preferred to look the other way. They found these vast Authorities with their dense bureaucratic thickets of vice-presidents and semi-autonomous offices not only a welcome barrier to accountability but also a fine source for white-collar patronage and potential cash cows to boot. Governor Cuomo, noted the *Times*, plundered Port Authority resources to balance his last budget by getting the Authority to "buy" a parking lot at Aqueduct Raceway from the state.[17]

Liberals, observed journalist Michael Powell, rightly railed about the unaccountable and often incompetent authorities, but did little to remedy the situation. But Giuliani, noted Ray Harding, the boss of the Liberal Party, was different. "Rudy is not looking for an independent authority to insulate him from responsibility, he wants to cut out all the circuit breakers that clever politicians put between themselves and the voters."[18]

In the face of the ongoing budget crunch, both Mayor Giuliani and Speaker Vallone looked to the bloated Port Authority for increased revenues. The Port Authority, modeled on the semi-autonomous agency running the London docks, was created at the end of World War I largely to build a rail tunnel connecting the city with the mainland. But thanks in part to the rancorous competition between the railroads, the tunnel was never built.

In its glory years, the Port Authority embodied the Progressive-era ideal of objective expertise. From the early 1930s to the late 1950s, the Port Authority did an impressive job of constructing the Lincoln Tunnel and the Outerbridge Crossing, Goethals, George Washington and Verrazano bridges linking New York to New Jersey by car and truck.

But over time, it evolved into a vast self-serving bureaucracy only half-jokingly referred to as "the sixth mafia family of New York." The Authority scanted its transportation mission to dabble in fishports, airports, teleports, and resource recovery centers as well as real estate. It used the billions collected from tolls to acquire a considerable art collection without ever building the tunnel for which it was chartered.

But what most concerned Giuliani and Vallone was the Port Authority's control of the city's airports and the World Trade Center, the Authority's most important real-estate venture. Both were providing the city with a fraction of the revenues that might be expected. The Port Authority had been systematically mismanaging the New York airports for thirty years while building up Newark International Airport. Dirty, outdated and subject to mob pilfering of cargo flights, LaGuardia was ranked thirty-first and Kennedy thirty-fifth amongst the country's top thirty-six airports.

In late 1995, Giuliani, squeezed by the ongoing budget crunch, filed an arbitration suit against the Port Authority alleging that the Port Authority had cheated the city out of $540 million in lease payments for JFK and LaGuardia. Morally and financially Giuliani was right but the suit went nowhere since the arrangements, while unfair, were entirely legal, the product, noted former Port Authority executive director George Marlin, of a bad agreement the city had entered into in 1947.

More promising, however, was the effort to receive a fair shake from the Port Authority-owned World Trade Center. In the late 1950s, the city, under pressure from Governor Rockefeller and his brother David Rockefeller of the Chase Manhattan Bank, co-operated with the Port Authority to make Port Elizabeth in New Jersey the primary harbor for the region while New York got that twin-towered white elephant, the World Trade Center, in return.

Critics said the Twin Towers should have been named David and Nelson after the Rockefeller brothers who devised the scheme to build the Towers as a way of rescuing their own real estate investments in depressed lower Manhattan. The trouble was the Towers came on line in the wake of the Lindsay-induced loss of 570,000 jobs between 1969 and 1974. By putting nine million more square feet into an already dismal real estate market, the World Trade Center helped to push the vacancy rate to 21 percent, the highest since the Great Depression.

Even after a long list of state agencies was moved into a building supposedly built to encourage trade, the Towers were only 85 percent occupied in 1980. They filled up during the boom of the 1980s but in the early 1990s, troubled by organized crime shakedowns, it had a thirteen point plus vacancy rate at a time when there were 150 million square feet of empty offices across the metro area—enough to fill fifteen World Trade Centers.

Pataki's 1995 arrival in the governor's mansion offered the city some hope. He wanted the Port Authority to get out of real estate and once again focus on its core transportation mission. He hoped to privatize the World Trade Center so that the building could go on the city and state tax rolls. But Pataki and Giuliani were blocked by objections from New Jersey, which made out quite well from the old arrangements.*

The Metropolitan Transportation Authority (MTA) was another of Rocky's follies. Governor Rockefeller created it in 1968 in order to seize control of the toll revenues from seven bridges and the Brooklyn Battery and Queens-Midtown tunnels from the city. Ever since then, the city has been subsidizing the metro area's poorly run MTA commuter rail lines even as Gotham's subways were allowed to deteriorate during the 1970s.

In his 1993 State of the City speech Council Speaker Peter Vallone argued, "the MTA doesn't work…. Let's break it up." Giuliani and John Dyson, his Deputy Mayor for Economic Development, .

---

*It wasn't until 2001 that the buildings of the World Trade Center were leased to Larry Silverstein, a private developer. Giuliani also achieved a small victory regarding the Port Authority's poor management of the city's cruise line docks which were losing $3.5 million dollars a year. Using his legal acumen, Giuliani pushed the Port Authority aside and brought in a private cruise management company that agreed to absorb any deficits and share the profits with the city. The upshot was a 28 percent increase in passengers and a small revenue stream for the city.

soon came to a similar conclusion. Describing the MTA budget as "a piece of junk" lacking "reasonable accountability," Giuliani fought it over many issues: fare hikes; who would subsidize student subway passes; workfare; the size of the vast MTA bureaucracy (with over 122 $100,000 plus employees); the MTA's and Port Authority's failure for fifty years to create rail access to Kennedy and LaGuardia; and his proposed police merger.[19]

Mayors starting with Koch had proposed merging the city's three police departments—the NYPD, the MTA-run Transit Police (where Bratton had initially made his mark) and the Housing Authority Police, which worked the public housing projects. "If they [the Giuliani administration] had been long-time New York politicos," explained Bruce Bender, "they would have never been able to achieve the police merger. They would have known that Koch and Dinkins tried it and failed, they would have known it couldn't be done."

The reasons for the merger were always the same, namely that it made no sense to have three duplicative bureaucracies that didn't always cooperate with each other. In his 1995 State of the City speech Giuliani added an additional reason: "having three separate departments impedes police investigations, because most criminals don't commit crimes exclusively on subways or in public housing."

It seemed like a compelling case, but opponents argued that the subways and the housing projects would be short changed. And the merger stepped on numerous institutional toes. Some of the Transit and Housing police unions objected ferociously. As always there was a bevy of lawsuits.

The biggest obstacle was the MTA. It refused to give up any part of its fiefdom. Here budget director Abe Lackman provided the key insight. Lackman noted that the city was paying a significant part of the salaries for the MTA's transit cops. Giuliani threatened to withdraw the money. "If the MTA wants its own force, let them pay for it," he snapped at Assemblywoman and MTA apologist Catherine Nolan. "Why should I write a $300 million check when they have executive pay and perks I couldn't tolerate?" The consolidation went through.[20]

In Albany, the union hirees of the Republican-controlled state senate voted fifty-four to one to undo the merger, but it was merely a gesture of obeisance. The merger would not be reversed. Looking back, Tony Coles saw the common denominator in many of

Giuliani's achievements. "He got things done," said Coles, "not only because of his fierce determination, but because he understood things better than the guys on the other side of the table."

TWELVE

Rudy on the Ropes

The mayor's lower lip began to curl, his eyes widened, and you could detect a faint smile beginning to spread across his face. The telltale signs were all there: he was about to tee off at the reporters peppering him with question about his feuds with former mayor Ed Koch and Tom Ognibene, the leader of the tiny rump of Republicans on the city council. Relishing the combat, variously annoyed and amused by the reporters' queries, Giuliani snapped, "Maybe I can make decisions they can't make. Maybe I don't spend my time worrying about getting re-elected." He mimicked a cowardly whine: "Will this political boss support me? Will..."

Fellow Republican Ognibene was offended. "The problem is," he exclaimed, Rudy's "got the personality of a lunatic bulldog, and slowly that's overshadowing everything else." Loneliness doesn't "appear to trouble Mr. Giuliani," noted journalist Michael Powell. Like his operatic heroes, he "never seems happier than when the bodies of foes are piling higher."[1]

From the spring of 1995, his second year in office, until the fall of 1996, Rudy was on the ropes, battered by both the city's ongoing fiscal crisis and the fallout from his take-charge approach to the city's failures.

A headline in the Daily News read CITY NEARING FISCAL ABYSS.

After two years in office Giuliani was still trying to fight his way out of wreckage he had inherited.

The city was so tight for cash that City Hall was delaying payments to companies it owed money to, while temporarily suspending contributions to city employee pension funds and offering discounts to businesses that paid their taxes early. Giuliani even tried to sell one of Gotham's treasures, its upstate reservoirs. But fortunately this ill-conceived move was blocked, over Giuliani's objections, by City Comptroller Alan Hevesi.

The fiscal monitors at the Financial Control Board and the bond-rating agencies were disturbed by both mounting city debt, which was three and half times greater than other large cities, and the mayor's reliance on one-shot revenues like the money from the sale of the city-owned television station. They warned of disaster ahead. In Albany, Joe Bruno, the Republican majority leader of the state senate, spoke of the coming fiscal chaos and warned that a takeover by the Financial Control Board was very possible.

Unable to borrow much or quickly cut much more, and unwilling to raise taxes on the 6 percent of the city residents who already paid almost 50 percent of the taxes, Giuliani was boxed in. He was under attack from both left and right. The liberal paternalists of the Citizens Budget Commission took to the op-ed pages to criticize him for not cutting labor costs far more sharply so as to preserve social spending and balance the budget. On the right, Giuliani's fiscal skills were being written off in the pages of the *New York Post* and *Commentary* on the grounds that despite cutting 20,000 city jobs he had been unable to reduce the city's labor costs. In *Commentary*, conservative economist Irwin Stelzer argued that Giuliani lacked the "nerve" to reverse the city's decline, while his limited budget cuts had "led both his popularity and his bond ratings to plummet just a notch above Marion Barry's D.C."[2]

For many, particularly those who benefited from the existing arrangements, slow decline was far preferable to a risky restructuring. Faced with an ongoing budget crisis, Giuliani's continued spending cuts, combined with all the enemies he had made in fighting the fiefdoms, made him, his accomplishments notwithstanding, an unpopular mayor who was losing ground with every major group in the city.

In 1994 the city suffered the sharpest drop in tax collections since 1946, but still there was broad public agreement that Giuliani's budget cuts, particularly for the schools, had gone too far. His standing dropped ten points among the outer-boro Catholics and Jews who were his core supporters, and twenty points among Latinos. He was so disliked by African-Americans that even with the cut in crime disproportionately benefiting minority areas, they believed the city had been safer under Dinkins. Giuliani's only gains were among well-to-do Manhattanites who had generally voted for Dinkins. Depending on the polls, between 44 and 62 percent of the city disapproved of the way he was conducting his mayoralty.

The relentless assault on the established arrangements at a time of budget cutting exposed him to counter-attacks from virtually every direction. Giuliani was accused of being a "control freak, the slasher of budgets, the taut face denouncing the vile stupidity of his enemies on television every night," who persistently disparaged and publicly humiliated those who disagreed with him. Thin-skinned and easily given to rages, he couldn't accept any criticism and he couldn't stand it when his commissioners got the headlines. Those, noted journalist John Tierney, were the charges leveled at La Guardia sixty years earlier, but they fit Giuliani just as well.[3]

The combative style of the immoderate centrist often made it hard to separate policy from personality. "People didn't elect me to be a conciliator," the mayor retorted. "If they just wanted a nice guy, they would have stayed with Dinkins. They wanted someone who was going to change this place. How do you expect me to change it if I don't fight with somebody? You don't change ingrained human behavior without confrontation, turmoil, anger."[4]

The intense passions Giuliani evoked were on display at his monthly town hall meetings when he brought his entire cabinet into a neighborhood for an extended question and answer session. In white outer-boro neighborhoods he was generally greeted with cries of "Roo-Dee, Roo-Dee." But even among his supporters there were sharp questions about the impact of his budget cuts. On Manhattan's liberal Upper West Side, he faced a healthy chorus of boos when he tried to explain his budget in light of the city's near bankruptcy. "Now, you owe it to me to listen to my answers," he responded. "You may disagree with it, but you've got to listen to the answers. Shouting and screaming is not the way for intelligent people to talk to each other." But when the boos and shouting didn't subside and he was unable to speak, he simply said "Good Night" and left after less than an hour.

In African-American Bedford Stuyvesent, where the local activists were lying in wait, he was greeted with shouts of "He's not *our* Mayor!" One woman waved a sign reading, "Ghouliani Is a Mark Fuhrman in Mayor's Clothing." When his criticism of school failure was met by more hostile shouts, he cracked back, "If you're happy with them [the schools], then go ahead and leave them the way they are."[5]

His relationship with the press was just as contentious. In October 1995, Yasser Arafat arrived in New York for a fiftieth anniversary party for the United Nations. In the midst of the Oslo peace process, Arafat was, for the time being, seen as more of a statesman than a terrorist. But for Giuliani, who as U.S. Attorney had investigated the murder of the retired New York Jewish businessman Leon Klinghoffer at the hands of Arafat's thugs, the Palestinian leader remained a man with American blood on his hands. When Arafat showed up uninvited to a concert at Lincoln Center's Avery Fisher Hall, the Mayor had him unceremoniously ejected. This produced howls from the State Department and the press as well as Ed Koch, who complained, "Giuliani has behavioral problems dealing with other people." Giuliani refused to back off. "My only regret," he told an aide, "was that I didn't throw Arafat out myself."[6]

When it came time to face press question about Arafat in the City Hall's Blue Room, Giuliani was primed. "It's like going into the arena," Giuliani says. "I look forward to it."

> "Some people," a reporter says, "think that if the party is financed by public money, then you have no right to exclude people."
> "Well," Giuliani replied, "some people think that, because you say that, but you're wrong."
> "Why?"
> "Why? Because you don't bother to check your facts, which is a very irresponsible thing to do."
> "I'm asking you the—."
> "Get your facts right in the premise of your question."
> "I'm asking you to get the facts."
> "No, you're not," Giuliani says, glaring at the reporter. "You asked the question, 'Some people think that'—the fact is, it is not funded by public dollars. The fact is that party is funded by private dollars."[7]

Giuliani and the press often spoke past each other. "I'm very different than what they're used to," Giuliani explained. "I'm the first Republican mayor in a generation and a half and only the third or fourth in this century. Many of the people in the press have a distrust of the Republican Party. Some of them have a hard time overcoming that."[8]

Beyond the confines of party identification, journalists shaped by Gotham's long liberal status quo were often genuinely mystified by what Giuliani was up to. The best of them acknowledged the failings of the Dinkins' years and struggled to be objective. A few even came to change their views on specific issues. But in general they were puzzled if not openly hostile to Giulinai and his staff.

"New York's mayors," explained *Times* columnist Joyce Purnick, "have always played by unwritten rules that demanded they get along with the leading players in government," including the city-funded interest groups. But the mayor made it clear that he was playing by a different set of rules. And to make matters more complicated, Giuliani's wrath could be directed not only at those richly deserving of his anger, but also, as in the case of his attempt to sell the city's water supply, against legitimate criticism as well.[9]

When the press corps got hot under the collar, Giuliani would question their intelligence, repeat his points about self-serving bureaucracies, or simply leave the Green Room, their questions hanging unanswered. But Giuliani's press secretary and right hand gal, Cristyne Lategano, young, intensely loyal and relentlessly hard-working, wasn't so lucky. The administration's aim, as one aide admitted to me, was "to obfuscate as best we can." It was left to Lategano to engage in the stonewalling. She became something of a piñata for the press, who in its frustration began to imagine that she was a power in her own right. Because she spent so much time with the mayor, never-substantiated rumors suggested that there was a love affair between them. But she later commented, "You're only as powerful as people allow you to be, or as much as they think you are. I was just the press gal, that's all." She was right; the mayor was calling all the shots.[10]

To make his insistence on controlling the message from City Hall perfectly clear, in February 1995 Giuliani fired the chief press spokespeople for five city agencies and thirty-six lower-ranking press aides on the same day. The dismissal of John Miller, Police Commissioner Bratton's highly respected personal friend, drew the most attention.

While the civilian mayor feuded with reporters, Bratton was beloved by the press as a great guy who made for good copy. The commissioner, along with the flamboyant Detective Jack Maple and their pals, were regulars at Elaine's, a lively celebrity-studded Upper East Side bar and restaurant. The ostensible reason for the firing was the high-living life-style Miller shared with Bratton. Lategano later contended that "Public Relations were put before any kind of substance. When you put glamour over fighting crime, it leads to serious problems."[11]

The Bratton and Giuliani crews rubbed each other the wrong

way. "The Bratton gang—cool dudes that they are," as Joe Klein of the *New Yorker* put it, saw Giuliani as "the sort of kid who never made it to school with his lunch." Miller responded to his firing: "Now loyalty is important.... I'm loyal to the mayor, I'm loyal to the police commissioner...but there were loyal Nazis too." From that moment on, it was clear that Bratton's days were numbered.[12]

The roots of Giuliani's problems with the press were far more than a matter of style. They went to the very nature of his administration. David Seifman, the *New York Post*'s City Hall bureau chief, got it right when he said, "They run the place like the U.S. Attorney's office" working on a mafia case. That meant that they were loath to release public documents that should have been readily available. And, contrary to the customary practice, the mayor forbade his commissioners from talking directly with the press. The message would at all times be controlled by City Hall. The reasoning was that, if, like prosecutors, you were going take down the bad guys, then you had to work as a team. Teamwork, as with the Mayor's beloved Yankees, meant that individuals had to subordinate their personal or agency agendas to the larger effort. Giuliani prized energy and intelligence, but just as important was loyalty, which he described as "the vital virtue." Rivalries like the one between chief of staff Randy Mastro and chief labor negotiator Randy Levine were unavoidable, but they were kept in check and largely out of the press.

There was vigorous internal debate, and Giuliani was sometimes convinced to change his stance. But once a decision had been made, he expected, as Tony Coles put it, "all oars into the water." Giuliani didn't take vacations, barely slept and conducted himself as a lawyer/soldier and expected the rest of the administration to do likewise. Bernard Kerik, who later became police commissioner, compared entering Giuliani's inner circle to becoming "a made man in a mafia family."[13]

▲ ▲ ▲

Giuliani's tense relationship with the press repeatedly came back to bedevil him. When he forced both Schools Chancellor Cortines and Police Commissioner Bratton to resign, the press had ample opportunity to express its resentments. In the words of a council member who didn't want to be quoted by name, "Anyone in the media Rudy ticked-off used the mayor's fights with Cortines and Bratton to get in some blows."

Giuliani and Cortines had seen eye to eye on some educational issues. Although at odds over how to respond to school crime, both men wanted the schools to implant conventional middle-class values. This enraged Dinkins loyalists. Dinkins' Human Rights Commissioner had attacked Cortines as inauthentic because he didn't speak enough Spanish. Cortines was "outed" as gay not by conservatives, but by the radical gay group ACT UP, which was angered by his seemingly conservative values. When Vergie Muhammed, a controversial principal sporting a Columbia University Ph.D., answered charges about stolen textbooks at her school with the comment, "There ain't no missing books and no books has been lost," Cortines was outraged. Her grammar, he said, was "unbelievable." When a reporter contacted her about Cortines' comment, she replied, "I'm too tired to curse you out."[14]

Giuliani's supporters were relentless in their criticism of the administrative bloat in the schools. "While they don't prepare kids for middle-class jobs," quipped an angry critic of the public schools, "the schools do provide middle-class union jobs with a ratio of one administrator for every 2.4 teachers not including support staff."[15]

A year into his job, Cortines came around to acknowledging that community school boards were "patronage mills" and admitted that the system for repairing the schools was broken beyond repair. He took to wondering out loud why an $8 billion system was still using textbooks that described the Empire State Building as the tallest in the world. "The city's schools are so troubled," he told *Newsday*, that "Jesus Christ couldn't remake this school system in one year, two years or three years."[16]

But Giuliani didn't have two or three years to deal with the city's budget deficit. Despite some areas of agreement, the fiscal pressures on Giuliani made his relationship with Cortines untenable. Their differences over the budget were so overwhelming, explained Giuiliani spokeswoman Cristyne Lategano, that "it's hard to pay any attention to our areas of agreement." Time and again Cortines was unable to seize control of the Board of Education's spending machine. When, under pressure from the mayor, Cortines admitted there were thousands more administrators than previously acknowledged, the headline in *Newsday* read "Look What I Found." When Cortines negotiated a weak contract with the custodians' union, which was famous for short hours, long pay, and bizarrely restrictive work rules, the mayor rejected the agreement. Randy Levine, wield-

ing the threat of privatizations, negotiated a new and better contract which was widely seen as a rebuke to Cortines.[17]

A local politician admitted to me, off the record, that Giuliani
had been proved right. Almost $2 billion had been cut from the
school budget with no discernable effect on student's educational
peformance. But, he went on, there was no way he would make that
argument to his constituents, many of whom were convinced that
the mayor was a racist cutting the budget to harm black and Latino
children.

"While Giuliani was repeatedly proven right," he said, "it's
also true that he always came away with a black eye." Under the
old charter, the mayor was partially insulated in his dealing with
the schools by the Board of Estimate, which had a big say on the
budget. But under the new charter, the mayor's fiscal priorities and
the claims of the schools rubbed up against each other for all to see.
The media, TV news in particular, was little interested in fiscal matters and the tensions were depicted as personality clashes with
Giuliani cast in the role of the schoolyard bully. Well aware of the
situation, Giuliani commented, "I don't dislike him [Cortines]. It
plays out that way because of the public impression of the two of
us—me being strong and tough, him being easygoing, friendly and
nice."[18]

The more they fought, the further Giuliani's poll numbers
dropped. By the time Cortines quit for good in September 1995,
polls showed the public backed the chancellor over the mayor by
two to one. When asked about Cortines' decision to leave, Giuliani
responded, "I won't quit" pushing for school reform.[19]

The response to Cortines' departure was mild compared with
the brou-ha-ha that followed Bratton's forced resignation six months
later in March of 1996. Giuliani and Bratton were cut from much
of the same cloth. They both hailed from working-class Catholic
families. They both brought a strong sense of right and wrong to
their careers in law enforcement. They were intense, ambitious men,
natural leaders who evoked strong loyalties from their troops. Anyone who had been around both of them quickly recognized that their
strong personalities and commanding intellects allowed them to
dominate any setting. Both were brilliant and brusque, short-tem-
pered with stupidity; their intensity was almost incandescent. They
were that rarity, cerebral men of action. Well-read students of government and management, each brought meticulous preparation and

private-sector techniques into the stagnant pool of public-sector bureaucracies. Giuliani was described by an admiring former aide as "a combination of Descartes and Patton," and the same could have been said for Bratton.[20]

Bratton was by far the more flamboyant; Giuliani had an ascetic streak. Bratton was given to grand pronouncements, which he then lived up to. Giuliani liked to under-promise and over-deliver. The basic tension between them was best summed up by one of the wise men of New York politics, Ed Costikyan, who said, "When you have the best mayor in the country and the best police commissioner in the same room one of them is bound to feel diminished."

From Giuliani's perspective, Bratton was a publicity hound, who, thinking he was the mayor's equal, had tried to carve out his own fiefdom. Bratton saw the mayor as a self-aggrandizer who wanted to hog the credit. In January 1996 *Time* magazine put Bratton, not Giuliani, on its cover, in a story describing the city's anti-crime successes. Two months later, Bratton, who said he had planned to leave by the end of the year, was pushed out of office. It was the single biggest mistake of the Giuliani administration, although its implications wouldn't be played out until Giuliani's second term.

In the short run, the damage was minimized by the continuing decline in crime rates under Bratton's successor Howard Safir. Safir, Giuliani's first Fire Commissioner and a trusted friend, had been at the Drug Enforcement Agency and the U.S. Marshal's office. Tight-lipped, square-jawed and competent, the stiff and distant Safir made life difficult for the press. But he passed his first test with flying colors. In June 1996, John Royster, the son of a murderer, went on a one-man crime-spree of his own. Known in the tabloids as the Zodiac killer, he had slain one woman and left three severely injured and the city in a panic. In a vindication for the "broken windows policing" Bratton and Kelling had brought to New York, Royster was captured when he was arrested for jumping a subway turnstile.

In 1996, there were less than a thousand murders in Gotham for the first time since 1968. The sharpest drops in crime came in minority neighborhoods. In the 44th Precinct of the South Bronx, there had been eighty-nine murders in the peak crime year of 1989. In 1996, there were eighteen. Even in the city's worst area for murder, Brooklyn's Bedford-Stuyvesant, there had been nearly a 25 percent decline in killings since 1993.

▲ ▲ ▲

The decline in crime was matched by a growth in jobs. Together they signaled a reversal of Giuliani's fortunes.

In the first half of 1996 the city's economy grew, albeit slowly, for the first time since 1988. The city had lost 361,000 jobs in the long recession that had ended nationally four years earlier. But the stock market revival of 1995, created in part by the conjunction of a Democratic president and a Republican Congress, produced a growth in private-sector jobs and income.

"The third quarter of 1996," explains Giuliani's budget director Joe Lhota, "was the first time we felt we could breathe a little easier. Our credit improved and the Financial Control Board finally backed off." New York's economy was still the weakest of the twenty largest cities in terms of unemployment, job growth and inflation. But Wall Street profits had produced a 14 percent jump in personal income and there were mounting signs of a tech boom in what would come to be called Silicon Alley.

There were also unexpected benefits from the tight budgets. The city had sharply reduced the number of building inspectors enforcing the city's rigid zoning codes, and that generally proved to be a very good thing. "Trying to enforce these rigid zoning laws" established when New York was a manufacturing city, was, said Joe Rose, Giuliani's Planning Commissioner, "like shouting at the ocean." Rose turned a creative blind eye to new uses for old spaces.

In the 1970s, artists in Manhattan's SoHo (for South of Houston) loft district were the first to circumvent the zoning codes by turning areas designated for manufacturing into live/work spaces. They were followed and sometimes displaced in the 1980s by retail and in the 1990s by tech firms that employed imaginative schemes to get around the zoning rules. In the 1990s, the dead zone between 14th Street and 23rd Street along Sixth Avenue was revived by major discount retailers like Bed, Bath & Beyond, which skirted the rules to open a nearly block long store between 18th and 19th Streets that became an anchor for a retail revival in the neighborhood. Paul Selver, Bed, Bath's lawyer, explained, "We developed a theory, which a receptive Building Department accepted, that Bed, Bath, as a type of establishment didn't fall into the categories that were prohibited— it wasn't a department store because there was no clothing, it wasn't a variety store, and it wasn't a home furniture store."[21]

But it wasn't always possible to get around the accumulation of rules and regulations that made it so difficult to upgrade or build in New York. In *The Death of Common Sense*, a book on how attempts to write perfection into the law stifle social and economic creativity, Philip Howard drew most of his examples from New York City. Howard, whose book drew great praise from President Clinton, told the story of how a group of nuns found a statue of the Madonna in the rubble of two burned-out four-story buildings on 148th Street in Harlem. Inspired, the Missionaries of Charity set aside $500,000 for reconstruction. Mayor Koch graciously sold the buildings for one dollar each. But that was only the start of it. Full transfer of title was another matter. For the next year and a half the nuns tried to navigate the bureaucratic processes extending from the local community board to the city planning commission. In 1989, after eighteen months of rigamarole, they finally began repairs only to discover that city ordinances required that they install elevators. Preferring to spend the money on worthy causes, they gave up and walked away from the project.

The Giuliani administration drew the right lessons from Howard's examples. Quietly, without fanfare or rhetoric, block-by-block, it broke with past failures by divesting itself of the tens of thousands of housing units it owned in Harlem. This was the quietest, and perhaps the largest successful privatization of any city in the U.S.

▲ ▲ ▲

A mere fifteen minutes from midtown Manhattan by subway, Harlem had long been an economic world apart. A virtual city within a city, the neighborhood, with more residents than Atlanta, didn't have a single supermarket or movie theater in 1994. More than two-thirds of Harlem's people shopped elsewhere for a lack of stores. Most of the area was in ruins, brought down not only by racism but also by the ongoing rolling riot of crime and dysfunction. More than 80 percent of births were out of wedlock. Unemployment was almost three times that of the city as a whole and median income was less than half of the rest of New York. Harlem lost a third of its population after 1970 as arson, crime and the city's self-destructive rent-control laws led to widespread property abandonment. As of 1994, the city owned almost one-third of Harlem's housing, and much of that was vacant.

Some blocks were a no-man's land. 129th Street was so frightening that cabbies wouldn't enter it all, while the police—who were sometimes greeted with rocks and bottles thrown from rooftops—received special warnings from their dispatchers when they were about to cross its threshold. In 1994, fifty-four people had been murdered on one block alone. Harlem, an old friend muttered, had been "liberated from mainstream mores."

▲ ▲ ▲

Deborah Wright, the architect of Harlem's real estate revival, learned about the housing industry from Kathy Wylde at the New York City Housing Partnership. Like Wylde, she recognized the powerful impact of owning one's own home. As commissioner of the city's Department of Housing Preservation and Development, Wright proposed to sell quickly all the city-owned buildings to residents, small local landlords and entrepreneurs, and community organizations.

Mayor Koch had begun to sell off abandoned houses to private owners, but when David Dinkins came to power those efforts had been largely halted. But thanks, in part, to the efforts of an organization called the Community Preservation Corporation that was funded by local banks, there was a cadre of Harlem-based small-scale owners, contractors and property management companies looking for new opportunities. If local black entrepreneurs as well as the building residents, whom Wright described as "the salt of the earth," bought the abandoned houses, she thought they would be deeply invested in a turnaround and might be able to make a go of it.*

By September 1994, Wright had spent all of her political capital to get the plan approved over the objections of Harlem's political firebrands, community development corporations, and white liberals. She would stand up at community meetings and say in her twinkly style, "I can continue to be your landlord [referring to the city's vast holdings of Harlem housing]. But before you can talk to me you'll have to go to them," she said pointing to a half dozen aides she had brought with her. Or, she went on, "you can have a more accessible landlord." That always produced nods of agreement.

---

*In the past, sales to local non-profit housing organizations produced mixed results. As had happened to the nuns, the groups sometimes had difficulty in circumventing the costly and confusing maze of regulations set up by the city. The properties then ended up getting recycled back into abandoned *in rem* housing.

White liberals feared that Wright's plan would displace tenants and squatters. Ideologically opposed to private ownership, they
set up what they hoped could be confrontation between Wright and
Harlem tenants. It turned out, says Wright, to be "an amazing meeting." Instead of the show-trial activists intended, the tenants, mostly
middle-aged black woman, were pleasantly surprised that a commissioner would spend time with them. Uninterested in squatters' rights,
they wanted the chance to get their basic services like plumbing and
heating improved. The tenants applauded when Wright told them,
"If your new landlord screws up, you'll see him at church or the corner market." When she finished her presentation, the audience gave
Debbie Wright a standing ovation.

Wright had undercut the advocates by selling tenants on her
plan, but she wasn't sure the mayor would buy what she was proposing. As Wright saw the situation, she was an unproven outsider, a
black woman from the Dinkins administration trying to initiate an
innovative but risky plan.

Respected players in the administration were opposed to
Wright's approach. Corporation Council Paul Crotty and mayoral
advisor Richard Schwartz, not unreasonably, wanted to buttress the
city's sagging bottom line by selling the vacant properties to the
highest bidders. But Wright saw that this could have produced a
political firestorm in Harlem. And although Giuliani didn't know it,
Wright was ready to resign if her plan for bringing home ownership
to Harlem was rejected.

Things came to a head in a tense meeting with the mayor and
the key players in the basement chapel of City Hall. But to Wright's
surprise, she found that Deputy Mayor John Dyson, a New Democrat, was strongly in her corner. Like Wright, he wanted to bring
capitalism to Harlem. He asked rhetorically, "Do we need more
absentee landlords, do we want to give the demagogues a bounty?"
Instead, he argued, "let's give local people a chance. If that doesn't
work, we can open it up to a wider circle of bidders." According to
Dyson, "Rudy's response to Wright's proposal was 'That makes
sense, let's try it.'" Wright had carried the day. Looking back, she
reflected, "I can't tell you how brave it was for the mayor and John
Dyson to back me on this strategy."

It was Wright's colleague Jerry Salama's job to bring the vision
to fruition. Salama, who described himself as "a slayer of bureaucracies," was the kind of guy who didn't take no for an answer. With

support from Salama and the city, the new owners went about the difficult task of removing squatters and drug dealers from their newly purchased properties. When new owners purchased three or four houses near each other, it began to change the character of a block. Both inspired and pressured by the possibility of improving their blocks, other neighbors received help from organizations like the Local Initiative Support Corporation to win bank loans to fix up their buildings. Over time the changes built on themselves. "No other housing commissioner," exulted Wright's deputy Jerilyn Perine, "could have pulled it off."

Important as the changes were in Harlem, the primary symbol of the economic upswing was the revival of Times Square. Famed as "the crossroads in the world" in the era before movies and television, Times Square had been in slow decline since the 1920s. But in the 1950s a series of ill-conceived court decisions granting pornography First Amendment protections produced a proliferation of sex shops that drove out conventional businesses. By the 1960s, when the movie *Midnight Cowboy* depicted the depravity of the strip, the "Deuce," as 42nd Street was known, had gone completely to seed. It was dominated by drug dealers, three-card monte games, pickpockets, prostitutes (child and adult, female and male, and transvestite thrown in), peep shows and porn theaters. By 1980 when plans for a revival were first laid, there were 2,300 reported crimes on the block between Seventh and Eighth Avenues alone, a fifth of them murder or rape.

In the early 1980s, the original plans for redevelopment called for a series of giant office towers with relatively little space for an entertainment district. In this case delay was salutary. When the 1987 stock market mini-crash waylaid the original designs for a series of office towers, a new and more appealing approach emerged that preserved Times Square's theatrical core.

Unnoticed at the time, innovative policing by Inspector Richard Mayronne, a cop's cop, who used broken windows techniques by making arrests for low-level crimes, began to make the area more appealing. In 1990 Viacom, the parent company of Nickelodeon and MTV, moved in. In 1992, a Business Improvement District was established. In the closing days of the Dinkins administration, an agreement in principle was reached for Disney to move on to 42nd Street and refurbish the historic but desolate New Amsterdam Theater. Disney received rich subsidies justly described as a sweetheart deal. But in this case the city also got to taste the sweetness. "Disney in fact and in perception created a sea change," explained Gretchen Dykstra of the Times Square Business Improvement District; before Disney, "property owners asked us to help them assuage fears of potential tenants. After Disney, brokers are all trying to get a piece of the action."[22]

Giuliani, who in 1993 had unsuccessfully chased a thief in Times Square after he saw him snatch a tourist's purse, was effective in zoning out many of the pornography dens. By 1996 when Giuliani and his new Police Commissioner Howard Safir went to Times Square to celebrate the New Year, the occupancy rates in the area's hotels, once the lowest in the city, were the highest. The transformation was too successful for would-be hipsters who complained that the area had been "Disneyfied," stripped of its sexual frisson and sanitized. One sex hustler was bitter about the revival. With Giuliani, he said, there was "more police and less money.... People be scared now.... Makes you wanna get a regular job."[23]

THIRTEEN

Racial Racketeering

I n New York, insisted Democratic political consultant Jim Andrews, "race isn't just part of politics, it is politics." Andrews had a point. Both of Giuliani's immediate predecessors had been brought down by racial incidents. Some of the other "new mayors" like Richard Daley in Chicago and Ed Rendell in Philadelphia worked overtime to avoid any action, including active policing in the inner city, that might spark a racial incident.[1]

Giuliani, aides note, had his worries when it came to Harlem, the symbolic center of African-American politics in the U.S. and the site of recurrent riots. Harlem's main shopping venue, 125th Street, had long been overwhelmed by African immigrant peddlers hawking bean pies, Afrocentric statues, t-shirts, pinwheels, and bootlegged and stolen goods, not to mention drugs. In one three-block stretch alone, there were 1,300 peddlers (on both sides of the street). The vendors who dominated the sidewalks left the area strewn with garbage that caught on fire and attracted rats to the walkways. Inspector Wilbur Chapman, a native New Yorker who had done thirteen years of foot patrol in Harlem and traveled abroad, said, "It was worse than what you'd see in a poverty-stricken third-world country."

The merchants, half of whom were African-American, lost business to the peddlers and got stuck with fines for the garbage. They were up in arms. "How can I compete with someone who pays no rent or taxes?" asked Jolena Matthews, owner of a small souvenir store. She and other merchants had complained bitterly to Mayor Dinkins and threatened to withhold their taxes to the cash-strapped city. But when Dinkins tried to clean up the sidewalks, the peddlers, organized by Morris Powell, an escaped mental patient, met the police with a near riot. Powell, an ally of Reverend Al Sharpton, had become a force to be dealt with. Dinkins, like Koch before him, backed off.[2]

When Giuliani entered office, he was privately beseeched by some of the same pols publicly denouncing him as a racist to do something about the peddlers. Congressman Rangel, a tireless Giuliani critic, and a host of lesser officials and business leaders met quietly with Giuliani to urge action. The mayor, well aware, as columnist E.R. Shipp put it, that they would cry "racism" as soon as there was tension, moved cautiously. Giuliani went up to the famed Apollo Theater on 125th Street and made the local pols put their requests for a clean-up in writing. Sharpton screamed about a "sellout," but the administration had some of the protection it needed.[3]

Giuliani's Commissioner of Business Services, Rudy Washington, then found a vacant lot nine blocks away from 125th Street that could be converted into an African-style open-air market, complete with electricity and bathroom facilities. But there was little chance the peddlers would leave of their own accord. In the 1970s a $3 million mall just off 125th Street had been built for them, but they refused to budge. This time their anger was augmented by black talk radio hosts who spoke of how moving the vendors was part of Giuliani's racist plot for a white takeover of Harlem. But if there was to be a Harlem renaissance, explained Barbara Askins of the local Business Improvement District, "there was no choice, the vendors had to be cleared out."[4]

Washington and Chapman, the duo that had taken on the mob at the Fulton Fish Market, took the lead. In some ways, explains Washington, the situation was more frightening on 125th Street than it had been at the fish market. "The mob guys," he said, "were semi-rational, but some of the knuckleheads on 125th were crazy. You could never know when you'd run into one of them toting a gun on the subway or in the streets."

Chapman and Washington spent months speaking with the peddlers about the new site. Then, in October 1994 when the colder weather had thinned the crowds, they made their move. Inspector Chapman moved a massive deployment of men on to 125th Street in the dead of night. He had barriers and police set up every thirty feet. When the peddlers arrived the following morning, there were some minor skirmishes but little more. Chapman's cops held the streets twenty-four hour a day for two weeks, while Sharpton probed for an opportunity. But gradually, with the help of Imam

Pasha, who ran Malcolm X's old mosque across from the new market, the peddlers, (many of them African Muslims) began to set up in the new site. The market became such a success it was eventually included on Harlem bus tours. For his part, Morris Powell, out of business, was looking for a new hustle.

▲ ▲ ▲

Mayor Koch had tried to rebuild parts of Harlem but ran into stiff opposition from the Harlem machine run by Congressman Charles Rangel and his allies who controlled most of the antipoverty funds coming into the neighborhood. "Anyone who wanted to do business in Harlem had to go through them," recalls Randy Daniels, a Harlem resident who had been the press officer for former City Council President Andrew Stein. They insisted, Koch explained, "everything had to be done through their Harlem Urban Development Corporation. It was flat up our way or no way."

"Over time," explains veteran nonprofit investor Kathryn Wylde, "the government displaced the private sector and destroyed any semblance of a free-market economy."[5]

But in the ferment of the early 1990s, both Democrats and Republicans were looking to break with the failures of the Great Society social programs and for new ways to revive inner city markets. "Cities," explained one official, "want to start over." Rob Gurwitt of *Governing* magazine thought, "If we could restore our older cities to the conditions they enjoyed before Lyndon Johnson declared 1965 'The Year of the Cities,' before *Newsweek* proclaimed John Lindsay 'The Hero of the Cities,' before the 1965 Watts riots transformed the urban landscape, it would be considered an historic achievement." The whole intellectual apparatus erected in the 1960s to deal with urban issues "was being dismantled."[6]

On a practical level the ferment produced bipartisan legislation to reduce federal taxes and regulation as well as provide low-interest loan funds in areas designated as Empowerment Zones. Harlem, due to Rangel's influence on the powerful House Ways and Means Committee, was awarded such a zone. But rather than break with the past, the congressman saw the zone as his new political money pot. When criticized because so many of the zone projects he proposed to subsidize were patronage-driven social service organizations, Rangel responded, "We cannot make an offer to business until the community has set the priorities."[7]

Pataki and Giuliani were pushing to bring in national retail chains like Blockbuster Video, which had been trying to get into

Harlem for two years. But they met stiff resistance from Rangel. One major site, an old abandoned wire factory that could be made into an ideal retail outlet store, became a major bone of contention after Rangel rejected a healthy private sector bid for the site. Rangel initially saw the factory land as the new site for the old idea of a third-world trade center. But failing that, he wanted a community college, government offices, a drug rehabilitation center—anything but private-sector development that might change the political economy of Harlem and loosen his grip on power. In the midst of this standoff, a racial conflagration on 125th Street threatened to derail the possibility of a Harlem revival.[8]

In the fall of 1995, Sharpton, well established as the city's leading racial demagogue, was in temporary eclipse. Shrewd and charming or thick and menacing as the occasion demanded, Sharpton's quick wit allowed him to make himself the master of a moment. One journalist tells the story of how tabloid photographers had staked out a beauty parlor where Sharpton was getting his permanent wave. When they burst in, Sharpton, unfazed, waved them closer, to record how a "real man" gets his hair done.[9]

But for the moment his touch seemed to have failed him. Sharpton, smarting from Giuliani's refusal to deal with him, organized a protest march in opposition to Governor Pataki's budget. But the episode produced only yawns. Sharpton's organization, the National Action Network, was treading water despite some successful shakedowns of Korean businessmen, he was out of the headlines. But in October 1995, first Louis Farrakhan's Million Man March in Washington and then Fidel Castro's visit to Harlem revived Harlem's third world and black nationalist passions.

Sharpton's ally Morris Powell, the escaped mental patient, had a long history of violence. (He had beaten three murder raps, once for breaking open the skull of a Korean woman.) As the head of the Buy Black Committee of Sharpton's National Action Network, Powell was feeling similarly displaced after Giuliani had moved the vendors off of 125th Street. And then a new opportunity presented itself in the form of a landlord-tenant dispute.*

The United Pentecostal House of Prayer, one of the largest

---

*In 1993 Sharpton drew closer to Farrakhan. When he introduced the Nation of Islam's leader in 1993 at the Javits Center he told the crowd, "We will stand together. Not in some private midnight meeting...but in the daylight. Don't ask who don't like it; we love it! Don't ask who's mad, we're glad." *New York Observer* 3/13/2000.

black landlords on 125th Street, raised the rent on the Fashion Mart owned by a Jew, Freddy Harari, who then raised the rent on his sub-tenant, Sikhulu Shange, who ran a record store. Recognizing that the quickest way to gain support was to turn a landlord-tenant dispute into a racial issue, Shange went to Sharpton's National Action Net-work.

Sharpton opened his public campaign against Freddy's on WWRL radio by warning, "We will not stand by and allow them to move this brother so that some white interloper can expand his busi-ness on 125th Street." His lieutenant Morris Powell, an intimidating figure, chimed in, "This street will burn. We are going to see to it that this cracker suffers."

On the streets, the picketers organized by Powell in front of Freddy's picked up their leader's themes. They not only ranted about Jews as "bloodsuckers"—a reference to the medieval charge that Jews sacrificed Christian children as part of the Passover ritual—but they also warned out loud, "We're going to burn and loot the Jews." While the protesters chanted, "bring a casket to work tomor-row" and made displays of striking matches and throwing them into Freddy's doorway, which stood just a few feet from the offices of Charles Rangel, the congressman professed to know nothing. After two months of rhetorical violence, protester Roland Smith, a man with a long criminal record, his already well-developed hatred of whites goosed by the protests, ran into the store guns blazing, and burned it down. When it was over, Smith, who liked to be known by his taken African name of Abubunde, had killed himself and seven others. He had killed three whites and a light-skinned Pak-istani he had mistaken for a Jew, and then set a fire that killed five Hispanics, one Guyanese, and one black, the security guard whom the protesters had taunted as a "cracker lover." When it was over, Congressman Rangel was angry, very angry—with Mayor Giuliani for having criticized Reverend Al.[10]*

In the wake of the massacre Rangel was forced to accept a highly talented and private-sector-oriented director for the Empow-erment Zone. The new director was the same Deborah Wright who as a member of the Giuliani administration had helped create a mar-

---

*In an anticipation of the 9/11 Islamist conspiracy theories, a few days after the killings Morris Powell postulated that the white owner of Freddy's had a secret pas-sageway out back through which, once the bloody rampage began, white employees were led to safety while black and Hispanic workers were left trapped inside.

ket for the stores on 125th Street by upgrading Harlem's aging brownstones. Naturally, prospective businesses interested in Harlem demanded that there would be no repetition of the massacre. At the same time Wright made it known to the Rangels and Sharptons that "this is the last, best shot the community has." She intended to "show taxpayers that investment in the inner city could produce results." Attacked as a tool of white interests, Wright asked, "Why can't the average shopper in Harlem have the same range of options that looks like any other neighborhood?"[11]

By the time the election year arrived in January of 1997, Rangel was still bitter. He complained, "The only thing I see that Giuliani has done is he bought some goods in Harlem from a Jewish merchant to show that 125th Street is coming back." But then again he had reason to be angry. *New York* magazine and *U.S. News and World Report* were speaking of "Harlem's Next Renaissance." With much of the country overrun by new malls competing with newer malls, Harlem was an untapped market. With crime down and Empowerment money available for the private sector, Disney, Sony, Magic Johnson Theaters, Pathmark, Cineplex Odeon, The Gap, Radio Shack, and Barnes & Noble had either opened or were in the process of opening stores. At the same time young black professionals were rediscovering the virtues of Harlem's beautiful and undervalued brownstones.[12]

Mike Tomasky, a left-liberal journalist, gave Giuliani credit. For six or seven years, he noted, "race was the city's obsession.... It unelected Koch, elected and unelected Dinkins. But Giuliani, who refused to play the racial bargaining game, seems to have cooled the city's racial politics down from its customary boil." The temperate racial climate wouldn't last. The beginning of competition from private-sector business was still far too limited to close down the race business. But there was a breather that lasted through the 1997 election season.[13]

FOURTEEN

The Mayoral Election: Ruth vs. Rudy

Rudy Giuliani's path to re-election in 1997 had been paved in 1996 by Bill Clinton's re-election. President Clinton, a Democrat, and the Mayor, a Republican, two cerebral centrists on the outs with the activists in their respective parties, had been very good for each other. New York's success in reducing crime—25 percent of the national decline in Clinton's first term came from Gotham alone—gave the president something to brag about. At the same time, Clinton's COPS program helped Giuliani pay for police overtime for his cash-strapped city. But more important, Clinton's support for welfare reform and his statement that "the era of big government is over" made it far harder for liberal Democrats to paint Giuliani as a right-wing extremist. On welfare reform, Giuliani actually positioned himself to Clinton's left by championing the right of legal immigrants to receive welfare.

As the 1996 presidential campaign took off, Giuliani was conspicuous as the only major New York State Republican not to have endorsed the candidacy of Republican Senator Bob Dole. The Republican vice-presidential candidate, former upstate New York Congressman Jack Kemp, was part of an all-out effort to woo the mayor. After a dinner with Giuliani, he gushed that he and Dole "want to do for the country what Rudy is trying to do here in NYC." But Giuliani kept his distance from the Senator. His political team was well aware that a Dole presidential victory would give the GOP control of all three elected branches and was sure to provoke an anti-Republican backlash in New York.[1]

When one of the mayor's key supporters explained that Giuliani's primary role "is to do what is best for the city," fellow Republicans fumed that Giuliani, might once again, as he had with Mario Cuomo, endorse the Democrat. One city council member critical of welfare reform quipped, "Clinton became a Republican to win. Now Rudy's becoming a Democrat to win." But though he appeared to flirt with the idea, Giuliani never endorsed Clinton. Instead he waited until the last minute when he gave Dole his pro-forma support.[2]

The left wing of the Democratic party was so frightened by the Republican victories in the 1994 elections that it was willing to give Clinton a blank check to battle the "barbarians." In a similar vein, Dole's defeat in the 1996 presidential election left the Republican right in a weakened position so that Giuliani became the first Republican mayor in the twentieth-century not to face a primary challenge. That left the mayor in a position to be as Clinton-like as necessary to win re-election in a city that was five to one Democratic.

▲ ▲ ▲

David Dinkins, tired of serving as Giuliani's rhetorical punching bag, made noises about running again. But chastened by the lack of enthusiasm, the former mayor gave his support to Manhattan Boro President Ruth Messinger, a close ally who insisted that Dinkins had made the city a "safer, healthier, smarter, and yes, far better place."[3]

In 1989, Dinkins had begun his campaign against Giuliani with attacks on Ronald Reagan. Messinger opened with the same tactic. Giuliani, she pointed out "won't talk about the fact that he is a member in good standing of a party whose brightest lights are Newt Gingrich and Al D'Amato, Bob Dornan and David Duke, Pat Buchanan and Jesse Helms."[4]

Messinger, a woman of considerable intelligence and enormous energy, was the prototypical Upper West Side Manhattan liberal. In the 1960s, she had lived in a commune and she had been involved in every left-liberal struggle from Vietnam and Civil Rights to gay rights and rent control. A formidable presence, she could be so focused as to seem brusque. She had little time for fashion: "with her straggly black hair and social worker's sense of fashion, she was the very image of a New York liberal."[5]

At first Messinger ran a full-throated liberal campaign. Her communications director was Leland Jones, a veteran of the 1993 Dinkins' campaign that depicted Giuliani as a racist reactionary, if not the forerunner of a fascist police state. This time around, Jones, in the rhetorical style of Congressman Rangel describing the mayor's reductions of the city payroll as the equivalent of "gang rape," depicted Giuliani's minority-hiring practices as "the local equivalent of Bosnia."[6]

Evan Mandery, an idealistic suburban liberal and Harvard graduate who signed up for the Messinger campaign, discovered that there was considerable irony in the Bosnia remark. He was shocked to discover that "the idea of addressing New Yorkers as citizens with potentially common public interests, rather than as members of various constituencies (blacks, gays, Latinos), seems to have been vacuumed out of today's Democratic Party in the city."[7]

In February of 1997 Messinger faced three challengers in the first debate of the Democratic Party primary campaign. They were Bronx Boro President Fernando Ferrer, the Reverend Al Sharpton and City Councilman Sal Albanese from Brooklyn. They were all critical of workfare and all talked about homelessness as if it were 1987 instead of 1997. Though many of the homeless were addicted to drugs or alcohol and suffering from mental disorders, these men insisted that more social services and more city-subsidized housing would solve the problem of homelessness. The only differences between the three were over gay marriage.*

Ferrer, who was never able to decide whether to run as an outer-boro Catholic moderate or as the leader of a third-world radical coalition, was the first to drop out. Albanese, a "lunch-pail liberal" who accused Messinger of being a "limousine liberal," was never a serious candidate. That left Messinger and Sharpton, who had described workfare as the equivalent of an "urban chain gang." It was widely assumed that she would have an easy go of it.[8]

Sharpton's role in the 125th Street massacre should have curtailed his political career. But a cowed media refused to press the issue. Sharpton was so sure that he was going to get a free ride from both the media and the other candidates in the Democratic primary, that in an act of bravado he himself brought up the Harlem massacre as he announced his candidacy. Correctly assessing the unwillingness of the press to contradict him, he blamed the 125th Street murders

---

*Senator Moynihan, commenting on the state of the New York Democrats, complained that "we were never able to accept or confront the social decline of our cities as something which was real.... It was something that was not easily turned around, but it was absolutely critical to try. We were in denial and learning disabled about it all." *New York Times* 1/14/97.

on Giuliani. "Only the city administration," he claimed, "knew of the hatred that was brewing" outside Freddy's Fashion Mart.[9]

Messinger couldn't gain any traction. She campaigned against under-funded schools, the unmet needs of children, and rural Republicans in Albany shortchanging the city. But Giuliani, in the style of Clinton and his political advisor, Manhattanite Dick Morris, triangulated on each of these issues. Thanks to the Wall Street windfall filling his fiscal coffers, the Mayor designated new funding for the schools and he made a point of repeatedly visiting classrooms with Rudy Crew, the new Schools Chancellor. He assailed those anti-urban Albany Republicans for both shortchanging the city and trying to kill rent control. Giuliani's support for rent control, at a time when Governor Pataki and Senate Minority Leader Joseph Bruno were looking to reform it, left his conservative admirers aghast, but with nowhere to go politically.

For reasons beyond rational explanation, the Messinger campaign decided not to rent a sound system for the "formal announcement" of her candidacy, and so the modest crowd of assembled reporters and supporters strained to hear the candidate over the wind, which whipped her prepared remarks to the ground, scattering them as she finally began to speak. "If you live high up in the sky, send your kids to private boarding schools, go to work in big black cars, eat at the finest restaurants, go to private doctors and need a team of accountants to figure out how much you really made last year, then Rudy is your guy," she shouted into the Lower East Side wind.[10]

While Messinger decried the New York of private schools, private doctors and hired accountants, the *Times* pointed out that she had attended the exclusive Brearley School on the Upper East Side, went to a private doctor, had an accountant, and lived in a three-bedroom apartment overlooking Central Park. And reporters could not resist pointing out that after Messinger finished attacking those "who go to work in big black cars," the candidate climbed into her chauffeured city-owned standard issue big black car and drove off.[11]

Messinger could never decide, noted political analyst Jim Chapin, whether the aim of the Democrats should be to "repeal Rudyism" or, like Clinton and Britain's Prime Minister Tony Blair, to seize the middle by accepting the changes that had been made in order to move on to a new set of issues. In her moderate mode, Messinger appeared before the 14th Street-Union Square Business Improvement District, a kind of organization that didn't even exist ten years earlier, and told the audience that "those of us who believe that government can be a force for good have a special duty to make it work as efficiently as possible." New Yorkers, she acknowledged, sounding like Giuliani, "don't get much bang for their municipal buck," and we "pay more for government services and receive less in return than the residents of nearly any other city in the United States." She was right; if Washington, D.C. with its fabulously felonious Mayor Marion Barry was excluded, New York topped the list for big city inefficiency.

Messinger also reconsidered the city's relationship to Washington. After hesitating to criticize the president whose support, however tepid, she was counting on, the candidate complained about the way Clinton had singled out New York State for a Medicaid veto. This long-time proponent of federal funding for city social programs noted that New York's Medicaid reimbursement rate was far below that of other states. Worse yet, "the average New Yorker," noted the boro president, "pays nearly $1,000 more in federal taxes than he or she receives in benefits."[12]

Messinger quietly promised that, if elected, no taxes would be raised to pay for more social programs. Stealing a page from Giuliani's playbook, she proposed privatizing some city services to come up with greater savings.[13]

While Messinger was moving toward the middle, Giuliani, in the manner of the liberals who preceded him, used the powers of an incumbent in command of a vast government to pad his margin through the time-honored tradition of buying votes. There were targeted tax cuts for parents, new domestic partnership benefits for gays, many millions for libraries and more housing subsidies for selected districts. There were also the inevitable jobs for the relatives of Democrat defectors like Brooklyn Councilman Noach Dear and the famed Manhattan political operative Jimmy McManus.

Former Mayor Ed Koch said Giuliani was the "most political patronage dedicated mayor, he had ever known." This suggested a lack of self-knowledge on the former mayor's part, since Giuliani was essentially following the path that Koch and all those before had laid out.[14]

It was hard not to sympathize with Messinger when she wailed about how "it might be more honest and direct if [Rudy] stood outside the voting booth on election day and gave everybody who was coming in a twenty dollar bill."[15]

Giuliani's grand strategy was to split labor away from its traditional social service allies. In 1995 his labor negotiator Randy Levine worked out a series of "double-zero contracts" that relieved some of the short-term pressure on the city by eliminating pay raises for two years. The workers would then get 13 percent raises over the final three years of the contract with the first raises coming due just before the 1997 elections.

The double-zeroes were an accomplishment compared to what Dinkins had wrought, but Giuliani's old foes at the Citizens Budget Commission (CBC) were angered by the way that social services were forced to bear a disproportionate percentage of the budget cuts while little was done to reform the city's grossly inefficient labor practices. The CBC, whose chairman was one of Messinger's chief fundraisers, noted that city public school teachers spent only 64 percent of their workday in the classroom, the lowest percentage in the country, about 20 percent less than their counterparts in Philadelphia, LA and Chicago. And at any given time 16 percent of the teachers, including those about to retire, were on sabbatical. In what education expert Sol Stern described as a "we don't do windows contract," the teachers were relieved of their duty to monitor the halls. The American Federation of Teachers stayed neutral in the election.

Subject to blistering criticism from the CBC and former mayor Ed Koch, who accused the administration of "giving the city away in the contracts," Randy Levine fired back. The city, he said, was divided between a mayor "protecting working people and the old guard who supported those who want to allow non-working people to receive a free pass, and unbridled entitlements." Levine blasted the "old leftist liberals who sought to protect welfare recipients at the expense of working people." The social services industry, he went on, had "hidden behind the unions for years and now that's over." The CBC, in its zeal to support Messinger, had overstated its case. The civil service redeployment designed by Levine produced substantial savings that wouldn't have been possible without union cooperation. But Giuliani's labor practices would come back to haunt Gotham down the road.[16]

▲ ▲ ▲

Giuliani's smooth ride to re-election tripped over the Abner Louima affair. Louima, a Haitian immigrant, had been arrested at a Flatbush Avenue nightspot in the early morning hours of August 9, 1997 by cops from the notoriously incompetent 70th Precinct. At the police station, the cops, one of whom had been sucker-punched by another man at the club, flipped out and brutally sodomized Louima with a plunger. The assault and the blue wall of silence erected by the other cops at the precinct appeared to validate the worst fears about the mayor's policing policies.

Giuliani's customary approach in cases where cops were accused of wrongdoing was to stand behind the men in blue first and ask questions later. But this time, accompanied by long-time foe Norman Siegel of the New York Civil Liberties Union, he quickly announced that the commander of the 70th Precinct had been fired, and that he already set in motion the prosecution of the alleged perpetrators. Norman Siegel was pleased. Giuliani, he said, has "had his best 48 hours as mayor of this city." Louima's uncle agreed. Influenced in part by the mayor's support for his fellow West Indian van drivers, he quietly urged the members of his Croisade Evangelique church to support Giuliani.[17]

Some of Giuliani's critics were not appeased. Dinkins insisted, "Not since the heyday of the Klan have African-American men been at more serious risk." The former mayor also mocked quality-of-life policing: "Killers and rapists are a city's real public enemies, not squeegee pests and homeless mothers." Dinkins' attack was accompanied by the claim by Louima (who was being advised by Al Sharpton), which he later admitted was untrue, that the cops who had violated him had shouted, "This is Giuliani time."[18]*

Messinger, not Giuliani, was the unexpected loser in the Louima affair. In the wake of the attack, Sharpton's campaign caught fire. Messinger's campaign manager, Jim Andrews, who had helped make Harold Washington Chicago's first African-American mayor, described race as the "Rosetta Stone" of big city politics. Andrews tried to play the race card when he asked, "Do you know what Rudy Giuliani was saying back in 1993 when he said he was going to get rid of squeegee men? He was telling every white person in New York City that he was going to close the sluice gates at 125th Street. Rudy

---

* The phrase nonetheless became common coin amongst more conspiratorially-minded foes of the mayor. In an incredibly awkward moment in John Singleton's 2000 remake of *Shaft*, the hero stops just before a burst of ultra-violence directed at Latino thugs and corrupt cops alike, and declares to the camera, "It's Giuliani Time."

was saying that he was going to make sure that they stay where they belong—up in Harlem and the Bronx." But Andrews was no match for Sharpton. Asked in the wake of the Louima affair if Giuliani was the worst mayor in the history of New York, Sharpton replied, "No, he is the worst mayor in the history of the world."[19]

In the September primary Sharpton took 32 percent of a record low turnout holding Messinger to slightly less than the 40 percent of the vote she needed to win the election outright. It looked as if Sharpton had unexpectedly forced the front-runner into a run-off. The "portly prince of provocation" was jubilant.

But a recount showed that by a scant margin of 793 votes Messinger had won enough support to gain the nomination without a runoff. The righteous Reverend Al, the candidate for mayor of New York who lived in New Jersey and sent his children to private school, the man who talked of "fraudulent lies," immediately cried foul. Leading followers in his trademark chant of "No Justice, No Peace," he warned, "we'll take our case to the streets, to the courts." There were once again murmurings about possible riots. He accused the Board of Elections of carrying out "schemes of voter suppression." In a cynical parody of the civil rights movements, Sharpton likened Messinger to Dixie's racist bosses, announcing, "We go to court Monday like we had to go to Southern courts in the Sixties."[20]

In the primary, Brooklyn Democratic boss Clarence Norman told Messinger that for "several hundred thousand dollars" she could win his organization's endorsement. A cash-strapped Messinger declined. Once the shouting by Sharpton was over and Messinger was clearly the nominee, the Reverend tried a similar shakedown. According to Messinger campaign insider Evan Mandery, Sharpton threatened to provide nothing but pro forma support if he wasn't given a generous contribution of several hundred thousand dollars. Messinger, trying to save her money for TV ads, declined. A few days later at a party for his forty-third birthday Sharpton announced, "I am going to launch a full scale anti-Giuliani campaign on our streets and if we have to support Messinger we will." The full-scale campaign he referred to would come two years later and would help define Giuliani's second term.[21]

▲ ▲ ▲

As the general election campaign began, Giuliani played off Messinger's fear of alienating black voters by tying her to Sharpton at every turn. He hammered Messinger on comments she made in defense of sex shops, while ads touting the mayor's popular quality-of-life campaign and the revival of the city's neighborhoods filled the airwaves.

In the debates Messinger was caught in contradictions of her own making. Her neighborhood, the Upper West Side, had once been overrun by wandering mental patients, druggies and panhandlers. But because they were serviced by her core constituency of social workers, she insisted, contrary to what was glaringly obvious, that the quality of life hadn't improved after Giuliani had removed most of these people from the streets. Listening to Messinger's denial, a veteran pol quipped to the author, "Ruth is suffering from a leakage of reality."[22]*

A Zogby poll found that the more Messinger campaigned, the less people liked her. Queens Boro President Claire Schulman and two African-American Congressman, Floyd Flake of Queens and Ed Towns of Brooklyn, joined the wave of Democratic pols deserting their party's nominee.[23]

As election day approached, not only the Giuliani team but the entire political class of the city was speculating on the possibility of a record win for the incumbent. Even assured of victory, Giuliani drove himself and his staff hard to achieve an historic result. When tensions erupted between his Liberal Party patronage appointees who were the key components of his field operation and his core staff, he pushed hard to whip the liberals back in line. A man of nearly unlimited energy, he campaigned almost non-stop for the final two days. The last twenty-four hours were devoted to a five-boro bus tour designed to stir up turnout.

In a very good year for incumbent mayors, Giuliani won with 57 percent of the vote to 41 percent for Messinger. It was a strong showing for a Republican but well below the margins obtained by

---

*My own favorite story about Upper West Side wackiness happened when I walked into a bodega on the Upper West Side in about 1990 and discovered a group of very large, very naked, very stoned women—presumably mental patients—prancing through the aisles knocking over boxes and bottles. It was an amusing scene. But there were, as in the notorious case of Larry Hogue, also serious cases of mentally ill and drugged-out patients assaulting children. Hogue became notorious because no sooner was he arrested and sent to a mental health facility than he was released. The mental health workers didn't want the menacing Hogue in their midst and the liberal courts wouldn't or couldn't find a way to confine him.

Wagner and Koch. In LA, a fellow Republican centrist, Richard
Riordan, who had accomplished far less, won mayoral re-election
with a similar coalition but with 61 percent of the vote.*

Giuliani lost only one boro, the Bronx, which lacked a
substantial private-sector economy. He also lost among African-
Americans, who went four to one for his opponent, and among those
voters who thought school spending was the key issue. Giuliani won
the female vote by nineteen points and he carried whites by nearly
four to one. Strikingly, he carried Messinger's Manhattan and he
captured a very respectable 43 percent of the Latino vote and an
extraordinary 75 percent of the Jewish vote. Giuliani won the new
swing voters, the moderately liberal middle class, many of them
Jews, who chose Giuliani over co-religionist Messinger.

▲ ▲ ▲

In the wake of Messinger's defeat, there was loose talk of a tectonic
shift in the plates of New York politics. Messinger's research director
wondered "if Rudy hasn't changed the very nature of New York politics." The *New York Observer* similarly saw "a sharp shift in the
city's psyche since Giuliani was "considered nothing less than the
messiah of a new urban pragmatism." Clinton's political advisor and
Upper West Side native Dick Morris said that when Messinger lost,
"white liberalism as a force in New York City politics died as well."
Michael Tomasky writing in *New York* magazine noted that with
Messinger's defeat a whole generation whose thinking had dominated New York liberalism for nearly thirty years appeared
discredited. "How much longer," he asked, "do people like Charlie
Rangel and David Dinkins who looked so small and bitter on election night think they can call the shots?"[24]

A very few prominent Democrats took Tomasky's question to
heart. Bronx Boro President Freddy Ferrer, back in his moderate pos-
ture, came out in support of quality-of-life policing and higher
academic standards. "We have let ourselves time and again," he

---

* "Giuliani is real, Giuliani is tough. There's no comparison. He's better than Riordan in every respect," said Riordan's opponent, ex-Sixties radical Tom Hayden. For
his part, Riordan, who visited the NYPD to study how it worked, envied the
accountability built into a system where the police brass can be held responsible for
their actions. "New York," says Riordan, has a "highly sophisticated system of
accountability that we should have in Los Angeles."

insisted, "be put in the position of defending an indefensible status quo—defending things that clearly haven't worked very well." Democrats, he argued, must, in the manner of President Clinton, "talk about giving people their money's worth from government."[25]

There was a sharp divergence along racial lines in the reactions of Messinger's core supporters. "Upper West Side white liberals accustomed to instructing the nation if not the world, were left in despair by a defeat on their home turf." But from Dinkins, Sharpton, et al. there came a piercing cry for revenge.[26]

As mayor, Dinkins had often been at odds with Sharpton, but as an embittered ex-mayor, Dinkins and the Gang of Five became Sharpton allies. At a fifty-sixth birthday party for Jesse Jackson, Dinkins, "arriving late as usual, pointed to Sharpton and proclaimed 'The is the first meeting of the Sharpton for Congress Committee.'" The former mayor wanted Reverend Al to run against Congressman Ed Towns as a way of punishing the Brooklyn representative for backing Giuliani. "I'm serious," Dinkins insisted, "Al ought to run against Ed Towns, and I'll be the first to back him." Dinkins laid out his reasoning for punishing the traitors. "I believe that those Democrats who have endorsed Giuliani in the face of brutality and all the things that are going on now—that I say are bad for black folks in this city—should be seen not as allies but as the opposition."[27]

Sharpton never ran for Congress, but the idea of preparing to take revenge on Giuliani took hold. Two years hence, a new racial incident would give Sharpton and his allies their opportunity.

PART III

The Second Term

FIFTEEN

Lame Duck Term

Rudolph Giuliani, the hard-charging moderate, went into his final four years with an ambitious agenda, some important staff changes, more than adequate confidence and his eyes elsewhere at times. From the outset, there was talk both among his supporters and in the national press of a run for the presidency.*

Some senior advisors, including Deputy Mayors Peter Powers and John Dyson, had left the cabinet but it still looked as if it would be a relatively smooth second term. Giuliani's restorationist regime had taken down both the deficit and the "riot ideology," the twin engines that had driven New York's self-destructive politics since the Lindsay years. For the first time in a decade, the economy was robust. As the stock market passed the 10,000 mark, the city boasted of a whole new tech sector dubbed Silicon Alley and total employment was nearing an all-time high. Harlem was bustling with new developments including a 275,000-square-foot entertainment and retail complex on 125th Street while a remade Times Square was studded with the stars of the infotainment economy. ABC, NBC, Time-Warner, Viacom, Condé Nast, Bertelsmann A.G., Bloomberg and ESPN had all set up offices around "The Great White Way." New York, with three times the population of Chicago, actually had fewer murders. The collapse of crime com-

---

*After winning reelection, Giuliani was deluged with invitations from Republican groups in thirteen states. He did little to discourage the attention. He even met quietly with a GOP activist from New Hampshire who planned to organize a grass roots Draft Giuliani for President Committee in 2000, but little came of the idea.

bined with the Wall Street frenzy turned Manhattan back into the 24-hour city of the past as New Yorkers reclaimed the public space that had for so long been denied to them.

▲ ▲ ▲

"It's all about changing [the political] culture," Giuliani repeatedly told his staff. Referring to his success in lowering the welfare rolls by more than the entire population of Buffalo, he exulted: "This city has really caught up with the rest of America."[1]

As the second term began, Giuliani and his team discussed how to ensure that their reforms would endure. The best outcome, as they saw it, would be for Giuliani to be succeeded by a fellow Republican reformer who could continue his agenda. But there was no obvious heir. None of the prominent players in Giuliani's administration had by 2005 tried to launch their own political careers. And there was almost no effort made to build up the institutions of the GOP, which were owned by Giuliani's Republican rivals Pataki and D'Amato.

There were discussions about introducing non-partisan elections into New York. By opening up the primary process to all voters and not just the tiny percentage of activists and city employees who dominated the Democratic Party primaries, non-partisan elections offered a way around the interest-group domination of Gotham's politics. But, despite the formation of two charter commissions that considered such electoral improvements, there was no structural reform of the political process. There was a poorly organized effort to institutionalize Giuliani's reforms of the city's fiscal practices, but that failed badly.

The Giuliani team expected to be followed by a Democrat, most likely Comptroller Alan Hevesi or former "Nader's Raider" Mark Green, although Giuliani hoped for the more moderate Peter Vallone. The lack of a successor seemed to make it all the more important to lock in reform by extending the CompStat accountability techniques from the Police Department to all city agencies. But in 1998 Giuliani was so thoroughly in command that he felt no immediate pressure to extend CompStat.

▲ ▲ ▲

When Mayor Giuliani stepped up to the lectern in mid-January 1998 to give the first major address of his second term, his State of the

City speech, he delivered a commanding performance. Describing New York as "the Comeback City," he spoke in whole paragraphs for ninety minutes, moving seamlessly across topics while drawing on a broad array of facts and figures. Confident in his delivery, at times he departed from both the podium and his nearly fifty-page text to wander into the audience delivering asides. His rivals in the audience of politicians, city council members and government officials, were, to judge by the expressions on their faces, more than a little intimidated.

Giuliani celebrated the "liberation" of New York and New Yorkers from the grip of "progressive" ideals, which valued welfare over work, and called on the city to rejoin America in emphasizing individual accountability. His goal, he announced, was "to make certain that all New Yorkers move from the prior era of dependency to the age of opportunity and advancement." "A truly progressive society," he asserted, "is one in which increasing numbers of people can take care of themselves and then, as a result, take care of others. A progressive political philosophy is one that improves the quality of people's lives, not one that fosters dependency, rationalizes deviancy and encourages educational failure."

Large sections of the speech were organized around a second-term agenda devoted to making his changes permanent by reforming policy towards children and education. There were some issues, such as the need for two-parent families, that he acknowledged were beyond the capacities of local government. But he bemoaned the effect of single female-headed families. The more than half of the city's children born "out of wedlock," he noted, are "three times more likely to fail at school," while "70 percent of long-term prisoners and 75 percent of adolescents charged with murder grew up without fathers."

Warming up to his theme, Giuliani, spurred on by applause, stepped out of the written text by threatening to "jail" parents who didn't provide child support. Then speaking directly to the people of New York, he suggested that they approach fathers who neglected their children and tell them, "You know something? You're a bum."

Turning to education, he called on the NYPD to replace inept school guards in protecting students from violence. And he called on the school system to protect students from those "social and political movements" that supported the failed policy of bilingual education. "The simple fact is a child has a much greater chance of success if they understand English."

But this was only the beginning of Giuliani's agenda. He also called for a longer school year and an end to social promotions, the practice of passing a student on to the next grade regardless of academic performance. Paraphrasing Machiavelli, he asserted that social promotion "may sound right, it may sound kind, but it's cruel in practice." He also called for the end of tenure for principals: "Is [the school system] a job-security system for the managers, or is it a system that's going to insist on accountability and excellence for children? Which is it? It cannot be both."

The mayor reserved his sharpest comments for the seventeen colleges and 200,000 students of what the *Daily News* described as "the second chance high school known as The City University." He noted that only "14 percent of incoming freshmen at CUNY community colleges pass...tests...geared to the 10th and 11th grade education standard." Describing CUNY as a failure by any standard, he pointed out that "the overall graduation rate for the two-year community colleges is approximately 1 percent in two years. The overall graduation rate for the four-year colleges [is] less than 9 percent in four years."

The mayor described the CUNY policy of open admissions, adopted in the 1960s, as a tragic mistake with cruel consequences. By eliminating any meaningful standards for admission and continually defining down standards, he warned that "the entire meaning and value of a college education has been put in jeopardy, [yet] the reaction of the people running CUNY to this disaster...was to do nothing about it but rationalize it."

Giuliani, limited by law to two terms, concluded, "If you think that I've run out of enthusiasm for this job because I'm a lame duck, watch out! This is my chance to do all of the things that I was too timid and restrained to do in the first administration." Then, with the room erupting in applause, Giuliani exited triumphantly, high-fiving his top aides as he left.

Supporters such as Queens Boro President Claire Schulman looked exultant; Mark Green looked downcast and said little. Few of the liberal big guns chose to respond, leaving that to second-stringers like Councilwoman Una Clarke who denounced criticism of CUNY's collapse as "an attack on the poor."[2]

▲ ▲ ▲

At the start of his second term, Giuliani's judgment, apparently impaired by talk of the presidency, lapsed and he became involved in a series of feuds that undermined his agenda for the second term. In November 1997, a few weeks after his re-election, Metropolitan Transportation Authority buses began running ads for *New York* magazine that read POSSIBLY THE ONLY GOOD THING IN NEW YORK RUDY HASN'T TAKEN CREDIT FOR. The mayor should have just laughed it off, but instead he forced the MTA to withdraw the ads. *New York* magazine went to court and a federal judge predictably ruled that the MTA had every right to run the ads. That left the magazine with a publicity bonanza and the mayor with egg on his face as an opponent of the First Amendment.

A few weeks later in mid-December, the administration, still stewing over the Citizens Budget Commission's ties to the Messinger campaign, began to hint broadly that it might not be the best thing for business people to attend the CBC's annual dinner. Asked his opinion of the CBC, the mayor, whose differences with them went back to the Kummerfeld Report, described them as "a dilettante organization" that issued "useless" reports. No stranger to nuance, Giuliani could have acknowledged the integrity of their reports even while strongly differing with their policy conclusions. But he didn't and the CBC, luxuriating in his hostility, went on to raise a record sum at their dinner.[3]*

Then in February 1998 Giuliani got into a misunderstanding with the Grammy Awards, an event that in 1997 had brought $2 million in direct spending to New York. He thought that he had been invited to make one of the presentations. Mike Greene, who ran the Grammys, disagreed and lit into one of the mayor's staff members. Giuliani stood up for his staffer by boycotting the event and he invited the Grammys to return to Los Angeles, which they did the next year.

But none of these contretemps was as politically problematic as the mayor's proposals for jaywalkers, sidewalk vendors and cabbies. Pointing to the very real problem of New York's high rate of

---

*The author, who rarely goes to such events, made a point of attending the CBC dinner that year. For the record the CBC dates back to the 1930s when they were among the very first to analyze and understand the enormous fiscal failings of the La Guardia administration.

pedestrian deaths at the hands of motorists, Giuliani had the police set up wooden barriers in Midtown to make sure that people "crossed at the green and not in between." The barriers elicited widespread derision in a city where the right not to obey the laws too well is considered a natural inheritance. But the derision turned to anger when the mayor announced that the police were being instructed to ticket jaywalkers.*

Giuliani referred to other, more civil cities "where pedestrians actually stop at red lights and don't walk signs, and tangos with cars are not considered part of street theater" as the norm to which New York should aspire. Reducing murder and muggings was one thing, but New Yorkers didn't want to be too much like the rest of America.[4]

The *Daily News*, generally friendly to Giuliani, teed off. "A CRACKDOWN on jaywalking? In this town? Where jaywalking is an art form? Surely Mayor Giuliani will come to his senses. If he goes ahead with the plan," the *News* warned, "he might as well deliver his State of the City address...in a jester's costume, complete with belled cap and elf shoes."[5]

Giuliani took the warning, but not the larger point. All references to jaywalking were dropped from the State of the City speech. But the mayor refused to stop talking about the importance of civility. He announced "a renewed quality-of-life campaign to reduce noise, traffic, and graffiti."

The inspiration for this quality-of-life campaign was an article, "Toward a More Civil City," written by journalist Jonathan Foreman for the Winter 1998 *City Journal*. But uncharacteristically Giuliani had misread the article. Foreman, who noted the common roots of the words "city," "citizen" and "civility," was inspired to write about public manners by his experiences living near Tompkins Square Park in the East Village. Foreman was contemptuous of the

---

*Rowdiness was an old New York story. Long before Rudy Giuliani preached civility to the unbelieving, Peter Stuyvesant described his seventeenth-century city by the sea as a "slovenly, drunken, disobedient community." Determined to restore discipline in New Amsterdam, Mayor Stuyvesant imposed fines on townsfolk who allowed pigs, goats and sheep to wander. He also ordered taverns to close at nine, and forbade residents from throwing "rubbish, filth, ashes, oyster-shells, dead animals or anything like it" into the street. At times La Guardia, who could be something of a raging bull, tried to handle the perpetual problem with a bit of humor. In a promotional memo by

city's "hipsters" but solicitous of the work-a-day people struggling to get by. In Tompkins Square Park, he found trustafarian radicals playing at anarchism were, along with homeless druggies, making the park unusable for the working-class Latino families with small children who were being driven away by the filth and noise.

But Foreman's article wasn't about jaywalking. Rather, it urged the mayor to "enforce the traffic laws" on motorists because pedestrians "feel under constant assault from cars that run red lights" and "cut them off." Unfortunately, the mayor, who was driven around the city, clearly hadn't spent enough time in the streets to take Foreman's insight to heart. In a city that prides itself on not being organized around the automobile, the *Daily News* nailed the mayor. Giuliani, they quipped, "left his heart in Detroit. First the barricades. Now this. Blame it on his shiny hood. He empathizes with cars."[6]

Reporters, only one of a number of groups looking to even the score, smelled hypocrisy in the civility campaign. How could a notoriously hard-edged mayor who described reporters' questions as "dopey," "jerky," "dumb" and "stupid" and who had gone on David Letterman's show to push the motto "New York City: We Can Kick Your City's Ass," talk about civility? The *Times* had fun with this headline: BE POLITE OR ELSE, GIULIANI WARNS IN ANNOUNCING CIVILITY CAMPAIGN.

▲ ▲ ▲

While the mayor was wasting political capital on secondary issues, racial demagoguery continued to simmer. Giuliani hadn't brought an end to the attempted shakedowns in which the city was threatened with riots unless it paid off demagogues with subsidies and city jobs for their friends. A new version of the old game emerged this time largely within the confines of the Democratic Party. Reverend Al couldn't win elections. But he could "win" as a spoiler. His minimal

---

"The Little Flower" entitled "Ten Misconceptions About New York," La Guardia insisted that out-of-towners are wrong about Gotham because "only the most courteous and considerate people could live under such conditions. Without good humor & without good temper the rush-hour crowd would become a disorderly mob." *Weekly Standard* 2/8/99; La Guardia's "Ten Misconceptions" is reprinted in Kenneth T. Jackson and David S. Dunbar, eds., *Empire City: New York Through the Centuries*, New York: Columbia University Press: 2002.

support for Ruth Messinger made it clear he had the capability of cutting down other Democrats who refused to play ball.*

When Sharpton first talked of running for mayor in 1996, Denny Farrell, a leading Democrat, referring to the Reverend's past alliance with Republican Senator D'Amato, called the prospective campaign "a Republican plot to disintegrate the Democratic Party." But by 1998 Farrell's tune had changed. The Reverend had every aspiring Democrat in New York kissing his ring. In late January 1998 on Martin Luther King Day, the three major Democratic candidates for senator—former vice-presidential nominee Geraldine Ferraro, Congressman Chuck Schumer and Public Advocate Mark Green—along with Peter Vallone and the other four Democratic candidates for governor gathered for the first time to pay tribute to Sharpton.[7]

Sharpton was setting the political tone. In the immediate wake of Giuliani's victory, Reverend Calvin Butts of the influential Abyssinian Baptist Church in Harlem had been mau-maued by Sharpton for getting too mainstream. "He's gonna have to explain his access to downtown money," warned Sharpton, who had long exploited his own contacts with Senator D'Amato. By the summer, Butts, backed by Pataki, got into a dispute with the Mayor's office over the development of a retail complex on 125th Street, and the Abyssinian pastor came out firing in full Sharpton mode. After accusing Giuliani of being a racist who was about to create a police state, he threatened, "We can get tough too.... Giuliani does not really want the kind of confrontation that could happen in the street." If Giuliani didn't back off, "we're going to have an explosion." Giuliani didn't back off (nor was he backed up), but racial threats were still very effective in immobilizing more run-of-the-mill politicians.[8]

---

*In the first year of Giuliani's second term, Sharpton suffered a series of setbacks, to little political effect. Sharpton had issued a public dare to Stephen Pagones, the young district attorney he had falsely accused of raping Tawana Brawley. "If we're lying sue us, so we can go into court with you and prove you did it." Pagones obliged and brought a defamation suit.

A slimmed-down Sharpton, attired in pinstripe suits and (somewhat) conservatively coifed in a toned-down version of his James Brown "do," was forced into an extended replay of the Tawana Brawley hoax. Pagones' lawyers played a video of the Rev "wearing a powder-blue jump suit and a big medallion—screeching that there was a 'racist cult'" in the Dutchess County Sheriff's Department. The cult, he charged, was responsible for the kidnapping of black teen Tawana Brawley by peo-

In late summer of 1998, Khalid Muhammad, a man so extreme
that Louis Farrakhan had expelled him from the Nation of Islam,
announced that he planned to stage a "Million Youth March in
Harlem." Harlem's business leaders were apoplectic. The 1995
Harlem massacre set off by Sharpton's operation had cost them
dearly. Giuliani waited in vain for prominent black leaders to
denounce Khalid. But instead State Senator David Paterson warned
that unless the mayor allowed the march there would be a "confrontation of monumental proportions." Only Michael Meyers of
the New York Civil Rights Coalition criticized Muhammad in
unequivocal moral terms, while Congressman Charles Rangel
adopted the for and against approach in which he condemned
Khalid for his inflammatory (and, in fact, anti-Semitic) rhetoric
while praising "the positive mission of encouraging our youth to be
more involved."[9]

Giuliani, describing the planned gathering as a "hate march,"
refused to issue a parade permit. Fearing another conflagration in
Harlem, he acknowledged that Khalid had "a right to demonstrate,"
but noted that the city had the right to "put reasonable bounds of
where, when, how and to what extent." A federal judge agreed and
the march was limited to six blocks and four hours.[10]

At a press conference Khalid revved up his followers. "I say to
every black man, woman and child...you have no need to be afraid
of Rudolph Giuliani any longer. Mayor Giuliani is an ordinary
cracker with no power. This devil has no power over you any
longer." He warned "riot police, riot horses, two-legged dogs and
four-legged dogs, any who will attempt to stop us, we have radical
revolutionary youth...who will be quite ready and quite prepared in
the numbers of hundreds and thousands and millions to fight the
devil in the streets." On the day of the event in early September,

---

ple using "IRA tactics" like "placing cotton in the noses of victims and smearing
them with feces." The trial degenerated into an eight-month circus in which Sharpton, after depicting himself as a latter-day Martin Luther King and a defender of free
speech, was found guilty as charged. Although Sharpton had become a court-
certified liar, this had little effect on his core supporters, while the damage he had
inflicted on the Messinger campaign when those supporters had sat out the election
only increased his political influence. Sharpton, who repelled swing voters, never
expanded past that core, but the verdict, explained Hank Sheinkopf, a Democratic
consultant who had worked with the Clinton campaign in New York, "doesn't mean
a thing" in a statewide race since the same "170,000 people will be with him for-
ever." *Daily News* 1/15/98.

Muhammad told marchers, "And if you don't have a gun, every one of them [New York City cops] has one gun, two guns, three guns.... If they attack you, take their guns from them and use their guns on them. Don't let nobody be arrested."[11]

The march itself was something of an anti-climax. There were at most 6,000 marchers. Some did attack the thick cordon of police Commissioner Safir had stationed along the streets. Fifteen cops were injured, but only one marcher was arrested, as more serious violence was averted. Giuliani had saved Harlem's economic renaissance from Harlem's political leaders to scant thanks. Instead, he was widely criticized for a heavy-handed police presence that curtailed Muhammad's First Amendment rights. As for Sharpton, the only prominent black leader to speak at the rally, he explained, "I have no problem with Khalid Abdul Muhammad. It is not Khalid who is talking hate, it's Rudy Giuliani."[12]

▲ ▲ ▲

After the low turnout and disciplined police presence rendered the march anti-climactic, public attention turned to the Democratic primary campaigns picking challengers to Governor Pataki and Senator D'Amato. In both cases, the more moderate Democrat emerged on top. City Council Speaker Peter Vallone easily won the gubernatorial nod while Brooklyn Congressman Charles Schumer won a vigorously contested senatorial primary.

Vallone's gubernatorial campaign brought him into conflict with Giuliani. The two men had cooperated closely to pull the city out of the fiscal morass of the Dinkins years. But in running for governor, Vallone needed to distinguish himself by emphasizing their differences. And while their differences were not fundamental, they weren't hard to find.

It got nasty as Giuliani and Vallone slugged it out over the city budget.

Deputy Mayor Randy Mastro went after Vallone's chief of staff Bruce Bender, a key figure in surmounting the fiscal crisis of the first term. Fight us, Mastro told Bender, and "we will bring you to your knees." The mayor warned that he would impound funds the council had appropriated if they passed a budget he opposed. But Bender was every bit as tough and talented as Mastro. Vallone countered that if Rudy got in their way, they would repeal the 12.5 percent income tax surcharge Rudy wanted to use to fund a new Yankee Stadium in Manhattan.[13]

There was broad public support, cheered on by Bronx Boro President Freddy Ferrer, to improve the stadium and the surrounding area with public money. But that wasn't enough for George Steinbrenner; he wanted a new stadium in Manhattan, complete with luxury boxes. And, invoking memories of how the Dodgers and Giants had departed for California in the 1950s, he threatened to leave if he didn't get his way. The sports talk radio airwaves were filled with angry fans hurling expletives at "the boss."

Vallone seized on the Yankee stadium dust-up to propose a referendum on keeping the Yankees in the Bronx, where they were an anchor for the weakest economy in the five boros. Giuliani denounced the proposal as a publicity stunt aimed at boosting Vallone's run against Pataki. But here again Giuliani was on the wrong side of public sentiments on a marginal issue. *Daily News* baseball columnist Mike Lupica caught the spirit of the city when he asked, "Why does he [Steinbrenner] want a new ballpark? He is exactly like Giuliani in this regard: He wants what he wants when he wants it.... This is about the greed of the Yankee owner and the arrogance of the mayor. They have pushed people around their whole public lives and won't stop now." The Yankees stayed put, and the brawl left Giuliani with another black eye.[14]

▲ ▲ ▲

While Vallone had the high ground when it came to moving the Yankees, he took a lower road regarding Giuliani's creation of a $6.6 million emergency command center being built on the twenty-third floor of 7 World Trade Center.

The criticism from politicians and pundits over what came to be known as "the bunker in the sky" referred only in passing to the 1993 terrorist attack on the World Trade Center. The press dubbed the command center "the bunker" (though it was so far above ground), a symbol of Giuliani's supposedly paranoid governing style.

The command center, which was capable of withstanding winds of over two hundred miles per hour, had to withstand gales of outrage and mockery. Elizabeth Kolbert writing in the *Times* caught the general tenor of the response: "Some people think it's New York's funniest bunker since Archie." It was called "Rudy's Nuclear Palace" and "the nut shell." Michael Daly of the *Daily News* compared it to Saddam Hussein's underground shelters.

Vallone, clearly stung by the acrimony between their camps said, "If [Giuliani] wants to build a bunker for the only people he trusts, all he needs is a phone booth." Former mayor Koch chimed in, "It's the joke of the week." "The trouble," said Kolbert, "is that the project seems to speak too clearly to the mayor's fears and, worse still, his hopes. Mr. Giuliani has always governed as if from a bunker, with chaos threatening from all sides and enemies all around."[15]

Lost in the press clatter was the fact that the Federal Emergency Management Agency, the Clinton White House and National Security Council, the FBI, CIA, and Secret Service (the latter three also had offices in World Trade Center) praised the mayor's plans for an emergency command center.

Some of the private criticism of the command center's location proved to be prescient. Louis Anemone, then Chief of Department for the NYPD, knew that the FBI's account of both the Kahane killing and the 1993 World Trade Center bombing were off the mark. The NYPD had quickly cracked the 1993 case, and then began to put together lineaments of a far larger terror threat—which the FBI disdained to look into. Referring to the 1993 bombing, Anemone argued that the command center should be in another boro in case the Towers were again the target of attack. But Anemone, knowing the criticism would be "futile," quipped, "You don't want to confuse Giuliani with facts."[16]*

---

*Journalists John Miller and Michael Stone note that prior to the 1993 bombing police had raided the apartment of El Sayyid Nosair, who had shot and killed racist rabbi Meir Kahane in front of witnesses in broad daylight, only to be acquitted in a giveback decision by a mostly black jury. Inside, police found sixteen boxes of evidence linking the murder to terrorists in Egypt, Saudi Arabia, Pakistan, Western Europe and the U.S. Already aware of Nosair's ties to the blind Egyptian cleric Sheik Omar Abdel Rahman, who preached holy war against America and was later convicted for his role in the 1993 World Trade Center bombing, they found bomb-making materials and maps of city landmarks. One of Nosair's papers urged his confederates to knock down the "tall buildings of which Americans are so proud." Police also found a hit list of prominent Jewish leaders and politicians.

According to Miller and Stone, when Detective Eddie Norris attempted to brief his superiors on the breakthrough, they wouldn't hear of it. "You, shut up," cracked Joe Borelli the chief of detectives. "You do murder cases. They," he said, pointing to startled FBI agents, "do conspiracies." At a news conference later, Borelli described the Kahane murder as apparently the act of a "lone, deranged gunman." Case closed. A few days later, FBI agents confiscated Norris's evidence, which wasn't examined until after the 1993 World Trade Center bombing. "The thinking was," Miller writes, "Don't take a high-profile homicide case that could be stamped 'Solved' and turn it into an unsolved conspiracy." John Miller and Michael Stone, *The Cell: Inside the 9/11 Plot and Why the FBI and the CIA Failed to Stop It*, New York: Hyperion, 2002.

The command center had emerged out of conversations between Giuliani and Jerry Hauer, a native New Yorker who had worked at both the Fire Department and at Emergency Medical Services, about the real meaning of the 1993 World Trade Center attack. Terror, they agreed, was an ongoing threat. While the public wasn't widely aware of it, the blind Sheik Omar Abdel Rahman had been thwarted in his plan to bomb New York landmarks including the Statue of Liberty, the George Washington Bridge and the Holland Tunnel. At the Sheik's trial in 1995, the prosecution opened by arguing, "The enemy in this war was the United States of America. The battlefield in this war was the streets and buildings and the tunnels of New York."

But if there was a war going on the press barely noticed it. The Sheik's trial was virtually coterminous with the O.J. Simpson case, so that the extraordinary testimony on the Sheik's plans to wreak havoc by killing "crusaders" and "Jews" was buried in the newspapers. But Giuliani was well aware of the case, which was effectively prosecuted by one of his former Assistant Federal Attorneys, Andrew McCarthy.*

Giuliani and Hauer were particularly worried about the possible precedent of a 1995 biological attack on the Tokyo subways. Their worries were heightened in 1997 by a plot by two Palestinian men to bomb Brooklyn's heavily used Atlantic Avenue subway station, which was only narrowly averted when a third member of their group alerted the police. Unlike the FBI, Giuliani and Hauer, in constant touch with the NYPD, were connecting the dots. They saw terrorism as far more than a matter of isolated criminal cases, and they prepared the city for the inevitable next attack.

Giuliani knew that the ongoing "battle of the badges" between cops and fire fighters could undermine the city's ability to respond to a crisis. He was also aware that fellow reform mayor Steve Goldsmith in Indianapolis had created a mayoral office to coordinate emergency response. Giuliani brought in Hauer to do the same for New York through the newly created Office of Emergency Management.†

---

*Coverage in the *New York Times* focused on whether the statutes used in the case violated the civil liberties of the accused.
†Giuliani was well ahead of the curve. It was only in the wake of 9/11 that President Bush created the Terrorist Threat Integration Center to push the FBI and CIA into cooperation.

Police Commissioner Howard Safir aside, Hauer won widespread cooperation. A big, plain-spoken and knowledgeable man, Hauer devised protocols for responding to an emergency that imposed a new and far higher degree of cooperation between the NYPD and the FDNY. He organized the first chemical weapons exercises, devised emergency drills in case of biological attack and integrated the hospitals into the emergency response system. He made New York the first city to put chemical antidotes on ambulances and the first to prepare for an anthrax attack. But his efforts, which were to pay handsomely down the road, were largely invisible to the general public at a time when the mayor's "bunker" was being widely ridiculed.

▲ ▲ ▲

Neither the Yankee Stadium issue nor his attack on Rudy's supposedly militarist overkill on the bunker could rescue Vallone's campaign against an incumbent governor who benefited from a booming economy. The vast patronage powers of the governor's office in the state with the highest debt and the highest percentage of public employees were too much to overcome. Pataki bought the support of the state's largest public-sector union leaving Vallone without a ground army. Vallone lost by twenty-two points, but he ran well in the city, preparing the way for a mayoral run in 2001 when Giuliani would be term-limited out of office.

The senate race was a different matter. Senator D'Amato, who already had re-election problems, courted more trouble for himself with his high profile role in the campaign to impeach President Clinton, who was extremely popular in New York. Senator D'Amato, known by friend and foe as Senator Pothole, continued to deliver on federal funds. He brought an unprecedented $6 billion in mass transit subsidies to New York. Tarred by repeated brushes with scandal, D'Amato tried without success to depict Schumer as an out-of-touch "Brooklyn liberal," deaf to the interests of moderate and upstate voters. D'Amato's political consultant Arthur Finkelstein had made his name with the very effective ads used by Pataki in 1994 describing Mario Cuomo as "Too Liberal, For Too Long." Against Schumer, Finkelstein tried "Liberal Chuck Schumer. Wrong on Taxes, Wrong on Welfare. Wrong on Crime. Wrong for Us." The Schumer camp replied with, "Too Many Lies for Too Long," turning the echo of the 1994 ad back on D'Amato.

Schumer campaigned relentlessly in upstate New York in general and the Western tier in particular, an area that had long felt neglected. He was also sufficiently independent and moderate to blunt the force of the D'Amato campaign at a time when Giuliani's achievements made it harder to fear liberals. When Schumer made the campaign a referendum on the Clinton White House, Hillary Clinton and Vice-President Al Gore came in to campaign for both Schumer and their own upcoming campaigns. Schumer's victory over the three-term incumbent made it clear that the campaign to impeach President Clinton was producing a backlash in heavily Democratic areas. Giuliani too would come to feel the force of that backlash.

SIXTEEN

Impeach Rudy!

Charles Schumer's November 1998 victory over Al D'Amato was followed a few days later by the announcement that the much revered Senator Daniel Patrick Moynihan, his health failing, wouldn't run for a fifth term. That left Giuliani, strengthened by the defeat of his Republican rival Al D'Amato, in position to run for the senate seat Moynihan was vacating. At the same time, Governor Pataki's weak electoral showing in the city suggested that the more articulate Giuliani might serve as the better standard-bearer of moderate Northeast Republicanism.

Giuliani, with his standard stump speech on how he brought New York's crime under control, became a hot item on the Republican fund-raising circuit. Ron Kaufman, a Republican strategist and the former political director for the Bush Administration, exclaimed, "I don't care where you are in the [political] spectrum of the party, you say, 'Man, I'm glad this guy is part of our party.'"[1]

Speaking in South Carolina on one of his many out-of-town engagements, Giuliani tried to reposition himself. Even as gay rights supporters were demonstrating on his behalf with signs that read "Thank You, Mayor Giuliani, for taking a Courageous Stand for Equal Rights," the mayor was downplaying his differences with Southern conservatives: "I think we have a lot more in common than maybe some people would think." He told them that they could all fit under "the big tent" of Republicanism.[2]

But while Rudy was looking beyond his lame-duck status to national office, Reverend Al, also a winner in the 1998 elections, was repositioning himself back in New York. No one in the Democratic Party was interested in bringing up the 1995 massacre at Freddy's, or

Sharpton's ties to Khalid Muhammad, because, in the three years since the fire, Sharpton had become the most powerful black leader in New York. It wasn't so much that there was a new Sharpton (though his apologists in the press spoke of how he had "gone mainstream") as the realization that while he might not help you to win, he could guarantee that you would lose. When Senator-elect Charles Schumer took his victory lap, he made Sharpton's Harlem headquarters his first stop.

While Sharpton was rising, the men who had long dominated the city's African-American politics, Harlem's Gang of Five led by Rangel and Dinkins, were slowing down. They had lost some of their power to Giuliani, Pataki, the Republican control of Congress and a high-profile scandal in which Rangel and his cronies had mismanaged Harlem's famed Apollo Theater into near bankruptcy. Sharpton's stature was further enhanced when he and his long-time enemy Ed Koch, united by their shared distaste for Giuliani, who had snubbed them both, staged a public reconciliation.

Sensing the opportunity to ingratiate himself with national Democrats, Sharpton threw himself into organizing rallies on behalf of President Clinton, who was in the midst of his impeachment hearings. In mid-December 1998, Sharpton and Dennis Rivera, the powerful New York labor leader, led a caravan of one hundred buses to a pro-Clinton vigil in Washington organized by Jesse Jackson. In early January, Sharpton, who had run in the 1992 and 1994 Democratic Senatorial primaries garnering first 14 and then 25 percent of the vote, announced, amid speculation, that if the First Lady was interested in running for Moynihan's seat, then he was willing to step aside. In anticipation of her entry, he organized a "minority summit" of city and state black and Latino officials that further established him as a key power broker.

The political tempo sped up dramatically in mid-January 1999. The cover of *New York* magazine featured a picture of Hillary Clinton slaying a Rudy dragon. The caption read "NY Democrats to first lady, save us." Talk of a Hillary Clinton for Senate run had come as early as September 1997. But it was the *New York* magazine story that brought a Hillary candidacy to center stage. The article, written by columnist Mike Tomasky, argued that New York liberalism, mired in the failures of the Dinkins years, needed a white knight— Hillary Clinton—to come in from the outside and revive a once worthy tradition.[3]

Giuliani's support in the polls never came close to matching his job approval numbers. He had made too many enemies, even if his successes were widely acknowledged. Still, should he run for Senate, Giuliani had a rising economy and declining crime to boast about. Like the Dow Jones average it closely tracked, New York's economic numbers were pointing skyward. In 1998 the city had created a record 84,000 private-sector jobs. All of the private-sector jobs lost in recessions had been regained. Unskilled minority workers were being drawn back into the economy so that 54 percent of adults were employed—a modern city record. And, if that weren't enough, for the first time in a decade, the city's economy grew faster than the nation's. At the same time, by 1998 crime was at a thirty-year low. The sharpest drops had come in minority areas like East New York and central Harlem, where overall crime had dropped 61 percent since 1994, and murders had fallen from 110 murders in 1993 (Dinkins' last year as mayor) to thirty-seven in 1998 and then none in 1999.

Then Sharpton struck political gold. In the wee hours of February 4, 1999, four cops from the celebrated Street Crime Unit were out on patrol in a Bronx immigrant neighborhood looking for both the killer of a cab driver and an armed rape suspect implicated in fifty-one assaults. Both men probably still lived in the neighborhood and both suspects were black. One was described as a man of slender build.

The Street Crime Unit (SCU) had been an extraordinary success. Just 1 percent of the police force, it had seized 40 percent of the guns pulled off the street while drawing minimal flak in the way of civilian complaints. But in 1997, Police Commissioner Howard Safir, Bratton's successor, tried to drive crime down even further by tripling the elite unit from 138 to 380 cops. Rapid expansion was achieved through diminished training and by sending untested units out without a veteran leading the team. The results weren't encouraging. "They quadrupled the number of people they stopped and frisked on the streets," said a one-time administration insider. But they only "confiscated the same number of weapons as when they were stopping one quarter as many people. It's just been a fucking disaster."[4]

The problem with specialized units, explained George Kelling, the father of "broken windows" policing, is that many, perhaps most, special units don't know the territory they're working. "They go to neighborhoods without knowing the players, or what's unusual." Rapidly expanding such units also caused problems. The killing that happened that night, Kelling believed, "was the result of officers who didn't know one another, because they had never worked together before."

The four men on patrol the night of February 4th were all new-comers to the SCU, unsupervised by a sergeant. They over-reacted when they saw a slim man matching the description of the perpetrator, nervously pacing in the doorway of an apartment building. Amadou Diallo, a Guinean vendor of bootlegged goods, had recently filed a phony application for political asylum after concocting a story about having been tortured in Mauritania. His illegal status may have been the source of his nervous motion as the police approached him.

Based on the trial testimony of the officers, it appears that when the SCU team told Amadou Diallo to exit from the doorway showing his hands, he misunderstood and reached into his pocket for what police assumed was a gun. Officer Sean Carroll screamed, "Gun, he's got a gun!" That set in motion a panicked response in which one officer, assuming he was in danger, fell off the steps while firing. The flash of the bullets reflected in a mirror at the far end of the darkened vestibule combined with the echo of the shots made it look and sound to the cops as though they were being fired upon. The other two cops, assuming a comrade had been shot, began firing at ricochets and the still standing figure of Diallo—the nine millimeter bullets passed right through him without knocking him down.

In little more than eight seconds, forty-one shots had been fired. When the officers searched Diallo's body, they found only a wallet. Sean Carroll broke down in tears by one account. By another, one of the officers screamed repeatedly, "Where's the fuckin gun?!"[5]

Neither Giuliani nor Safir recognized the significance of what had happened. The mayor expressed his sympathy for Diallo's family and asked people to reserve judgment until the incident could be investigated by the Bronx DA. He reached out to the Diallo family, but Sharpton beat him to the punch. Sharpton went to Guinea to court Amadou Diallo's mother as a political prop. He returned to announce, "Amadou Diallo will be the end of Rudolph Giuliani's burgeoning political career." A day after the shooting, Giuliani, distracted at home by ongoing tensions with his estranged wife, Donna

Hanover, was further diverted by a Republican speaking engagement in Pennsylvania. Safir, who lacked Bratton's shrewd sense of politics and the press, left for the Academy Awards in Hollywood.[6]

With Giuliani and Safir slow to grasp the situation, what took hold was nothing short of political hysteria. The fact that panicked cops tragically shot forty-one times at Diallo—essentially firing at their own ricochets and flashes—was repeated literally thousands of times as if malevolent intent could be deduced from the number of shots fired.

Giuliani responded with statistics. He trotted out the numbers showing that the NYPD's use of deadly force had dropped sharply since the Dinkins days and that it was the most restrained big city police force in the United States. The police in Washington and Detroit, cities with black mayors and police chiefs, were seven times more likely to use deadly force than Gotham cops. In Prince George's County, adjacent to Washington, with a black executive and police chief, the police were nine times more likely to use deadly force. And half of those killed in Prince George's were unarmed. These facts had no impact in the court of public opinion.*

This was the moment Giuliani's enemies had been hoping for, the moment that proved that the man in City Hall was the fascist they had said he was since 1993 when he defeated Dinkins. New York was said to be "UpSouth" and Giuliani was "Bull Giuliani," a reference to the Southern segregationist sheriff in Birmingham who had attacked peaceful protest marchers with dogs and fire hoses. Sharpton's allies in the New York Civil Liberties Union ran a "41 shots" fundraising ad which read, "On Feb. 4, 1999, the NYPD gave Amadou Diallo the right to remain silent." Within a few days,

---

*An unjustified police killing in a hail of bullets doesn't by itself create a cause célèbre, noted James Fyfe, a former New York police officer turned professor of criminal justice. Fyfe, who usually testified against the police, was an expert witness for the defense in the trial of the four Diallo cops. He noted a Camden, New Jersey case involved a mentally disturbed man who, during the course of a long confrontation with the police, pulled from his pocket a talcum powder bottle wrapped in a sock. Eleven officers, some as far as 280 feet away, responded by firing at least 106 shots at him. The media coverage of this killing consisted of one small newspaper story. There was no discipline, no criminal trial, no outrage. "In such places, where people are not paying attention, the need for change is not recognized and the police come to believe that such behavior is appropriate." Washington Post 7/8/01.

A Washington Post article, "Officers Killed with Impunity, Officials Ruled Shootings Justified in Every Case—Even of Unarmed Citizens," described similar and repeated excesses in Prince George's County, Maryland, which like Camden was run

Sharpton was organizing rallies near City Hall. The placards read
NYPD = KKK and IMPEACH GIULIANI. "If they can shoot anyone
forty-one times," screamed Reverend Al, "they can shoot everyone
forty-one times."[7]

Sharpton's message received amplification from the press. NY1,
Gotham's all-news cable TV station, virtually put itself at the disposal of Sharpton and his allies. The *Times*, which was giving the
story wall-to-wall coverage, stoked the anger by insisting that the
city was under siege from its own police force. The running theme in
the *Times*, as expressed in an editorial, was that New York had
"exchange[d] the fear of crime for a fear of the police." Television
reporters, echoing Sharpton, repeatedly cited the motto of the Street
Crime Unit, "We rule the night," as evidence of bullyboy ways.
What they ignored was that the motto was part of an emblem depicting a silhouette of an old lady bent over a cane.[8]

President Clinton, his eye on his wife's upcoming Senate race,
got in on the act. The President dispatched the FBI to aid the Bronx
DA's office in its investigation. And soon both the U.S. Civil Rights
Commission and the Justice Department announced that they were
looking into civil rights violations by the NYPD. Nothing substantial
came of either inquiry, but the announcements of the investigations
dominated the headlines.

The main show was at One Police Plaza in front of NYPD
headquarters where demonstrations and "designer arrests" were
choreographed daily. Celebrities and political figures such as Susan
Sarandon and Jesse Jackson showed up to be briefly placed in plastic
handcuffs and soon released. The highlight was Dinkins' arrest.
"The image of New York's first black mayor being handcuffed by

---

by minority officials and a minority police chief. "By any measure, Prince George's
County police have shot and killed people at rates that exceed those of nearly any
other large police force in the nation. Since 1990, they have shot 122 people, killing
47 of them. By one standard—the number of fatal shootings per officer—they killed
more people than any major city or county police force from 1990 through 2000.
Almost half of those shot were unarmed, and many had committed no crime. Unlike
many departments, Prince George's top police officials concluded that every one of the
shootings was justified. Among the shootings ruled justified: An unarmed construction
worker was shot in the back after he was detained in a fast-food restaurant. An
unarmed suspect died in a fusillade of 66 bullets as he tried to flee from police in a car.
A homeless man was shot when police mistook his portable radio for a gun. And an
unarmed man was killed after he pulled off the road to relieve himself." *Washington
Post* 7/1/01.

Rudy Giuliani's police force was," noted journalist Andrew Kirtz-man, "a searing symbol. After weathering six years of defeat and humiliation, Dinkins finally exacted his revenge."[9]

In the month that followed the killing, the local papers ran more than 600 stories on the shooting, all based on the same paltry set of facts. Giuliani's approval rating dropped by twenty points. With Sharpton's flacks in the press stirring up fear and hatred, a *Daily News* reporter insisted that the cops that killed Diallo had set out to "prey" on black people, while Art Spiegelman did a *New Yorker* cover in which a smiling cop takes target practice at cutouts of civilians. Giuliani confidante and Liberal Party boss Ray Harding complained, "This is a political operation against Rudy, and the core group is made up of the usual cast of characters."[10]

He was right. The protestors at One Police Plaza who came daily to be arrested came from all the left-wing groups Giuliani had upset, ranging from opponents of welfare reform to the Free Mumia movement dedicated to springing a convicted Philadelphia cop-killer from jail. Tom Reppetto, the historian of the NYPD, captured their reasoning: "There are people who are very unhappy that crime has gone down since it undermines their root causes argument for increased social spending."

Some of the anger went beyond the usual suspects. A Democratic City Hall insider complained in the wake of the Diallo tragedy, "I love Rudy's philosophy but I've come to despise him and his bunker mentality." The Diallo affair crystallized legitimate resentments that had been building because of the expansion of police stop-and-frisk efforts. Filmmaker Majora Carter, a resident of the South Bronx, explained that, while she liked "the message the cops were sending to criminals," she "disliked some of the messengers," particularly the special unit cops unfamiliar with her neighborhood, who had hassled her.

There was a problem with New York policing, but it was a matter of policy, not racism. "There is no racism or tolerance of brutality in the NYPD," argued former Police Chief Bratton. "The racism comes from Sharpton." Bratton, author of the administration's early anti-crimes successes, had been forced out of the Giuliani administration in 1996, depriving the city of a Police Commissioner who would have been up to the situation. Bratton had long argued that after street crime had been reduced through broken windows policing, community policing should have been given a bigger role.[11]

The problem, Bratton recognized, was that it's very hard to drive crime below the level a community has set for itself without incurring considerable resentment. One way to keep pushing it down is to establish a better rapport between police and the citizens in order to minimize understandable black ambivalence about anti-crime efforts. Most African-Americans are conservative on crime until their fifteen-year-old nephew gets unfairly arrested. The dilemma is that while fifteen- to twenty-five-year-old minority toughs live in fear of the police, much of the rest of the city lived in fear of those same toughs.

The key to black middle-class anger about New York policing is found in what sociologist Jan Rosenberg described as "the failure of success model." The more the objective conditions for African-Americans improve as they move up the social ladder into integrated situations, she notes, the more opportunities there are for slights, real and perceived. A similar situation is set in motion when broken windows policing radically cuts crime. The more Giuliani's police department tried to reduce crime, the more cops came into contact with innocent people. So as crime went down, fruitless frisks went up and resentments multiplied. Or, as Bill Stephney, a hip-hop record producer put it, "As fear from knuckleheads declines, fear from police pursuing knuckleheads has been rising."*

A better-connected administration, one with a wider range of allies or at least a greater willingness to listen to friendly dissent, might have picked up on such complaints and modified its tactics. But when Bratton left, the primary channel for feedback was closed. His replacement Howard Safir was a highly competent administrator who had integrated civilian complaints about the police into the daily CompStat reports. He had also begun the CPR (Courtesy, Professionalism, Respect) campaign to improve relations with the public, but as Guiliani himself later acknowledged, it wasn't effective. Safir, a stiff and distant man, was even more estranged from the press than his mayor. Isolated at his command headquarters, Safir had a scant feel for the mood of his own force (which strongly disliked his rigid bureaucratic style), let alone public sentiment.

New York Post police reporter Murray Weiss saw the Diallo affair in terms of the over-centralization of power that followed

---

* Jan Rosenberg, the author's wife, is a sociology professor at Long Island University's Brooklyn Campus.

Bratton's departure. In a police department where accountability was the byword, no one, he noted, had lost his job or was demoted for his role in the Diallo affair. "No one is in trouble," a former top official told Weiss, "because everyone views this as being about the mayor. It is not a police hierarchy issue because everything is run by [Giuliani]."[12]

Although his back was up against the wall, Giuliani wasn't yet prepared to fire the loyal Safir and rethink his policies. The mayor dismissed Herman Badillo's suggestion to organize a counter-demonstration of police supporters. Still, he did ask the pollster Frank Luntz to convene a focus group on his handling of the Diallo tragedy. But when Luntz's subjects found Giuliani insufficiently sensitive, the mayor, never much of a politician, roared, "This is a waste of time.... I am not going to give in to the mob mentality. I'd rather not be mayor than do something unprincipled."[13]

The feeding frenzy that had begun with Diallo's death in early February 1999 began to wane in mid-April. But it wouldn't end fully for another fourteen months.

Sharpton, bankrolled by the hospital, communications and municipal workers' unions, blanketed sympathetic neighborhoods with a mailing for a planned mid-April protest. The promotional budget for radio and TV alone was $300,000. The march across the Brooklyn Bridge was backed by dozens of Democratic bigwigs including prospective mayoral candidates Mark Green and Freddy Ferrer. Two top-notch political operatives out of Dinkins' shop, Bill Lynch and Ken Sunshine, who were also part of the Hillary Clinton Senate campaign, were the key organizers. For his part, David Dinkins pumped up the rhetoric. When asked in an interview about the drop in the city's crime, the former mayor answered, "[T]here was no crime in Nazi Germany." But the march, expected to draw 25,000, drew less than 5,000. It was a bust. The anti-Rudy rage had played itself out for the time being.[14]

SEVENTEEN

CUNY and the Genius
of American Life

While the anti-Rudy rage waxed and waned, a new issue emerged to agitate the anti-change activists. "Once," said Giuliani advisor Tony Coles, "the City University of New York had been the escalator that moved the poor up into the middle class." But the school, once known as the "Harvard of the Poor," which numbered among its graduates General Colin Powell and Dr. Jonas Salk, had long been caught in a downward spiral.

CUNY, the city's public university, with dozens of campuses and colleges scattered around the five boros, briefly caught the mayor's attention in 1995 when a protest march in opposition to higher tuition in the midst of the city's fiscal crisis was marked by clashes with the police. Giuliani was taken aback by the placards that misspelled the mayor's name as well as "tuition" and "priority." Responding to the protesters, Giuliani asked, "Do we spend" scarce dollars "on every single young person's performance? Or do we spend it on those who show some ability to be able to function better?" CUNY professor Sandy Cooper replied that Giuliani was pushing the city to the brink. The only choices for New York high school graduates, she insisted, were either CUNY or jail.[1]

But CUNY as an issue then faded for several years until the school's failings unexpectedly came back on to Giuliani's radar screen by way of welfare reform. When the administration tried to move CUNY students on welfare into the workfare program, they met stiff resistance from CUNY Chancellor Ann Reynolds, who insisted vehemently that a work requirement would prevent students from graduating.

But when Giuliani advisor Tony Coles took a look at the graduation rates, he was taken aback by the figures that showed only 1.3 percent of community college students finished their two-year program in two years. At Hostos Community College, it was .05 percent, or one of every 2,000 students. Only 25 percent completed their two-year degrees after six years.

Looking for answers about CUNY, Giuliani turned to Herman Badillo, who had a long and intense relationship with CUNY. A tall ruggedly handsome man, Badillo understood the value of good education. He had been a twelve-year-old orphan in 1940 when he arrived in New York from Caguas, Puerto Rico, unable to speak a word of English. He made it through high school, then worked his way through City College as a short-order cook, graduating magna cum laude. Badillo went on to become a lawyer, finishing first in his class at Brooklyn Law School, a Certified Public Accountant, and a member of Congress.

Nearly thirty years earlier, in the summer of 1969, the young Herman Badillo, then Boro President of the Bronx, pushed the City University to bring more blacks and Hispanics into its fold. As the first Puerto Rican boro president of the Bronx, he had already created Hostos College, New York's first bilingual college, to entice Hispanics into higher education. Badillo wanted to create a California-style tiered system at the City University of New York. One tier of the system could bring in students who had failed to do well in high schools while other tiers would continue to preserve the traditionally high academic standards of the tuition-free City University. But Badillo's carefully laid plans to expand academic opportunity were swept away by the high tide of the 1960s.

Under the influence of the Kerner Commission report on the 1960s riots, which was primarily authored by New York Mayor John Lindsay, older ideas about education as a pathway to upward mobility for individuals were pushed aside by the emerging concept of group rights. The group-rights approach argued it was fundamentally unjust that, in a city where African-Americans and Hispanics were half of all high school students, they should make up only 10 percent of the CUNY student body. Instead, they should immediately be given a proportional share of the university's slots. Students at Badillo's alma mater and CUNY's flagship school, the City College of New York, acting in the name of group rights as racial redress, seized control of the school, briefly renaming it "Malcolm X-Che

Guevara University." They demanded that anyone who graduated from high school be admitted into the university. In a 1999 report commissioned by Badillo, the section entitled "Policy by Riot" described what happened next. In the words of Deputy Chancellor Seymour Hyman:

> I was telling people what I felt when I saw smoke coming out of [the Great Hall at City College], and the only question on my mind was can we save City College? And the only answer was, Hell, let everyone in.[2]

Hyman's solution saved City College by destroying it. Badillo came out against open admissions as a threat to the upward mobility of New York's minority youngsters. But he was told that there would riots if it was blocked.

Forced to admit students unready or unable to do college work, the nine four-year colleges of the City University of New York became heavily remedial institutions. As it became impossible to maintain even a shadow of the old standards for the new students, academic success was redefined. A perverse logic took hold in which the more remediation failed to bring students up to the level necessary to do college work, the more money was poured into remediation and the more college work was defined down. Intellectual achievement was defined as discriminatory and excellence was replaced with the idea of "adequacy." "One of the things that changed" explained Bernard Sohmer, a City College math professor supportive of open admissions, "was that the students said, 'You shouldn't make us do anything we don't want to do.'" In the words of a personnel director who ceased to be interested in CUNY graduates, "after open admissions, it wasn't a college anymore." But one sort of hiring did flourish. CUNY's many remedial programs hired advisors, jobs counselors, teaching coaches, reading and writing specialists, and a host of administrators. Remediation generated its own bureaucracy.[3]

This was bad enough, but the contrary consequences of open admissions flowed down into the high schools creating a unified system of failure. Roughly 60 percent of New York City's high school teachers were CUNY graduates. As CUNY's academic level declined, so did the quality of high school teachers. With college standards sharply lowered, there was less pressure on high school students and teachers to perform. Both were caught in the same downward spiral. The *Daily News* summed it up: "to paraphrase the old cliché, teachers who can teach, do and those who can't were trained at the City University."[4]

But for all its failings, the CUNY administration was in denial. As a member of CUNY's Board of Trustees, Badillo pointed out that in the mid-1990s half of CUNY's education school graduates were failing the none-too-rigorous state teacher certification exam. CUNY administrators responded that those who failed really were good teachers, just poor test takers.

At Hostos, whose president, Isaura Santiago Santiago, had turned the school into a largely monolingual Spanish-speaking institution, only a fifth of the seniors could pass the very basic English writing test required of all graduates. But when failing students protested, the school dropped the requirement that they be able to write in English before they graduated. Hostos Dean Eugenio Barrios explained: "Allowing teachers to assess a student's success from a variety of angles is an advancement forward, rather than a step back or a lowering of standards."[5]

Feeling pressure more from the students than the CUNY trustees, the faculty responded by introducing an even easier test, but the vast majority of Hostos students failed that as well. Badillo wasn't surprised. He had spent a good deal of time at the college talking directly with students who were confused and angry. When Badillo spoke with them, he had to use Spanish, since most of the students couldn't understand English. "What employers will be hiring these kids?" he asked.

The Bronx Democratic Party, which used Hostos, as it used the local school boards, as a source of patronage, was outraged. Bronx Boro President Fernando Ferrer denounced an end to remediation as racist, warning that higher standards meant that vast numbers of minority students would be barred from CUNY.

But with Badillo in the forefront, Giuliani and Pataki worked in tandem to upgrade CUNY. Together they would make Herman Badillo the Chair of the CUNY Board of Trustees.

For all of Badillo's ardor and intelligence, he might not have succeeded if his opponents at CUNY hadn't been so rigidly dogmatic. The academic left, committed to CUNY as a working class college for "people of color," had fused their own identities with the futile programs they defended. Their own sense of virtue challenged, they refused to admit to even minor errors of policy and that allowed Badillo, backed by the *Daily News* and the *New York Post*, to marginalize them.

In presenting his 1998 budget, Giuliani explained his cuts to CUNY: "There comes a point, after fifteen years of tragically plummeting graduation rates and a total evisceration of standards, that somebody has to say: 'This isn't working.'" Then, in an inspired stroke, Giuliani brought in Benno Schmidt, former president of Yale and the Dean of Columbia Law School, to oversee a thorough outside evaluation of CUNY. The Schmidt-directed report, "An Institution Adrift," called for remediation to be confined to the two-year colleges. This created a firestorm, and in late June 1999 Badillo and Schmidt were called on the carpet by the City Council Committee on Higher Education.[6]

The City Council hearing room bristled with hostility. Councilman Steve DiBrienza, famous for screaming at Giuliani administration officials, set the tone. He described one member of the panel that had issued "An Institution Adrift" as "a flack for workfare," and he described another as a "right-wing fanatic" and suggested that the panel's chair, Benno Schmidt, who had left Yale to work for the Edison Corporation (which managed for-profit charter schools), was "a shill for privatization." It got worse. Councilman Bill Perkins, a rising member of Rangel's Harlem machine, opened by denouncing "the racist stereotypes and innuendos that are implied in this report, as well as some of the political agendas that are quite apparent." Then the exchanges became heated:

> *Dr. Schmidt:* There is none of that in this report.
> *Council Member Perkins:* Let me just read a line from the report.
> *Dr. Schmidt:* What is outrageous is for you to suggest there is.
> *Council Member Perkins:* Let me read a line in the report. "We found that being Asian or white was often associated with strong performance, while being black or Hispanic was often associated with weak performance."

After a brief and nasty verbal scuffle between Perkins and Councilman Marty Golden, one of the five Republicans on a council with fifty-one members, the exchange between Perkins and Schmidt continued:

> *Council Member Perkins:* I am waiting for a response.
> *Dr. Schmidt::* You got the response. The response is that it is a fact,

and there is no more important or alarming fact about public education in New York City than the fact that black students and Hispanic students tend to be in public schools that are not raising their academic achievement to appropriate levels. There is no more important civil rights issue than addressing that fact.

The committee chair, CUNY graduate Helen Marshall of Queens, continued Perkins' line of innuendo.

> *Council Member Marshall:* In reading this report, I get a feeling of ethnic cleansing, all right?
> *Dr. Schmidt:* You are wrong.
> *Chairperson Marshall:* Just a minute.
> *Dr. Schmidt:* Look, I am not accusing you or the people who disagree with me of these preposterous and outrageous things-
> *Chairperson Marshall:* Dr. Schmidt, today-
> *Dr. Schmidt:* Do me a favor, will you? I mean, give me a break.
> *Chairperson Marshall:* Today we have to be careful where things are coming from. We have to read between the lines.

Then Herman Badillo jumped in.

> *Mr. Badillo:* Councilwoman Marshall, the public school system is already over 80 percent African-American and Hispanic.
> *Chairperson Marshall:* Yes, I know.
> *Mr. Badillo* That number is going to increase. This cannot be a racist report, because there is no chance that anybody is proposing importing whites from anywhere else. We are talking exactly about an African-American and Hispanic institution, there is no choice. So, therefore, we are talking about improving the situation.

Badillo went on to talk about the importance of leveling up, not down, so that, in Schmidt's words, the system could "raise standards to raise opportunity." Badillo and Schmidt carried the day.

After state approval, the problem of implementing the reforms fell on the shoulders of both CUNY's new chancellor, Mathew Goldstein, who had already raised standards as the president of Baruch College, and Louise Mirrer, his able vice-president for academic affairs. Mirrer understood that CUNY would have to reach down into the city high schools to achieve the goals Badillo and Schmidt had laid out. Under the old CUNY system, students didn't have to think about applying to CUNY in advance, in part because the SATs weren't required. Instead they could decide at the last minute to attend. Mirrer wanted high school students to take CUNY seriously, so she made the SATs an entrance requirement. That sent a message to the high schools. At the same time she dramatically expanded the sort of outreach Badillo had proposed in the pre-open admission days for promising minority high school students. Mirrer credits then-Schools Chancellor Harold Levy with creating "a serious partnership" with CUNY. Its College Now program reached down into the high schools and allowed 50,000 promising but deficient students to enhance their skills before they arrived in college.

The combination of College Now, higher admissions standards based on how students did in the more difficult high school courses, and an honors college all administered by Mirrer raised the quality of the incoming students. Then, once in CUNY, the elimination of remedial classes at the senior colleges and rising junior exams, which prevented weak students from sliding by, along with generally heightened expectations, all increased the level of academic achievement.

In 2003, five years after his "CUNY Adrift" report, Benno Schmidt, by then chair of CUNY's Board of Trustees, delivered a speech entitled "CUNY: The Pride of the City" before the Center for Educational Innovation. He described a much improved institution. Referring to a spiral of improvement in which "academic progress builds on itself," he exulted in both the ability of the honors college to attract top-notch students and a doubling of the gifts the colleges received from alums and others who were increasingly aware of the turnaround.[7]

Despite the elimination of remedial classes at the senior colleges, the racial and ethnic composition of CUNY remained roughly constant. The higher standards attracted not only better but more students even as tuition rose by 25 percent. The headline in the *New York Post*—The City University of New York Is Looking Like 'The Poor Man's Harvard' Again—was a stretch, but the gains were significant. In 1997, only 75 percent of CUNY's education graduates could pass the state's teacher licensing exams. In three years that rose to 90 percent. This was the virtuous circle Giuliani and Badillo had been hoping for.

EIGHTEEN

The Grand Guignol

B y September 1999, First Lady Hillary Clinton had been campaigning for the Senate seat Daniel Patrick Moynihan was vacating for the better part of a year. Yet Giuliani still hadn't made up his mind if he was running. Republican Congressman Rick Lazio of Long Island had made it clear that he was itching to get into the race. But he had to wait for Giuliani's decision.

The mayor wasn't acting like a candidate—or at least not like a conventional candidate. The rules of New York state politics said that if a Republican were going to win statewide, he had to have the support of the small but influential Conservative Party whose core supporters were both Catholic conservatives and conservative Catholics. But Giuliani had kept his distance from the Conservative Party when he ran for mayor and showed little inclination to join them now. Mike Long, the gruff Brooklyn liquor storeowner who ran the Conservative Party, made it clear that he would support Giuliani only if the mayor dropped his support for partial birth abortion and his ties with Ray Harding's Liberal Party. But Giuliani refused on both counts. And with his beloved Yankees headed to the World Series, the mayor, a frequent visitor to the stadium, seemed uninterested in riding the rubber chicken circuit of upstate campaign events.

Nonetheless, in September 1999, events at the traditionally staid Brooklyn Museum, which was partially funded by the city, gave Giuliani his chance to score campaign points with conservative Catholics without the drudgery of a conventional campaign.

The 102-year-old museum, best known for its extraordinary Egyptology collection, had languished during the years of Brooklyn's decline. But the revival of brownstone Brooklyn, which had begun in the late 1970s and accelerated as crime declined in the 1990s, gave the Museum a chance similarly to remake itself. Arnold Lehman, who had angered Catholics in Baltimore with art they found profane, was brought in to give the institution more aggressive leadership.

Lehman in turn looked to Charles Saatchi, the British advertising executive who had helped make Margaret Thatcher prime minister. Saatchi, who had learned how to dissolve the boundaries between art and commerce, was a force in the modern art world. In 1997, the "Sensation" exhibit of transgressive "art" pieces owned by Saatchi helped rescue the financially strapped Royal Academy in London. The show included mannequins of children with penises and vaginas for facial features. There was also a portrait composed of children's handprints depicting "Myra," a woman who had been convicted of the sexual torture and murder of five children. The show was a box office bonanza for the Royal Academy.

Saatchi, explained Bruce Wolmer of *Art and Auction* magazine, "creates his own reality. First he goes around and buys up enough young artists' works to create his own movement. Then he gets the Royal Academy to show it, and then he holds an auction to test out the market on these artworks, donating the proceeds to charity to drive up the prices." Most New York institutions, recognizing the conflict of interest in a show whose full name was "Sensation: Young British Artists from the Saatchi Collection," kept away from the project. Unable to find corporate backers for the show (even Trojan Condoms refused), Lehman financed it with money from art dealers like Christie's which would then be selling the paintings they had helped promote. Asked if he was marketing controversy to sell the $9.75 tickets to "Sensation," the fifty-four-year-old museum chief replied, "We're not denying it."[1]

Proceeding with all the integrity of a World Wrestling Federation promoter, Lehman drew fire from animal rights groups angry about the presentation of chopped-up creature parts preserved in formaldehyde as art. But, as in Baltimore, Lehman struck publicity gold with Catholics.

Chris Ofili's painting of the Virgin Mary splattered with elephant dung drew the intended outrage. (Less noticed were the depictions of vaginas and rectums cut out from porno magazines also attached to the painting's surface.) Lehman banned children under sixteen unless accompanied by an adult and explained, "Some visitors may find the material difficult, even offensive." Jed Perl, writing in the *New Republic*, caught the game: "Once art provoked controversy. Now it seems that controversy can give anything the aura of art. Andres Serrano, Robert Mapplethorpe, and Ofili are nothing without their controversies; that's what gives their work meaning."[2]

Giuliani seized the opportunity to circumvent the Conservative Party. He told reporters, "the city shouldn't have to pay for sick stuff." The issue, he insisted was not the museum's First Amendment rights but taxpayer subsidies. Liberals could barely contain their rage over Giuliani's attack on the First Amendment; attendance at the Brooklyn Museum temporarily skyrocketed, as did Giuliani's standing with conservative Catholics. Margaret O'Brien Steinfels, editor of *Commonweal*, a liberal Catholic magazine, summarized the situation. It was, she said, a win-win for everyone: the museum made money, Catholic and First Amendment activists had a cause, and the press releases for Giuliani's unofficial Senate campaign touted his courageous stand against religious desecration.[3]

The off-Broadway production played on for months. But by March 2002, when each side had achieved its aims, a settlement was quietly reached after the case was brought into court. The court proceedings exposed Lehman's financial manipulations, and the museum agreed to drop its First Amendment lawsuit in return for a restoration of its city funding. The city had been put through the predictable paces. But what won the mayor votes in the Westchester and Long Island suburbs helped create a backlash in the city when the mayor placed a crucial charter reform proposal on the November ballot.

▲ ▲ ▲

With a Rudy vs. Hillary Senate race looming in 2000 and a mayoral election the following year, 1999 was the last year in which Rudy Giuliani and Peter Vallone could achieve the tax and spending reforms New York badly needed. The two men were sometimes vehemently and very publicly at odds as in the fight over moving the Yankees to Manhattan, but they trusted each other and shared the fear that a new round of fiscal follies would follow after they had both been pushed out of office by term limits. Typically, Giuliani, Vallone and their key staffers met privately on Friday mornings to talk things over quietly and work out issues. The gatherings were generally cordial and relatively non-political. In the spring of 1999 they talked with increasing urgency about how to lock in the spending restraints they had achieved through their sometimes prickly personal cooperation.

Vallone feared the free-spending council he had held in check "could go crazy raising taxes." But where the mayor was thinking about amending the city charter to impose fiscal restraint, Vallone opposed the charter change route as restricting the council's institutional powers. With his eyes on the mayoralty, he wanted a package of reforms including lower taxes on business achieved not through a charter referendum, but by legislation from his city council.

The possibility of an agreement was complicated by national politics. In the first term, the extensive cooperation between Mayor Giuliani and President Clinton muted partisan animosities. But a new element, the Senate campaign of the still undeclared Hillary Clinton, increasingly became the unspoken issue clouding the Giuliani-Vallone deliberations. Vallone was under considerable pressure from political consultant Harold Ickes and the national Democrats to give Ms. Clinton as much help as possible. On the speaker's side, as Vallone advisor Bruce Bender described the situation, "You weren't just dealing practically with Rudy on local issues," but with "real Republicans like Peter Powers and Joe Lhota who were carrying water" for the national party. From the mayor's corner, Deputy Mayor Randy Mastro saw the Hillary campaign as "coloring every discussion." It produced, he said, "uniform Democratic opposition to the mayor."

The Friday morning meetings so useful in working out issues grew tense and even ugly. In the end, the failure of Giuliani and Vallone to come to an agreement had long-term consequences for Gotham. Bruce Bender, looking back at the ill-conceived and massive property tax hikes imposed by Giuliani and Vallone's successors in the midst of a recession, commented, "We're living now with the ramifications of their failure to cooperate as they had earlier."

The mayor fatally attempted to impose reform without the speaker's cooperation. The charter commission he had appointed proposed such urgently needed fiscal reforms as holding city spending to the rate of inflation. Typically, Gotham's spending expanded at well over the rate of inflation. Giuliani's charter reforms also called for a rainy day fund and required supermajorities for all tax increases except on the property tax. But the vital matter of fiscal reform barely came to the public's attention. Instead press coverage and public interest, such as it was, locked on to the secondary issue of mayoral succession.*

Vallone was open to changing the rules of succession so that his likely mayoral rival in 2001, Mark Green, who held the post of Public Advocate, wouldn't automatically become mayor if Giuliani left for the Senate. The office of Public Advocate, the mayor and the speaker agreed, had no function other than to serve as a campaign platform and should be abolished. But where Giuliani wanted a charter change requiring a quick election in the event that he left for the Senate, Vallone wanted the office of Public Advocate itself abolished. The speaker worried that an attempt simply to change the rules of succession without abolishing the office would be seen as a personal attack on Mark Green rather than as a principled reform. Vallone was proven right.

Giuliani, his eye on the Senate, was afraid that if Mark Green succeeded him his achievements would be undone. But his attempt to change the rules in midstream through the charter commission he had appointed backfired. It was widely seen as a power grab, and even the Rudy-friendly *Post* compared it to a Bill of Attainder. With the Brooklyn Museum fight going on in the background, the proposed rules change reinforced the Rudyphobes' worst fears of an out-of-control tyrannical mayor. At the first public hearing on the charter changes, a sarcastic Mark Green commented: "I'd like to thank Mayor Giuliani and Chair Mastro for launching an unprovoked, unprincipled and unprecedented attack on the office of Public Advocate."[4]

Forced onto the defensive, Charter Commission chair Randy Mastro insisted, "This isn't about any one man, or any one issue," referring to the 250-page commission report and its fourteen proposals, but to little effect. A private poll done by the mayor found that the charter changes were seen largely as both a personal attack on Green and an extension of the arbitrary policies associated with the mayor's handling of the "Sensation" show. Responding to the

---

*Holding spending close to the rate of inflation was important because, while tax revenues typically tracked the business cycle, spending grew regardless, ratcheted up during each boom, thus creating increases that then had to be paid for in the downturns.

polls, the Giuliani-selected charter commission dropped the succession proposal. But even so, the attack on Mark Green continued to define the charter changes for both the press and the public. As Vallone explained, "Mark Green was widely disliked but Rudy was disliked even more."[5]

The succession proposal wasn't the mayor's only mistake. Holding a charter vote in an off year with no major electoral contests on the ballot was a major blunder. "Off-year elections are dominated," explains political consultant Jerry Skurnick, "by super-prime voters," the hard-core Democrats "who are sure to turn out even when no one else does." For the city as a whole, which was basking in the best of economic times, there was no reason to see fiscal reform as urgent. But for the Democratic base already angry with Giuliani, fiscal reform was a serious threat to their livelihoods.

Giuliani made the case for a rainy day fund and spending restraints in a forty-minute speech that called on the city never to return to the discredited policies of the past: "Every sense that someone has of logic, history, sociology, would say that after the end of this administration the city was going to go back in the other direction."

But Giuliani's wonkish appeal to the city's long-term interests made no sense for an off-year election. The political campaign against the charter reform was led by the newly formed Working Families Party (WFP), a creation of the city's public sector unions. While the WFP was organizing rallies, Mark Green's key aide Richard Schrader was very effectively targeting the super-prime Democrats in twenty key districts. Few were listening to the mayor's policy insights, while radio airwaves were filled with the messages of mayors past. Former mayors Abe Beame, Ed Koch and David Dinkins, each of whom had seriously mismanaged the city's fiscal affairs, cut an ad urging voters to defeat the charter initiatives.[6]

With an opposition coalition composed of Vallone, Green, the unions and the so-called good government groups, most of whom live off the public sector, the outcome was never in doubt. Only 11 percent of the voters turned out on November 2, 1999, and 76 percent voted against the changes. Giuliani quickly and uncharacteristically acknowledged, "I made a mistake in presenting charter revision this year. The vote against it makes it clear that it was a mistake, and I accept responsibility for it and certainly respect the views of the voters." Vallone called the outcome "a severe blow" to Giuliani's Senate aspirations. "He put everything into this," said the speaker. "He hasn't got a chance [in the Senate race] if he gets less than 30 percent in the city." The Democratic Party faithful did nothing to conceal their jubilation; though Giuliani was still leading in the polls, they saw the charter defeat as paving the way to Hillary victory in the Senate race.[7]

NINETEEN

Rehearsal for Terror

I t was December 1999 and Jerry "Hands on Everything" Hauer, director of the city's Office of Emergency Management, was getting ready for the big one, the anticipated Y2K meltdown and Millennium celebration. Hauer, who made things happen "fast, on time, and the way he wants it," was getting ready to step down after being worn out by a seemingly endless series of routine emergencies.[1]

As head of what was not so jokingly known as "The Office of WHAT IF?," the publicity-shy Hauer had been banging up against the sheer density and aging infrastructure of a city whose iconic buildings and bridges made it a tempting target. "Everyone," said Hauer, "thought we were crazy for preparing for terrorism." But he and Giuliani took the threat of more attacks very seriously.

Based on intelligence that emerged from the Blind Sheik's thwarted attack on Gotham's bridges and tunnels and newly developed information, it looked as if either the bombing of the bridges and tunnels and a biological or chemical attack were the most likely threats. Hauer and his staff engaged in "game playing." They tried to put themselves inside the mind of a terrorist planning an attack to anticipate how the city should respond. To make sure they stretched their imaginations as far as possible, Hauer brought in Richard Clarke, then President Clinton's head of counter-intelligence, to lead an intense brainstorming session attended by forty top members of the Giuliani administration. A theme that repeatedly emerged from the various anti-terror briefings and probes was the attackers' fascination with the city's bridges, tunnels and subways, far more than buildings. The World Trade Center was not much discussed by

Hauer's group, because in the years since the 1993 attack cement barriers surrounding the building blocked off a potential car bomb attack and both people and dogs checked each delivery truck. Further, a battalion of security guards searched food deliveries and carefully matched visitors with their picture IDs before they were allowed to board an elevator. Besides, the intelligence suggested that terrorists seemed most interested, among the city's buildings, in the New York Stock Exchange and City Hall. But in all the scenarios of possible threats, no one anticipated an airplane exploding into a skyscraper. Explains Hauer: "We never looked up, [we] never conceived of airplanes used as missiles."[2]

After working eighteen hours a day seven days a week since a July 1999 blackout, Hauer had been six hours into a vacation out at Long Island's Montauk Point—but still in constant touch with the command center—when reports of the covers blowing off manholes in upper Manhattan's Washington Heights made him realize that Con Ed was mishandling the power problems created by a brutal heat wave. Hauer remembered that a similar heat wave in 1995 had killed 525 people in Chicago, and he worried that a blackout in upper Manhattan could trigger a rerun of the 1993 drug runners' riot in Washington Heights.

Giuliani was on his way to Massachusetts; they both turned back. As Hauer returned to the city, Spike Lee's *Summer of Sam* was in the theaters, reminding the city of the terrible summer of 1977 when a blackout produced mass looting and massive despair over the city's future.

This time was different. Although 300,000 people were without power, Washington Heights stayed calm while urgent appeals by the mayor to reduce power use averted a Brooklyn-wide blackout. The power was out in sections of Washington Heights for a week, but police and fireman directed traffic where the signals were out and received widespread cooperation from the Dominican population. The city's preparation and the cooperation of citizens held the death toll from overheating to just two elderly people.

Giuliani barely slept during the crisis. Hauer describes how on the first night he took a ninety-minute rest at 4 a.m. But Giuliani, Hauer noted, "just kept going."

But so did the crises. Because Hauer and Neil Cohen of the Department of Health, described by Giuliani as an "unsung hero," had developed a syndromic surveillance system, the Office of Emergency Management discovered the West Nile virus very early. In late August, a Queens hospital spotted the first case in the U.S. of the pathogen that came to be known as the West Nile virus. The reporting system Hauer had set up to deal with a biological or chemical attack worked to perfection.

The city was ready to respond. The potentially deadly encephalitis virus was spread by mosquitoes. As more cases were reported, the city moved decisively to spray its parks with the pesticide malathion. The city made mosquito repellent available free at nursing homes, precinct houses and fire stations. Some of the spraying was done by truck and helicopter. Nighttime helicopter spraying was accompanied by warnings to stay indoors when the choppers came overhead. The warning produced a paranoid reaction from some New Yorkers. Normally sensible people talked about how they were under a state of siege, forced to run at the sound of the copters.

Wild rumors were spread about how the fascist Giuliani and his sidekick Jerry "Strangelove" Hauer were poisoning the people. The health department sent out a small army of people to educate the city, but the *New Yorker* ran an article entitled "West Nile Mystery" by Richard Preston suggesting that the virus was probably part of a biological attack by Saddam Hussein. When the worst was over, there were only four confirmed deaths. As the disease spread to forty-six other states, Hauer and Giuliani were widely praised for a model effort.[3]

Ever since the July blackout, Hauer had been forced to live on two tracks. One track was the relentless pressure to prepare the city in case Y2K problems produced havoc as the computers that ran the city's vital services failed. The other was on whatever new crisis emerged.*

With a subway strike set for just two weeks before the Millennium, Hauer drew up elaborate contingency plans to bring in buses from all around the Northeast and boats from Boston and Baltimore. As the union or individual transit workers engaged in minor

---

*There was always something. To offer just one example: There are usually about 600 water main breaks a year along the city's 6,048 miles of pipes. In the past they had taken months to repair. In mid-November a major water main break on Broadway near City Hall spewed rocks, sand and torrents of water. Worse yet, it threatened to topple a fifteen-story construction crane. Three buildings had to be evacuated; subway service was ended along Broadway's N and R lines. But in just a few days the repairs were made and the city was back to what passed for normal.

acts of sabotage, Police Commissioner Safir was forced to assign an additional 2,000 cops to the subways. But Giuliani's reputation, and his tough talk to transit workers primed for a walkout by the rise of a militant caucus, averted a shutdown.

Hauer told friends that he was burned out. The job was tough enough, but, as one insider put it, Police Commissioner Safir "did everything he could to make Hauer's life miserable." Safir, a former fire commissioner, had left that post with a sour taste in his mouth. He once famously quipped that the FDNY was "an organization with 150 years of tradition and no progress." He wanted the NYPD to run everything, even though, Hauer noted, "that would have guaranteed an endless battle of the badges."[4]

A senior official at a city agency explained the lack of cooperation between Police and Fire as "just a PD inherent thing.... If you're not cops we're not going to tell you, no matter who's running O.E.M. That's just the cop mentality." But that mentality meant that the police refused to use "inter-operable radios" that allowed police and fire to talk to each other in an emergency. That had been a problem during the 1993 World Trade Center attack and it would be a problem again.[5]*

Hauer announced plans to step down after the New Year. First he had to get the city through the Y2K scare and the Millennium celebration at a time of rising fears about terrorism. The early Y2K speculation centered on planes falling from the skies, elevators crashing down sixty stories and a financial panic. But as the date approached and the wilder fears had been discounted, the Y2K preparations were divided into two areas. The first, led by Brian Cohen of the city's Year 2000 Project Office, had spent three years and $400 million pushing city agencies to patch their computer software originally programmed to express dates in two digits to accommodate the four digits of the year 2000. The second "What if?" was terror.

On December 8, Hauer, operating out of his World Trade Center headquarters, organized a real-time run-through for a crisis. If it

---

*Fire Commissioner Thomas Von Essen was more cooperative on inter-operable radios. He adopted them, but then backed off when firefighters complained about the technical inadequacies of the model the city had purchased, which worked poorly within buildings, where firefighters needed their radios most.

were Broadway, they would have called it a dress rehearsal. "Everyone," said a top official, "has to be prepared for the worst, and has to have a fallback position." "We expect this real-time drill to be far more stressful than New Year's Eve," Hauer warned. "It's going to have a lot of scenarios we don't think will happen."[6]

Hauer organized numerous drills and tabletop scenarios, which Giuliani usually attended and in which the first responders, hospitals and even non-emergency services could play through a variety of scenarios. One of the first drills was a mock attempt to respond to a Sarin gas attack of the sort that had already occurred in the Tokyo subways. The simulation was a mock attack on a rally being held at the base of the World Trade Center with a thousand injured. There was considerable study, planning, and preparation. It was like a good football team, explained Deputy Mayor Joe Lhota: "You drilled and prepared over and over so that when the trouble comes you don't have to consult a manual or think things through again, you can react instinctively." If any city was ready for trouble it was New York.

In late October, Egypt Air Flight 990 crashed into the sea just after taking off from Kennedy airport. Was it terrorism? Two weeks later Diana Dean, an alert customs agent in Port Angeles, spotted a suspicious car and driver arriving on the ferry from Victoria, B. C., in Canada. The man turned out to be Ahmed Ressam, who was associated with an Algerian terrorist group. His car's trunk was loaded with powdery explosives for blowing up either Seattle's Space Needle or LAX airport. Shortly after the arrest, an Algerian man associated with Ressam was caught trying to enter Vermont with a fake Canadian passport.* The Seattle arrest had direct implications for New York. Ressam's phone calls were traced by the FBI's Paul O'Neill, a close friend of Hauer's, to a building on Newkirk Avenue

_____

*Seattle had been shaken a few weeks earlier by another manifestation of globalization, the violent anti-World Trade Organizations protests that had been poorly handled by the police. An editorial from the very liberal *Seattle Times*, rarely know to have sympathized with the police, complained that Mayor Paul "Schell endorsed a strategy that essentially put the protesters and the WTO on an equal footing." Shaken by the demonstrations and then the terror threat, Schell called off the city's New Year's celebrations. Asked about Seattle's decision, Giuliani responded, "If you probably tried to cancel it, instead of two million people showing up, four million people would show up." *New York Post* 12/2/99; Murray Weiss, *The Man Who Warned America: The Life and Death of John O'Neill, The FBI's Embattled Counterterror Warrior*, New York: Regan Books, 2003: 256-61.

in a Pakistani section of Brooklyn near Coney Island Avenue. On the last day of the year, the anti-terrorist task force closed in and arrested Ressam's Brooklyn accomplice. Giuliani had no intention of calling off the Times Square New Year's Eve celebration despite a statement by former FBI regional director James Kallstrom that, "I, personally, wouldn't go to any event in Times Square. If there is a strike, it will be in a large gathering." An angry Giuliani responded that there was no guarantee of absolute safety, but that the city was doing its utmost to guard against an attack.

As New Year's Eve approached, nervous New Yorkers made runs on flashlights, canned food, bottled water and propane stoves. But in case they didn't prepare or if they had to evacuate, Hauer's office had 50,000 ready-to-heat beef dinners stowed away, plus an additional 5,000 cots for shelters. Hospitals had long been prepared to identify the symptoms associated with a biological or chemical attack and they were ready to begin decontamination procedures. Brian Cohen, in charge of Y2K preparation, had a vast stockpile of spare parts and ready response teams set aside for emergency computer repairs if they were needed.

The Police Department's plan for Times Square on New Year's Eve was three years in the making. It included flooding the area with 7,000 uniformed cops, seven hundred supervisors and three hundred plainclothes officers, as well as bomb-sniffing dogs, roof top and helicopter surveillance and high tech bomb disposal units. The assigned officers were given special training to identify suspicious people as they moved through tightly controlled corridors in and out of Times Square. In the rest of the city, virtually the entire force was on patrol, including two hundred cops assigned to walking the subway tracks in search of suspicious objects.

"Climbing to the top of the scaffolding in Times Square to drop the ball making the new year was," says Giuliani, "one of the few times I genuinely feared for my life." While Giuliani and Safir were in Times Square overseeing the two and a half million revelers waiting for the ball to drop, Hauer and Deputy Mayor Joe Lhota were in the World Trade Center command post accompanied by three hundred crisis managers from city departments, Con Edison, Verizon, the Red Cross, the Coast Guard, the Federal Emergency Management Agency, the FBI and the National Guard. And although the public didn't know it, the National Guard had been quietly prepositioning in Brooklyn as part of an emergency plan for evacuating Manhattan.

All the work added up to an anti-climax. The celebration went off without a hitch. The city's computers, which had been tested repeatedly, continued to work in the year 2000. There were no major incidents in Times Square or anywhere else. When the revelry had ended in the wee hours, Giuliani joined Hauer and Lhota and the other crisis managers in the command center to lean back, light up stogies and celebrate. They and the city had passed the test. Gotham was ready for a future emergency.

TWENTY

The Best of Times/
The Worst of Times

As the new Millennium arrived, Gotham was giving birth to new industries while once dying neighborhoods were coming back to life. But for Giuliani, as a politician and a man, 2000 would prove to be the worst of years. Anger over police practices was intensified by a new and badly handled incident that sent his popularity plummeting. At about the same time, his personal life came apart with the very public end of his second marriage. Meanwhile, the discovery that he was suffering from prostate cancer led to his withdrawal from a Senate race that he had never fully entered.

The year began with the mayor, fresh from his Y2K/terror scare triumph, standing in front of a huge panoramic picture of a packed Times Square on New Year's Eve, delivering his State of the City address. Politically, the speech was both a long goodbye to the Giuliani mayoralty and the kickoff for his "undeclared United States Senate campaign."[1]

The speech opened with the mayor first holding up the 1990 *Time* magazine cover with the blazing headline: THE ROTTING OF THE BIG APPLE. Then, to encapsulate his accomplishments, he held up the current issue of *Time* showing Times Square packed with happy revelers. "It's a lot better cover," he smiled to a round of applause.

"This could be," he began referring to his prospective campaign for the Senate, "my last State of the City speech..., it might not be my last State of the City speech. We don't know—but it could be. So today," he went on picking up the themes that had been obscured in his mishandled fight for charter reform, "I'd like to discuss with you the ideas behind the changes in the City. We need to understand those changes and the ideas behind them. Otherwise, there's no question in my mind that the City will go back to the way it was to the policies that produce predictable failure."

But it took another forty-five minutes of a ninety-minute speech, delivered in whole paragraphs without notes, before Giuliani discussed the ideas he had referred to. "America soars," he explained, "when we have the genius of America working for the poorest people in America. One of the tragedies of New York, and of American urban areas, is that we actually blocked the genius of America from working for the poorest people in America."

The key to pulling people out of poverty, he argued, was the economic opportunity that derives from vigorous economic growth. He boasted that in 1999 New York had almost doubled the national rate of job growth. Praising the affordable Nehemiah homes built by the East Brooklyn Congregations, he lamented that only 30 percent of New Yorkers owned their own home compared to 50 percent in most cities and 66 percent nationwide. To increase New York's rate of minority home-ownership, the city, he announced, would create building incentives in three outer-boro minority neighborhoods, Ocean Hill-Brownsville, Morrissania, and East Harlem.

When Giuliani had finished speaking and began to leave the stage, he was called back by Peter Vallone who had shouted out, "You don't want to mention the tax cuts?" Giuliani responded "Yes, I do want to mention the tax cuts" which had made the over-burdened city more economically appealing. "So far," he continued, "together, we've done $2.2 billion as a partnership. We believe that over the next four years we should do another $2 billion in tax cuts."[2]

▲ ▲ ▲

At the end of 1994 the Dow Jones average was at 3,834. But by the end of 1996 the combination of a Republican Congress and a Democratic president helped nearly double the market to 6,448. The country had been out of the recession for nearly four years, but only then did the city that prides itself on being smarter than the rest of America emerge from the doldrums. By the end of 1997, the city had grown 1.1 percent over the previous three years compared to a national growth rate of 2.7 percent. Then things took off. On the last day of December 1998, the Dow was at 9,181 and it nearly reached 11,000 by the end of 2000—a climb of more than 6000 points since 1994. The federal treasury's increasing dependence on the revenues that flowed from the stock boom meant that quietly, without the issue ever being discussed, power was flowing back to New York from Washington.

Driven by the stock market, which nearly tripled between 1994 and 2000, Gotham's job growth was the fastest since 1951 as private-sector jobs increased by a record 84,000. By the end of 1998 the city had recovered all the private-sector jobs that had been lost in the Dinkins recession. By the end of 1999, after a 9 percent increase in employment since 1993, more New Yorkers were employed that at any time since before Lindsay induced the 1975 fiscal crisis. Public-sector jobs dropped slightly although the city's non-profit sector, which was politically aligned with the public sector, continued to grow. Fifty-four percent of New Yorkers considered themselves part of the labor force, still well below the national average of 64 percent but the highest percentage since the Bureau of Labor Statistics began calculating labor force participation in 1978.

Population in a democracy is a marker of both power and pride, a sort of civic scorecard. New York was one of the big winners in the 2000 census count. Thanks to immigration, the once-dying city grew in the 1990s by 456,000 people to surpass eight million for the first time, despite the loss of more than 250,000 white residents in the same decade.

Immigrants, largely from Asia and Latin America, with their entrepreneurial energy, represented 40 percent of the population as whites declined to 35 percent. The change was least visible in Manhattan where the rush of white commuters gives an appearance at odds with the outer boros. The new immigration transformed neighborhoods as Koreans placed their stamp on Flushing in Queens, Mexicans on East Harlem, and Eastern Europeans on the Belmont section of the Bronx.*

▲ ▲ ▲

The combination of crime reduction, population growth, strong mayoral leadership and the stock market boom coincided with the

---

*The newer immigrants—a hodgepodge of Koreans, Vietnamese, Chinese, Filipinos, Pakistanis and Indians from Asia; Romanians, Russians, Ukrainians and others from the former Soviet Bloc as well as Lebanese and Egyptians—all arrived in numbers too small to achieve gains through politics. Only the Dominicans among the new arrivals could think of moving up, as had the Irish, Puerto Ricans and African-American before them, though winning office. Dominicans were also the one group experiencing severe downward mobility.

end of the transition out of a manufacturing economy. Together these trends were reshaping the city. Thanks not only to Giuliani but to the Nehemiah housing program, the New York City Partnership and the Community Preservation Corporation, home-ownership rates, which change only slowly, grew from 28 to 33 percent, still half that of the nation at large, but a big step forward for the long-term stability of the city. The Harlem and outer-boro housing markets, which had collapsed in the 1970s, were finally restored so that, as private developer Richard Richman explained, "there are now functioning housing markets in virtually every nook and cranny of the city."

If, as Jane Jacobs has argued, healthy cities are places where old buildings are put to new uses, the mid- to late-1990s New York saw recycling on a grand scale. New York's burgeoning software industry, Silicon Alley, found space in the aging and underused office buildings of lower Manhattan. The thick, sturdy floors, high ceilings, abundant electrical power and easy access to fiber-optic cables that have been laid along the old water lines close to the grand old buildings all made the area ideal for tech firms. In the Garment District, sweatshops morphed into internet incubators and Lower East Side tenements became million-dollar work/live lofts. The upper stories of the Woolworth Building, the famed turn-of-the-twentieth-century "Cathedral of Commerce," were converted into condominiums.

Outer-boro neighborhoods like Mott Haven, St. George, Williamsburg, Fort Greene, East New York and Coney Island were also reviving. In the city's ten poorest neighborhoods, the median price of a single-family home grew by 37 percent in the course of the late 1990s, four times the rate of increase in the ten wealthiest neighborhoods. In East New York and Mott Haven, two of the city's ten poorest neighborhoods, median income grew by 39 and 47 percent during the same period. New York as a whole hadn't been so healthy in a half century.[4]

With Brooklyn and Lower Manhattan intertwined by the best mass transit connections anywhere in the county, "The restoration of the Brooklyn brownstone belt," explained Carl Weisbrod of the Downtown Alliance, "was a crucial element in the revival of Lower Manhattan. Just as at the turn of the twentieth century, Brooklyn's tony neighborhoods were once again filled with "location decision-makers, senior managers in investment banks, partners in law firms, and bank executives."

A whole new Brooklyn neighborhood called Dumbo (Down Under the Manhattan Bridge Overpass) emerged, signalling new possibilities for the once declining boro. Dumbo was largely the creation of one man, David Walentas, who began acquiring property in the 1970s when the area was filled with abandoned buildings. But in the 1990s it became one of the prime sites along the Brooklyn littoral for Silicon Alley companies that had crossed the river. Next to Dumbo, the nearly moribund Brooklyn Navy Yard was brought back to life by Giuliani appointee Marc Rosenbaum, who enticed a variety of new companies, including movie production facilities, into the historic and previously all-but-abandoned facility.

Next door to the Navy Yard was Fort Greene. In the 1990s as crime receded, it blossomed as an integrated district defined, in part, by a number of independently owned African-themed boutiques, stores and restaurants. The adjacent BAM (Brooklyn Academy of Music) cultural district benefited from over-heated Manhattan rents that sent a stream of nonprofits, including the Mark Morris Dance Company, into the "outer" boro. Brooklyn had become hip. Brooklyn, said urbanist Joel Kotkin, has "become the exciting urban experience people once went to Manhattan for before it became too expensive and too filled with chain-store retailers."

North of Canal Street in Manhattan, the traditional boundary between downtown and what was once the machine tool and loft manufacturing district of SoHo was effaced. In the 1970s local artists augmented by arrivals from the Rhode Island School of Design and the Chicago Institute of Art remade SoHo. In the 1990s, young software executives, fledgling investment bankers, and anyone else who could afford to live in a hip area within walking distance of Wall Street largely displaced the artists who moved to Williamsburg in Brooklyn.

While "hip" young bankers were moving south to "funky" designer lofts and chic shopping, parts of Wall Street were migrating north to Times Square. In the new Times Square, noted Tom Wolfe, "out-of-town financial types must be perplexed to find the mighty Morgan Stanley shank-to-flank with a pink-neon girlie bar called Runway 69."[4]

In the new Times Square, Wall Street firms and the giants of information and infotainment—ABC, ESPN, Reuters, Condé Nast, Time-Warner, Viacom, NBC, Bertelsmann A.G., Bloomberg L.O.— were located side by side with KMPG, and Deloitte Touche. New

York, glowed Mitchell Moss of New York University, "was the capital of the information age...companies that now define our economy."[5]

For all the positive change, probably the best indicator of the city's revival was the feel of street life. Cities, noted Milwaukee's innovative Mayor John Norquist, offer the pleasures of public life unavailable in suburbs where "life is filtered through a two-screen experience—the TV and the windshield." One sign of the change came on Kings Highway in Brooklyn. An elderly lady waiting at a bus stop watched as a group of young teens were throwing pebbles at passing cars. The lady turned to the kids and said, "You better stop that or Rudy is going to get you." The boys, startled for a moment, thought about it, dropped their pebbles and walked away.

▲ ▲ ▲

When Mayor Giuliani stood in front of the huge blow-up of Times Square to deliver his 2000 State of the City speech, New York was without a School Chancellor. In his speech Giuliani spoke of a "school system today" that "protects jobs before it educates children. It's essentially a job protection system." He proposed, in addition to his usual suggestion for giving the mayor direct control of the schools, a position strongly backed by Peter Vallone: merit pay for teachers so that "the teachers who do a great job" aren't "paid the same as the teachers who do a bad job." Throwing caution to the winds, he argued that there should be not only merit pay, but an end to tenure for teachers as well. He noted with some anger that if a "teacher commits a crime, it takes years to remove him or her. Commits a crime! That's job protection at its worst, and we have to have the courage to reverse it."

If that weren't enough to stir the fires, he came out strongly in support of school vouchers so that public money would follow the pupils rather than the other way around. In making his case, he referred to Milwaukee Mayor John Norquist's voucher program that was raising student scores. If vouchers "don't improve the education of children, then we'll move on to something else. That's what an innovative, creative society does. It embraces new ideas."

Giuliani had thrown down the gauntlet, and the city held its breath. But the sparks he had thrown out never ignited the debate New York needed to pick a new school chancellor. The past chancellor, Rudy Crew, who had until recently had been a Giuliani ally, had been forced out by the mayor in December 1999 following a series of minor scandals and, more significantly, his opposition to Giuliani's plans for school vouchers.

Crew, appointed in 1995, had been the longest serving chancellor since 1983, but test scores had barely improved on his watch. Worse yet, despite efforts to root out patronage and corruption, School Inspector Edward Stancik, a Javert of a man, uncovered widespread teacher involvement in doctoring test scores. The response from the teachers' union was to attack Stancik as another Kenneth Starr pruriently looking into people's private lives.

Displacing Crew, an African-American, had the potential of turning into a racial firestorm. (And Chancellor Crew, anticipating Giuliani's response to his limited achievements, had been meeting with Al Sharpton.) Crew's de facto firing also risked angering the powerful teachers' union with which Crew had been closely aligned. The teachers had remained neutral in the 1993 and 1997 campaigns, but it was clear that in the upcoming Senate race they would support Hillary Clinton.

Robert Kiley, who had turned the Metropolitan Transit Authority around in the 1980s, was the big business choice for a new School Chancellor. But he was narrowly passed over. In mid-February 2000, the Board of Education chose Harold Levy, an IBM lawyer and the choice of Assembly Speaker Shelly Silver and the United Federation of Teachers. Levy, a conventional liberal, who was on record as saying that the chief problem with the schools was a lack of money, had to be pushed into accepting higher standards for CUNY. Levy was white; his recent predecessors had been Hispanic and black. For the moment the interests of the teachers trumped the usual game of racial politics, but not for long.

▲ ▲ ▲

Racial tensions were rising during the trial of the four officers who killed Amadou Diallo when the major Democratic presidential candidates, Vice President Al Gore and former senator and Knick Bill Bradley, came to Harlem's famed Apollo Theater on 125th Street for a debate. If the candidates wanted to strike a positive note, there was plenty to talk about. Nationally, African-American home ownership had reached record levels during the Clinton administration and for the first time since the 1950s black income was rising at a faster rate than white income. In New York, the average income of a black household residing in Queens had surpassed that of whites. The candidates had only to look around 125th Street to see the changes. Mainstream companies and middle-class professionals were moving into Harlem as never before. Duane Reade, Rite Aid, Pathmark, Blockbuster Video, Starbucks and Sterling Optical had set up shop with major retail complexes and multiplex movie houses on the way.

Had the national journalists covering the event done their homework, they would have known that the famed Apollo nearly went bankrupt the previous year while under the control of old-time liberal Congressman Charles Rangel. The publicly owned theater had generated a great deal of money for Rangel's cronies but very little for itself. The fact that the theater had revived after control was wrested from Rangel was a symbol for Harlem and black America more generally.

But the presidential primary debate was held under the auspices of Rangel and Sharpton, the very men who had done their best to retard Harlem's revival with their relentless focus on resentments and their own "claim" to the neighborhood. "Auspices" may not be the right world. Gore had come because Sharpton had threatened him with protests if he didn't comply with the Reverend's wishes. This could have been Gore's Sister Souljah moment. Gore, who had quite rightly criticized George Bush for kowtowing to "Confederate flag waving" white racism in South Carolina, decided to capitulate to black racism in New York.[6]

The Gore/Bradley debate degenerated into a pander fest. Both candidates went out of their way to denounce supposed "racial profiling" by the NYPD. No proof was necessary nor was any available since there was no credible evidence that the NYPD did any such thing.

Four days later the verdict in the trial of the cops who had killed Diallo was announced in Albany, where the case had been moved to get a jury that hadn't been inundated with press reports on the case. The Bronx District Attorney had over-charged the police with intentional murder so that acquittal on all counts was as predictable as the outcry that followed. The Reverend Calvin Butts, a Pataki ally, spoke of the "evil that permeates City Hall," and even the usually cautious Reverend Floyd Flake, a one-time Giuliani ally, denounced the mayor as a "megalomaniac and a paranoid schizophrenic." Others weren't so kind.[7]

The game was on. Less than a week later, on March 1, when a heroin dealer was killed in a struggle with a cop, the racial racketeers and the press had a new "victim." The Malcolm Ferguson killing, only a few blocks away from where Diallo had died in the Soundview section of the Bronx, set off a small-scale riot as two hundred local residents threw bottles and bricks at the police. Ferguson, who had been arrested nine times on drug and burglary charges, was one of only two protesters arrested a few days earlier in a violent demonstration occasioned by the Diallo verdict. Louis Rivera, the officer in the struggle with Ferguson, had a distinguished record and had never fired his gun before. The police found six cellophane-wrapped packages of heroin rolled into the waistband of a pair of sweatpants Ferguson wore under his jeans. Nonetheless, the local CBS and NBC television affiliates turned Ferguson into a martyr to Giuliani's police state.

There was no case. In June the Bronx District Attorney's office found that "on balance, the evidence supports Police Officer Louis Rivera's statement that the death of Malcolm Ferguson occurred accidentally, in the course of a struggle. Accordingly, the Bronx District Attorney's criminal investigation is now closed."[8]

But tensions were inflamed, and the worst was yet to come. On March 16th aggressive policing intersected with an innocent man, producing tragic results. An undercover cop on narcotics patrol approached twenty-six-year-old Patrick Dorismond, an off-duty security guard, in the drug-trafficking area not far from the Port Authority Bus Terminal. In an attempted sting, the officer asked if Dorismond was interested in buying crack. Dorismond got angry and was reputed to have said, "What are you doing asking me for that shit?" A fight broke out and during the struggle Dorismond was killed.

The angry surface of Giuliani's public persona was usually a mask for calculated political judgments. But the Dorismond case was different. Giuliani initially called for calm until all the evidence was in. But whether under the strain of the Diallo and Ferguson cases or the tension from his own dissolving marriage, he ignored his own counsel and soon released Dorismond's scant juvenile arrest record. Challenged, he said that a dead man can't be libeled. This was a clear violation of both city rules and elementary fairness. Appalled, even his allies at the *New York Post* came down hard on the mayor. The Reverend Butts threatened riots. He compared the death of Dorismond to a "lynching." Then, saying he feared a repeat of the urban unrest of the 1960s, he explained that "Every urban rebellion, every riot, whether in Newark, New Jersey, or Harlem, New York, was started because of police violence and misconduct."[9]

The man who had saved New York City saw his job-approval rating drop to 32 percent. And for the first time, he fell narrowly behind Hillary Clinton in their hypothetical match up for the Senate. Candidate Clinton, who had run a very restrained campaign, sensed an opening and tore into Giuliani, who responded in kind. It looked as if the Senate fight was truly joined. But it wasn't.

Pundit and polls alike were puzzled by Giuliani's lukewarm approach to a Senate race that had much of the country abuzz. He seemed to want the job but only if that meant he didn't have to miss too many Yankee games or campaign too often in the frigid areas of upstate. One source of the ambivalence became clear when on April 26 he announced on television that he had prostate cancer. The mayor spoke of how he was considering different treatments but said that he was still a candidate for the Senate. As the press conference was winding down, he was asked if his cancer might mellow him. "No way," he replied, a half smile on his face.

Giuliani's marriage had been dissolving for years. Friendly politicians who visited the mayor at Gracie Mansion would, as early as 1996, speak in hushed tones of the frosty relations between the mayor and his second wife, TV anchor Donna Hanover. Some of their musings made it into the tabloid gossip pages, which lit up when Hanover accepted a role in *The Vagina Monologues*.

On May 10, two and half weeks after the announcement about his cancer, Giuliani went public with what the gossip world already knew. His marriage to Donna Hanover was over. For nearly a year, Giuliani had been keeping increasingly public company with Judith Nathan, a forty-five-year-old divorcee with one child, whom he would eventually marry. Hanover learned on TV that the marriage had fully ended. Furious, she went before the cameras herself to allege that Giuliani had ruined their marriage with two affairs, one of them with his former press secretary.

The mayor's critics saw the obvious hypocrisy of a man who "had been the scourge of illicit pleasures" being forced to confess to his own. "Usually quick to assign blame," wrote Elizabeth Kolbert in the *New Yorker*, "he has, on the subject of his own marital difficulties, been magnanimous to a fault," refusing to assign blame and musing about "who knows why these things happen." Giuliani quietly moved out of Gracie Mansion and into the spare bedroom of an apartment of a gay couple with whom he was friends. The fallout might have been far more severe if it hadn't played out against the larger backdrop of the Monica Lewinsky affair and Hillary Clinton's run for the Senate.[10]

On May 19, 2000, Giuliani announced, "This is not the right time for me to run for office" at a hastily convened press conference in the City Council hearing room. He insisted that his marital breakup had little to do with the decision, which he insisted was strictly a matter of his health. "I've decided that what I should do is to put my health first, and that I should devote the focus and attention…to being able to figure out the best treatment and not run for office."[11]

The press was given a very different, very sentimental Giuliani. "The reason I'm such a fortunate man is that I have people that love me and I love them and they care for me and I care for them." This was an apparent reference to Judy Nathan. A day later he told Tim Russert of NBC news, "I tend to think that love is more important than I thought it was."*

Giuliani, who had preached strength and self-discipline, had been humbled not only by disease but also by his own personal disorder. A lame duck, who had flaunted his affair and publicly humiliated his wife, Giuliani, it was widely assumed, would have to change his political ways. And for the moment, there was a great deal of talk of a kinder, gentler Giuliani.

▲ ▲ ▲

The Senate race that followed between Hillary Clinton, and the little-known Republican congressman from Long Island, Rick Lazio, was anti-climactic. Her brilliant campaign, which focused on paying attention to the neglected voters of upstate's Western tier, produced a crushing victory. But then again there was something disingenuous about the earlier claim that the Rudy match would be the great struggle of Right and Left. Both had been defined by their enemies as far more extreme than their actual policy positions. Their

---

*Giuliani credited his paramour, Judith Nathan, a trained nurse, with helping him choose his course of treatment, radioactive seed implantation, rather than surgery. It proved successful.

symbolic images diverged far more than their substantive stances on issues such as welfare reform and policing where, as befitting Bill Clinton's centrist presidency, they were in substantial agreement. Once in the Senate, Hillary Clinton backed Giuliani's call to abolish the Board of Education.

The mayor's withdrawal began to temper the anti-Giuliani frenzy. It obviated the organized campaign to undermine him that had begun even before the Diallo affair with Hillary's entrance into the contest. The animus was further tempered by his personal troubles and talk of a "new Rudy."

But just as important, when the city's African and Haitian livery cab drivers were subjected to a wave of murders followed by the vicious mass murder of minority workers at a Wendy's, there were second-thoughts about the anti-Rudy animus. The bloodshed reminded the city that, while the emergency might be over, there was no such thing as a tipping point, a natural process, which produced a self-sustaining collapse in crime. A better metaphor for a city in which there are 650,000 single-parent, generally fatherless families with at least one child under eighteen, is a pressure cooker. The police are crucial for keeping the lid on it. But it was only after the June 11, 2000 Puerto Rican Parade that many grasped what they stood to lose if the lid were removed.

That Sunday, what began as friendly-flirty boy-girl rough-housing in Central Park near the parade route turned into a wave of fifty or more sexual assaults. "This is better than Disneyland," shouted a "youth" caught on one of the amateur videotapes the TV stations played over and over. There, visible on the videos of women besieged, were the "gregarious youths" the police had been accused of harassing. The same "youths" the *New York Times* had portrayed as victims of Giuliani's attempt to "mindlessly impose the mores of Mayberry" were, in a most un-PC manner, harassing upper-middle-class women in Central Park, and right across from the Plaza! There are limits to multiculturalism. The wilding was part of a weekend of murder and mayhem in which three were killed and fifty-nine assaulted with knives or guns; there was also a bias attack against Orthodox kids on the Coney Island Boardwalk.[12]

Suddenly the idea of a kinder, gentler Rudy didn't seem so appealing.

Newsday, which had been flaying the police for months, captured the change of mood. "Has Giuliani given up on keeping order?

It's over. Suddenly Mayor Rudolph Giuliani sounds like a tired and defensive guy forced to wrestle with a city of ingrates." The fear was that the mayor who had kept the city's enemies at bay for nearly seven years was now more preoccupied with personal than public issues.[13]

But whatever changes he had gone through, the core of his public persona remained unchanged. Giuliani went on to reassert his authority and that of the police. By November 2000, Giuliani's poll numbers stood at 55 percent approval, 37 percent disapproval—his highest rating, according to the Quinnipiac poll, since November 1998 prior to the start of the Senate race and the Diallo killing.*

---

*For all of Giuliani's personal troubles, the revival of cities in general and New York in particular played an important role in the 2000 presidential election. In the 1992 and 1996 elections, the big cities had generally been shunned by the candidates. But 2000 was different. The reform currents in American life, namely school, welfare and crime reform, were coming out of City Halls. Gore took pains to wrap himself in the mantle of Democratic mayors such as Wellington Webb of Denver, Dennis Archer of Detroit and Ed Rendell of Philadelphia. When Texas Governor George W. Bush described himself as a "compassionate conservative," he was following in the path of Richard Riordan, Los Angeles's Republican mayor, who called himself a "bleeding-heart conservative." In a period before we realized we were at war with 1,300 years of Jihad, both Gore and Bush talked so much about schools and quality-of-life issues that at times they seemed to be running for the office of America's mayor.

TWENTY ONE

Bernard Kerik and Jason Turner: Round Two of Crime and Welfare Reform

For those who assume that crime is basically an expression of income and demography, the 2000 census numbers comparing Philadelphia with 1.5 million people and the city's poorest boro, the Bronx, with 1.3 million, is revealing. If age, income, race, family structure and education are proxies for crime, then they should have had a similar murder rate. The percentage of the population fifteen to twenty-nine years old was slightly higher in the Bronx; 55 percent of Philadelphia and 70 percent of the Bronx were minority. A Bronx family was one-third more likely to be headed by single parent; 18 percent of Philly and 28 percent of Bronx families lived below the poverty line; per capita income was $16,500 dollars in Philly, $14,000 in the Bronx. In other words, the Bronx was worse off in every category. Yet Philadelphia's murder rate was more than twice that of the Bronx, with twenty-three per hundred thousand people to ten per hundred thousand in the Bronx. No doubt other factors were involved, but clearly the quality of Gotham's policing had made an enormous difference. Nonetheless, the city's reforms fell short when it came to police/minority relations.

In August 2000, the stiff and bureaucratic Howard Safir decided, on his own, to step down after four years as police commissioner. A distant figure who rarely strayed from his office, Safir had little contact with either African-Americans or his own rank and file. The cops on the beat had never forgotten his trip to the Academy Awards two days after the Diallo killing. Delighted to see him go, they had mocked him as "Hollywood Howard."

Bernard Kerik, Safir's replacement, was an improbable choice. Kerik, who had earned a college degree late in life and had never made it beyond the title of Detective Third Grade, was chosen over men with far higher ranks. But it was, despite Kerik's tendency to bend the rules, an inspired appointment.

Abandoned by his streetwalker mother, Kerik had grown up with a series of relatives in the down-and-out mill town of Patterson, New Jersey. After dropping out of high school, Kerik joined the army where he served in Korea as an MP. He later worked in Saudi Arabia as a private security guard. When he returned to New Jersey, Kerik used the skills he'd acquired in the army to rise to the position of warden of the Passaic County jail. Restless and ambitious, Kerik, a bullet-headed hulk of a man who had a black belt in karate, joined the NYPD in 1985 for half the pay he enjoyed as the warden. An undercover cop in 1991 along the infamous "Deuce" (42nd Street), Kerik was nicknamed "Rambo." He was a legendary cop who was described by another officer "as about the toughest guy you'll ever come across." In 1992, he won the NYPD Medal of Valor in a case where he cracked part of the Cali cocaine cartel.

Kerik, who lived a life of huge leaps, came to Giuliani's attention in 1993 when he served as the candidate's driver for the mayoral campaign. He first came to public attention in 1995 when Giuliani brought in a new team led by the talented Michael Jacobson to head the Department of Corrections which ran the city's troubled Rikers Island jail complex. The newspaper headlines captured the situation at Rikers. *Newsday* spoke of ARMED RULE BY INMATES, and the *Daily News* read, BRUTAL GANGS ROAM RIKERS. The *Post* headline, referring to the frequent riots, read POWDER KEG AT RIKERS in the expectation of more outbursts. But they didn't come. Jacobson and Kerik made Corrections the second department to apply the principles of broken windows policing and CompStat successfully.

Though constantly on the edge of riot, Rikers had had its staff sharply cut by the Dinkins administration even as the prison population was rising. Meanwhile, judicial decisions had shifted the balance of power inside the prison toward the inmates. The management of the prison was constrained by a 1975 prisoners' rights decision that asked little of inmates, but minutely regulated prison management down to holding officials accountable if food wasn't served at its proper temperature. Public school cafeterias were generally mopped only once a week; at Rikers it was done twice daily by court order. The city had to seek federal court permission to change the court-ordered cook-chill protocol regarding the proper temperature of prison food, to ban gang jewelry, and to provide law books to violent prisoners in their cells rather than in the prison library. Abstractly, Rikers was never better off. The prisoners' rights were scrupulously protected by the courts in a way that left the milder inmates at the mercy of the most murderous among them, the roughly ten percent who belong to gangs.[1]

There were more than one hundred slashings or stabbings a month among the 26,000 prisoners. Inmates who attacked other prisoners were almost never punished and the same held true for prisoners who assaulted guards. That left the guards angry and alienated. Frustrated, they held their own protest, blocking the short bridge connecting the island to Queens.

Just as when Giuliani asked Chancellor Cortines how many people worked for the Board of Education, when Kerik and Jacobson asked the wardens how many inmates there were in Rikers' ten different jails, they couldn't get an answer. When managers couldn't give a good account of what they had been doing, they were removed. Jacobson and Kerik quickly moved to paint over the graffiti and generally clean up the areas on the grounds that "appearance improves performance." When they moved to bar prisoners from wearing their gang colors, they prevailed over the protests of the Legal Aid Society and began making arrests of prisoners who were attacking other inmates. Arrests within the prison increased dramatically. The prisoners who had been most likely to stab their fellow inmates with razor blades had their hands swaddled in a foot-long tube. These measures began a drop in violence that was then accelerated when Jacobson and Kerik began applying the CompStat approach to managing the prisons. They called their version TEAMS (Total Efficiency Accountability Management System).

In August 1995 when Jacobson and Kerik took over there had been 115 stabbings that month; by August 1998 there were three. They had created a virtuous circle. Less violence meant better morale, which meant fewer guards out for sick days, which meant less overtime, which meant more money could be put into improving security, which meant even lower violence. Serious crime within the Rikers complex dropped by more than 90 percent while overtime spending had been cut nearly in half. Prison officials from around the country came in to see how it was done although some in the

local press were raising their eyebrows over the way Kerik had surrounded himself with cronies.[2]*

When Jacobson returned to academia, Kerik became Corrections Commissioner and continued the good work that made him
Giuliani's choice to succeed Safir. By picking his friend Kerik, a mere
detective, Giuliani bypassed the NYPD's top brass, who were more
than a touch resentful. But within the ranks of the NYPD his
appointment came as a relief. "Bernie Kerik knows the foot cop's
story, knows the detective's story and knows the boss's story," said
Sergeant Jerry Kane, who had worked with Kerik in the Midtown
South narcotics squad in the late 1980s. "He's going to be able to
relate to all those people."[3]

In line with the broken windows concept, Kerik saw that there
was a link between how the line cops were treated by their commanders and the way the cops on the beat treated the public. "Cops
don't like the way they're talked to, how they're treated by bosses.
And if you embarrass or insult a cop in front of peers or prisoners,
what is the cop going to do? Take it out on a prisoner or the public."[4]

From the start, said Julia Vitullo-Martin of the Vera Institute of
Justice, the earthy Kerik "was a very different kind of commissioner" than the dour and distant Safir. Kerik made community
relations his top priority. His commissionership was the unspoken
response to the Diallo tragedy.

Kerik made it his mission to heal "the deep rift between the
NYPD and the city's minority neighborhoods." In what amounted to
a political campaign, he visited one black church after another making personal contact with the pastors, assuring them that he would
be accessible to their worries. Having set the example, Kerik
instructed his commanders to assign at least one sergeant in each
precinct as a specialist in community and family affairs. Even more
important, he instructed officers to explain to people why they were
being stopped and frisked and, if the frisk was in error, to apologize
for any inconvenience. Kerik was putting in place the strategy Bratton had outlined a half a decade earlier.[5]

In February 2001, Kerik and the entire Giuliani cabinet were in
Harlem for one of the mayor's town meetings. When the mayor

---

*There is no doubt that the situation at Rikers had been dramatically improved. But in
the wake of the withdrawal of Kerik's nomination as Secretary of Homeland Security,
questions were raised in an article in the *New York Post* on 12/27/04 about whether
he hadn't jiggered the numbers to make them look even better.

referred to recent statistics describing the continued decline in crime, an elderly man red in the face with anger described how he was repeatedly hassled by drug dealers around Amsterdam Avenue and 146th Street. A raft of similar stories buttressed the man's account. Giuliani was visibly taken aback. The next day Kerik announced a series of transfers that brought in a top-notch detective commander to take charge of the NYPD in Harlem.[6]

Kerik's approach calmed tensions even as crime continued to fall an additional 18 percent during the first quarter of 2001, when there were no murders in fourteen of the city's seventy-six police precincts. One measure of his success was that there were fewer murders in all of Manhattan (105) during this period than had occurred in just once precinct (119)—Washington Heights, home of 1991 drug runners' riot—a decade earlier. Part of what kept the reduction rolling was Kerik's emphasis on going after people with outstanding warrants: "Every time you have a major crime incident and look at the people involved, they are either on probation or parole or already wanted. This is about going after the bad people and taking them off the streets."[7]

Speaking at the Manhattan Institute six months into his term, Kerik told the audience, "I haven't seen racism [on the NYPD], but I have seen arrogance. It's up to the front line supervisors to change it." To illustrate the problem of police arrogance, Kerik gave the example of how he was treated when he was an undercover cop with long hair, a ponytail and six earrings. "No one says hello when you come in." He described how on one occasion, he was ignored by two desk cops in the middle of a personal conversation who assumed he was a civilian. The sergeant turned to him and said, "Can't you see we're talking here?" Then Kerik paused dramatically and added, "I'm still looking for that guy."

"Commissioner Kerik," noted civil rights leader Michael Meyers, is about "accountability. That's why there have been transfers, retirements, and shake-ups." The cops were still gruff, but under Kerik the force lost some of its hard edge of arrogance tinged with pride and improved relations with blacks and Latinos even as it kept reducing crime.*

---

*Kerik's insecurity in his new, elevated post as Police Commissioner was revealed by his misuse of cops to find one of his lover's lost cell phones and the use of police officers to research his autobiography. Worse, Kerik started to believe his own press clips. He began to lose the trust of some of the rank and file who had welcomed him

In 2001, crime started to go back up in other major cities including Boston, where there was a 60 percent jump in murders. Boston had long been cited as a city whose police methods represented a kinder, gentler alternative to New York. In Gotham, crime registered its biggest drop in five years in 2000. That year, Chicago, with a third of New York's population, passed the five boros in its murder count.

Immigration is usually associated with rising crime rates. But in Queens, even with its heavy immigrant population, policy triumphed over demography. The Queens murder rate of three per hundred thousand people in 2001 was half the national rate. Murder declined so sharply in Queens that it "rival[ed] wealthy suburban communities."[8]

The success was due not only to Kerik and New York's policing methods but also to something that has been largely ignored, something that might be described as "broken windows parole." Journalists and academics who kept predicting a return to higher crime rates invariably pointed to the growing number of released prisoners who were totally unprepared to re-enter society. When prisoners were discharged from Rikers, they left with "little more a $4.50 subway pass and the clothes they arrived in." This wasn't as much of a problem in New York as nationally, because crime control had come in Gotham without a sharp increase in the prison population. Still, New York State prisons released 20,000 to 30,000 inmates annually, "85 percent of whom returned to one of the city's 'dead zones,'" the high-crime neighborhoods.[9]

But then why didn't these returnees produce a soaring crime rate? The answer, in part, was that broken windows policing has been augmented by broken windows probation. In the past when individuals left jail, they would disappear into the streets only to show up again as a welfare case, a patient at a city hospital with a stab wound or too often as a suspect in another crime. Each agency dealt with them unaware of the others. But increasingly, a joint task force of police, probation and parole officers who shared information on the ex-offender supervised the parolee. And better yet, New York under Welfare Commissioner Jason Turner was increasingly using the money saved from the decline in the welfare rolls to pro-

---

when he awarded himself the NYPD's highest medal and had busts of himself made to be given out as gifts.

vide drug treatment and job readiness training for people leaving prison.

▲ ▲ ▲

When it comes to welfare as with policing, Jason Turner explained, "neither the economy nor demography is destiny." A balding, heavy-set man with a passion for 1960s blues and folk music, Turner had left his family behind in Wisconsin, where he had been a key player in the country's leading welfare reform experiment. Turner, the most important addition to Mayor Giuliani's second-term team, said that his mission was to "make work central in the lives of every able-bodied New Yorker receiving public assistance."[10]

After three and a half years of moving New York's welfare system from an emphasis on giving out benefits to a focus on placing people in jobs, Turner, as he came before the committee, finally had the resources to replicate what had been done in Wisconsin. Thanks to Giuliani's first-term welfare reforms, there had been a 60 percent decline in the number of people on public assistance. That left the city with far more money to spend on each of the harder-to-place people that remained. In 1993 under Dinkins there had only been $317 dollars to help each client find and hold a job. By 2001 spending had risen to nearly $3,000 dollars per participant. In 2001, the city was spending more money per capita on childcare for each adult recipient with a family than the Dinkins administration had extended for all supplemental services. Reducing the rolls had become a self-sustaining process as declining numbers freed up more money to spend on the remaining and generally harder cases. That allowed Turner and his deputy Mark Hoover to transform the old welfare intake offices into work placement centers that found employment for 133,000 people in 2000.

When Jan Rosenberg visited the Greenwood Job Placement Center in 1999, she was greeted with "Welcome! How can I help you? Are you a participant or a visitor?" The contrast with old welfare centers was startling.

The chaotic old welfare centers were of a piece with inner-city disorder. The new Job Centers were clean and well organized. They looked like any other office. The receptionist greeted the "participants" (the very term connoted more initiative than "clients" or "recipients") and handed them a Profile to fill out. Signs on the walls announce that "Welfare is Temporary and Time Limited" and "The

Clock is Ticking," as videos replayed a similar messages and offered job information as participants waited to see the Financial and Employment Counselors. Then came a one- to two-hour interview with a "Financial Planner" who helped the participant explore any alternatives to welfare (from family or charitable assistance to other benefits, like Medicaid, Food Stamps, Unemployment Insurance, emergency cash, and so forth). Next, an Employment Planner (another recently retrained HRA worker) helped the participant began a search for a private-sector job with workfare as the second option.[11]

Giuliani took great pleasure in visiting the former welfare centers that Turner and his staff had turned into Job Centers. He exulted in the changed atmosphere. In place of the once somewhat seedy offices were clean, well-organized operations that took themselves and the people they were working for seriously.

This should have been good news. For years, social service advocates like Councilman Steve DiBrienza had complained that workfare was merely punitive, that it didn't do enough to place people in jobs. But when Turner was brought before DiBrienza's council committee in May 2001, he was greeted with hostility. DiBrienza, who was a candidate in the 2001 Democratic primary to replace Mark Green as Public Advocate, only grew red-faced and visibly annoyed as Turner described his successes at job placement.

While Turner broke down the population of 43,000 people faced with the end of their federal welfare eligibility into categories, DiBrienza gestured derisively to his ally, Councilman Bill Perkins, a junior member of the Harlem machine, as if to say, can you believe this nonsense!? Each time Turner turned one of his flip charts to present more statistics by way of making his argument, DiBrienza made his disdain clear.

Bill Perkins, who played a key role in opposing both reform at CUNY and new housing for Harlem, was a key DiBrienza ally. Both seemed to believe that they were representing the little people in the face of the powerful. Perkins' oft-repeated line was that Turner's primary goal was to "increase the stress" in the life of already harried welfare recipients.

Turner, who had made a point of trying to avoid confrontations, clearly dreaded the anticipated browbeating. Speaking softly in a monotone, he described the spectrum of available opportunities his deputy Mark Hoover was providing. He explained that those who were currently working while continuing to receive welfare were eligible for a program that supplied scholarships and subsidies to upgrade their skills and hopefully move them off the dole altogether. A second group was eligible for the state wage subsidy program. A third population was those in substance abuse program who couldn't yet be expected to work and had been routed into drug rehabilitation programs. Hoover, a talented administrator, had also created a program for people who needed to improve their English in order to work and another for prisoners on probation who were given an intense employment re-entry program. There was even a "wellness" program for people with chronic but not debilitating health problems that kept them from working.

But DiBrienza showed very little interest in these efforts. His concerns were focused on those who faced a loss of support for refusing to work and for people whose five years of federal benefits were coming to an end. Both groups were eligible to become part of Safety Net, the state/city program that would pick up when the federal money was cut off. But Turner wanted them to reapply to continue receiving aid in the hopes of further winnowing out those capable of working. This enraged DiBrienza. The more people left welfare, the fewer clients were available to the social service agencies DiBrienza represented. Worse yet, Turner's emphasis on results and accountability put the social service providers in danger of losing their contracts if they didn't become more effective.[12]

In the past, when DiBrienza started shouting at Turner on behalf of the welfare rights advocates, the commissioner would generally walk out of the hearings until Peter Vallone could arrange a compromise basis for his reappearance. When Turner reiterated his position on having people whose federal eligibility had expired reapply for the local Safety Net program, an angry DiBrienza got personal. "And during whatever period of time you think they should take to reassess their circumstance in life," he bellowed, "Do you think they could come live with you?" Turner, shaking his head, told the committee he was ready to walk out when DiBrienza barked, "Don't go through this stupid show again. I talk the way I speak. I speak the way I speak because I am energetic and passionate, I didn't yell at this Commissioner, I just raised my voice because these issues interest me, and besides the fact it is not up to him to determine the level of my voice."

Despite the theatrics, the attempts by DiBrienza and his allies to replace welfare reform with make-work city jobs and to return to an emphasis on job training rather than job readiness and placement failed. Welfare reform continued to roll on. As with CUNY, the interest groups invested in failure tried to slow or even reverse welfare reform in court, but the Giuliani administration fought them vigorously and, although slowed at times, won most of the cases.*

The wild predictions of the social service advocates about the massive suffering that was inevitable if welfare was reformed had clearly failed to come true. Welfare reform was popular with both the general public and, according to 1998 interviews with 126 families who were able to leave welfare, former recipients as well. Both the public and the former welfare clients embraced the idea of reciprocity in which those in need received help and in turn made an effort to help themselves.[13]

The old-line liberal organizations like the National Association of Social Workers, whose ideology had been preserved unchanged since the 1960s, tried to block reform politically. Activist groups like ACORN took direct action. It was ACORN, in fact, that initiated Jason Turner and Mark Hoover into Gotham's politics of posturing. Shortly after their arrival in Gotham, Turner and Hoover went to the Greenwood welfare facility in Brooklyn where they sat down for a meeting with the Greenwood staff only to have activists from ACORN well familiar with the facility come up the back stairs to storm the room. The ACORN protesters jumped up on the conference table shouting insults and holding placards which read WORKFARE = SLAVERY. But true to his low-key style, Turner never made much of the disturbance except subsequently to ignore ACORN.

Turner wasn't bereft of support. He discovered welcome allies in most of the Human Resources Administrations frontline employees. A good number were only a few notches removed from welfare themselves, but got to work on time daily and resented those who thought they were entitled to welfare with no questions asked. Others, who were recent immigrants from Africa, the Caribbean and Russia, wanted to make it in America and helped impose a no-nonsense business-like approach on the formerly disordered welfare offices.[14]

---

*Term-limited off the council, DiBrienza eventually lost his race for Public Advocate, but his heirs on the city council repeatedly tried to reverse the welfare reforms of the 1990s.

Critics of welfare reform credited the robust economy with reducing the rolls. But the welfare explosion had begun during the boom years of the 1960s, and welfare case loads had increased in New York during the great days of the 1980s. Wendell Primus, a Clinton welfare expert who had quit the administration to protest the president's embrace of reform, had changed his mind by 2001, admitting welfare reform "is working better than I thought." To make his point about how welfare reform produced a new set of expectations, Primus noted that the percentage of children living with a single mother fell 8 percent (from 19.9 percent to 18.4 percent) between 1995 and 2000. Most of the drop took place among those most likely to have been affected by welfare reform—that is, low-income and minority households headed by woman.[15]*

New York City in 2002 had declining rates of child poverty and single-parent-headed households. Those changes were connected to a "remarkable rise in job holding by single mothers." Between 1996 and 2000, the number of single mothers in the New York work force grew by 17 percent compared to 10 percent nationally. There was an even more remarkable change among unmarried mothers without high school diplomas. In 1996 only 16 percent had jobs, but by 2000, 42 percent were working. These women not only found jobs in the good times, but, because the market for low-end work remained healthy even as the city went into recession, they also tended to keep their jobs or find new ones. Their work was made all the more viable because President Clinton's earned income tax credit supplemented low-wage work.[16]

Poverty still persisted, but what it meant to be poor had changed. Welfare had isolated generation after generation of the

---

*Giuliani never commissioned a large-scale social scientific study of welfare reform's effects. Given the time and expense of a longitudinal study to track a large group of former recipients over time, neither the critics nor independent scholars chose to pick up the burden Giuliani had avoided. There was another less discussed reason for deferring a full-scale study. In Wisconsin, Jason Turner had a reputation among researchers for offering extraordinary access to his work. But New York with its highly politicized courts and far more activist judges was another matter. Reform efforts were fought in the courts at every step. At one point, for instance, welfare rights advocates sued to set up their own counseling operations inside the job centers. Turner refused to allow the creation of an adversarial situation and he eventually won in court. But he was left with the fear that any study would, even if generally positive, necessarily contain ambiguous findings sure to be seized upon by those who wanted to roll back the idea of reciprocity. The upshot is that reform's effects have had to be inferred from less precise studies and other forms of evidence.

poor in benighted neighborhoods. Work pulled people out of their inner-city cocoon and into the possibilities provided by the larger world. They then brought the values of the larger society back into their neighborhoods. "Work," Jason Turner summed up, "was the basis of full citizenship."

The decline in crime and welfare and the increase in work changed the texture of poor neighborhoods. The urbanist Tony Proscio summed up the way the cumulative changes, including the construction of new housing by the New York City Partnership, affected the South Bronx. "The neighborhood was not saved the way decades of reformers insisted it would have to be saved: by eliminating poverty." Poverty levels in the South Bronx at the end of the 1990s were somewhat lower than those at the start of the decade, but that wasn't the most important change. "What changed the South Bronx from Fort Apache to a functioning community," explained Proscio, "was not a sudden influx of wealth, but a careful restoration of order—in the built environment, in public spaces, and in people's lives."[17]

TWENTY TWO

Running after Rudy—
Part I

W hen the campaign to succeed Rudy Giuliani began in earnest during the spring of 2001, it was widely assumed that the winner of the Democratic primary would be the next mayor. The campaign attracted scant attention in a city still bathing in the glow of the 1990s boom and not yet aware of the signs of a sinking economy. When the tech bubble on Wall Street burst, the city lost 60,000 jobs in the spring and summer prior to the September 11, 2001 Democratic party primary. But the prevailing mood was still optimism, "with much of the credit going to Giuliani." There were "few worries about what happens after Giuliani," a *Times* poll found, since "few are paying much attention to the election."[1]

But while the city at large was indifferent, the so-called "prime voters" who drove Democratic primaries were ideologically or financially invested in reversing the gains of the Giuliani years. That presented the four major candidates—Public Advocate Mark Green, Bronx Boro President Freddy Ferrer, Comptroller Alan Hevesi, and City Council Speaker Peter Vallone, all of whom were term-limited out of their current offices—with a dilemma. The "prime voters" were at odds with the majority of their own party, whose members wanted to see the Giuliani policies continued by a 52 to 40 margin.[2]

The candidates all understood that the election was likely to be a two-stage process. There was a good chance that in a four-way race, none of the contenders—two of whom were Jewish and two of whom were from Queens, thus dividing those constituencies—would garner the 40 percent of the vote needed to win the nomination outright. Instead a runoff between the two top finishers seemed likely.

The candidate best positioned to make it into the second round was Ferrer, who was running as the anti-Rudy. That set up a competition between the other three, Green, Vallone, and Hevesi, who were the candidates of continuity. They all had to get it right on Rudy whose not-so-hidden hand would be an ongoing factor in the primaries.

Mark Green, who had at one time denounced the idea of workfare as a device for making the poor "dance for their supper," now admitted, "I was wrong." Alan Hevesi who described himself as having a "100 percent voting record from the ACLU," nonetheless agreed that Giuliani was right to curtail aggressive panhandling. In retrospect, he agreed that it wasn't a civil liberties issue.[3]

Each of the candidates of continuity insisted that they could carry on Giuliani's legacy of success while also addressing the concerns of the African-American, Latino and white liberal voters the mayor had alienated. Ferrer, as the anti-Rudy, had the best chance to make it into the runoff. But being the anti-Rudy also made him the weakest general election candidate. The political team behind the likely Republican nominee, billionaire businessman Mike Bloomberg, was hoping for Ferrer.

Hevesi, the incumbent Comptroller, was the early front-runner, with support from Jews, older African-Americans and that special New York ethnic group, white liberals, as well as the teachers' union. His intelligence, speaking abilities and the broad support he got from his former colleagues in the New York State Assembly made him appear a formidable candidate.

Hevesi, however, was caught in a crossfire. Looking to distinguish himself from Giuliani, Hevesi championed the cause of the small social service providers in their opposition to Welfare Commissioner Jason Turner's pay-for-performance reforms. It produced an ugly but inconclusive fight over what turned to be minor ethical violations by Turner and Maximus, a privately owned social service company with ties to Turner. But what was conclusive was the enmity it produced. Giuliani, convinced that Hevesi would roll back his welfare reforms, made a point of telling his fervent admirers among the moderate-to-conservative Democrats known as "Rudy-crats" not to vote for the comptroller, which cost Hevesi dearly.

Hevesi's dilemma on his left came from his earlier, relatively amicable relations with "Rudy." That dilemma became visible when the Comptroller announced his candidacy. "Our city," he told an audience of supporters, "is going in the right direction. Some people want to pretend that's not true: they root for bad things to happen in our city on Rudy's watch because they don't like Rudy Giuliani personally, or just because he's a Republican. I say that is wrong." Today, New York's "can-do spirit is back. Crime is down, private-sector jobs are up, tourism is setting records...[the] welfare rolls are down [and the] quality of life is improved. The squeegee men are off the streets. We've had budget surpluses and raised the city's bond ratings. Our population is growing again." He went on: "My challenge as mayor will be to include everyone in that progress and to keep our city moving in the right direction." This was a good speech for a general election audience, but it left the hard-core Democrats in the auditorium cold. Hoping for something in the way of Rudy-bashing, they responded with just polite applause.[4]

Hevesi, the descendant of Hungarian rabbis, had an even bigger problem with Al Sharpton. His criticism of Sharpton's ties to Khalid Muhammad had sent the Reverend into a rage. So while he didn't want or need Sharpton's endorsement, after what Sharpton had done to Messinger during the 1997 mayoral election he didn't want to be the object of Al's ire either. When Hevesi appeared at Sharpton's National Action Network on Martin Luther King Day, he tried to make amends by acknowledging that he hadn't done enough to speak out against police brutality. "I didn't get it. I got it later. I got it with the Dorismond case and the rest of the city ought to get it as well." But Sharpton was unappeased and suggested that Hevesi, known for his support of Jewish Holocaust victims, needed to learn that African-Americans too had suffered a holocaust.[5]

Ferrer, who was trying to reassemble David Dinkins' 1989 black-Latino coalition, faced no such dilemma. He announced his campaign by declaring that he would be the advocate for "the other New York" Giuliani had mistreated for eight years. In the "other New York, law-abiding people of color approach their police with fear rather than trust." The "other New York" theme, which he made the leitmotif of his challenge, was borrowed from Sharpton's 1997 mayoral campaign. Ferrer mocked his rivals as "sheep" who had "routinely supported the policies of Mayor Rudolph W. Giuliani."[6]

In 1997, when he made his first run for mayor, Ferrer dropped out after being unable to decide whether to run as an outer-boro Catholic moderate or as the candidate of the third-world peoples of color coalition. In 1997 his key advisors, Hank Sheinkopf and

Dick Morris, convinced him, after the brutal murder of a Bronx cop, to come around in support of the death penalty. That earlier Ferrer had been an enthusiast for the policing policies of Bill Bratton. In 2001, firmly allied with Al Sharpton, Ferrer suffered from no such ambivalence. The only brutality he spoke of was police brutality. He made Bratton (by then aligned with Green), the special object of his ire, accusing the former top cop of having brought racial profiling to Gotham.

Ferrer ripped the other contenders for running as "Rudy-lite." His chin jutting, he asserted, "I am...no faint imitation of Rudy Giuliani.... I ain't Rudy lite. I'm not Rudy with a smile. I'm not a kinder, gentler Rudy. My name is Fernando. I want to lead this city in a different direction." Ferrer dismissed welfare reform. "Don't give Rudy so much credit," he said. The sharp drops in both crime and welfare, were, he insisted, all a matter of the economy. Ferrer credited Federal Reserve Chairman Greenspan, as "the greatest welfare reformer this nation has ever known."[7]

At times, the boro president cast himself simultaneously in the roles of arsonist and fireman. Ferrer told a forum at the CUNY Graduate Center that the city was in crisis and that he was running for mayor "because this horror show needs to come to an end." Then, after stirring tensions, he insisted that he was the man to calm them. This approach brought him support from less than 3 percent of white voters. But the us vs. them stance gave him a newfound standing among Latino voters who felt neglected by the city's white politicians.[8]

Mark Green, long associated with the left wing of the Democratic Party, derived much of his black support from his repeated clashes with Giuliani. But Green tired to run as a crossover candidate who could appeal to all the elements of the Democratic Party.

Hammered in his 1998 Senate bid for being too liberal, Green tried to broaden his appeal by running as Gotham's version of Bill Clinton. "I don't accept the premise," he explained, "that candidates should be seen through the lens of Rudy Giuliani. I reject this simplistic post-Giuliani bipolarization that requires candidates to be either General Patton or Mr. Rogers. There's a new way to run and govern that ideally will produce someone who's tough and smart, and can be persuasive in boardrooms and civic meetings, with beat cops and high-school seniors." To make his point, Green, who had brought Bill Bratton and Jerry Hauer into his campaign, embraced both broken windows and CompStat policing.[9]

Vallone ran as the candidate of experience whose proven success could guarantee a continuation of Giuliani's achievements, albeit under kinder and more consensual management. "I think everyone will agree," he stated, "that I've always been able to work things out, with three different mayors, whatever the problems were." While the others were positioning themselves to solidify their base (Ferrer), or to reach out to new constituencies (Green, white moderates; Hevesi, younger blacks), Vallone's pitch was practical, telling voters, "I only have to walk 65 feet across City Hall to keep things going."[10]

Vallone was the clear winner in the first mayoral debate. His insistence that "this is not the time for on-the-job training," effectively separated him from his rivals. The *Post*, which endorsed him, praised his "average-man sensibilities." But Vallone fell into the Bob Dole mode of speaking of himself in the third person, as in "Peter Vallone will..." Hampered because he and Hevesi, both of Queens, were splitting that boro's vote, Vallone never caught his stride.

There were few divisions among the challengers when it came to seeking the support of the city's public-sector unions. At one point Hevesi came out for repealing the Taylor Law that prohibits public employees from striking. He also called on the city to provide a major pay increase for those unions, which hadn't won raises during the fiscal crisis of the early and mid-1990s. Not to be outdone, Ferrer called for a 30 percent pay increase for teachers. And while the other candidates, backed by Hillary Clinton, called upon Albany to give the next mayor control of the schools by eliminating the Board of Education, Ferrer wanted to maintain the Board.

Ferrer could call for a 30 percent raise the city clearly couldn't afford because he generally avoided the issue of New York's slowing economy. In their attempt to be responsible, the other candidates had a problem. Both Hevesi and Green spoke frequently about how the economy was already in a serious slowdown that would affect the next mayor. But Hevesi in particular, as the city Comptroller and hence the guardian of fiscal virtue, was caught between his attempts to buy the union vote with the public treasury and the need, as a future mayor, to balance the budget.

Hevesi, Green and to a far lesser extent Ferrer tried, without success, to make an issue of Giuliani's budget-busting spending increases in 2000. But it was hard for them to score points by

warning of the very real danger of looming deficits at the same time
as they were supporting sizeable union wage hikes and union pension enhancements.

Giuliani was in fact open to substantial criticism. Facing a
fiscal crisis when he entered office, Giuliani, in his "October Plan" of
1994, had said he was "looking for a permanent not just a temporary reduction in the size of City government." Although not as
irresponsible as Koch, Giuliani, after coming into office with a promise of reducing government, had opened the spending spigots during
the boom of the late 1990s.

His earlier compromises with the municipal labor unions,
essential for cooperation on welfare reform and getting through the
fiscal woes of his first-term, came back to haunt the budget. The
turning point on spending came in 1999 when Giuliani began considering a Senate run. The city payroll, noted the Citizens Budget
Commission (CBC), actually grew to record levels by the end of Giuliani's second term. 2001 was a blowout year in which Giuliani spent
almost as recklessly as Albany. In his last year, Giuliani's expenditure
of city revenues, driven in part by an unsustainable expansion in
state Medicaid spending, grew by nearly 10 percent, melting away
much of the massive surplus that had been built up in the boom.[11]

In its fight with Giuliani over the Kummerfeld Report, the CBC
had been wed to outmoded assumptions about New York's local-
ized version of the welfare state. But looking at matters in the long
run they had been right on two key points: the city's payroll was far
too large and it was insufficiently productive. In rebuttal, Giuliani's
staff pointed out that there was a shift in the composition of the city
work force toward more teachers and cops. That was also true, but
the CBC argued that without major gains in labor productivity the
city would repeat the old cycle of boom and bust. They proved correct. Giuliani had earlier spoken of a possible "revolution" in labor
negotiations through the introduction of merit pay so that high per-
forming workers would be better rewarded than their fellow union
members. But little came of this. For all his achievements, and
despite the threat of privatization, which waned during the boom of
the second term, productivity gains had been limited.[12]

The political culture of spending was still intact after eight
years of Giuliani. Some of the problems with the city budget had
been imposed by the state, which recklessly raised pension benefits
during the upswing. Anticipating the downturn, the administration

cut costs in its final budget, but it had already allowed school spending to skyrocket to little educational effect. The city's debt in 2001, noted Diana Fortuna of the CBC, was a record 19 percent of the total budget. Even before 9/11, the old pattern of maximal spending in good times leading to severe, sustained downturns was intact despite Giuliani's first term pledge to tame the boom-bust cycle.

Jim Chapin worked for the Green campaign, but he was also independent minded and the city's best political analyst. He summarized the campaign as the September 11 primary approached. "Green," he said, "is running right with his advisor Hank Sheinkopf sealing off all the lines of attack, Vallone and Freddy are running left. Hevesi, with the misguidance of campaign advisor Hank Morris, is running all over the place incoherently assembling interest groups."

Ferrer, aided by former Dinkins Deputy Mayor Bill Lynch, remained focused on bringing out new Latino and black voters by playing up racial resentments. When, in the final debate, Vallone criticized Ferrer's talk of "two cities" as "divisive" and asked Ferrer to repudiate his endorsement by racial racketeer Sonny Carson, Ferrer responded by saying that just bringing up such issues was "meant to inflame the divisions in this city." Sharpton couldn't have said it better.[13]

▲ ▲ ▲

On the morning of the primary, political insiders thought that Green, who had succeeded Hevesi as the front runner, had himself been overtaken by Ferrer with Vallone and Hevesi well behind. The polls opened at 6 a.m.; at 8:47 the first plane hit the World Trade Center.

PART IV

9/11 and After

TWENTY THREE

Terror from the Skies

O n the morning of the Democratic Party primary, the skies over New York were cloudlessly clear. While voters were arriving at the polls, Mayor Giuliani and his alter ego Denny Young were at the Peninsula Hotel on 55th Street for a breakfast. If terrorism was on their minds, it was in part because on the next day, September 12, one of Osama bin Laden's associates was scheduled to be sentenced for killing 213 people in the 1998 bombing of the U.S. embassy in Kenya. But then came an unexpected phone call from Deputy Mayor Joe Lhota. At 8:47, a plane had crashed into the World Trade Center. It was about 8:48. Giuliani and Young rushed to the scene.

At the same time, Richard Sheirer, Jerry Hauer's successor at the Office of Emergency Management, was at City Hall for a meeting about the proposed Jackie Robinson–Pee Wee Reese memorial planned for Coney Island. "I was in heaven, sitting between Ralph Branca and Joe Black," he remembers. "We were about to select the statue, and then we heard the pop."

The meeting about the memorial for the two Brooklyn Dodger heroes had been a welcome break from preparation for the big event scheduled for September 12, when Sheirer was supposed to lead a drill on biological terrorism at Pier 92 along the Hudson. The drill was designed to test the city's ability to respond to the casualties from a major terrorist attack by quickly setting up ad hoc medical facilities. "For an audience, Sheirer had lined up Mayor Rudy Giuliani, the police and fire commissioners, and representatives of the FBI and the Federal Emergency Management Agency (FEMA). He had hired over 1,000 Police Academy cadets and Fire Department trainees to play terrified civilians afflicted with various medical conditions, allergies, and panic attacks." Sheirer, like the mayor and thousands of firefighters and cops, raced to the World Trade Center.[1]

A fire official later remembered that it was still "beyond our consciousness, unimaginable that a second plane would hit the South Tower." Shortly after the first plane hit, Brian Clark, a broker working in the South Tower, heard the announcement over the PA system: "Building 2 is secure. There is no need to evacuate Building 2. If you are in the midst of evacuation...return to your office."[2]

At 9:03 the second plane hit the South Tower. While people were fleeing for their lives, Giuliani and his crew arrived downtown at 9:20 to witness what he later described as "the most horrific scene I've ever seen in my whole life." The second plane had already hit, leaving no doubt that this was a terrorist attack. At least two hundred firefighters were on the scene, as were Fire Commissioner Tom Von Essen and Police Commissioner Bernie Kerik.

Shocked by the sight of a man jumping from one of the top floors of the Trade Center, Giuliani was quickly briefed by the FDNY Chief of Department Pete Ganci, who was running the fire command post. According to Giuliani, Ganci told him, "My guys can save everybody below the fire [at the point of impact on the 94th floor], but I can't put a helicopter up there because the smoke is too dangerous." Chief Ganci perished in the collapse of the North Tower.[3]

Giuliani quickly saw that the city's Emergency Command Center, in the smaller adjoining building of 7 World Trade Center, was in danger. He gave the order to evacuate. "I immediately had two priorities," he explained. "We had to set up a new command center. And we had to find a way to communicate with people in the city."[4]

At about 9:50, the mayor set up an ad hoc command center at Barclay Street about a block away from the World Trade Center where his staff made contact with both the White House and the governor. No one yet thought the towers, which had survived the powerful 1993 blast, would collapse.

Just as Giuliani was about to talk with the White House, a powerful rumble was heard as the South Tower began to collapse, creating an architectural avalanche that reached 2.4 on the Richter scale. The mayor and his team momentarily appeared to be trapped in a Barclay Street building as the debris began to rain down. Giuliani, Kerik and Von Essen were led to safety by two janitors who showed them a little-known passage out through the basement. Retreating to Chambers Street and West Broadway, Giuliani held an impromptu news conference interrupted by the collapse of the North Tower. As it crumpled, hundreds of firemen who had gone running up the towers as the civilians had been running down them were killed.*

From the time the first plane hit to the collapse of the second tower at 10:26, all of one hundred minutes had elapsed.

For almost an hour, Giuliani and his staff entered what they described as "uncharted territory" as they worked to re-establish a command center in the midst of the chaos. City Hall, which seemed like it might be another target, was covered in ash. There was a concern, explained Giuliani aide J.P. Avlon, that Times Square and the United Nations might be the next targets. But Giuliani never gave voice to his fear that more attacks and perhaps hostage-taking might be on the way. Nor did he dwell on his own narrow escape from death or the likely deaths of people close to him such as fire department hero Terry Hatton, husband of his personal secretary Beth Hatton.

While Giuliani was in limbo, Deputy Mayor Rudy Washington was taking charge at City Hall. Acting on what he had learned about anti-terror procedures during the preparation for Y2K, Washington contacted the Pentagon, which ordered air cover for the city in case more attacks were on the way. He called in the Navy to guard against a sea-borne assault. Then he ordered all bridges and tunnels, the targets of an earlier thwarted attack, shut down. He also ordered heavy machinery (to move rubble) and medical supplies to be sent to Ground Zero. And then the second tower came down and he had to flee City Hall.[5]

Lower Manhattan's landlines were down and Giuliani's cell

---

*The engineers who had built the Twin Towers had anticipated the possibility that the buildings might be hit by an airplane. They had designed its steel skeleton to withstand the shock of a Boeing 707 accidentally crashing into the building. What they hadn't anticipated was that planes fully loaded with jet fuel would intentionally crash into the buildings at high speed, creating an inferno. "The towers' innovative external engineering...redistributed the walls' structural forces around the gaping holes after the attacks and kept the buildings standing long enough for a vast majority of their occupants to escape.... Had the towers possessed conventional steel skeletons, they would have probably snapped and immediately fallen over, causing more catastrophic collateral damage than they did by crumpling onto their footprints." *New York Times* 12/17/03.

phones all but dead. At that moment, as he described it, "I grabbed Andrew Kirtzman [of New York 1] by the arm and said to him and other members of the press, 'Come with us. We'll talk as we walk.'" At one point, Kirtzman recalled, the Mayor bumped into a young black police officer: "she said something to him, and, like a father, he touched her on the cheek."[6]

Giuliani wanted to get on the air as soon as possible. Fearing further attacks, he wanted to lay out contingency plans for an orderly evacuation of lower Manhattan. At his best in a crisis, he was prepared to face the pressure on 9/11 as buildings buckled all around him. A little more than two hours after the second plane had hit, he went on NY1 in a talk that was picked up by all the other TV and radio outlets. In the calm voice of authority the city would hear frequently in the coming days, he said in the phone interview:

> The first thing I'd like to do is to take this opportunity to everyone to remain calm and to the extent that they can to evacuate lower Manhattan.... The end result is going to be some horrendous number of lives lost...the only thing to do now is remain calm.

The heroism of the firefighters, police and Port Authority personnel, their steely resolve in the face of near-certain death, calmed the civilians trying to escape. Giuliani later testified before the 9/11 Commission that the first estimate of possible death he had been given suggested that as many as 12,000 to 15,000 of the roughly 25,000 people in the buildings were likely to have been killed. Thanks to the bravery of the rescuers, many of whom lost their own lives, fewer than 3,000 civilians died, all of whom had been in the high floors above where the airliners, fully loaded with jet fuel, had exploded into the buildings. Fewer than one hundred people who had been below the point of impact were murdered. The 9/11 commissioner Slade Gorton concluded that 99.5 percent of the people who could be saved had been saved.

Twenty-five thousand people were successfully evacuated from the Towers. It was the largest mass rescue in American history. But the 2,800 who died made Ground Zero the largest mass grave on American soil in the nation's history. The New York Fire Department had lost 778 men while fighting fires since its inception in 1865; it lost nearly half that many on September 11 alone. Some of the losses probably could have been avoided had the fire and police radios been fully able to speak with one another. But that was as much a matter of human error and the limits of the available technology as of the problems in integrating the fire and police response to the crisis.*

By noon, the mayor, assuming the role of a wartime leader, had gathered not only the police and fire commissioners, but also representatives of all of the city's emergency agencies, at the Police Academy on 20th Street, which served as makeshift command center. There, Giuliani replicated the crisp tenor of his 8 a.m. meetings. Congressman Gerald Nadler, usually a critic, "was amazed at the efficiency of the meeting.... It was magnificent really." The mayor went around the table to each agency head, "told them what the city needed from them, and it was immediately done." "That process," wrote Deputy Mayor Tony Coles, "created an immediate sense of discipline for a government that otherwise could have spun in confusion. And the mayor was able to use the media to reflect that sense of discipline and order to the city at large."[7]

At 2:35 p.m. he went on live TV. With Fire Commissioner Thomas Von Essen at his side, he asked people to remain calm and "to go about their lives as normal." At a 6 p.m. briefing he said, "the city is going to survive.... New York is still here. We've undergone tremendous losses, but New York is going to be here tomorrow morning, and this is the way of life that people want throughout the world."[8]

Time and again, through his union of anger, indignation and resolve, Giuliani, who returned to Ground Zero five times that fateful day, connected with the heart and soul of the city. He gave people

---

*For all the low-level rivalry between police and fire, cooperation between the two services was probably never higher than when they were led on 9/11 by Bernard Kerik and Tom Von Essen, who got along famously. Kerik told the 9/11 Commission that radio problems in such an emergency are difficult to avoid. "Show me one radio that they will guarantee you this radio will go through that metal, it will go through the debris, it will go through the dust, and you will have 100 percent communications 100 percent of the time—there is none," said the former police commissioner.

But the very "regimental pride" and camaraderie that defined the internal life of the NYPD and FDNY and gave them their habits of virtue and courage were seen after the attack as problematic. The 9/11 Commission spoke of the Battle of the Badges as an important problem, but when asked to point to specific problems caused that day by the inter-service rivalry the expert witnesses were at a loss to point to any. The

both practical advice and reassurance at a time when many assumed more attacks were to come. Fearing that there might be attacks on innocent Arabs, he told the city that "hatred, prejudice, and anger are what caused this terrible tragedy, and the people of the city of New York should act differently.... We should act bravely. We should act in a tolerant way. We should go about our business, and we should show these people that they can't stop us."[9]

President Bush was in Florida reading to schoolchildren when the attacks on the World Trade Center and the Pentagon occurred. His first response was a less-than-inspiring speech on the night of September 11th. In his book *The Right Man*, David Frum, a former Bush speechwriter, acknowledged that the president "had given not one indication all day long of readiness for his terrible new responsibilities." Bush, noted *Washington Post* columnist E.J. Dionne, "finally seized the moment three days after the attacks when he visited the Trade Center site and shouted to a rescue worker: 'The people who knocked these buildings down will hear all of us soon.' Until then, Rudy Giuliani was the de facto spokesman for a grateful nation."[10]

Within a few days, Giuliani established a crisis command center on Pier 92 along the Hudson River, the site of the terrorism exercise that had been planned for September 12th. The ongoing rescue aside, Giuliani's focus was on trying as quickly as possible to recreate a sense of normalcy. He pushed the theater owners to reopen Broadway on the 13th. He tried to get the stock market, located just a few blocks from Ground Zero, to reopen on the 12th. They couldn't, but by mid-day on Friday the 15th they were back in business. "Every day," explained Deputy Mayor Tony Coles, "the frozen zone around Ground Zero had to shrink, even if by only one block, or another street had to re-open to pedestrians."

Commission's final report was critical of the FDNY: "Understandably lacking experience in responding to events of the magnitude of the World Trade Center attacks, the FDNY as an institution proved incapable of coordinating the numbers of units dispatched to different points within the 16-acre complex." But it then went on to say, "It is clear that the lack of coordination (within the FDNY and between the NYPD and FDNY) did not affect adversely the evacuation of civilians." But it did cost the lives of some—it's impossible to specify how many—firefighters.

There had been failures on 9/11 of technology, human judgment and foresight. The 911 system, for example, had been overwhelmed by the volume of calls and unable to provide the trapped people calling from the Towers with useful information. But any massive undertaking, let alone a surprise attack, has its failures and so it was on 9/11.

When a shaken David Letterman returned to the air he captured the sentiments of most New Yorkers:

> If you're like me and you're watching and you're confused and
> depressed and irritated and angry and full of grief and you don't know
> how to behave and you're not sure what to do, because we've never
> been through this before, all you had to do at any moment was watch
> the mayor. Watch how this guy behaved. Watch how this guy con-
> ducted himself.... Rudolph Giuliani is the personification of courage.

Rick Hertzberg of the *New Yorker* described Giuliani as
"exactly the leader the city needed. His demeanor—calm, frank,
patient, tender, egoless, competent—was, as carried to the city and
the world through the intimacy of television, profoundly reassur-
ing." His stature had grown so that "the governor defers to him. The
president seems somehow inadequate beside him."[11]

Revered in the aftermath of the attack, Giuliani looked ahead
to the reconstruction. He began to give members of Congress and
foreign dignitaries tours of the devastation at Ground Zero. He lectured visiting President Jacques Chirac on the importance of firmness
in fighting terrorism and walked countless national politicians
through the help New York would need to recover. Through it all
he maintained an upbeat tone:

> We're mourning, we hurt and we're going to hurt tomorrow, the next
> day, for a month, a year, and maybe forever. I think we are going to
> hurt forever. But we have to be optimistic. There's no reason for us not
> to be optimistic. All the same things about our economy are there that
> were there before. We have a big problem to overcome. But overcom-
> ing the economic problems is the least of it. I mean I have no doubt
> the city is going to be economically stronger six months and a year
> from now."[12]

Giuliani was an enormous comfort to the families of the
bereaved firefights and cops. At one of the many funerals he attended
he spoke caringly to the children of the fallen hero:

> Nobody can take your father from you. He is part of you. He helped
> make you. He and your mom are an integral part of who you are. All
> the wonderful things that everybody...for the rest of your life tells you
> about your dad, about how brave he was, what a decent man he was,
> how strong he was, how sensitive he was to the needs of people—all
> those things are inside you. They're all part of you. People will say the
> same things about you ten, fifteen, twenty, twenty-five years from

now.... I can just see it in your family. This is a great family. He's with you—nobody can take him away from you. You have something lots of children don't have. You have the absolute, certain knowledge that your dad was a great man.[13]

The congregation was in tears.

In August, a month before the attack, fireman Michael Gorumba died fighting a blaze. In late September, Gorumba's sister Diane was scheduled to be married but there was no one to give her away since she had also lost her father and grandfather in the last year. The mayor had promised that he would stand in. The mayor kept that promise. With a wide grin that told the city that life went on, Giuliani walked Ms. Gorumba down the aisle.

TWENTY·FOUR

Running after Rudy—
Part II

The first hint that the mayoral campaign was about to resume came so subtly it barely made it into the newspapers. When Peter Vallone accompanied Giuliani at most 9/11 funerals, he became, all but officially, the designated heir. Mark Green was also at many of the funerals, but conspicuous by their absences were Alan Hevesi, the early front-runner who seemed to have dropped out of the race, and Freddy Ferrer. The Bronx boro president's absence was heatedly discussed in political circles and more than duly noted by the uniformed services.

For a moment it seemed that, if they could, New Yorkers would re-elect Giuliani by acclamation. Wherever he went, he was met by the chant of "four more years, four more years." One woman summed up the sentiment when she said of the other candidates, "They look so trivial, compared to our king." Asked by television interviewer Larry King if he would try to find a way around term limits, Giuliani responded with uncharacteristic indecision: "I don't know the right answer to that at this point."[1]

With the primary suspended on 9/11 coming up on Tuesday, September 25, Giuliani made his own sentiments plain not by what he said, but by what he did. He had Peter Vallone at his side at virtually every press conference and public event of those hectic days. People quipped that they were "surgically attached." But the Vallone campaign team, which was well to the candidate's left, was ambivalent about Giuliani. Vallone, who showed fatigue in the aftermath of 9/11, never stepped up to take full advantage of the situation.

Given Vallone's hesitation, the conventional wisdom was that Mark Green would win. Surely, it was argued, in the wake of 9/11 the city would reject Ferrer's divisive "two cities" message. But it was the Democratic primary electorate and not the city at large that would go the polls.

Amid rumors that Governor Pataki was going to postpone the election again, there was little in the way of visible campaigning. In an appeal to post-9/11 sentiment, Mark Green spoke of how he would rebuild lower Manhattan. Ferrer said less, but behind the scenes, he was, with the help of the Health and Hospital Workers Union, organizing a formidable get-out-the-vote operation targeted not just at prime voters but at Latinos who had never voted.

On the rescheduled Election Day, voters were given an immediate reminder of 9/11 when information about a potential truck bomb had the police stopping and searching trucks across the city. Overall turnout was low, more than 300,000 short of the 1989 Koch vs. Dinkins primary. As in 1989, many white moderate-to-conservative voters sat it out. But in a surprise, Ferrer's voter operation, organized by the Health and Hospital Workers Union, brought out a 70 percent increase in Latino turnout and a first-place finish for the Bronx boro president.

But while Ferrer's 36 percent bested Green's 34 percent, it was shy of the 40 percent needed to avoid a run-off. Vallone, who, thanks to Giuliani, had gained white votes since 9/11 at Green's expense, finished a distant third with 20 percent. With Vallone's votes up for grabs, the run-off between Ferrer and Green on October 5th promised to be a donnybrook.

The exit polls from Edison Media Research found that Latinos as a percentage of the vote had tripled since the Koch vs. Dinkins primary in 1989 from 8 to 23 percent of the vote. In the same stretch, white voters declined from 61 to 50 percent of the primary voters. Only one in sixteen white voters were for Ferrer, who carried half the black vote.

The assumption after 9/11was that everything had changed, but little seemed to have changed for the Democratic primary voters who ranked terrorism and rebuilding lower Manhattan at the bottom of their priorities, well below the liberal staples of more money for social services and education. Just 3 percent of the Democratic Party primary voters wanted someone who would be a strong leader in a crisis. All of 1 percent of Ferrer voters thought that rebuilding lower Manhattan should be a top priority.

The primary voters took little notice of the staggering economic loss that had been inflicted on the city. In the week after the attack, the Dow Jones average suffered its second biggest weekly downturn since 1915 with losses totaling $1.38 trillion in market value. The businesses below 14th Street were the hardest hit, but the lights were going out along Broadway and hotels were half empty, while department store sales, down 10 to 15 percent nationally since 9/11, were down 40 percent in New York.

The attack turned what had been a mild recession into a steep economic slump for the city, which faced massive cleanup costs and many months of economic disruption. "The city," exclaimed Felix Rohatyn with some exaggeration, "is in greater economic jeopardy today than it was in the fiscal crisis of 1975." The insurance industry estimate set the total economic losses suffered by the city at somewhere between $40 and 60 billion. The losses doubled the city's projected budget gap. Giuliani, sizing up the situation, prepared to sell a billion dollars in city debt to bring in money for cleanup and repair quickly until federal aid could arrive.[2]

Behind the immediate numbers describing the economic losses lay something even more frightening for the long run. The losses from 9/11 hid the long-term trend toward the geographic decentralization of financial services that had been gaining strength even before the attack. The Internet made it possible to locate financial services jobs virtually anywhere. In the 1990s, there was a sharp rise in financial services employment nationally, but none of that growth took place in Gotham. 9/11 accelerated the trend to decentralize.

Giuliani recognized the threat. He saw that an unprecedented attack required an unprecedented response. In what became the defining issue of the run-off, he proposed to stay on an additional three months to smooth the recovery. If the candidates wouldn't agree to that, he threatened to circumvent term limits. But practically, there was no way to evade term limits. Talk of running again was clearly a bluff aimed at winning the additional three months. Legally speaking, there was no problem with an extension. The state constitution made explicit provision for just such a delay in case of an emergency.

Time was of the essence in mitigating the impact of the attack. Much of America had grown up despising New York's pretensions and the arrogance of the "Damn Yankees." But for a moment, the country embraced its half-foreign city on the Hudson. Giuliani and the firefighters and police had become symbols of American resolve.

It was important to seize the moment. By the time the next mayor was fully in control of the city's government, the 2002 political season would have already begun along with new issues, and a new budget year in which the national recession would place both the federal and state governments in fiscal difficulty. New York needed to move quickly on its rebuilding agenda before its needs got caught up in the inevitable complication of congressional, state legislative and gubernatorial elections.[3]*

Giuliani's enormous national popularity was an invaluable asset for the rebuilding of New York. The man who escaped near death as the World Trade Center collapsed was now "America's Mayor." If he could stay in charge for an additional three months, he could help move the federal money through Congress with a maximum of speed and minimum of restrictions while magnifying the city's say in how the money was used. Even more intriguing, Giuliani proposed to use the country's passing embrace to redo the federal funding formulas that consistently shortchanged the city. "We should not go back to the tin cup era," Giuliani explained. "We just have to ask for equity."[4]

Michael Bloomberg, the Republican candidate for mayor, agreed to the three additional months as did, much to many people's surprise, Mark Green, who agreed to the three-month extension for Giuliani without consulting his dismayed political team. When the issue of Green's support for the ninety-day extension came up during a rally at Brooklyn's Boro Hall, "about a dozen Democratic officials who were endorsing him were asked by reporters to display, by a show of hands, whether they agreed with Mr. Green.... Only one hand went up."[5]

The audience on the Letterman show might be chanting "RUDY, RUDY, RUDY," but Green's staff knew that Ferrer, running on resentment, would seize on Green's support for the ninety-day

---

*In retrospect, the slow pace in reconstructing lower Manhattan, the long delays in even thinking about how to redo the area's transportation connections and the inability to use much of the money and credits on offer from the federal government, which until the attack had systematically shortchanged the city when it comes to anti-terror funding, make Giuliani's proposal to stay on look better and better. President Bush promised $20 billion in reconstruction aid. He kept his promise, but much of the aid was in the form of tax credits the city and state were unable to use. Nearly three years after 9/11 Governor Pataki tried to trade the tax credits for transportation money needed to ensure the long-term business viability of lower Manhattan.

extension to morph Mark into Rudy. Green, a lifelong leftist, was suddenly "unmasked" on Sharpton-friendly black media outlets as a stealthy racist. With some of the anti-Rudy rage and resentment that had been cultivated for eight years transferred to Green, the Public Advocate lost 15 percent of his black support in forty-eight hours. In a week Green lost a fifth of his support among white woman. Under attack from the tandem of Reverend Sharpton and Representative Rangel, who accused the Public Advocate of truckling to the racist Rudy, Green's support collapsed in the Bronx and Harlem.

Appealing to his base, Ferrer promised, despite the attack, to initiate the costly spending programs he had been promising. He said he would pay for them with new taxes. "The towers of the World Trade Center have crumbled," he explained, "but our priorities have not." Ferrer who bragged that "I'm not from Mars, I'm from the Bronx regular [political] organization," was in synch with his core voters.[6]*

The candidates who accepted the extension, argued Ferrer, "lacked the leadership to run the city." The Bronx Boro President implied that an additional ninety days for Giuliani was part of a white establishment coup to deny the city's people of color their chance to control the government.[7]

Green, surrounded by a solid cast of outer-boro advisors, had, up until the extension flap, run the well-grounded campaign of a man whose focus was on governing. But the extension flap rattled him. Green was under attack from both his left and his right. On his right, former mayor Ed Koch had warned that Ferrer would owe

---

*The key to the response of both Ferrer and his supporters lies in the economics and politics of the Bronx. The Bronx was the only boro without a Chamber of Commerce. That's because the Bronx has very little in the way of a private-sector economy. Nearly half the jobs in the Bronx come directly from local government or from government subsidized health and social service programs.

Ferrer's unstinting support for city spending won him the trifecta of support from the city's three largest public sector unions: The United Federation of Teachers, District Council 37 of the American Federation of State County, and Municipal Employees and Local 1199 of the Health and Hospital care workers. DC 37 leader Lee Saunders boasted that in 2001 the unions had the chance to "elect our own employers." But the 1199 support was the most significant. Health care workers alone represent nearly 25 percent of all employment in the Bronx, where politics has often been organized around competing Medicaid empires. The Health and Hospital Workers provided the ground troops for the Ferrer campaign.

his election to Sharpton, who "will have the power to either appoint or veto commissioners, including the police commissioner." But Koch, who was carrying water for Republican Michael Bloomberg, the candidate he would support in the general election, backed Ferrer to hurt Green, whom he accused of being "craven" for supporting the ninety-day extension. Under pressure, Green reverted to an earlier political persona that had been marred by arrogance: "I would have done as well or better than Giuliani on 9/11."[8]

Fear of what was sometimes known as the "Freddy Sharpton" campaign drove the city's police and fire unions, as well as most of the city's private-sector unions and businessmen, into the Green camp. One business leader told *Crain's,* a business weekly, that Ferrer has "run an 'us vs. them' campaign and we are 'them.' He's made business the enemy." Similarly, fear of Freddy pushed the *Times* to warn that Ferrer's policy proposals might threaten the city's recovery.[9]

Green capitalized on how white voters heard Ferrer's "other New York" rhetoric as "we're owed and you're going to pay for it." He responded to Ferrer's attacks by arguing that the Bronx boro president viewed 9/11 through "the lens of the Bronx." Green didn't need to exploit the Sharpton-Ferrer connection overtly—the Reverend did it for him. Eager to put himself in the center of things, the Reverend mocked those who thought Giuliani had performed brilliantly. He insisted at a rally attended by Ferrer that "We [the city] would have come together if Bozo was the mayor."[10]

Green was well aware that Sharpton's support for Ferrer was a double-edged sword. Early in the race, he told political reporter Arthur Nitzburg that he had "received feelers from Sharpton." "I'd like to get his constituency, but the real question is how to handle Sharpton if he winds up endorsing me." Then they related to each other the old Jewish joke about the woman who shows her friends the huge diamond ring on her finger. "It's the world-famous Finkelstein diamond," the woman says. "But it comes with a curse." "What's the curse?" her friend asks. "Finkelstein," the woman sighs.[11]

Four days before the October 11 run-off, Ferrer's effective mobilization of Latino and black voters put him in the lead. But Green closed strong with endorsements from the police and firefighters' unions and Mario Cuomo. In the preposterous politics of New York's racial spoils system, Mark Green, the former Naderite, became the establishment candidate supported by the *New York Post* and its arch-enemy, the *Village Voice.* What held them all together was fear of Freddy.

In the Democratic primary, voters didn't so much elect Green, who benefited from an anthrax scare that terrorized the city in the weeks before the primary, as reject Ferrer, who with Sharpton at his side, bitterly acknowledged his 48 to 52 percent defeat. Of those voters who told the exit pollsters that they had cast a negative vote, 78 percent supported Green. In a sign of trouble for the general election, only 40 percent of Green's voters were enthusiastic about their choice.

On Election Day, there were, as the Ferrer campaign had hoped, two New Yorks. The lower your income and years of education, the more you were likely to vote for Ferrer; the more educated and wealthier, the more likely you were to vote for Green. Ferrer's mobilization had produced a counter-mobilization. Without 9/11 Ferrer probably would have won the primary.*

Green's victory pitted a chastened liberal who had accepted Giuliani's policing and welfare reforms against a liberal Democrat turned Republican, Michael Bloomberg, who had also signed on to the Giuliani reforms as the price of the incumbent's endorsement. In the topsy-turvy world of New York, a campaign pitting these two liberals against each other meant that at least part of Giuliani's legacy was safe.

▲ ▲ ▲

In the summer of 2001, polls found Bloomberg losing to any of the Democratic candidates by forty points. David Garth, who had worked for the winner in seven of the last nine mayoral elections, was hired by Bloomberg to do his TV ads. But at the outset, not even Garth thought that his candidate had a chance. The unwritten rule

---

*Ferrer's identity-politics campaign of rolling back the Rudy-reforms had carried 84 percent of the Latino and 71 percent of the black vote, but only 16 percent of whites. Sharpton proved a big plus for Green since according to exit polls 36 percent of voters said that his support of Ferrer pushed them to Green while 16 percent, less than half as many, said it drew them to Ferrer. Of the voters who had come out for the run-off, 14 percent of Green's voters shifted to Ferrer while the reverse traffic was only 5 percent. But in the midst of the anthrax scare Green won 57 percent of those who hadn't voted in the earlier rounds.

A look at the broader election picture suggests it was not minority candidates who had been rejected in the primaries but rather Ferrer and Sharpton. In 2001 African-Americans would for the first time win the offices of Comptroller and Queens Boro President. There were no Republican candidates fielded for those offices in the general election. The victor in the Comptroller race, Bill Thompson, a black moderate, defeated Herb Berman, a white Jewish candidate. Both were from Brooklyn. Thompson became the second most powerful elected official in the city and a future candidate for mayor.

of Gotham politics said that Republicans never succeed one another. They are elected once every thirty years and only when an incumbent Democrat has bungled things badly. 2001 proved different because of the Rudycrats as well as 9/11.

The city's one-party politics had been modified ever since Giuliani first ran in 1989. For mayor, at least, Giuliani made the general election important again. The Rudycrats, the moderate white Catholic and Jewish voters who had first elected Koch, began deserting the Democratic Party primary in droves. They preferred to wait and vote for Giuliani in the general election in 1989, 1993 and 1997. This produced Democratic Party mayoral nominees who, chosen by the remaining rump of the Democratic Party, were well to the left of even New York's electorate.*

▲ ▲ ▲

After winning the run-off, Mark Green's thoughts jumped ahead to governing. Green all but dismissed his political consultant Hank Sheinkopf, who was attuned to the Rudycrats, and began assembling his transition team. But the expected reconciliation between the rival Democrats never took place. Green made the standard moves; he praised Ferrer for running an "extraordinary, passionate, principled, inspiring race," and welcomed the support of Sharpton, whom he described as "inarguably a leader."[12]

Green's generous words weren't reciprocated. Just as in 1997 when Sharpton had submarined Messinger, what followed the run-off was a Sharpton/Ferrer vendetta, this time directed against Green. Depicting Green as a raving racist was no easy matter. But New York's entrepreneurs of ethnic antagonism were up to the task. The city's Democratic primaries are often competitions for ethnic power masked by the pretense of ideological differences.

Green was accused of making Sharpton into the Willie Horton of the run-off. "Some of us are incredibly unhappy," said Dennis

---

* White liberal candidates for the Democratic nomination have been whipsawed by the Giuliani factor. If they fail to gain sufficient minority support they lose the primary, as Ed Koch lost to David Dinkins in 1989. But if they defeat a minority candidate, like Messinger in 1997 and Green in 2001, they generate resentments that come back to haunt them in the general election. A similar dynamic played out in the 2002 Democratic primary for Governor between State Comptroller Carl McCall, an African-American, and the moderately liberal Andrew Cuomo. Racial politics forced Cuomo, the stronger candidate and one with a well-developed critique of why Albany was dysfunctional, out of the race.

Rivera, president of 1199, the powerful hospital workers' union. "Mark tried to divide this city by using code words. He has a lot of work to do. All is not well in the Democratic Party." According to Sharpton, doubtless an expert on the matter, "The race card was played; there were certainly racial overtures made. We just are going to inspect the decks to see whose fingerprints are on the card." By Sharpton's reckoning, a campaign phone message—"stop Al Sharpton," because "Sharpton cannot be given the keys to the city," so "please go to the polls tomorrow and vote against Freddy Ferrer and Al Sharpton"—was inherently racist.[13]

Initially it appeared as though, in the traditional fashion of New York's version of racial collective bargaining, the Ferrer/Sharpton anger, real and feigned, would be used as leverage for jobs and patronage in a Green administration. But Green, while wanting to propitiate the anger, was determined to govern effectively in the wake of the 9/11 attacks and during a severe downturn. He had spent eight years as Public Advocate thinking about how to govern, and he had assembled a first-rate staff. Confident that he would win, he wasn't willing to bargain that away.

Emboldened by their success in creating a black-Latino coalition, Ferrer and Sharpton soon began to cozy up to Bloomberg and his vast fortune. "There will not be silence and consent to the insult that we've been dealt in this race," Mr. Sharpton said to loud applause, addressing about two hundred people. "I'm not endorsing Bloomberg," Mr. Sharpton said. "But I'm not endorsing nothing that doesn't stand for us. And if I could survive eight years of Giuliani, I can survive four years of Bloomberg." Rangel followed suit. The Congressman and Ferrer's political strategist Bill Lynch met with Bloomberg. After the meeting, Rangel said he had encouraged the financial-media mogul to run for mayor as a Democrat. Asked if he might endorse Bloomberg, Rangel said, "Wasn't John Lindsay a Republican? I was one of the first Democrats who supported him, so I'm out of the business of ruling out" any candidates based on their party affiliation.[14]

▲ ▲ ▲

Michael Bloomberg, who'd donated $1,000 to the 1997 Green for Public Advocate re-election campaign, had been a Democrat until a year before he entered the 2001 mayoral race as a Republican. He owned a financial news TV channel and radio station both of which bore his name, and the Bloomberg logo was plastered on bus stops and billboards, the walkways to the La Guardia shuttle flights, and the entrances to the Holland Tunnel. But outside of Wall Street, most New Yorkers had little idea of who he was.

The scion of a middle-class family from Medford, Massachusetts, Bloomberg attended Johns Hopkins and Harvard Business School and then worked his way up on Wall Street, becoming a partner at Salomon Brothers until the firm was bought out and he was forced out in 1981. He used his $10 million share of the buy-out to form his own financial information firm. Bloomberg saw the demand for real-time financial information was growing rapidly. He developed the Bloomberg terminal, which provided up-to-the-second pricing information on stocks and bonds along with background information for free. All you had to do was pay for the dedicated Bloomberg information terminal. The idea succeeded brilliantly. In the 1990s Bloomberg moved into magazines, radio and television.

Restless, he divorced his wife in 1991 and became a man about town. He was selected as both one of the Forbes 400 Richest Men in America and as New York's "most eligible bachelor" (beating out Donald Trump). Bloomberg, who made no secret of his love for fine wine and beautiful woman, was frequently featured in the city's gossip columns. He also became a philanthropic force through his membership on the Board of Johns Hopkins University Hospital. In 2000, he donated more than $100 million to charities, many of them devoted to improving public health.

One of his first forays into local politics came in 2000, when he hosted a dinner party at his Upper East Side townhouse to discuss the problems of Central Park. Guests at the feel-good occasion were given a Bloomberg-logo umbrella, a radio that received only Bloomberg's radio station and gourmet cookies as party favors. It was a successful effort at "dialoguing," and he later cited it as an example of how he would govern.

Why did Bloomberg run for public office? A statement he made before his mayoral run gave a strong hint: "Once you've accumulated wealth, you've got a serious problem. You can only eat so many meals, have so much domestic help, travel to so many places and live in so many rooms. You can only sleep in one bed at one time." The mayoralty, it seems, would be a new experience, the personal challenge to cap his career.[15]

Despite the advice of talented political pros like former Moynihan operative William Cunningham and pollsters Doug Schoen and Frank Luntz, Bloomberg's campaign got off to a rocky start with disclosures about sexual harassment suits that had been filed against him. In one case that was settled out of court, it was alleged that when a female employee informed him she was pregnant, he told her, "Kill it!" In what was described as a "What, me worry?" interview with Elizabeth Bumiller of the *New York Times,* Bloomberg blanched at having his wealth held against him. "Would you rather elect a poor person who didn't succeed?" he snapped.[16]

While Mark Green was making a series of well-wrought speeches on how to respond to the physical and financial aftermath of 9/11, Bloomberg, closely supervised by his political team, confined himself to generalities.

A stranger to most of the city outside of Manhattan, Bloomberg talked about how New York brought down crime with "community policing." It didn't; it used "broken windows" policing, which is quite different. He insisted that the city alone should handle the reconstruction of Ground Zero, but the World Trade Center stood on state land, and Mr. Giuliani and Governor George Pataki went ahead and named a state-city commission to oversee the rebuilding. The doubters, such as *New York Post* columnist John Podhoretz, described Mr. Bloomberg as a man with an "elemental misunderstanding" about how New York is governed.[17]

It looked at first as though Bloomberg was just a wealthier version of the famously failed Republican candidacies of Ron Lauder and Pierre Rinfret. He was mocked as a "slightly taller not so nutty version of Ross Perot," an "ego in search of an office," with no ideas and no program except resolving his own mid-life crisis. Political guru Dick Morris described him as "a series of TV ads in search of a candidate, a bank account running for office."[18]

Even after he easily won the Republican nomination by defeating Herman Badillo in September, Bloomberg's campaign was largely ignored. But then events turned Bloomberg's way as he began drawing one card after another to an inside straight. 9/11 and the bitter brawl between the Democrats allowed him time to work on his political skills while attention was focused elsewhere.

Green, hampered by the public financing rules he helped create, had a hard time garnering public attention. The news coverage was focused on the aftermath of 9/11, the fear that the anthrax sent in the mail was part of a terrorist attack, and the Yankees' path to another World Championship. That enabled Bloomberg to match Green's almost five to one advantage in party registration with a better than five to one advantage in advertising.

Saved from scrutiny by the perfect political storm that followed 9/11, a bitter, racially divisive Democratic primary, and a $75 million campaign, Bloomberg was barely questioned, let alone tested. While Green's campaign receded in the public eye, Bloomberg was defined to the voters by his ads that depicted him as a Rudy-like guy who got things done. In a lavishly funded and very effective TV campaign in English and Spanish, David Garth struck just the right note by emphasizing Bloomberg's managerial skills and independence. Bloomberg wasn't given the chance to make many gaffes. He made few public appearances and rarely answered questions. Then, after defining the candidate in gauzy terms at a time when the free media's attention was elsewhere, the Bloomberg campaign turned to driving up Green's negatives very effectively. The attack ads, noted Green campaign advisor Rich Schrader, piled atop one another "like snow on a roof," until Green's lead collapsed. Particular damage had been done by the ad that simply quoted a smug Green declaring he could've "done better" than Giuliani on and after September 11.

The Bloomberg camp waited to play its key card. It saturated the airwaves and mailboxes with Giuliani's endorsement of Bloomberg. The Bloomberg commercials created their own Garth-inspired reality. They exploited the Giuliani endorsement so persuasively that, said Rich Schrader of the Green campaign, "Bloomberg morphed into post-World Trade Center Rudy, almost as if the city would get a third Giuliani term if Bloomberg was elected." Strangely, Green never played his aces in the hole. He never ran ads appealing to white Catholic swing voters featuring the police and firefighters, Bill Bratton, Bill Clinton or Mario Cuomo, all of whom had endorsed him.

Both Green and Bloomberg had created such contradictory coalitions that it would make it difficult for either to govern effectively. Green, the long-time critic of police brutality, was the candidate of the Police Benevolent Association. Bloomberg, the CEO of a non-union company, was effectively the candidate of labor leader Dennis Rivera. But while Green didn't play off the possibilities presented by his mesalliances, the Bloomberg campaign did. Lenora Fulani, the leader of the cultish New Alliance Party, had been shunned by all the major Democratic candidates for her extreme and anti-Semitic statements. Bloomberg accepted her endorsement. On Election Day 60,000 voters supported Bloomberg on Fulani's Independence line, although it wasn't clear if they were voting for her or the idea of political independence or they just couldn't bear to vote for Bloomberg on the Republican line.

While Green was losing the air and tactical wars, Ferrer and Sharpton were waging a ground war that undermined Green's standing with minority voters. It is no accident, as the Marxists say, that on Election Day, the offices of the Bronx Democratic Party headquarters were closed, the phones turned off. Bloomberg eked out a narrow 4,200 vote victory with an incongruous coalition of Rudycrats and Rudyphobes united only in their opposition to Mark Green in one or another of his incarnations. Asked by Maureen Dowd about the importance of Giuliani's endorsement, Bloomberg replied, "Rudy was two or three points." On his first morning as mayor-elect, Bloomberg met not with Rudy Giuliani, but with Freddy Ferrer. On his second day as mayor-elect he went out of his way to shake hands with the Reverend Sharpton. From the start, plain "Mike," as he wanted to be known, wanted to try to shake the shadow of the man who had made his victory possible.[19]

TWENTY FIVE

City Hall after Rudy/
Rudy after City Hall

Most mayors have departed from New York's City Hall defeated by the ungovernable city. Lindsay, Beame and Dinkins all left under a cloud. La Guardia left with his local achievements intact, but La Guardia, out of synch with the immediate post-war electoral mood, was already fading politically in his final term. Rudy Giuliani's departure was different. Rudy Giuliani, the merciless moderate, presided over a New York Renaissance. His heroism on 9/11 and his prescience on terrorism made him a rising national political figure.

There was a remarkable thematic unity to Giuliani's mayoralty. His inaugural speech in January of 1994 centered on the 1993 attack on the World Trade Center and on the promise of American life embodied in the story of his own immigrant family. He returned to those same themes eight years later in his farewell address delivered from the dais of St. Paul's Church, a stone's throw from where the World Trade Center had once stood. St. Paul's, where George Washington had prayed after he had been inaugurated as the first president, had, almost miraculously, emerged from the firestorm of 9/11 virtually untouched.

Giuliani explained to a crowd of loyalists but only a skeleton's crew of reporters that, when he took office, he "believed rightly or wrongly that we had one last chance to" save New York, "to really turn it around in a totally opposite direction from the direction it was going in. And that created a lot of hostility." There had been, he argued, a war of ideas between himself and those with different "political philosophies and political creeds" whose ideologies "had the city headed in the wrong direction." Giuliani discussed liberal judges who were "cruel" even as they thought they were being kind by exempting the homeless from all responsibility for their actions. On a more defensive note, he mocked the editorialists at the *New York Times* whose judgments he had almost systematically ignored, although on the question of the city's long-term fiscal prospects, those critics were increasingly getting the better of the argument.

He made two pleas: One was to treat the World Trade Center site as "hallowed ground" like Gettysburg, Valley Forge and Normandy; the other was never to return to the anti-development, high-tax policies that had laid the city low. It was advice destined to be ignored. Bloomberg returned the city to the failed tax policies of the Dinkins years. Mayor Bloomberg backed development, although that often meant support of vast Rockefeller-like stadium projects with questionable economic benefits.

There seems to have been an implicit deal between Giuliani and Bloomberg in which the new mayor agreed, despite his liberal proclivities, not to tamper with Rudy's policing and welfare reforms and in return the former mayor would refrain from criticizing his successor. Despite occasional sniping, the bargain has held up. Crime has continued to decline under Ray Kelly, Bloomberg's capable police commissioner, and welfare backsliding has been limited.

But rarely has a mayor of a major city been less prepared to govern. Asked what he did in his first one hundred days, Bloomberg answered, "I got ready for the next thousand." At the same stage, Giuliani had already spent years immersing himself in the details of government. In office he worked long hours keeping a close watch on day-to-day operations without losing sight of the big picture. His successor, far less skilled as a manager, has had neither an animating vision nor a direct hand in running the city's maze of bureaucracies. In almost every major instance where Bloomberg has tried to make his own mark, his approach has failed.

Giuliani was able, at times, to embody higher purposes that transcended ordinary contradictions. Bloomberg has little of that policy magic. As befits an administration that came to power with electoral support from both Giuliani's most ardent admirers and his most agitated enemies, the Bloomberg mayoralty attempted to use Dinkins-like means to attain Giuliani-like ends and has ended up a moderately competent muddle. The political neophyte's conciliatory attempt to reach out to every major interest group was initially well suited to the post-9/11 sense of trauma. Bloomberg's we-can-all-do-business-together approach allowed him to distinguish himself from Giuliani's driving, contentious style. But it came at the cost of cutting him off from the substance of his predecessor's achievements. In a city where there is no countervailing power to the public sector, Giuliani generally governed by serving as the representative of widely-shared goals. Bloomberg, in savoring good relations with every pressure group, has had a hard time representing the city as a whole.

The problem, in part, was that while most public officials are consistently insincere, Bloomberg was sincerely inconsistent. He ran for office on a ringing no-new-taxes pledge. In his first major speech as mayor, he declared, "We cannot drive people and business out of New York. We cannot raise taxes." But when faced with the post-9/11 recession, rather than look for spending cuts, he sharply raised property, sales, income and cigarette taxes, thus deepening and prolonging the city's recession.* And when the billionaire Bloomberg explained that he would be glad to pay the additional taxes, he only highlighted the vast differences between himself and most New Yorkers.

Like Rockefeller and Lindsay before him, Bloomberg is a liberal paternalist, who despite his own success story has a scant understanding of what's needed to give people a chance to rise in life. When Mayor Bloomberg spoke of "opportunity," he referred, as if it were still the age of La Guardia, to new public works projects. Bloomberg's comments on Gotham as "a luxury city" for the very rich and the people servicing them was world's apart from Giuliani's vision of a city embracing the "genius of American life."[1]

Giuliani's attacks on the Board of Education set the stage for its elimination and gave his successor direct mayoral control of the schools. Given the opportunity to manage the city school system, Bloomberg and his School Chancellor Joel Klein imposed an oft-

---

*Both Giuliani and Bloomberg faced massive budget holes but the city Bloomberg inherited in 2002 was in far better shape than the city Giuliani had taken over in 1994. Not only was crime under control, but, even with 9/11, the recession Bloomberg faced was shorter and less severe than the downturn of the early 1990s. Despite the destruction of the World Trade Center, the city in 2002 had 200,000 more jobs than in 1994.

failed curriculum straight out of the "progressive" education fever swamps of Columbia Teachers College. "The teacher," says the progressive education slogan," shouldn't be a sage on the stage, but rather a guide on the side." Klein has imposed the postmodern attack on knowledge, which assumes that students learn as much if not more from each other than from their teachers, on every classroom. The educational results have been predictably disappointing.*

One area of continuity between the two very different mayors has brought Bloomberg considerable political grief. Giuliani generated heated opposition with his plan to move Yankee Stadium from the Bronx to the West Side of Manhattan. Bloomberg has scanted the rebuilding to try to construct a football stadium for the Jets on the same West Side location as part of a still-grander plan to bring the 2012 Olympics to New York. It is a plan about which New Yorkers, already burdened with a mammoth city debt, feel at best ambivalent. The idea of massive subsidies to a sports franchise at a time of rising taxes and subway fares has provided an opening for his 2005 re-election opponents. Win or lose in 2005, Bloomberg seems unlikely to escape Giuliani's shadow.

Giuliani's anti-crime achievements and his success in reviving neighborhoods will endure. But whereas La Guardia, New York's other great twentieth-century mayor, was part of a broader reform movement, Giuliani *was* the reform movement. With its Prince gone, the city has reverted to its predictable pattern in which public-sector unions and their liberal activist and social service allies, temporarily divided in the Giuliani years, have reasserted their dominance. Not even the next fiscal crisis, which looks to be coming in the next few years, is likely to challenge the city's archaic politics. Gotham's fiscal follies are like those lead-weighted toy soldiers, which, even after being knocked over, always return to their original position. The upshot is that the chasm between the country and the city, which Giuliani narrowed and 9/11 closed temporarily, reopened as wide as ever during the intensely polarized 2004 presidential election.

▲ ▲ ▲

In the aftermath of 9/11, Giuliani became a major national and even

---

* The Klein/Bloomberg centralized curriculum fiasco made Giuliani's call for vouchers all the more compelling.

international figure. On October 11, 2001, the country got to see what a Giuliani presidential run might look like when Prince Alwaleed Bin Talal of Saudi Arabia, the home country of fifteen of the nineteen 9/11 terrorists, presented the mayor with a check for $10 million at a memorial service for the victims of the attack. American qualms about Saudi Arabia's radical brand of Wahhabi Islam had long been quieted by similar exercises of checkbook diplomacy. But the Saudi Prince was in for a surprise. After giving Giuliani the check, he released a statement blaming the attack on the Arab-Israel conflict as the root cause of terrorism. Giuliani responded by rejecting both the check and its rationalization to cheers from the American public, which had already adopted him as a hero. Giuliani explained, "To suggest that there's a justification for [the terrorist attacks] only invites this happening in the future." There was, he insisted, no moral equivalence between liberal democracies like the U.S. and Israel and "those who condone terrorism." He concluded that Alwaleed Bin Talal's comments were not only "wrong, they're part of the problem."[2]

Dubbed America's Mayor by Oprah Winfrey, knighted by the Queen of England, Giuliani's stature was further enhanced by the corporate scandals of 2002, which created a demand for public rectitude that the former slayer of Wall Street dragons was only too happy to fill on behalf of his new firm, Giuliani Partners LLC. Giuliani Partners, which offered not only security but also management and public relations advice to everything from hospitals to horse racing operations to South American police forces as well as to pharmaceutical and communications companies, quickly moved into the top tier of American consulting companies.

In October 2002 his book *Leadership,* ostensibly a guide to management but in fact an unselfcritical replay of Rudy's greatest hits, was published to enormous fanfare. The book, a turgid read, became a national bestseller as long rows of fans lined up around the country to have America's matinee idol mayor sign their copy. In the 2002 election, his luster undiminished, a self-confident Giuliani, who now combed his hair straight back to reveal his balding pate, vigorously campaigned for Republicans in nineteen states as the GOP went on to recapture the U.S. Senate.

In the 2004 elections, Giuliani, with an eye on national office, emerged as a tough critic of Democratic presidential nominee John Kerry. Questioned about his swing from a relatively non-partisan mayor who had once endorsed Mario Cuomo for Governor to GOP spokesman, Giuliani never explained his shift but merely responded, "Look, I'm a partisan. I am a Republican. I have always preferred to be straight-out with people."

Giuliani's speech, delivered at the August 2004 Republican Convention held in New York so that the Bush campaign could draw on the images of 9/11, was a smash hit. The speech wasn't as coherent as John McCain's well-reasoned case for the war in Iraq, but it was far more of a crowd-pleaser that completed Giuliani's move from the local to national stage. Giuliani appeared at the podium to a standing ovation while the crowd cheered "Rudy, Rudy." A smiling Giuliani responded, "It feels like a Yankees game."

The former mayor praised Kerry's service in Vietnam. But then in an implicit comparison with his own steadfastness, he mocked Kerry as someone who "at one point, declared himself an anti-war candidate. Now, he says he's pro-war. At this rate, with sixty-four days left, he still has time to change his position at least three or four more times." Giuliani brought the crowd to applause and laughter when he added, "Maybe this explains John Edwards' need for two Americas—one where John Kerry can vote for something and another where he can vote against the same thing."

Mixing humor with substance, he made the case for Bush's foreign policy better than the president himself was able to do. Pointing to how Bin Ladenism had grown out of the international appeasement of Palestinian thuggery, he condemned the way that "Terrorist acts [had] become a ticket to the international bargaining table." Then, in a reference to the incident in which he had Yasser Arafat unceremoniously tossed out of Lincoln Center, he continued, "How else to explain Yasser Arafat winning the Nobel Peace Prize when he was supporting a terrorist plague in the Middle East?.... President Bush will not allow countries that appear to have ignored the lessons of history and failed for over thirty years to stand up to terrorists, to dissuade us from what is necessary for our defense."

Giuliani's rollicking New-York-style sarcastic speech connected with both the Madison Square Garden and television audiences. The headlines around the country echoed the *Daily News*, which reported, "America's Mayor hits a Homer for W."

Many in the crowd responded as did Laurie Forcier, a Wisconsin delegate. "This is a leader," she said, "This man knows how to lead. Every single one of us. We sat here like a church saying 'Yes!'

'Yes!'" But there were doubters on the religious right of the Republican Party who warned that if Giuliani with his liberal stands on abortion and gay rights were nominated for president by the 2008 GOP convention, "you would have a walkout by social conservatives."[3]

In America, the election season is now a matter of perpetual motion. Two days after George Bush's re-election, a McLaughlin & Associates poll found America's mayor had emerged as the clear front-runner for the 2008 Republican nomination with 30 percent, while John McCain was second with 18 percent. Giuliani's strong numbers raised the question of whether the mayoralty, even of New York, prepares a politician to be president. Running New York's vast bureaucracy certainly provides a more rigorous test of accountability than serving in the Senate. President Lyndon Johnson, in talking about his own troubles, once noted that not a sparrow falls in a city that the mayor isn't blamed for and then quipped, "When the burdens of the presidency seem unusually heavy, I always remind myself that it could be worse—I could be a mayor." A mayor and a president are similar in that the public relates to them in a far more personal, direct and even visceral manner than other elected offices.

Before the Republican convention, there had been speculation about Giuliani, first that he, his eye on the presidency, would take over the troubled Securities and Exchange Commission, then he would replace an ailing Dick Cheney as the vice-presidential nominee on the Republican ticket for 2004. After the election, when President Bush began a cabinet reshuffle, Giuliani was mentioned prominently as a possible Attorney General, Secretary of Homeland Security or even Secretary of State.

But in the end, Giuliani showed little interest in subordinating himself to the needs of the Bush administration. Consistent with his presidential ambitions, which date back to his mayoral re-election in 1997, he remained in the private sector, continuing to amass wealth as the CEO of Giuliani Partners, which a few months after the election acquired the investment-banking arm of the accounting giant Ernst & Young. The Bush administration acknowledged the former mayor's influence when it announced that his former police commissioner and business partner Bernard Kerik had, partly on Giuliani's recommendation, been picked for the Homeland Security post. It looked as if Giuliani would have the best of both worlds, personal wealth and his own voice inside the administration.

Kerik, who had gone to Iraq to train the police force and then campaigned vigorously for the Bush re-election campaign, had established his own ties to the administration. He was a far cry from the usual buttoned-down cabinet secretaries. An administration insider explained the choice in personal terms: Bush, he said "likes Kerik. He gets a kick out of him." The appointment was initially received with great enthusiasm across New York's political spectrum. Kerik promised both to bring a beat cop's broken windows sensibility to the post and to redirect anti-terror funds to New York, which had been badly shortchanged by Senate formulas that gave Wyoming, an unlikely target, nine times more in per capita aid than New York.*

But it all quickly unraveled as Kerik withdrew his nomination on the grounds that he hadn't paid the social security taxes for a nanny who may or may not have existed. This was followed in short order by revelations that the married Kerik had maintained a post-9/11 love nest for one of his two paramours in an apartment near Ground Zero that had been set aside for rescue workers. The underside of his life, including a close friendship with a reputedly mob-related contractor, continued to pour out. He was soon forced to resign from Giuliani Partners as well as the cabinet nomination.†

Although he didn't seem to suffer in national popularity, Giuliani had badly damaged his relationship with the Bush clan, which will have a crucial say in who receives the 2008 GOP nomination. Giuliani's judgment was also called into question and charges of cronyism were given credibility when it was revealed that Kerik was not given an updated background check when he had been appointed Police Commissioner in 2000. And worse yet for the New Yorker's presidential hopes, his rivals for the nomination were given a way to go after Giuliani without even mentioning his social issue shifts on abortion and gay rights. Instead, references to cronyism, deceit, and sloppy background checks would serve to remind conservative voters of the enormous gap between the political culture of Gotham and the heartland. The Kerik scandal reminded politi-

---

*The 12/16/03 *Washington Post* described how New York policing provided insights that led to the capture of Saddam Hussein: "Following a strategy similar to that pioneered by New York City police in the 1990s, who cracked down on 'squeegee men' only to discover they knew about far more serious criminals, Maj. Gen. Raymond T. Odierno said his analysts and commanders spent the summer building 'link diagrams,' graphics showing everyone related to Hussein by blood or tribe."
† The next nominee, Michael Chertoff, first came to public attention as an assistant federal prosecutor working for Giuliani in the Justice Department.

cians of all stripes of why the New York mayoralty has long been a graveyard for political ambitions. No New York City mayor has gone on to higher office since the mid-nineteenth century.

Still, it's far too early to count Giuliani out. His Machiavellian realism has given him the ability to play deftly with whatever hand he has been dealt. His extraordinary management skills, his evolving speaking abilities, his prescient stand on terrorism, and his appeal to moderate voters would all serve him well as a general election candidate. He could campaign as few others can on a record of extraordinary accomplishments and a demonstrated capacity to lead in a time of peril.

Giuliani achieved his success in New York by living up to Churchill's maxim that courage is the most important political virtue because it guarantees all the others. Putting partisanship aside, he governed in the broad interests of the city regardless of whom he enraged. He's become far more of a partisan Republican to try and win the 2008 GOP nomination. But even so, the man reviled by Gotham's leftists as a ruthless "fascist" and criticized by heartland social conservatives as a "liberal" has an enormous appeal for a considerable majority of Americans.

His future as a hard-edged moderate may depend on whether the 2008 election is again fought on a polarized landscape in which left and right, blue and red, mobilize their bases, or whether the country, which is largely purple, turns back to the center. And that in turn will depend on which issues come to the fore. Another major terror attack will shake the political terrain, and the criticisms of Giuliani as "ruthless" may turn to his advantage as the public looks for a resolute leader. But in a calmer climate, his tendency, even in the name of good causes, to bulldoze people who get in his way, will be a liability.

In the meantime, one thing is certain: Giuliani, the student of management, will be scrutinizing the GOP nominating process and the operations of the federal bureaucracy, including our problematic intelligence services, with the same extraordinary attention to detail he gave to New York City government. Should he win the nomination, his mayoral record of promoting opportunity and upward mobility along with his clear-eyed prosecutorial sense of why "it is better to be feared than loved" by our Islamic enemies would make him a formidable candidate.

A Short History of Terror Attacks on New York (Real and Seriously Imagined)

L ong before 9/11, New York, as both source and symbol of Yankee capitalism, attracted external enemies who hoped to destroy the city. New York's dynamism and modernity offended those who held to a rooted, organic conception of the world. While Gotham embodied American and capitalist power, its skyscrapers expressed the vulnerabilities of a city whose very hubris seem to invite attack. The bottlenecks and chokepoints—bridges, tunnels and towering elevators so appealing to mobsters—were tempting to terrorists as well. And while New Yorkers, looking to the future, may have had scant time for history, Islamists, whose faded greatness was rooted in the distant past, remembered that the once majestic cities of Athens, Rome and Constantinople had each been humbled by energetic enemies.*

The first attempt to destroy all of Manhattan came in the mid-nineteenth century. By the time of the Civil War, Manhattan, tied to the world of global commerce first by its docks and then by the telegraph, was a city of one million and Wall Street was already a metonym for financial markets. With their commercial ties to the slave South, New Yorkers had been opposed to the fight for the Union despite Lincoln's stirring Cooper Union Address. There had

---

*In 1920, thirty-eight people were killed and three hundred wounded on Wall Street as both part of an anarchist attack on the command center of world capitalism meant to avenge the arrests of Sacco and Vanzetti. And in the 1970s and 1980s there was a terrorist campaign by advocates of Puerto Rican independence that culminated in the 1983 New Year's Eve bombing of four government buildings, including NYPD headquarters. I mention these attacks only in this note because these were targeted attacks; they didn't involve the idea of bringing the entire city to its knees.

even been talk of seceding and becoming an independent city. But once the war began, New York, long despised by the southern planters in debt to the Yankee bankers they saw as money-grubbing parasites, had become integral to the war effort and the object of Dixie's opprobrium.

In November 1864, a dozen agents of the Confederacy set up a bomb-making factory off Washington Square. They succeeded in setting fire to major hotels, public buildings and ships in lower Manhattan. Given the city's vulnerability to fire, they hoped for a major conflagration, but they were disappointed. Despite rumors of a planned germ warfare attack and speculation about mysterious fires, this was the most effective Southern attack of the war.[1]

A little more than thirty years later, the more than slightly mad Kaiser Wilhelm II restored absolute monarchy to Germany. The Kaiser thought in racial terms—in one diatribe he attacked the French and the English as "not Whites at all but Blacks," while Jesus of Nazareth, he claimed, "had never been a Jew." Anticipating both Hitler and contemporary Islamofascists, the Kaiser saw a vast conspiracy of freemasons and Jews as his ultimate adversary.[2]

The future, according to Wilhelm, belonged to young, virile Germany. But he saw the U.S. as a great obstacle. He wanted "to put America in its place." He gave officer Eberhard von Mantey the task of planning an assault on New York and Boston. Sixty German ships laden with 100,000 soldiers were to attack the Northeast. Several thousand soldiers would land at Cape Cod and march into Boston, while heavy cruisers would enter New York's Lower Bay and bombard Manhattan. "This is the core of America and this is where the United States could be most effectively hit and most easily" brought down, wrote von Mantey. He assumed that "the greatest panic would break out in New York over fears of a bombardment" so that President Theodore Roosevelt would be "forced to sign a peace treaty."[3]

The closest the Kaiser came to carrying out his plans came shortly after the U.S. entered World War I. Sleeper cells of German saboteurs blended in easily with the city's considerable German-American population. Activated with the onset of war, their greatest feat was the Black Tom Explosion. Black Tom was an artificial island built on landfill in a shallow portion of the upper harbor near the Statue of Liberty and just off Jersey City. It was used during the war as a lightly guarded munitions depot. In the early morning hours of

July 30, 1917, the Germans succeeded in destroying not only the munitions but the entire island. Only four people were killed, although the explosion felt like an earthquake to the sleeping people of Jersey City, Staten Island, Brooklyn and lower Manhattan. The windows of thousands of homes and in almost all the skyscrapers of lower Manhattan were shattered. Shrapnel from the explosion shot across the entire harbor area as the explosions continued until dawn. When it was over the entire island and everything on it had disappeared into the waters of the bay. The saboteurs were never caught.[4]

In 1942, President Franklin Roosevelt, who had been Assistant Secretary of the Navy in charge of intelligence during the Black Tom attack, was informed that the Germans had landed saboteurs on Long Island. Hitler had been eager to attack the U.S. even before Pearl Harbor gave him the opportunity to declare war on America. He established Operation Pastorius to train German-Americans in the use of explosives. In 1942 a German U-boat landed eight saboteurs off Amagansett on the South Fork of Eastern Long Island. The landing party soon ran into a lone Coast Guardsman on patrol. He quickly informed his superiors who informed the navy, which dismissed the report and made no attempt to capture the submarine even though it was stranded on a sand bar a short distance from a Coast Guard station.

Fortunately, the would-be saboteurs, all of whom were former Americans who had returned to Germany to train for the Fatherland, were a group of bungling misfits. The eight caught a Long Island Railroad train and headed for Manhattan where they began their career in sabotage by taking in the nightlife. Two of the eight had such a good time that they decided to change sides and tried to hand themselves over to the FBI. But the Bureau, like the Coast Guard, treated the matter as a crank call. One of them had to go directly to FBI headquarters in Washington in order to get himself arrested. The surrender turned into a bureaucratic turf war that enraged Roosevelt.

Remembering his chagrin over the Black Tom affair, Roosevelt sought to make an example of the German agents. They were tried not by a civilian court but by a military tribunal. Six of the eight were executed within six months. The deterrent seems to have been effective. There was only one subsequent landing. FDR's use of a military tribunal was challenged and produced the *Quirin* case, which is the legal backdrop to the current wrangling over how to treat enemy combatants who are U.S. citizens.[5]

▲ ▲ ▲

In 1908, five years after the Wright brothers' flight and at time when the Kaiser was experimenting with dirigibles, H.G. Wells added a new and imaginative twist to schemes for destroying New York. Wells, a proponent of eugenics, who sometimes took a pestilential view of modern man, worried that presumptuous Jews were diluting New York's British stock. In his 1908 book *The War in the Air*, German airships wipe out New York, which is described as the new "Babylon," "the wickedest city the world had ever seen" with its "black and sinister polyglot population." Smug, "barbaric" New York, Wells makes it clear, deserves to be destroyed because of its decadence. Its purposeless swirl of individual wills demanded that it be remade by men of commanding organization and efficiency. Wells, the prophet of a scientifically managed world who later embraced Stalin, was repulsed by the individualist culture of New Yorkers:

> And over all that torrential confusion of men and purposes fluttered that strange flag, the stars and stripes, that meant at once the noblest thing in life, and the least noble, that is to say, Liberty on the one hand, and on the other the base jealousy the individual self-seeker feels towards the common purpose of the State.[6]

Hitler too was disgusted by polyglot New York. In his prison journals Albert Speer recalled how Hitler consoled himself near the end of World War II with films showing London and Warsaw burning, "but I never saw him so besides himself as when in a delirium he pictured New York going down in flames." He described skyscrapers being turned into "gigantic, burning torches, collapsing upon one another, the glow of the exploding city illuminating the dark sky" in a Wagnerian Götterdämmerung. After Hitler died in his bunker, his legacy lived on in men like his ally the Palestinian leader Haj Amin al-Husseini, the Grand Mufti of Jerusalem. Talking on the air over Radio Berlin during the war, al-Husseini urged Arabs, "Kill Jews wherever you find them for the love of God, history and religion."[7]

The Wells/Hitler/al-Husseini fantasy of a cleaning fire became part of post-war fears: "In a 1946 congressional hearing, the nuclear physicist J. Robert Oppenheimer acknowledged that a few people could smuggle components of a nuclear bomb into New York. Asked how such components could be detected in a crate or a suitcase, he answered: "With a screwdriver."[8]

In *Here Is New York*, E.B. White caught the fears World War II's mass destruction brought to Gotham:

> The subtlest change in New York is something people don't speak much about but that is in everyone's mind. The city, for the first time in its long history, is destructible. A single flight of planes no bigger than a wedge of geese can quickly end this island's fantasy, burn the towers, crumble the bridges, turn the underground passages into lethal chambers.

White saw New York's appeal to madmen. "This riddle in steel and stone," he wrote, "is at once the perfect target and the perfect demonstration of nonviolence, of racial brotherhood, this lofty target scraping the skies and meeting the destroying planes halfway, home of all people and all nations, capital of everything." As the capital of everything modern from racial mixing to money making, New York, "in the mind of whatever perverted dreamer, might loose the lightning...must hold a steady, irresistible charm."[9]

White might have been referring to Sayyid Qutb in his reference to perverted dreamers. Qutb, the sheltered offspring of a devout Muslim family from Upper Egypt, was more than any other individual the intellectual godfather of Al Qaeda. A student of architecture and literature, the defining moment in his life was his visit to New York in 1948. He quickly came to despise what he saw. He had earlier been shocked by seeing a Muslim woman without her veil in Cairo; what he saw in seductive New York was far worse. He saw New York as a "giant brothel," the home of "usurious Jewish financial institutions." He found Gotham a "noisy" and "clamoring" city in which even the pigeons looked unhappy and people could speak of nothing but "money, movie stars or car models." In his essay "The America that I saw," he described the U.S. as "materially prosperous but morally rotten." The Americans, he concluded, were a "people drowning in dirt and mud" because they insisted on a separation between the sacred and the secular. "No one, he wrote, "is more distant than the Americans from spirituality and piety."[10]

When he returned to Egypt, where he would remain celibate for the rest of his life, he joined the Muslim Brotherhood in the hopes of overthrowing Gamel Abdel Nasser's insufficiently Islamic dictatorship. The Muslim Brothers, influenced by the fascist mantra "believe, obey, fight," adopted as its slogan "action, obedience, silence."

In Saudi Arabia, Qutb's brother Mohammed taught his doctrines to Osama bin Laden. In 1989, another of Qutb's disciples, the blind Sheik Omar Abdel Rahman, was given sanctuary in Brooklyn where he was the inspiration for the 1993 World Trade Center attack and a foiled 1994 plot to blow up the Holland and Lincoln Tunnels, events that were later understood as advertisements for terrorism.*

▲ ▲ ▲

The short fuse that led to 9/11 was lit on November 5, 1990 when Egyptian immigrant El Sayyid Nosair, an acolyte of Sheik Omar Abdel Rahman, assassinated the demagogic Rabbi Meir Kahane in the lobby of a lower Manhattan hotel.

Within fourteen hours the FBI announced that Nosair was a lone gunman so there was no need to go through the forty-nine boxes of documents and materials captured from his New Jersey apartment. The cache, none of which was studied until after the 1993 World Trade Center attack, included his diary in which he called for "jihad against the enemies of Islam" by destroying the structure of their civilization. The cache also included a hit list of public figures including Kahane, paramilitary training materials, detailed pictures of famous buildings (including the World Trade Center), and sermons by Sheik Omar urging his followers to "destroy the edifices of capitalism."[11]

William Kunstler, one of New York's left-wing lions, rushed forward to offer his services as Nosair's defense lawyer. His most celebrated recent case had been his defense of Larry Davis, who later

---

*The desire for revenge on New York was not confined to Islamists in the Arab world. In his 1971 poem " The Funeral of New York," the modernist poet Adonis (Ali Ahmed Said) describes a nameless narrator wandering through Wall Street and Harlem, looking in vain for Walt Whitman's ghost and angrily imagining "an eastern wind" uprooting skyscrapers, "a cloud necklaced with fire" and "people melting like tears." One verse reads:
> New York is a woman
> holding, according to history,
> a rag called liberty with one hand
> and strangling the earth with the other.

changed his name to Adam Abdul Hakeem, an admitted Bronx drug dealer who had killed four men and wounded a half a dozen cops when they tried to capture him. Kunstler depicted Davis as a primitive rebel who was being framed by the corrupt police for trying to go straight.

Kunstler was elated by the Nosair case. In his autobiography he says it made him fell like it was 1969 all over again. Kunstler had elective affinities with Nosair. His close aide Ron Kuby acknowledged that "movement lawyers" like Kunstler and himself identified with men like Nosair. *"In the best of cases we identify with their determination, with their courage, and we see the people that maybe we could have been had we the courage to do what they did."*[12]

In the Nosair case, Kunstler, aided by liberal Judge Alvin Schlesinger, who made little effort to conceal his sympathies for defense, was able to pick a credulous jury. Osama bin Laden himself contributed $20,000 to the Nosair defense fund to pay for Kunstler. The jury acquitted Nosair, who had been caught at the scene with the murder weapon, of second-degree murder. He was, however, sent to Attica on secondary charges. In Attica, Nosair, who had become a hero to radical Muslims, helped plan the 1993 World Trade Center attack.

In his book *The Cell*, John Miller, who had been Police Commissioner Bill Bratton's top press officer, described the scene when the Nosair verdict was announced. "Any reporter could read their thoughts…America really was a spineless nation just as the imams had been preaching. Here you could murder your enemy in public…and receive nothing more than a slap on the wrist. Here, the jihadi will be victorious."[13]

Early on, Giuliani saw the ties between Nosair and the wider threats that were developing. Referring to the Nosair verdict, he commented, "In this case the result is so jarring that it has tempted people to talk about taking the law into their own hands." Giuliani asked Manhattan U.S. Attorney Otto Obermaier to have the FBI reopen the Nosair investigation. The Justice Department refused,

---

In 2002, he told the *New York Times* that New York, "to me, is both heaven and hell," adding, "When I read this poem today, it frightens me." *New York Times* 7/13/02. On Adonis and how his hatred was so great that it could be directed both at the West and his own society and how this combination led him despite his secularism to embrace the Ayatollah Khomeini in 1979, see Fouad Ajami, *The Dream Palace of the Arabs*.

and the case dimmed from public memory, save for a few mentions following the 1993 World Trade Center bombing.

In tracing the links between Arab immigrant jihadis and 1960s vintage black radicals turned black Muslims, detectives such as Tommy Corrigan and Louie Napoli, men who knew the local territory as the FBI did not, saw early on the kinds of conspiracies that were emerging. The NYPD quickly cracked the 1993 Trade Center bombing by ignoring the FBI's instructions. As an anonymous police official put it later, "Why should we wait for some special agent from Iowa to tell us where terrorist cells in Brooklyn are located when we have the best detectives in the world?" Had New York's Comp-Stat techniques been used to break down the walls within the FBI, not to speak of those between the FBI and other federal intelligence agencies, 9/11 might have been prevented.[14]

But there is one way in which the Giuliani administration, which was so often prescient on these issues, contributed to the intelligence failures. That was immigration. When Cuomo spoke of his immigrant grandparents, he usually invoked the prejudice they suffered at the hands of WASPs; Giuliani, however, invoked his immigrant father who fought in World War II against the land of his forebears. But as part of his vigorous, and generally well-considered, policy of supporting immigrants and immigration, Giuliani defied national rules that required local government to cooperate with the Immigration and Naturalization Service. He fought those rules in court, and even when he lost he continued a sanctuary policy that made it clear that city workers didn't have to cooperate too well with the federal authorities. Not all Muslims are jihadis, but a more vigilant approach would have looked into the ease with which the Islamists of 9/11 could meld into the Arab and Pakistani neighborhoods of Brooklyn. The Al Farooq mosque on Atlantic Avenue, for instance, had been funneling money (roughly $20 million) and probably information to bin Laden for more than a decade, while three of the highjackers blended seamlessly into the Pakistani neighborhoods along Brooklyn's Coney Island Avenue.[15]

Acknowledgments

I owe considerable thanks to the friends who read earlier versions of this manuscript. Todd Brewster, Ben Haimowitz, E.J. McMahon, Tony Proscio and Sol Stern all made helpful comments on my very rough second draft.

My editor Peter Collier of Encounter Books improved my prose and made my arguments more accessible. My son Jacob Siegel provided the title and my cousin Carol Ross the legal advice. Medical detective Dr. Kenneth Jaffe, his wife Linda and Dr. Nella Shapiro helped get me healthy enough to write the book. President George Campbell and Dean David Weir of The Cooper Union for Science and Art went out of their way to arrange my schedule so that I could work on the book. Mark Steinmeyer and the Smith Richardson Foundation generously provided time off from teaching to study American urban life.

Friends Joel Kotkin, Eric Foner, Lloyd Greene, Will Marshall, and Julia Vitullo-Martin allowed me to bend their ears trying out the arguments that would make their way into the book. Adam Wolfson of *The Public Interest*, Jody Bottum of *The Weekly Standard*, Neil Kozodoy of *Commentary*, Peter Range of *Blueprint*, Karl Zinsmeister of *American Enterprise Magazine* Edith Kurzweil of *Partisan Review*, Chuck Lane of *The New Republic*, Murray Friedman of the Myer and Rosaline Feinstein Center for American Jewish History at Temple University, and Herb London of the Hudson Institute allowed me to work through some of my ideas in print. Richard Caldwell of Denver University's Institute for Public Policy Studies, Stanley Moses of Hunter College, Henry Wollman and Ellen Posner of the Newman Real Estate Institute of Baruch College and Dean James Wilburn of Pepperdine University's Public Policy Institute gave me the opportunity to present my ideas to audiences ready to provide criticism.

Diana Chapin, Harvey Robbins, John Mogelescu and Henry

Stern, four of New York's finest public servants, gave me their time and insights. Larry Mead and Doug Besharov shared their research findings. Dan DiSalvo, my brother-in-law Howard Naft and cousin Cecil Taman provided comparative material on other cities, and I benefited from the insights of Jerry Skurnick, Ed Hochman, Eli Lehrer, Danica Gallagher, Fipp Avlon, Joe Mercurio, Arthur Zabarkes, Eamon Moynihan, Louie Menashe and Jack Schwartz. Roger Hertog provided counsel and encouragement at a crucial moment. The librarians at New York's Municipal Archives and The Cooper Union were helpful to both Harry Siegel and myself.

If this book has been interesting or pleasurable, much of the credit goes to my wife, Jan Rosenberg, who both patiently listened (in sections) to the entire manuscript read aloud (deadpan) and took on much of the household load to give me time to write.

Interview List

Michael Anton
Mario Argote
Herman Badillo
Bruce Bender
Herb Berman
Andrea Bernstein
Dan Biederman
Lee Bowes
Gail Brewer
James Brigham
Wilbur Chapman
Anthony Coles
Daniel Connolly
Edward Costikyan
Peter Cove
Steve Cushman
Randy Daniels
John Dyson
Virginia Fields
Ken Fisher
Jonathan Foreman
Coleman Genn
Rudolph Giuliani
Lorna Goodman
Mark Hoover
Michael Jacobson
George Kelling
Edward Koch
Liz Krueger
Adam Kurtz
Abe Lackman

Michael Lapin
Richard Larkin
Crystine Lategano
Randy Levine
Joseph Lhota
Bill Lynch
George Marlin
Randy Mastro
Andrew McCarthy
Joseph Mercurio
Ruth Messinger
Louise Mirrer
Larry Mone
Daniel Patrick Moynihan
Steve Newman
David Osborne
Jerilyn Perine
Peter Powers
Jennifer Raab
Mark Rosenbaum
Jerry Salama
Richard Schwartz
Richard Schrader
Hank Sheinkopf
Marla Simpson
Jerry Skurnick
Andrew Stein
Norman Steisel
Sol Stern
Henry Stern
Jason Turner

Peter Vallone
Rudy Washington
Carl Weisbrod
Susan Wiviot
Barbara Wolf
Deborah Wright
Kathy Wylde

In addition, there were others whose request for anonymity I have honored.

Notes

Part I

Chapter 1

1 Martin Shefter, "New York City's Fiscal Crisis: The Politics of Inflation and Retrenchment," *The Public Interest*, Summer 1977: 111.

2 Edward Robb Ellis, *The Epic of New York City: A Narrative History*, New York: Old Town Books, 1966: 549.

3 Thomas Kessner, *Fiorello H. La Guardia and the Making of Modern New York*, New York: McGraw-Hill, 1989: 241; Ronald Bayor, *Fiorello La Guardia: Ethnicity and Reform*, Chicago: Harlan Davidson, 1993: 29.

4 Alyn Brodsky, *The Great Mayor: Fiorello La Guardia and the Making of the City of New York*, New York: St. Martin's, 2003: 330.

5 Brodsky 552.

6 Kessner 291.

7 Brodsky 286; Robert Moses, *La Guardia, A Salute and a Memoir*, New York: Simon & Schuster, 1957: 30; Brodsky 292.

8 Kessner 338.

9 Kessner 300, 555.

10 Kessner 406, 407, 560.

11 Kessner 556.

12 Ibid.

13 Kessner 561.

14 Kessner 288.

15 Charles R. Morris, *The Cost of Good Intentions: New York City and the Liberal Experiment, 1960-1975*, New York: Norton, 1980: 22.

16 Vincent Cannato, *The Ungovernable City: John Lindsay and His Struggle to Save New York*, New York: Basic Books, 2001: 36.

17 Cannato 139.

18 Cannato 215, 223, 95.

19 Joshua Benjamin Freeman, *Working-Class New York: Life and Labor Since World War II*, New York: New Press, 2000: 264.

20 James Ring Adams, "Why New York City Went Broke," *Commentary*, May 1976.

21 Edward C. Banfield, review of Charles Abrams' *The City is the Frontier*, *Commentary*, March 1966.

22 *New York Times* 12/27/02.

23 Fred Siegel, *The Future Once Happened Here*, New York: The Free Press, 1997: 204.
24 Charles J. Orlebeke, *New Life at Ground Zero: New York, Home Ownership and the Future of American Cities*, Albany: Rockefeller Institute Press, 1997: 7.
25 Bernard J. Frieden and Lynne B. Sagalyn, *Downtown, Inc.: How America Rebuilds Cities*, Cambridge: MIT Press, 1989: 296.
26 Chris McNickle, *To Be Mayor of New York: Ethnic Politics in the City*, New York: Columbia University Press, 1993: 288.
27 Edward Koch, *Mayor: An Autobiography*, New York: Simon & Schuster, 1984.
28 Jerome Charyn, *Metropolis: New York as Myth, Marketplace, and Magical Land*, New York: Putnam, 1986: 205. On October 19, 1987 the stock market dropped 508 points or 22 %. It was the biggest one-day drop since 1929 and the start of the Great Depression.

Chapter 2
1 *New York Times* 9/12/93. Purdum stood out for his consistent effort to make race the only issue in the 1993 mayoral campaign. *Newsday* 11/11/89.
2 *Newsday* 10/3/93.
3 "A Victim of the Law of Unintended Consequences?," *The National Journal* 2/7/87; *Wall Street Journal* 1/19/87; *New York Times* 2/15/87.
4 *New York Magazine* 6/20/88. Reagan's personal popularity rebounded. He left office with a 68% approval rating, the highest of any president since WWII. But Reaganism as an approach to governing faltered.
5 *Newsweek* 9/5/88.
6 *Newsday* 5/10/87.
7 Ibid. The original Kerner Commission was a blue-ribbon panel created in the wake of the 1960s riots to investigate the causes of the outburst. New York Mayor John Lindsay was one of the key members of the commission, which concluded that white racism was the source of the violence.
8 *New York Times* 4/27/88.
9 *Newsday* 10/24/88.
10 "Is the ACLU a Threat to Freedom?," *New Politics*, 1970; *Wall Street Journal* 2/15/1990.
11 Jonathan Rieder, *Canarsie: The Jews and Italians of Brooklyn Against Liberalism*, Boston: Harvard University Press, 1985: 6.
12 *Newsday* 11/8/89.
13 Ibid. For Stein's remarks, see *Newsday* 9/4/89.
14 Roger Biles, "Mayor David Dinkins and the Politics of Race in New York City" in David R. Colburn and Jeffrey S. Adler, eds., *African-American Mayors: Race, Politics, and the American City*, Urbana: University of Illinois Press, 2001: 139.
15 Scott McConnell, "The Making of the Mayor," *Commentary*, February 1990.

16 Biles 135.
17 *Newsday* 8/29/89.
18 *New York Times* 4/7/91.
19 Andrew Kirtzman, *Rudy Giuliani: Emperor of the City*, New York: Harper Collins, 2001: 3.
20 Wayne Barrett, *Rudy!: An Investigative Biography of Rudolph Giuliani*, New York: Basic Books, 2000: 163.
21 Kirtzman 2.
22 George J. Marlin, *Fighting the Good Fight: A History of the New York Conservative Party*, South Bend: St. Augustine's Press, 2002: 281.
23 *New York Times* 9/9/89.
24 *Village Voice* 3/14/95.
25 Barrett 91.
26 Ibid.
27 Ibid. There was little anticipation from Giuliani that four years later he would adopt an innovative crime-fighting strategy. Both he and Dinkins declined to endorse a plan of the Transit Authority to keep vagrants from sleeping on the subways. Giuliani's big crime initiative was using drug forfeiture money to fund drug treatment.
28 *Newsday* 10/30/89, 11/5/89.
29 Kirtzman 27. Questions about Dinkins' capabilities weren't confined to the Giuliani campaign. A minority political leader said of him: "I think Dave's a wonderful guy, but let me tell you three things about him running for mayor: First, he'll make a lousy candidate. Second, in the unlikely event that he does win, he'll make a terrible mayor. Third, I will support him."
30 *Newsday* 11/5/89.
31 Ibid.
32 Kirtzman 27.
33 McConnell 38.
34 *Newsday* 11/8/89.
35 Ibid.
36 Ibid.

Chapter 3
 1 *Newsday* 11/10/89.
 2 Ibid.; *Newsday* 1/2/94.
 3 "The Promise of the Peace Dividend," Municipal Archives.
 4 Dick Kirschten, "More Problems, Less Clout," *The National Journal*, September 12, 1989.
 5 *Daily News* 6/13/90; *Governing* April 1991.
 6 Jim Sleeper, *The Closest of Strangers*, New York: Norton, 1990: 207-208. The "chop suey" comment was overheard by the author, who lives a short walk from the scene of the confrontation.
 7 Tamar Jacoby, *Someone Else's House: America's Unfinished Struggle for Integration*, New York: Free Press, 1998: 205-206.
 8 Tamar Jacoby, "Sonny Carson's Politics of Protest," *City Journal*, Summer 1991: 30, 31.

9   *Newsday* 2/13/90.

10 Ibid. For the notion that the boycott wasn't racial, see *Daily News* 5/11/90.

11 5/11/90 Dinkins speech, Municipal Archives; the court proceedings are recounted in Eli B. Silverman, *The NYPD Battles Crime*, Boston: Northeastern University Press, 1999: 74-75.

12 Sharpton wrote to Dinkins during the Church Avenue affair rebuking the mayor for saying that "I don't think most African-American agree with Al Sharpton." Sharpton warned Dinkins that while "*I do not endorse violence and will not participate it . . . its likelihood is real and imminent.*" Municipal Archives.

13 Andrew Kirtzman, *Rudy Giuliani: Emperor of the City,* New York: Harper Collins, 2000: 34.

14 *New York Times* 12/10/89.

15 "Helplessly, Hopelessly Teaching," *Washington Post* 5/13/91.

16 "The Decline of New York," *Time,* 9/17/90; James Lardner and Thomas Reppetto, *NYPD: A City and Its Police*, New York: Henry Holt, 2000: 297.

17 Lardner and Reppetto.

18 Siegel, *The Future Once Happened Here*, New York: The Free Press, 1997: 222. The income tax surcharge required Albany's approval and Dinkins did work with Vallone to get Safe Streets/Safe City through the state legislature.

19 *Newsday* 10/3/93; *Newsday* 9/20/90.

20 Andres Torres, *Between Melting Pot and Mosaic*, Philadelphia: Temple University Press, 1994: 116. In 1975 when the city's massive short-term debt shut it out of the credit markets and made it impossible for New York to pay its bills, then-Governor Hugh Carey asked the Viennese-born Rohatyn of the French-American investment firm of Lazard Frères to take charge of the newly created MAC and the city's future. MAC, because it was guaranteed a portion of the city's share of sales tax revenues, was able to borrow money on Gotham's behalf. Rohatyn had backed the ill-fated campaign of Richard Ravitch in the 1989 election, but, already a close advisor to Governor Cuomo, he became a power in the Dinkins administration. Norman Steisel, his former junior associate at Lazard Frères, had been the sanitation commissioner under Mayor Koch and had been appointed as a Dinkins deputy mayor.

21 CBS 880, 8/18/90.

22 Felix Rohatyn, *New York Review of Books*, 11/8/90.

23 *Newsday* 3/7/91.

24 *Newsday* 1/31/92.

25 *Newsday* 12/10/91, 7/8/91. Gail Collins also quotes from a 1971 Rockefeller-commissioned report, which, in an attempt to embarrass Lindsay, concluded that "Not only are there clear indications that municipal services have deteriorated while promises go unfulfilled, but there is also a sensation of helplessness—a feeling that there is no one or no place in city government to go for assistance or redress, and that no one

is held accountable. Productivity reports issue from City Hall, yet nothing appears to change. Increase in municipal employment has not meant an increase in service delivery." She was right, little had changed.

26 *New York Times* 9/14/90. "Cities," Dinkins told audiences, "are the soul of the nation," the places where "the gorgeous mosaic of America must be brought together again." At a time when the tech revolution of the 1990s was beginning to take off in exurbia, and while economists were unable to identify a single infant industry gestating in New York, Dinkins insisted that "Like a mighty engine, urban America pulls all of America into the future."

27 The short book published on the summit was edited by Ronald Berkman, *In the National Interest: The 1990 Urban Summit: With Related Analyses, Transcript, and Papers*, New York: Twentieth Century Fund, 1992. For the "demands," see "35 Mayors Convene In New York City To Discuss Problems," *The Bond Buyer* 11/13/90; for "mad as hell," see *Boston Globe* 11/14/90.

28 Municipal Archives.

29 *New York Times* 3/31/91.

30 Ibid.

31 *New York Times* 5/17/92.

32 *New York Post* 1/25/94.

33 *New York Post* 11/11/94.

34 *New York Times* 6/18/92.

35 *Houston Chronicle* 8/9/92; *Newsday* 6/18/92.

36 Siegel 216.

37 Siegel 207.

38 Siegel 242. The aide asked to remain anonymous.

Chapter 4

1 Richard M. Bernard, "The Death and Life of a Midwest Metropolis," in Richard M. Bernard, ed., *Snowbelt Cities*, Bloomington: Indiana University Press, 1990.

2 John Norquist, *Wisconsin Interest* Winter/Spring 1992.

3 Fred Siegel and Will Marshall, "Rediscovering Liberalism's Lost Tradition," *The New Democrat* September/October 1995.

4 Kenneth Baer, *Reinventing Democrats,* Lawrence: University Press of Kansas, 2000.

5 Attendees included Newt Gingrich, Sidney Blumenthal, Hernando De Soto, Julian Simon, Bruce Bartlett, Congressman Rob Andrews, Jim Pinkerton, Elaine Kamarck, E.J. Dionne, Joe Klein, William Galston, Peter Cove, Lee Bowes and Fred Siegel.

6 *New York Times* 12/31/93.

7 *New York Observer* 3/15/93.

8 *Newsday* 7/1/91.

9 *New York Times* 7/31/91.

10 Ibid.; *Newsday* 8/1/91.

11 *New York Times* 12/29/91.

12 *New York Times* 2/27/92.

Chapter 5
1 *Village Voice* 5/11/93; *New York* 8/16/93.
2 *Newsday* 9/29/93.
3 *New York Times* 12/29/91.
4 *Newsday* 9/24/93.
5 *New York* 12/20/93; *Newsday* 5/27/93.
6 *Crain's* 2/17/92.
7 *Newsday* 911/02.
8 *New York Times* 4/9/93.
9 Ibid. The affable Stein was candid about his strengths and weaknesses. He once told the author, "I know I'm not the brightest guy around, but I'm smart enough to know what I don't know and surround myself with top-notch people."
10 Rudolph Giuliani, *Leadership*, New York: Miramax Books, 2002: 327-329.
11 *New York Times* 12/29/91.
12 *New York Post* 3/27/93.
13 *Daily News* 7/26/92; *Newsday* 9/01/93.
14 *Newsday* 2/22/92.
15 *New York Times* 10/8/93; *Daily News* 10/31/93; *Newsday* 9/2/93.
16 See Fred Siegel, *The Future Once Happened Here*, New York: The Free Press, 1997, Chapter 14, "The Moral Deregulation of Pubic Space," for a discussion of the concept of "victimless crime."
17 *Village Voice* 9/1/93.
18 The Industrial Policy Proposals were laid out by Chief Economist James Parrott for Deputy Mayor Barry Sullivan in a 180-page brief entitled "STRONG ECONOMY, STRONG CITY: JOBS FOR NEW YORKERS: Job Creation Strategies for the Global City of Opportunity"; *Newsday* 10/8/93. While the mayor spoke of a city industrial policy, the city had not even been able to maintain its much touted "Fields of Dreams," the forty vacant lots that had been, temporarily as it turned out, turned into ball fields at the cost of $750,000. Revisiting the sites, *Newsday* found that many had returned to weeds while others had never been cleared in the first place.
19 *New York Magazine* 7/21/92.
20 *Newsday* 5/26/93.
21 *New York Times* 9/19/93.
22 *New Yorker* 11/18/93; *Newsday* 11/02/93. But in New York, as earlier in LA, when Clinton had endorsed a conventional liberal Asian-American Mike Woo over reformer Richard Riordan, the race card backfired.
23 *Newsday* 11/2/93; *Daily News* 11/31/93.
24 George Marlin, *Fighting the Good Fight: A History of the New York Conservative Party*, South Bend: St. Augustine Press, 2002: 311.
25 Zoltan L. Hajnal, "White Residents, Black Incumbents, and a Declining Racial Divide," *Wilson Quarterly*, Winter 2002.

Chapter 6
1 Municipal Archives.

2 Andrew Kirtzman, *Rudy Giuliani: Emperor of the City,* New York: Harper Collins, 2000: 65.

3 *Washington Post* 12/27/94; David Axelrod, who had worked for Harold Washington in Chicago as well as Archer and White, argues that race mattered less because voters were driven by "an unparalleled sense of pragmatism.... They are in a battle for survival, looking for allies rather than enemies to blame."

4 *Boston Globe* 10/31/93.

5 James Atlas, "The Democrats Then and Now: The Daleys of Chicago," *New York Times Magazine,* 8/25/96.

6 *New York Times* 12/23/93.

7 *Newsday* 5/26/93. Donald Kummerfeld was a former NYC Budget Director and a former Executive Director of the New York State Emergency Financial Control Board

8 *New York Times* 12/20/93.

9 *New York Times* 12/4/93.

10 Municipal Archives.

11 *Washington Post,* 3/27/94.

12 *New York Times* 12/3/93.

Part II

Chapter 7

1 *New York Times Magazine,* 12/3/95; *New York Times* 6/2/96.

2 Jim Dwyer, David Kocieniewski, Deidre Murphy, Peg Tyre, *Two Seconds Under the World: Terror Comes to America—The Conspiracy Behind the World Trade Center Bombing,* New York: Crown Publishers, 1994: 72.

3 *New York Times* 1/5/94.

4 William Bratton with Peter Knobler, *The Turnaround: How America's Top Cop Reversed the Crime Epidemic,* New York, Random House, 1998: 314.

5 NY1 8/16/93; *New York Magazine* 12/20/93.

6 *New York Magazine* 1/15/93. "It's not like he didn't ask black people to help" during the campaign, noted the Reverend Calvin Butts of the Abyssinian Baptist Church, "but few would even return his calls." Butts told Giuliani, "I've got to go with Dinkins. That's the reality of it."

7 *New Yorker* 2/21/94.

8 For accounts of the 1972 Harlem mosque incident, see Vincent Cannato, *The Ungovernable City: John Lindsay and His Struggle to Save New York,* New York: Basic Books, 2001: 484-491, and Eli B. Silverman, *The NYPD Battles Crime,* Boston: Northeastern University Press, 1999: 21-24.

9 Bratton and Knobler xii, xiii.

10 *New York Times* 1/14/94.

11 *Newsday* 1/16/94, 1/17/94; *Daily News* 1/16/94, 1/17/94; Andrew Kirtzman, *Rudy Giuliani: Emperor of the City,* New York: Harper Collins, 2000: 71, 72.

12 Rudolph Giuliani, *Leadership,* New York: Miramax Books: 29.

13 Kirtzman 78, 79.

14 *New York Times* 12/19/03.

15 For more on Dyson's verbal gaffes, see *Rudy* 29.

16 Giuliani called for digital imaging not fingerprinting which only agitated his critics. Favorable comments came from developer Samuel Lefrak and former MAC chair Felix Rohatyn. Lefrak, who had deserted Gotham to build in Jersey City, was excited. "When," he asked, "was the last time a big-city mayor said he wanted to cut taxes? It's like 'man bites dog.'" Rohatyn liked the way Giuliani had "showed no favoritism" by stepping "on every toe in town." *Crain's* 2/7/94; Kirtzman 77.

17 *New York Post* 2/24/94.

18 *New York Post* 2/7/94; *Newsday* 2/7/94. *Newsday* and the *Daily News* chipped in with criticism of the chancellor's inability to gain control of school repair and construction with the former suggesting that it was time to take the responsibility for repairs "away from 110 Livingston Street and give it to the local school districts." For a brief account of how the Ocean Hill-Brownsville dispute bitterly divided the city, see Chapter 3 of Fred Siegel, *The Future Once Happened Here*, New York: The Free Press, 1997.

19 *Newsday*, 2/20/94, 1/29/94.

20 Ibid.

21 *Newsday* 10/6/93.

22 *Newsday* 10/6/93; *New York Times* 1/28/94; on the history of the HHC, see *Power Failure*.

23 *Newsday* 1/13/94; Kirtzman 78; *New York Times* 1/14/94.

24 *Newsday* 2/1/94.

25 *New York Post* 2/1/94; *Newsday* 6/11/94; *New York Post* 2/25/94. Norman was later indicted on a variety of charges including the sale of judicial decisions.

26 *Newsday* 6/16/94.

27 *Daily News* 3/18/94; *New York Observer* 2/8/94; *Newsday* 2/16/94, 3/18/94. The *Daily News* on 1/29/95 ran an expose of how Assemblyman Larry Seabrook's Youth Programs, which had received nearly $400,000 in social services monies and an annual payroll of 114,000 yet had no programs and no children.

28 *New York Times* 2/29/94; *Newsday* 1/18/94.

29 *New York Times* 5/11/94; Keilin declined repeated requests for an interview.

30 *New York Times* 3/22/94, 5/11/94.

31 Kirtzman 78.

32 *New York Times* 4/9/94.

33 Ibid.

34 Kirtzman 78.

35 Kirtzman 81.

Chapter 8

1 This account is based on a conversation with Moynihan and *New York Times* 12/7/93; *Daily News* 1/22/94 and 2/6/94.

2 *New York Times* 3/11/94.

3 "Clinton and the Crime Bill," *Governing*, October 1994; *New York Times* 8/13/96. In a thoughtful 1/18/95 speech on "The New Urban Agenda" given at Yale Law School, Giuliani discussed the failings of federalism as it had developed since the New Deal. The mayor complained that the federal government simultaneously drained $8 to $9 billion a year from New York while micromanaging cities in areas like policing and education where it wasn't competent to govern. Giuliani argued that the original version of President Clinton's Crime Bill "offered no help to cities which didn't need more police officers." "In fact," he went on, its offer of 25 percent of federal money to 75 percent of local dollars "could almost act as an inducement to spend money unwisely. Because sometimes the cities are led by the federal government to spend money on things they don't need because that's the money that's available." Not wanting to be embarrassed politically by turning down federal money, cities distort their priorities. But in the case of the new version of the Crime Bill supported by the mayors of Philadelphia, Los Angeles and New York, a city could spend its money on new technology or overtime, not more police officers. "That," he concluded, "is the kind of responsive relationship that has to exist between Washington and the cities." Giuliani wanted that same approach applied to education and welfare. Municipal Archives.

   Giuliani's argument here is similar to the case against federal micro-management laid out by then first-term Mayor Ed Koch in a famous article, "The Mandate Millsone," *The Public Interest* Fall 1980.

4 Charles Mann, "The Prose (and Poetry) of Mario Cuomo," *The Atlantic*, December 1990.

5 *New York Times* 9/23/90.

6 *Crain's* 9/20/90.

7 Wayne Barrett, *Rudy!: An Investigative Biography of Rudolph Giuliani*, New York: Basic Books: 2001: 200; Municipal Archives. Giuliani and Peter Powers had been in substantive budget discussions with Cuomo since shortly after the November 1993 election. They discussed giving the city's sales tax revenues to Albany in return for a state takeover of the city's Medicaid costs, but nothing came of it.

8 *New York Post* 10/24/94 and 10/26/94; *New York Magazine* 10/13/94.

9 *Newsday* 9/19/94. The article "One Interest Group at a Time" noted that Cuomo "will be sending letters to about 36,000 businesses in poor neighborhoods that haven't gotten economic development zones telling them they qualify for a wage tax credit for being part of a 'Zone equivalent area.'" In 1994 Pataki bitterly criticized Cuomo's tax-funded vote-buying, but by 2002, when Pataki ran for his third term in the

midst of a recession, he had adopted Cuomo's "Santa Claus" technique of traveling around the state to hand out money.

10 *New York Times* 10/27/94. Traveling with Cuomo, noted R.J. Apple of the *Times*, "you realize how much of his time the governor spends in telling stories about the past...what he does not talk about very much are his plans." Cuomo began to frequently quote from E.B. White's 1947 *Here is New York* on how Gotham "is to the nation what the church spire is to the village. The visible symbol of aspiration and faith, the white plume saying, 'This way is Up.'" The nostalgic Cuomo talked to reporters about the 1911 Triangle Shirtwaist fire, Apple went on, and called New York "the engine of the economy as if it were 1950 and California and Texas were still the sticks."

11 Andrew Kirtzman, *Rudy Giuliani: Emperor of the City,* New York: Harper Collins, 2000: 133.

12 Ibid.

13 Barrett 133; *Daily News* 10/7/94. Giuliani wasn't entirely wrong about Pataki. On October 5 of that year, Pataki held a news conference in front of mounds of regulations piled up as books—at which he was unable to name a single regulation he would abolish. Pataki did say that the city had seventeen state agencies authorized to issue permits and licenses in 1982—but by 1993 there were fifty-five such agencies, which had combined to file 536 "new" regulations and 68 "revised" regulations in the last year.

14 Kirtzman 134, 304; Barrett 304.

15 *New York Times* 11/6/94. A Penn and Schoen poll published just before the election anticipated the outcome. Two-thirds of all voters thought New York was headed in the wrong direction; 29 percent said they had become more conservative, 16 percent said they had become more liberal.

16 *New York Post* and *Newsday* 11/9/94.

17 Barrett 305.

Chapter 9

1 *Boston Globe* 6/13/93.

2 *New York Times* 3/17/94; *Daily News* 3/17/94.

3 Vincent Cannato, *The Ungovernable City: John Lindsay and His Struggle to Save New York*, New York: Basic Books, 2001: 477.

4 *Newsday* 5/3/91.

5 For a comparison of Chicago and New York, see Fred Siegel, "Two Tales of Policing," *The Public Interest*, Winter 1998 and *The Chicago Tribune* 5/3/2002.

6 Fred Siegel, *The Future Once Happened Here*, New York: The Free Press, 1997: 194.

7 Siegel 195.

8 Jack Maple, *The Crime Fighter: Putting the Bad Guys out of Business*, New York: Doubleday, 1999: 31; William Bratton with Peter Knobler, *The Turnaround: How America's Top Cop Reversed the Crime Epi-*

demic, New York: Random House, 1998: 253; Eli Silverman, *NYPD Battles Crime: Innovative Strategies in Policing,* Boston: Northeastern University Press, 1999: 87; Maple 33.

 9 Bratton xxix; Silverman 22; Bratton 88.
10 Maple 23.
11 Maple 160; Silverman 142.
12 Bratton 219.
13 Silverman 108.
14 Silverman 84; Bratton 224.
15 *Boston Globe* 8/6/95.

Chapter 10

 1 Professor Steve Savas, one of Pataki's 1993 campaign advisors, pioneered the case against Washington while working for the Reagan administration in *"The President's National Urban Policy Report"* (1982).
 2 Municipal Archives. In his speech before the National Press Club on March 30, 1995, Giuliani invoked the oft-forgotten Tenth Amendment to the Constitution, which reserved *for* the states and the people all powers not specifically enumerated in the Constitution. He went on to call for a roll-back of the federal powers over localities that had been expanding ever since the 1930s when La Guardia and Roosevelt had forged an alliance. He then praised President Clinton, Senate Majority Leader Bob Dole and House Speaker Newt Gingrich for supported new legislation "prohibiting Congress from imposing new unfunded mandates" on the cities. But that, he said, was only a first step.
 3 *New York Post* 3/16/94
 4 *Daily News* 2/14/95.
 5 *Newsday* 2/15/95; *New York* 3/27/95.
 6 Fred Siegel, *The Future Once Happened Here,* New York: Free Press, 1997: 211.
 7 *Newsday* 2/14/95; *New York Magazine* 4/29/95; Mark Green budget speech 2/28/95. Giuliani wasn't the only object of ire. *Times* columnist Bob Herbert responded to the Pataki budget cuts by warning that "the anger, the fear, and the despair are building." He concludes: "the rage will be like nothing we have seen before." Congressman Charles Rangel, displaced from his accustomed position in the majority, expressed some of that rage. He accused the Congressional Republicans of planning "economic genocide" after Gingrich spoke of dramatically downsizing the welfare state. Gingrich and other supporters of the "Contract with America," said Rangel, are "worse than Hitler." *New York Times* 2/4/95; *Newsday* 2/30/95.
 8 *New York Times* 4/9/95.
 9 NYU Conference on Workfare and the Future of Welfare Reform, 11/20/96.
10 NYC Department of Planning Report on Immigrant Incomes.
11 This paragraph is based on Roger Waldinger, *Still the Promised City?:*

African-Americans and New Immigrants in Postindustrial New York,
Cambridge: Harvard University Press, 1996.

12 *Daily News* 4/16/95.

13 Siegel, *The Future Once Happened Here* 226. In Cuomo's first term, his
wife Matilda repeatedly spoke out against teen pregnancy. For this she
was derided by some members of the Cuomo administration for being
Nancy Reagan-like.

14 Municipal Archives, Speech before United Jewish Appeal 12/12/95.

15 Ed Koch, *Mayor*, New York: Simon & Schuster, 1984: 143; *New York
Times* 12/29/94.

16 E. S. Savas, *Privatization in New York: If you can make it here you
can make it anywhere*, Washington, DC: CQ Press, forthcoming: 41.

17 *New York Times* 5/7/87; Douglas Besharov and Peter Germanis, *Work
Experience in New York City* (unpublished manuscript), 2003: 72-74;
Fred Siegel and Jan Rosenberg, "Taking Stock of Welfare Reform," *The
New Democrat*, 3/1/99.

18 *Newsday* 11/2/94. Supporters of the status quo like Councilman Steve
DiBrienza argued that "We talk about all this waste, fraud and corruption, all this double-dipping, and there is very little hard data that it
exists;" *Daily News* 12/15/94. Fourteen city workers got in on a fraud
by funneling $600,000 in phony assistance to 131 bogus welfare recip-
ients.

19 *New York Times* 9/22/96. Workfare was also an organizational success.
A study done for Price Waterhouse by Steven Cohen, dean of the
Columbia School of Public Affairs, "Managing Workfare, The Case of
the Work Experience Program in the Parks Department," found that
"the most significant lesson learned...is that a large-scale workfare program can be successfully implemented. The Department has absorbed
a workforce of over 5,000 part-time, diverse, and untrained workers
and put them to productive use with visible results."

Chapter 11

1 "The robbed at both ends" quote comes from a merchant interviewed
for a 1993 Giuliani campaign commercial; for a discussion of the paradox of regulation that caught the eye of President Clinton, who feted its
author, see Philip Howard, *The Death of Common Sense*, New York:
Random House, 1994. Most of Howard's examples come from
Gotham.

2 *New York Times* 10/14/93.

3 Ibid.; *Newsday* 3/25/95.

4 *New York Times* 4/19/95; *Newsday* 7/23/92; *New York Observer*
3/14/94.

5 *Newsday* 3/24/94; also the author's own experience.

6 Municipal Archives; *New York Times* 6/28/95; Katz's was the location
of the famous orgasm scene in *When Harry Met Sally*.

7 *Newsday* 11/18/95.

8 James B. Jacobs (with Coleen Friel and Robert Radick), *Gotham
Unbound: How New York Was Liberated from the Grip of Organized*

Crime, New York: NYU Press, 1999: 154. Jacobs also describes how the mob used the Fulton Fish Market to move guns and drugs.

9 *New York Times* 3/27/94.

10 Andrew Kirtzman, *Rudy Giuliani: Emperor of the City*, New York: Harper Collins, 2000: 164.

11 Jacobs 162.

12 This section draws on Jacobs' fine *Gotham Unbound*. Fear of driving out small carters proved unfounded. Several hundred small carters remained in New York even with the arrival of the national companies. Municipal Archives, an 11/14/96 letter to the mayor from Martin Sokol, president of a lower Manhattan leather goods company bearing his name, substantiates Mastro's claim. Upon learning that he was going to "save each month about $460 dollars on garbage removal," Sokol thanked Giuliani for "a de facto huge tax cut."

13 *Crain's* 3/20/95. The center was named after the last of the major New York liberal Republicans, Senator Jacob Javits.

14 *New York Times* 3/19/95. Rob Rosenfeld is the author's nephew. A show manager concurred with Rosenfeld. He explained anonymously, "Chicago is no labor paradise, [but] at least the politicians and unions there realize they have to stay competitive. In New York the unions did what they wanted, and until this year [1995]," he said speaking of Giuliani and Pataki, "we couldn't get anyone at City Hall or Albany to stand up for us."

15 *New York Times* 5/7/95.

16 *New York Post* 7/6/95; *Daily News* 5/2/95. As a small consolation, the Philadelphia convention hall situation may have been even worse and largely persists to this day under the ethically challenged Mayor John Street.

17 *New York Times* 2/7/96.

18 *Newsday* 4/11/94.

19 *New York Observer* 9/11/95; *Daily News* 2/27/94. High-level mayoral aides Tony Coles, Katy Lapp, and Giuliani confidant Denny Young worked with Vallone's staff to overcome the objections of the officers in the heavily African-American Housing Police by assuring them that they would be given suitable positions in the NYPD.

20 *Daily News* 4/10/94.

Chapter 12

1 *Guardian* 2/29/06.

2 *Wall Street Journal* 8/22/96, 6/10/96; *Commentary*, December 1995.

3 John Tierney, "The Holy Terror," *New York Times Magazine* 12/3/95.

4 *Time* 1/1/02.

5 *New York Times* 2/9/95, 3/9/95.

6 Andrew Kirtzman, *Rudy Giuliani: Emperor of the City*, New York: Harper Collins, 2000: 162-163.

7 *New York Times* 12/3/95.

8 *New York Times* 7/4/94.

9 Kirtzman 123.

10 Kirtzman 142.
11 Wayne Barrett, *Rudy!: An Investigative Biography of Rudolph Giuliani*, New York: Basic Books, 2001: 408.
12 William Bratton, *The Turnaround: How America's Top Cop Reversed the Crime Epidemic*, New York: Random House, 1998: 283.
13 *Time* 1/1/02.
14 *Newsday* 11/18/94.
15 *Daily News* 9/2/93.
16 *Newsday* 6/24/94.
17 *New York Times* 12/18/95; *Newsday* 1/15/94.
18 *Time* 1/1/2002.
19 *New York Times* 6/16/95.
20 *New York Times* 6/22/95.
21 *New York Times* 4/21/96.
22 *Insight* 7/21/97. The story of the Times Square revival is told in Lynne B. Sagalyn, *Times Square Roulette: Remaking the City Icon*, Cambridge: MIT Press, 2003. Mayronne's role is discussed by Bill Stern, "The Times Square Revival," *City Journal* Fall 1999.
23 Samuel R. Delany, *Times Square Red, Times Square Blue*, New York: NYU, 1999: 10.

Chapter 13

1 Evan Mandery, "The Campaign—*Rudy Giuliani, Ruth Messinger, Al Sharpton, and the Race to Be Mayor of New York City*, Boulder: Westview Press, 1999: 126.
2 *New York Times* 9/12/93.
3 *Daily News* 5/24/94.
4 Ibid.
5 Tamar Jacoby and Fred Siegel "Growing the Inner City," *The New Republic*, 9/23/99.
6 *Governing*, August 1995.
7 *Crain's* 1/23/95.
8 *Crain's* 3/18/96.
9 *National Review* 11/10/97.
10 Fred Siegel, *The Future Once Happened Here*, New York: Free Press. 1997, 233-34.
11 *New York Magazine* 1/17/97; *New York Times* 3/2/8/97.
12 *New York Magazine* 1/27/97.
13 Ibid.

Chapter 14

1 *Daily News* 9/17/97.
2 *Crain's* 9/18/95; *New York Post* 1/15/97; Municipal Archives. In a speech before the heavily African-American Urban League, Giuliani denounced Patrick Buchanan as a "figure...whose message is one of division, of intolerance and of fear." 3/26/96 Address to the Urban League. *Crain's* 9/18/95; *New York Post* 1/15/97.

3 *New York Post* 2/14/97.

4 *The Hotline* 2/14/97.

5 Andrew Kirtzman, *Rudy Giuliani: Emperor of the City,* New York: Harper Collins, 2000: 196.

6 *Daily News* 5/19/96.

7 Evan Mandery, *The Campaign: Rudy Giuliani, Ruth Messinger, Al Sharpton, and the Race to Be Mayor of New York City,* Boulder: Westview, 1999: 39.

8 *Newsday* 2/15/97.

9 *New York Post* 1/21/97.

10 John Avlon, *Independent Nation: How the Vital Center is Changing American Politics,* New York: Harmony Books, 2004: 307.

11 Ibid.

12 *New York Post* 7/12/97.

13 *New York Times* 7/18/97. Messinger's belated recognition of fiscal realities did nothing to endear her to the city unions. When she remedied her moves toward fiscal conservatism with talk of achieving parity with the higher salaries of suburban teachers and police-officers, the *Times* again took a shot across her bow: "The talk about parity with the suburbs may just be Ms. Messinger's attempt to mend her bridges with a little old-fashioned Democratic pandering. If so, she is playing right into conservative claims that liberals can no longer govern New York City."

14 *New York Post* 10/4/97. For all his talk about "poverty pimps," Koch made political peace with the social service industry because its leaders, like Ramon Velez of the Bronx, were such a rich source of votes. Giuliani followed the same script as Koch. He sent city money to the poverty empire of Velez—once a subject of a Giuliani-led criminal investigation—in return for political support.

15 Ibid.

16 *Daily News* 11/20/95.

17 *Village Voice* 10/21/97. The author and his family live in the 70th Precinct.

18 *New Yorker* 9/8/97.

19 Mandery 126, 272.

20 *New York Times* 9/21/97; *New York Post* 9/21/97.

21 Kirtzman 293; *New York Post* 6/19/03.

22 Kirtzman 317.

23 *Washington Post* 9/9/97.

24 *New York Observer* 10/27/97; Mandery 265; *New York Magazine* 11/17/97.

25 *New York* 11/17/97; *New York Post* 11/20/97. Clintonian moderation was just a passing phase for Ferrer, who reappeared in 2001 as Sharpton's candidate for mayor.

26 *New York Post* 9/20/97. Even before the results were in, Sharpton, who had given Messinger only token support, was railing against the mayoral ambitions of City Comptroller Alan Hevesi, a Democrat from Queens who was on good terms with Giuliani and who, like Sharpton,

had given Messinger only token support. The Rev denounced Hevesi as a "little Giuliani-lite," a crack Ferrer would repeat during his own 2001 mayoral campaign. Hevesi's real offense was to say that "Sharpton has exploited anger and hatred." Sharpton said he planned to call a black and Latino summit within a week to decide how to punish Hevesi before he would be willing to rally his supporters behind Messinger. "Progressive Democrats need to meet before I make another step. We've got people on the ticket that have openly [collaborated] with Rudy Giuliani."

27 *Village Voice* 10/21/97.

Part III
Chapter 15

1 *Daily News* 12/20/97.
2 The author was present as Clarke was interviewed by radio reporters following the address.
3 *New York Times* 12/20/98.
4 *New York Times* 1/13/98.
5 *Daily News* 1/13/98.
6 Ibid.
7 *New York Post* 9/25/96.
8 *New York* 1/26/98; *New York Post* 5/21/98.
9 *New York Times* 8/12/98; *Daily News* 9/12/98.
10 *New York Post* 8/7/98.
11 *Daily News* 8/12/98; *New York Post* 8/27/98; *Daily News* 8/27/98.
12 *New York Post* 8/18/98.
13 *Daily News* 6/2/98.
14 The preceding paragraphs draw heavily on Neil Sullivan, *The Diamond in the Bronx: Yankee Stadium and the Politics of New York*, Oxford: Oxford University Press, 2001.
15 *New York Times* 6/18/98; *Gotham Gazette* 9/12/01; *New York Times* 6/15/98.
16 *New York Times* 6/15/98; Murray Weiss, *The Man Who Warned America: The Life and Death of John O'Neill, the FBI's Embattled Counterterror Warrior*, New York: Regan Books, 2003: 191.

Chapter 16

1 *New York Times* 12/6/98
2 Ibid.
3 *New York Magazine* 1/25/99.
4 *New York Magazine* 4/19/99.
5 *Village Voice* 2/23/00.
6 *New York Post* 3/7/99.
7 Andrew Kirtzman, *Rudy Giuliani: Emperor of the City*, New York: Harper Collins, 2000: 234.
8 *New York Times* 4/2/99.
9 Kirtzman 244.
10 *The New Republic* 4/19/99.

11 *The National Review* 4/19/99.
12 *New York Post* 4/31/99.
13 Kirtzman 252.
14 *New York Post* 4/18/99; *New York Observer* 4/26/99; Kirtzman 253.

Chapter 17

1 *Newsday* 3/24/95.
2 From the appendix of Benno Schmidt, et al., "An Institution Adrift," 17.
3 *Daily News* 11/23/97. Asked by the author at a forum if there was a tension between open admissions and academic achievement, Sohmer replied that in practice that was the case but in principle the tension could be resolved.
4 *Daily News* 7/14/94.
5 *Daily News* 5/21/95.
6 Municipal Archives, 1/24/98 budget address.
7 Municipal Archives 12/16/03 speech. There was an element of improvement Schmidt didn't mention, but which was immediately visible to visitors to the City College campus in Harlem. In the early 1990s, guests coming to City College's Great Hall (modeled on Oxford's) for evening events saw the campus as a collection of graffiti-ridden decaying buildings. Like much of New York at night, it was largely deserted and scary. A decade later, the graffiti were gone, the buildings had been repaired and visitors to the Great Hall found the welcoming sight of a bustling campus.

Chapter 18

1 *New York Observer* 10/4/99; *Daily News* 9/16/99.
2 *Daily News* 9/16/99; *The National Review* 4/3/00.
3 *Daily News* 9/23/99.
4 *Daily News* 8/8/99.
5 Ibid.
6 *New York Times* 11/16/99.
7 *New York Post* 11/3/99.

Chapter 19

1 Tom Manigold and Jeff Goldberg, *Plague Wars: A True Story of Biological Warfare*, London: Macmillan, 1999: 353-354.
2 Hauer's testimony on 5/19/04 before the 9/11 Commission; Clarke would go on to fame for his 2004 book *Against All Enemies*, an attack on the Bush administration's anti-terror policies. Information from the FBI's John O'Neill led the city to erect barriers and tighten security around the stock exchange, federal buildings and City Hall.
3 Councilman Victor Robles, Chair of the Health Committee, 10/12/99 City Council public hearing.
4 *Newsday*, 3/31/97.
5 *New York Times* 12/14/99.
6 *New York Times* 12/27/99.

Chapter 20

1 *New York Times* 1/14/00.
2 *New York Post* 12/11/00. Earlier in the week, Giuliani had told an Association for the Betterment of New York breakfast that Vallone deserved to "share the credit for the $3 billion plus in tax cuts since 1994."
3 Glynis Daniels and Michael Schill, "The State of New York Housing and Neighborhoods, 2001," New York University Furman Center for Real Estate and Public Police.
4 *New York Observer* 12/17/01.
5 *New York Observer* 1/10/02. Less visible but very present were NAS-DAQ, MTV, Starmedia Network, Oxygen.com and Earthweb.
6 *New York Observer* 3/13/00.
7 *New York Post* 2/29/02; *Newsday* 3/3/00.
8 "The Death of Malcolm Ferguson: An Investigative Report," Office of the Bronx District Attorney, June 10, 2000.
9 *New York Post* 3/18/20, 3/20/00, 3/24/00.
10 Elizabeth Kolbert, *The Prophet of Love and Other Tales of Power and Deceit,* New York: Bloomsbury, 2004: 43. When Hanover won a court order preventing Nathan from attending city functions at Gracie Mansion, Giuliani's divorce lawyer, Raoul Felder, attacked Hanover as an "uncaring mother" with "twisted motives."
11 Ibid.
12 *New York Times* 4/1/00. "Antidrug Tactics Exact Price On a Neighborhood, Many Say." The neighborhood on which Giuliani supposedly tried to impose the mores of Mayberry is the author's own. As written by the pen of *Times* reporter David Barstow, a small-time heroin dealer becomes a friendly family man unfairly hounded out of the city by Giuliani's intolerance. The gullible Barstow referred to one alleged victim of police harassment as a "gregarious youth," though he was, in fact, a notorious thug wanted for slashing a man's throat on the subway.
13 *Newsday* 6/17/00.

Chapter 21

1 For a discussion of the courts and prisoners' rights, see Ross Sandler and David Schoenbrod, "Prison Break," *City Journal,* Summer 1996.
2 The previous paragraph draws on Kerik's memoir, *The Lost Son: A Life in Pursuit of Justice,* New York: Regan Books, 2001: 257, 262, 274-277. Kerik doesn't mention either the affair he had with a corrections employee or his personal connections to shady characters.
3 *New York Post* 8/20/2000. Questions, however, were raised about his use of the revenues from a tax-exempt foundation used to collect rebates from cigarette purchases by prisoners. The use of the money—much of which was ear-marked for counseling violent prisoners—was never clearly accounted for. *Daily News* 2/9/03.
4 Julia Vitullo-Martin, "Commissioner Bernard Kerik and the Three Priorities," *Gotham Gazette* 3/3/01.

5 Julia Vitullo-Martin, "The Heritage of Amadou Diallo," *Gotham Gazette*, 1/25/01.
6 *New York Post* 6/24/01.
7 *New York Post* 5/01/01.
8 *Chicago Tribune* 12/21/01; *Newsday* 6/29/01.
9 Jennifer Wynn, *Inside Rikers: Stories from the World's Largest Penal Colony*, New York: St. Martin's, 2001: xii, 35. In a revealing quote about the pressures of living in a meritocracy, one inmate told Wynn, "I live in the best fuckin' country in the world and I keep asking myself, Why can't I make it?"
10 *Daily News* 2/11/1998. Welfare reform in Wisconsin had begun in 1986 with bipartisan backing that included Republican Governor Tommy Thompson and Milwaukee's reform Democratic Mayor John Norquist. The bipartisan deal was based on a combination of tough work requirements and generous financial and in-kind support to bring people into the workforce. Strongly paternalist, the program worked with clients to reshape their lives so they could re-enter mainstream society. A good account of the Wisconsin program and its paternalism can be found in Larry Mead, "The Culture of Welfare Reform," *The Public Interest*, Fall 2002.
11 Jan Rosenberg and Fred Siegel, "Welfare Reform So Far," *The New Democrat*, January/February 1999.
12 Some social service groups like the Doe Fund welcomed the change in outlook. Genuinely committed to helping the poor, they thrived under the new result-oriented rules. JobStat, Turner's version of CompStat, measured the performance of the non-profit social service contractors. JobStat is discussed in Swati Desai and Michael Wiseman's "Inside the Help Factory: Public Assistance, Process, Outcome and Opportunity in New York City," a paper prepared for the Association for Public Policy and Management's November 2002 conference.
13 Even the usually astute Moynihan predicted calamity in a speech before the Senate (reprinted in the 1/11/96 *New York Review of Books* as "Congress Builds a Coffin"). Work was a considerable source of self-respect among former recipients. But these 126 interviews, part of a working paper done for the city by respected social scientists including Lawrence Mead, made too small a sample to satisfy the skeptics, let alone the critics. The study was "Leaving Welfare: Findings from a Survey of Former NYC Welfare Recipients" by Andrew Bush, Swati Desai and Lawrence Mead, HRA Working Paper 98-01 September 1998.
14 Turner was described by welfare expert Douglas Besharov of the University of Maryland as "a fabulous manager." See also Douglas Besharov and Peter Germanis in "Work Experience in NYC: Successful Implementation, Uncertain Impact and Lessons for TANF's Participation Requirements." Besharov and Germanis say that "almost every objective observer agrees that the implementation of NYC's welfare reform program was a tremendous administrative and management accomplishment.... It is widely seen as a model."

15 *New York Post* 8/8/01.

16 Mark Levitan and Robin Gluck, "Mother Work: Employment, Earnings and Poverty in the Age of Welfare Reform," done for the Community Service Society of New York: 3. In a similar vein a 2002 Rockefeller Institute study, "Leaving Welfare Post-TANF," found that of those who left welfare in the late 1990s, "48% of the former recipients considered themselves much better off, and another 23% said somewhat better off. And the ones with jobs had more than twice the income, $1,965 per month, on average as those who went back on welfare."

17 Paul Grogan and Tony Proscio. *Comeback Cities: A Blueprint for Urban Neighborhood Revival.* Boulder: Westview Press, 2000: 13. A similar sentiment came from Joe Hall, the spokesman for a Bronx Community Development Corporation, quoted in a June 4, 1996 *U.S. News & World Report* editorial. Referring to the decline of the Bronx as "the Destruction," Hall insisted that "the only way to get back where we were before the Destruction is to make sure we never again have a reliance on government funding built on social service models—those that create dependency." Revival, he argued, can be built on home-ownership, private-sector jobs and community self-help that minimizes the role of "credentialed professionals."

Chapter 22

1 *New York Times* 8/15/01.

2 NY1 Poll 3/5/01.

3 *New York Times Magazine* 2/11/01.

4 *New York Times* 3/21/01.

5 *Forward* 1/19/01.

6 *New York Times* 6/19/01.

7 *Newsday* 2/15/01; *New York Post* 7/14/01.

8 *New York Post* 2/17/01.

9 *New York Magazine* 2/26/01.

10 Vallone interviewed by Gabe Pressman 9/9/01. Writing in *New York* on 2/26/01, Michael Tomasky described Vallone as presenting "an admirably universalist appeal."

11 1994 "October Plan" issued by the Office of Budget and Management, 3. City spending on Medicaid grew from $2.5 billion dollars in 1998 to $3.7 billion in 2002. In the same period the city went from 21 to 30 percent of its population on Medicaid.

12 *New York Times* 1/28/2000.

13 Jim Chapin memo to the Green campaign.

Part IV
Chapter 23

1 *New York Magazine* 10/15/01.

2 9/11 Commission hearing held in New York on 5/18/04. The announcement came from the protocols established after studying the problems of the 1993 World Trade Center evacuation. In 1993 many of the

injuries had been caused by the rush to evacuate, which also hampered emergency workers. In the future, the Port Authority, which owned the Towers, decided it would "defend in place" against fires rather than evacuate as quickly as possible. But the lessons of 1993 did not apply to the situation in 2001.

3 Giuliani testimony before 9/11 Commission, 5/19/04. In the wake of the 1993 attack the Port Authority had spent $100 million on upgrading its security measures. In 1993 cops and firefighters had a hard time communicating by radio, so the PA had installed a repeater system that amplified and extended the range of radio signals. In what was the most important communication failure on 9/11, human error led the firefighters to assume that the repeater wasn't working in the South Tower, thus limiting their ability to communicate with their commanders. When the words MAYDAY, MAYDAY, MAYDAY were sent out at 9:00 as a signal to evacuate, some of the firefighters who had been climbing the stairs didn't hear the call.

4 Rudolph Giuliani, *Leadership*, New York: Hyperion, 2002: 6.

5 *Daily News* 5/20/04.

6 *Leadership*, 11; *New Yorker* 9/17/01.

7 Steven Cohen, William Eimicke and Jessica Horan, "Catastrophe and the Public Service: A Case Study of the Government Response to the Destruction of the World Trade Center," *Public Administration Review* September 2002; *New York Post* 9/9/02.

8 Andrew Kirtzman, *Rudy Giuliani: Emperor of the City*, New York: Perennial, 2002: 303-304.

9 *New Yorker* 9/17/01; *Washington Post* 5/21/04. Roy Jenkins, a left-of-center British politician who had written a biography of Churchill that had influenced Giuliani, told *Time* that, in the aftermath of 9/11, "What Giuliani succeeded in doing is what Churchill succeeded in doing in the dreadful summer of 1940: he managed to create an illusion that we were bound to win."

10 *Washington Post* 5/21/04.

11 *New Yorker* 10/8/01; *New York Times* 9/20/01.

12 *Washington Post* 8/14/01.

13 *Time* 1/1/02.

Chapter 24

1 *New York Times* 9/20/01.

2 *New York Times* 10/9/01, 10/30/01.

3 House speaker Dennis Hastert of Illinois found that a $20 billion package "was not an easy sell" among conservative Republicans, many of whom were openly hostile to New York and its interests. Hastert himself complained New Yorkers engaged in an "unseemly scramble" for money, and in fact when applying for the promised emergency 9/11 aid, Governor Pataki sent in what amounted to a wishlist for state projects, many of them upstate and not in the least connected to anti-terror measures or the attack; *New York Post* 8/25/04.

4   *New York Times* 10/10/01.

5   *Newsday* 9/29/01; *New York Times* 9/30/01. Explaining his decision to support an extension for Giuliani, Green unselfishly declared, "There aren't many examples of the greatest criminal act inflicted on a city ever before…. And balancing everything, the most urgent thing was not precedent, but was unity."

6   *Newsday* 10/8/01.

7   *Newsday* 9/29/01.

8   *New York Magazine* 10/8/01; WLIB 10/1/1. Koch was also motivated by an intense personal dislike for Green, who, whatever his failings, responded with honor and integrity to the World Trade Center attack.

9   *Crain's* 10/1/01; *New York Times* 10/4/01. In their first debate Ferrer repeated his promise to use federal recovery money to build up sections of the Bronx and Staten Island. The "danger" of that approach, argued a *New York Times* editorial, is "that Mr. Ferrer's plan would reduce the city's chances of getting needed federal aid." Some Republicans in Congress drew the same conclusion as the *Times*: "There are some people out there who say 'Whoa, this is a chance to get some money,'" Rep. Bill Young (R-Fla.), told the *New York Post*'s Vincent Morris. "We do not want to view this tragedy as an opportunity for more spending," added Rep. Pete Sessions (R-Texas), an influential conservative. "It should not be some kind of open book." *New York Post* 10/11/01.

10 *New York Post* 9/30/01.

11 *Newsday* 10/16/01. Ferrer was saddled with Sharpton and in the public mind that conjured up Tawana Brawley, Freddy's Fire and a host of lesser incidents. The *New York Post* led the way in linking Ferrer and Sharpton in the public mind. One of its cartoons showed Ferrer planting a big wet kiss on the behind of the rotund Reverend. In Brooklyn fliers with the cartoon printed on them were distributed in Jewish neighborhoods.

   The Green TV ads never referred to Sharpton. They warned Ferrer would run a patronage regime that would raise taxes and divide the city. Green's "Can we take a chance?" ad quoted from the *Times* editorial warning that Ferrer's reaction to 9/11 was "borderline irresponsible." One particularly hard-hitting ad was shot in a grainy tone and set to the music from *Jaws*. It asked of Ferrer, "Can we risk this?" Hazel Dukes of the NAACP called the commercial "the height of racism" and a "lynching," adding: "I woke up and thought I was in Mississippi." *New York Post* 10/11/01.

12 *Newsday* 10/30/01.

13 *Newsday* 10/12/01. On election night Green's supporters spontaneously broke into the hoary Sixties chant "THE PEOPLE (brief pause) UNITED (brief pause) WILL NEVER BE DEFEATED." The chair of Green's election night victory party was the raucous Bertha Lewis, the African-American leader of ACORN, a group that had fought against both school and welfare reform. For better or worse it was hard to mistake Green for Giuliani.

14 *Newsday* 10/16/01.
15 *Washington Post* 12/31/01. Bloomberg was compared to outgoing Los Angeles Mayor Richard Riordan, a fellow businessman. But Riordan had long been involved in the civic life of the city, where Bloomberg prior to his run was scarcely involved.
16 *New York Times* 1/18/01.
17 *New York Post* 11/5/01.
18 *New York Post* 11/4/01.
19 *New York Times* 11/11/01.

Chapter 25
1 Bloomberg's 2005 State of the City speech.
2 CNN 10/12/01.
3 *Daily News* 8/31/04.

Appendix
1 These paragraphs have been drawn from Edward K. Spann, *Gotham at War: New York City, 1860-1865*, Wilmington: Scholarly Resources Inc., 2003.
2 This section draws on John C.G. Röhl. *The Kaiser and His Court: Wilhelm II and the Government of Germany*, London: Cambridge University Press, 1994.
3 This new material on a planned invasion was first published in the German paper *Die Zeit* 5/9/02 and then in English in the *Daily Telegraph*.
4 The best source on the Black Tom Explosion is Jules Witcover, *Sabotage at Black Tom: Imperial Germany's Secret in America, 1914-1917,* New York: Workman, 1989.
5 The previous paragraphs are drawn from Michael Dobbs, *Saboteurs: The Nazi Raid on America*, New York: Knopf, 2004.
6 H.G. Wells, *The War in the Air,* New York: Penguin, 1908: 242, 243.
7 Robert Wistrich, "The New Islamic Fascism," *Partisan Review*, Winter 2002.
8 *New York Post* 8/16/2002.
9 E.B. White, *Here Is New York,* New York: The Little Bookroom, 1949: 54.
10 Ian Buruma and Avishai Margalit, *Occidentalism: The West in the Eyes of Its Enemies,* New York: Penguin, 2004: 32; Kenneth Timmerman, *Preachers of Hate: Islam and the War on America,* New York: Crown, 2003: 14.
11 Quotes from material entered into evidence by prosecutor Andrew McCarthy in the Blind Sheik case.
12 *New York Times Magazine* 9/23/02.
13 John Miller and Michael Stone, *The Cell: Inside the 9/11 Plot, and Why the FBI and CIA Failed to Stop It,* New York: Hyperion, 2002: 66.
14 *New York Post* 9/7/02.
15 On Giuliani's immigration policy, see Heather MacDonald, "Keeping New York Safe from Terrorists," *City Journal*, Fall 2001.

Index

abortion, 26, 28, 249, 329
Abrams, Robert, 23, 134n
Abyssinian Baptist Church, 222
Abzug, Bella, 114
ACLU, 19–20
ACORN, 288
ACT UP, 185
Adams, Eric, 79, 104
AIDS, 13, 51, 53, 109, 123
Ailes, Roger, 27
Albanese, Sal, 127, 203
Al Farooq mosque, 340
Al Qaeda, 337
American Federation of State,
    County and Municipal Employ-
    ees (AFSCME), 47, 72, 116,
    121; and privatization, 161
American Federation of Teachers,
    206
America Works, 59–60, 66, 116,
    161
Anastasia, Albert, 6
Andrews, Jim, 195, 207–8
Anemone, Louis, 226
anthrax, 315, 319
Apollo Theater, 232, 271, 272
Arafat, Yasser, 19, 32, 182, 328
Archer, Dennis, 86, 277n
Askins, Barbara, 196
Association for a Better New York,
    74
Auletta, Ken, 32
Avlon, J.P., 303

Babbitt, Bruce, 17
Badillo, Herman, 21n, 79, 80, 124,
    125, 239, 319; and CUNY,
    242–47
Baltimore, 51
Barrett, Wayne, 106
Barrios, Eugenio, 244
Barry, Marion, 205
Barwick, Kent, 42
baseball, 107; Yankees, 184,
    224–25, 249, 251, 319–20
Beacon Schools, 129
Beame, Abe, 7, 9–10, 20, 112, 254,
    323
Beckles, Arlene, 116
Bed, Bath & Beyond, 188
Bell, Daniel, 6
Bender, Bruce, 108–9, 127, 174,
    177, 224, 252
Benenson, Joel, 137
Berman, Herbert, 117, 126,
    127–28, 138, 315n
Bernard, Richard, 57
Bernstein, Blanche, 160, 162
bin Laden, Osama, 301, 338, 339,
    340
Bin Talal, Prince Alwaleed, 327
Blackburne, Laura, 73
blackouts, 258
Black Tom attack, 334–35
Blair, Tony, 204
Blockbuster Video, 197–98
Bloomberg, Michael, 292, 312,
    314, 315; benefit from 9/11,
    319–20; inconsistencies, 325;
    mayoral campaign, 318–21;
    media ownership, 317–18;
    Olympics plan, 326; party

369

change, 317; paternalism, 325;
philanthropy, 318; policing, 324;
policy changes, 324–26; short-
comings, 319; on Wall Street,
318; welfare policy, 324
Blumenthal, Joel, 17
Board of Education, 78, 90, 111,
126, 271; abolition of, 295, 325;
and budgets, 115–16, 119, 124,
166; and corruption, 166, 167;
and local autonomy, 114–15;
trimming of, 113
Board of Estimate, 21, 31, 35–36,
37n, 83, 89, 160, 276
Boesky, Ivan, 25
Borelli, Joe, 226n
Boston, 87, 94, 284
Boston Globe, 150
Bowes, Lee, 59, 66, 161
Boyd, Gerald, 41–42
Boyle, Robert, 173–74
Bradley, Bill, 271, 272
Bradley, Tom, 86
Brandeis, Louis, 58–59
Brandon, John, 104
Bratton, Bill, 62, 92–95, 102, 143,
145, 146–50, 294, 320; "broken windows" policing, 147–48,
237; Catholicism, 186; "CEO
cop," 147; on community rela-
tions, 237–38, 282; on
corruption, 146; and Cosa Nos-
tra, 170; flamboyance, 187;
forced resignation, 184, 186–87,
237; friction with Giuliani,
183–84; Harlem mosque incident, 104–6; likeness to Giuliani,
186–87; and press, 183–84, 187;
"reengineering" of NYPD,
146–49
Brawley, Tawana, 22–23, 106,
222n
Breaux, John, 59
Breslin, Jimmy, 25, 53, 157
Brewer, Gail, 40, 54
Brezenoff, Stanley, 66, 160
Bronx, 44, 156, 210, 272–73; crime

decline, 187, 279; demography,
279; economy, 313n; revival,
290
Brooklyn, 44, 156; Arab/Pakistani
neighborhoods, 340; Canarsie,
20; crime decline, 187; Dumbo
neighborhood, 269; revival,
268–69
Brooklyn Museum, 249–51
Brown, Jerry, 49–50
Brown, Joe, 67
Brown, Lee, 51, 52, 144–45
Brown & Ferris, 171
Bruno, Joseph, 180, 204
Buchanan, Pat, 202
Buckley, William F., Jr., 7
budget, 7, 29, 87–89, 110–22,
131–33, 179–80, 295–97;
competitive bids, 113; council
cooperation on, 125–28; and
crime, 45; Cuomo, 131–32,
153, 174; debt, 2, 4–5, 10, 11,
99, 101–2, 103, 180; Dinkins, 36,
38–39, 45–47, 57, 77–78; federal
aid, 48–49, 53–55, 70, 129–30;
fine collection, 69–70; hospitals,
117–19; infrastructure, 112;
Koch, 11; Kummerfeld Report on,
90–92; La Guardia, 4–5; Lindsay,
9–10; payroll, 102, 120–22, 127,
136, 296; and Port Authority,
174–77; reform efforts, 251–55;
and schools, 110–11, 114–16,
117, 119, 124, 154, 167, 185–86;
social services, 13, 62, 91,
153–57, 206; state aid, 110–11,
112, 131, 135, 137–38; trash
hauling, 172; Vallone vs. Giuliani,
224–25; and Yankee Stadium,
224–25; *see also* taxes
Buffalo News, 135
building permits, 166, 188
Bumiller, Elizabeth, 319
Bush, George H. W., 15, 19
Bush, George W., 227n, 272, 277n,
foreign policy, 328; Kerik nomination, 329–30; reconstruction

aid, 312n; re-election, 328–30; on Sept. 11, 306

Business Improvement Districts, 192–93, 196, 204–5

Butts, Calvin, 18, 157, 222, 272, 273–74

Buy Black Committee, 198

Byrne, Edward, 144

Caldwell, Earl, 79

Cannato, Vincent, 8

Cardillo, Philip, 105

Carey, Hugh, 10, 110–11

Carroll, Sean, 234

Carson, Sonny, 24, 32, 297; Korean grocery boycott, 40–42; prison sentence, 41

Carter, Marjora, 237

Castro, Fidel, 198

Catholicism, 26, 27, 28, 186, 316, 320; and Brooklyn Museum scandal, 249–51; support for Giuliani, 33, 83, 180

Cato, Gavin, 81n

Chambers Paper Fibres, 171

Champy, James, 147

Chapin, Jim, 204, 297

Chapman, Wilbur, 169–70, 195, 196

Cheney, Dick, 329

Chertoff, Michael, 330n

Chicago, 40, 87, 173, 195, 206, 207; crime rate, 145, 215, 284

Chiles, Lawton, 59

Chirac, Jacques, 307

CIA, 226

Citizens Budget Commission, 4, 29, 91, 180, 206, 219, 296–97

city charter reform, 35–36, 83, 85, 89, 101, 160, 252–55

City College of New York, 242–43

City Journal, 60, 62, 72, 88, 220–21

City University of New York (CUNY), vii, 218, 241–47; and budget, 241, 245; English writing test, 244; graduation rates, 242; and high school standards, 243–44; open admissions, 243–44; outreach, 247; racial issues, 242–47; SAT requirement, 246–47; Spanish language, 244; tuition hike, 241; and welfare reform, 241

civil service system, 11, 13, 29, 102; restructuring, 120–22, 206; *see also* municipal employees; public-sector unions

"civility" campaign, 220–21

Civil War, 333–34

Clark, Brian, 302

Clarke, Richard, 257

Clarke, Una, 113–14, 154, 218

Cleveland, 86–87

Clinton, Bill, xv, 49, 50, 52–55, 59, 65, 68, 116, 137, 189, 252, 320; budget issues, 129–30; as centrist, 276; crime bill, 129–31; on Diallo case, 236; on "entrepreneurial government," 70; impeachment, 228, 229, 232; race card, 80; re-election, 201–2; "Stimulus Package," 54; tax increases, 54–55; triangulation, 204; welfare reform, 162, 201, 289

Clinton, Hillary, 229, 232, 295; Senate campaign, 236, 239, 249, 252, 274, 275; policy agreement, 275–76

Cohen, Brian, 260, 262

Cohen, Neil, 258

Cohen, Richard, 103

Coles, Anthony, 160, 177–78, 184, 241, 242, 305, 306

Collins, Gail, 47

Colon, Rafael, 69

Commentary, 180

Community Preservation Corporation, 190, 268

CompStat (NYPD), 148–49, 216, 238, 294, 340

Con Edison, 258, 262

Conservative Party, 26–27, 82, 83,
    133, 249, 251
Cooper, Sandy, 241
Corley, Gloria B., 115n
Corporation Counsel's Office, 168
Corrigan, Tommy, 340
Cortines, Ramon, 113, 114–16,
    117, 124–25, 154, 281; forced
    resignation, 184–86; "outed,"
    185
Cosa Nostra (the mob), 5–6, 166;
    at Fulton Fish Market, 168–70;
    and Javits Center, 172–74; RICO
    suit, 171–72; and trash hauling,
    170–72
Costikyan, Edward, xi–xii, 63, 124,
    187
Council of Trade Waste Associa-
    tions, 171
Cove, Peter, 59, 66, 161
Craig, Stephen, 62
Crew, Rudy, 204, 270–71
crime, xiii, 8, 11, 12, 13, 19, 67,
    74, 116, 141–50; under
    Bloomberg, 324; in Boston, 284;
    and "broken windows" policing,
    62, 72, 94–95, 147–48, 187,
    192, 237, 284–85, 294, 319;
    and budget, 45; in Chicago, 145,
    215, 284; and civic education,
    142; Clinton bill, 129–31;
    declines in, 149–50, 187, 215,
    233, 238, 283, 284–85; in
    Detroit, 143; Dinkins era,
    42–45, 94–95; Giuliani view of,
    141–42; Harlem mosque inci-
    dent, 104–6, 143; and
    immigration, 284; juvenile vio-
    lence, 103; and Midnight
    Basketball, 129; murder rate, 44,
    45, 99, 143, 149, 215, 276, 279,
    283, 284; Operation Pressure
    Point, 144; panel discussion on,
    141–42; parolees, 284–85; in
    Philadelphia, 279; and "quality
    of life," 143–44; and race,
    43–44, 72, 143, 237–38; "root

causes," 141, 143, 150n, 237;
    and social programs, 141;
    squeegee arrests, 102–3; in
    Times Square, 192; "victimless,"
    77, 143, 147
Crotty, Paul, 191
Crown Heights riot, 76, 81–82,
    144, 145, 170
Cunningham, William, 319
Cuomo, Andrew, 65–66, 316n
Cuomo, Mario, xi, 16, 20, 51, 53,
    113, 129–39, 320; budgets &
    taxes, 131–32, 153, 174; on
    Crown Heights riot, 81; and
    Dinkins, 25, 30, 32, 38, 39, 57,
    77–78, 80; Giuliani's endorse-
    ment, 136–37, 153, 202, 328;
    and Javits Center, 173; loses
    governorship, 138–39, 151–52;
    and MAC, 136; as "philosopher-
    politician," 131; re-election
    campaigns, 133–38; and Sharp-
    ton, 134–35; on teen single
    mothers, 159
Cuomo, Matilda, 135

Daily News. See New York Daily
    News
Daley, Richard, xiv, 40, 48, 87, 195
Daly, Michael, 225
D'Amato, Alphonse, 27, 28, 69,
    134, 137–38, 202, 216; re-elec-
    tion campaign, 224, 228–29,
    231; and Sharpton, 222
Daniels, Randy, 197
Davis, Larry (Adam Abdul
    Hakeem), 338–39
Dear, Noach, 205
Death of Common Sense, The
    (Howard), 189
debt, 2, 4–5, 10, 11, 99, 101–2,
    103, 180; see also budgets
decentralization, 62–63, 89
Democratic Leadership Council
    ("New Democrats"), 58–59,
    86–87
Democratic Party, 26, 27, 28, 129,

202; dominance of, 29, 31; mayoral primaries, 70–71, 203–4, 291–97, 309–10, 312–15; national convention, 51, 52–53; race issues, 221–22, 316n; and "Rudycrats," 81, 316

Democratic Socialists of America, 22

Department of Health, 258–59

Department of Housing Preservation and Development, 92, 190

Department of Investigation, 169

Department of Sanitation, 165–66

Detroit, 86, 91, 235

Dewey, Tom, 25

Diallo, Amadou, 234–37, 277, 279, 282; immigration status, 234; officers' trial, 271, 272–73

DiBrienza, Steve, 169, 245, 286–87

DiCarlo, Richard, 69, 81

Dinkins, David, xi–xii, xiii, xiv, 15–25, 29–33, 35–55, 168, 232, 254, 323; and Board of Estimate, 21, 31, 36; as boro president, 20–22; on Brawley hoax, 22–23; budgets, 36, 38–39, 45–47, 70, 77–78, 102; business flight, 29–30, 39, 70; as city clerk, 20; and Clinton presidency, 53–55; as "coalition politician," 22–23, 25, 81; on Cold War, 39; and crime, 42–45, 94–95; and Crown Heights riot, 81–82; in debate, 82; and Democratic National Convention, 51, 52–53; and Diallo case, 236–37, 239; and Giuliani re-election, 202; on "gorgeous mosaic," 16, 32, 37, 80; and Harlem, 21, 195–96; on homelessness, 21, 37; indecision, 37; interest-group offices, 37; lame-duck appointments, 90; on Louima incident, 207; March on Washington, 50–51; on Moynihan, 74; as national figure, 15–17; National Urban Summit, 48; policing,

144–45; race issues, 22–23, 24–25, 32, 40–42, 68, 74; re-election campaign, 68–69, 77–84; reform agenda, 63–64; revenge, 211, 237; scandals, 36, 72–73; staff expansion, 37; taxes, 30–31, 38–39, 112; on "victimless crimes," 77

Dionne, E.J., 306

Disney, 192–93

Dole, Bob, 201–2

Dorismond, Patrick, 273, 293

Dornan, Bob, 202

Dowd, Maureen, 321

Down, Michael, 145

drugs, 13, 21, 51–52, 79, 192, 283; Ferguson shooting, 273; policing, 146; sting operation, 273

Dukakis, Michael, 15, 19

Duke, David, 202

Dykstra, Gretchen, 193

Dyson, John, 101, 107, 108, 109–10, 176, 191, 215

Economic Development Corporation, 109

economy, 38, 47, 99; business climate, 29–30, 39, 70, 110, 112–13; and crime, 141–42, 143, 150n; Dinkins era, 29–30, 39, 70; growth, 188, 215, 233, 266–67; Harlem revival, 197–200, 215, 272; job losses, 29–30, 82, 99, 153, 176, 188; and September 11, 310–11; Silicon Alley, 188, 215, 268, 269; state, 132–33; tech-bubble burst, 291; *see also* budget

Edelman, Marian Wright, 93

education. *See* City University of New York; schools

Education of Sonny Carson, The (film), 41

Edwards, John, 328

Egypt Air Flight 990 crash, 261

Eimicke, Bill, 66

Elder, Elizabeth, 163

Eldridge, Ronnie, 127, 169
emergency command center,
    225–28; ridicule of, 225–26; on
    September 11, 302, 303, 305,
    306
Empowerment Zones, 197–200
Erasmus High School, 166
Eristoff, Andrew, 76n
Exxon, 29, 30

family breakdown, 155–56, 159,
    217, 276
Family Support Act (1988),
    157–58, 160
Farrakhan, Louis, 22, 24, 105, 223;
    Million Man March, 198
Farrell, Denny, 222
Federal Bureau of Investigation
    (FBI), 226, 262, 301, 335; in
    Diallo case, 236; failures of,
    226, 227, 340; on Ressam,
    261–62
Federal Emergency Management
    Agency, 226, 262, 301
Federation of Protestant Welfare
    Agencies, 158
Feinstein, Barry, 38, 47, 65
Felissaint, Gieslaine, 40
Ferguson, Malcolm, 273
Fernandez, Joe, 114
Ferraro, Geraldine, 134n, 222
Ferrer, Fernando (Freddy), 203,
    210, 225, 239, 244; mayoral
    race, 291–95, 297, 309–10,
    312–15; and Sharpton, 293–94,
    316–17, 321
Fields, C. Virginia, 113
Financial Control Board, 10, 47,
    63, 74, 90–91, 101, 102, 111,
    127, 180, 188
Finder, Alan, 53
fine collection, 69–70
Finkelstein, Arthur, 27, 134, 138,
    228
Fisher, Ken, 168–69, 172
Flake, Floyd, 209, 272
Fliegel, Sy, 62

Florio, Jim, 100
Flynn, Ray, 50, 87
Forbes, George, 86
Forbes, James, 104
Forcier, Laurie, 328
Ford Foundation, 61
Foreman, Jonathan, 220–21
Fortuna, Diana, 297
Frankfurter, Felix, 3
Freddy's Fashion Mart, 199, 203–4,
    231
Friedman, Stanley, 12, 26
From, Al, 58
Frucher, Meyer "Sandy," 133
Frum, David, 306
Fulani, Lenora, 320–21
Fulton Fish Market, 168–70, 196
Fyfe, James, 235n

Gambino family, 171
Ganci, Pete, 302
Garcia, Kiko, 51–52
Garth, David, 80, 315, 320
Genn, Colman, 62
Gilder, George, 60
Gingrich, Newt, 151, 202
Girgenti, Richard, 81
Girgenti Report, 81–82
Giuliani, Rudolph: annulment, 31;
    "band of brothers," 89–90; and
    baseball, 107; budget reform,
    75, 87–89; cancer, 274–75;
    Catholicism, 31; divorce,
    234–35, 274–75; farewell
    address, 323–24; as federal
    attorney/prosecutor, 25–26, 27,
    28–29, 69, 90; film portrayals,
    25; inaugural speech, 99–101;
    knighthood, 327; management
    thinking/style, 107–10; mayoral
    campaigns, 25–33, 68–72,
    83–84, 201–11; as mayor-elect,
    90–95; and New York Times,
    90, 92; State of the City
    speeches, 116–17, 152–53,
    216–18; at Patterson, Belknap
    and Webb, 90; poll ratings, 119,

180–81, 186, 233, 237; presidential prospects, 215, 219, 329, 330–31; and the press, 182–84; "Reaganism," 119–20; quality-of-life issues, 72, 75–77; Senate race, 254–55, 265–66, 274–75; on September 11, 301–8; staff meetings, 108–9; term extension, 311–14; Vietnam deferment, 31
Giuliani Partners LLC, 327, 329, 330
Gladwell, Malcolm, 93–94
Glazer, Nathan, ix–x, 11, 63, 92
Godfather, The, 7
Goetz, Bernie, 18
Golden, Harrison, 23n
Golden, Marty, 245
Goldsmith, Steve, 87, 130, 227
Goldstein, Mathew, 246
Goodling, Bill, 130
Goodman, Roy, 28, 29, 69
Gore, Al, 19, 53, 229, 277n; at Apollo Theater debate, 271, 272
Gorton, Slade, 304
Gorumba, Diane, 308
Gorumba, Michael, 308
Gotbaum, Victor, xiv, 9, 90
Gottehrer, Barry, 8
Governing magazine, 197
Grammy Awards boycott, 219
Grand Council of Guardians, 95
Granger, Elie, 76n
Great Depression, ix, xiv, 58, 141, 157
Great Society, 48n, 154, 197
Green, Mark, 53–54, 85–86, 119–20, 123, 157, 171–72, 216, 218, 222, 239; on Giuliani term extension, 312–14; mayoral race, 239, 253, 291–92, 294–95, 297, 309–10, 312–17, 319–21; and Public Advocate's office, 253–54; and Sharpton, 316–17
Green, Mike, 219
Greenspan, Alan, 294

Greenwood Job Placement Center, 285, 288
Griffith, Michael, 18
Gross, Michael, 67
Gunn, David, 94
Gurwitt, Rob, 197

Hammer, Michael, 147
Hammett, Bill, 60–61
Hanover, Donna, 27, 234–35, 274–75
Harari, Freddy, 199
Harding, Ray, 109, 174, 237, 249
Harlem, 189–92, 195–200; Castro visit, 198; crime rates, 150, 189–90; Empowerment Zone, 197–200; entrepreneurship in, 190, 191; Freddy's Fashion Mart, 199; home ownership plan, 190–92; Khalid Muhammad, 223–24; Korean businesses, 198; mosque incident, 104–7, 143; presidential debate, 271–72; Salem Baptist Church, 104; "second renaissance," 200, 215, 272
Harlem machine, 21, 22, 197–200, 245, 286
Harrington, Michael, 21
Harris, Lou, 73, 74
Hartford, 87
Hatton, Beth, 303
Hatton, Terry, 303
Hauer, Jerry, 227–28, 257–63, 294
Hawkins, Yusef, 24
Hayden, Tom, 210n
Health and Hospital Workers Union, 310
Health and Hospitals Corporation (HHC), 72, 75, 78, 117–19; privatization, 113
Heckscher, August, 8
Hellenbrand, Leonard, 124
Helms, Jesse, 202
Hertzberg, Rick, 307
Hevesi, Alan, 32, 180, 216; mayoral race, 291–93, 295–96, 297, 309–10

Hill, Stanley, 47, 116–17, 121
Hitler, Adolf, 336
Hoffman, Abby, 8
Hogue, Larry, 209n
Holtzman, Elizabeth, 87–88,134n
Home, Philip, ix
homelessness, 21, 37, 42, 51, 65, 76–77
Hooks, Ben, 51
Hoover, Mark, 285, 286–87, 288
Horton, Ray, 29
Hostos Community College, 242, 244
housing: abandoned, 93–94; divest-ment of, 189; Nehemiah program, 267, 268; ownership, 266, 268, 271; rehabilitation, 12; rent control, 91, 93; 204; and welfare subsidies, 11n; *see also* homelessness
Housing Authority Police, 122, 177
Houston, 32
Howard, Philip, 189
Human Resources Administration, 72
Hunt, Leslie, 55
Hussein, Saddam, 259, 330n
al-Husseini, Haj Amin, 336
Hyman, Seymour, 243

Ianello, Mattie "The Horse," 171
Ickes, Harold, 82, 252
immigrants, 73, 158–59, 267; African vendors, 195; and crime, 284; sanctuary policy, 340; and welfare, 201, 288
Immigration and Naturalization Service, 340
inaugural speech, 99–101
Indianapolis, 87, 227
infrastructure, 74, 112
Iraq, 100–1n
Israel, 327

Jackson, Jesse, 24, 50, 211; and Arafat, 19, 32; and Diallo case, 236; and Dinkins campaign, 80; DLC convention, 58, 59; on Giuliani, 32, 119; presidential campaign, 17–18, 19, 22
Jackson, Maynard, 48
Jacob Javits Convention Center, 172–74
Jacobs, Jane, 268
Jacobson, Michael, 280, 281–82
James, Henry, ix
Jang, Pong Ok, 40
jaywalking, 219–21
Jersey City, 39, 87
Jews, 180, 210, 316, 336; bias crime against, 276; vs. blacks, 81, 199–200; as terrorism tar-gets, 226n
Johnson, Brad, 134
Johnson, Lyndon, 48n, 59, 60, 197, 329
Jones, Billy, 118
Jones, Leland, 202–3

Kagann, Steven, 88n
Kahane, Meir, 100, 226, 338
Kallstrom, James, 173, 262
Kamarck, Elaine, 59, 65
Kane, Jerry, 282
Kaplan, Fred, 150
Kaufman, Ron, 231
Keilin, Eugene, 101, 117, 120–22, 136
Kelling, George, 62, 63, 72, 94–95, 233–34
Kelly, Ray, 82, 95, 101n, 102, 145, 324
Kelly, Sharon Pratt, 141
Kemp, Jack, 201
Kempton, Murray, 167
Kennedy, Edward, 32
Kennedy International Airport, 175, 177
Kerik, Bernard, 184, 280–84; com-munity relations, 282–83; and Homeland Security, 329–30; Medal of Valor, 280; police accountability, 283; Rikers Island management, 280–82;

scandals, 330–31; on September 11, 302–3, 305n
Kerner Commission, 19, 242
Kerrison, Ray, 27
Kerry, John, 327–28
Kessner, Thomas, 3, 5
Khalid Muhammad, 223–24, 232, 293
Kharfen, Michael, 50
Kiley, Robert, 94, 101, 271
King, Larry, 309
King, Rodney, 50
Kings County Hospital, 117, 118–19
Kirtzman, Andrew, 125, 127, 237, 304
Klein, Joe, 59, 75, 184
Klein, Joel, 325–26
Klinghoffer, Leon, 182
Koch, Ed, 1, 10–13, 17, 18, 26, 28, 29, 48, 80, 168, 179, 210, 254, 313–14; on Brawley episode, 23; budget, 11, 111; crime, 11, 12, 13; on Dinkins, 24; on emergency command center, 226; on Giuliani, 182, 205; and Harlem, 196, 197; on homelessness, 21; and housing, 94n; and middle class, 92; Parking Violations Bureau scandal, 65, 73; on police merger, 177; and public-sector jobs, 13, 136; racial policies, 18–19; and riots, 18; and Sharpton, 232; social services, 13; taxes, 112; welfare reform, 160
Kolbert, Elizabeth, 225, 226, 274–75
Koreans, 40–41; Harlem businesses, 198
Kotkin, Joel, 269
Kramer, Marcia, xiii, 117
Kuby, Ron, 339
Kudlow, Lawrence, 72
Kummerfeld Report, 90–92, 120, 219, 296

Kunstler, William, 338–39
Kuttner, Bob, 59

labor unions. *See* public-sector unions
Laboratories of Democracy (Osborne), 58
Lackman, Abe, 108–9, 111, 115, 118, 127; civil service restructuring, 120–22; on police merger, 177
La Guardia, Fiorello, ix–x, xiv, 1, 2–5, 6, 36, 39, 48, 63, 81, 84, 156, 168, 323, 325, 326; anti-business, 4; budget, 111, 125; on disorderliness, 220–21n; and FDR, 3–4, 5, 54; legacy, 11, 26; paternalism, 2–3; spending, 4–5
LaGuardia Airport, 175, 177
Lane, Eric, 36n
Lane, Maureen, 158
Lanier, Robert C., 130
Larkin, Richard, 91–92, 101–2
Lategano, Cristyne, 183, 185
Lauder, Ron, 27–28, 69, 319
Lazio, Rick, 249, 275
Leadership (Giuliani), 327
Leake, Joe, 105
Lee, Spike, 24
Legal Aid Society, 281
Lehman, Arnold, 250–51
Lehman Brothers, 39
Leichter, Franz, 154
Letterman, David, 221, 307
Levine, Randy, 90, 121, 161, 184, 185–86, 206
Levy, Harold, 247, 271
Lewinsky, Monica, 275
Lhota, Joe, 107–8, 188, 252, 261, 262–63, 301
Liberal Party, 26–27, 28, 81, 109, 138, 209, 237, 249
Liebling, A.J., ix
Lindsay, John, x, xii–xiii, xiv, 1, 7–10, 23, 27, 48, 60, 80, 81, 197, 317, 323, 325; and Kerner Commission, 242; on murder of

policeman, 105; and race, 8;
  taxes, 112
Lloyd, Emily, 123
Local Initiative Support Corpora-
  tion, 192
Logan, Andy, 80
London, Herb, 133
Long, Mike, 249
Los Angeles, 86, 206, 209–10, 261;
  riots, 50–51, 86
Losing Ground (Murray), 60
Louima, Abner, 206–8
Lucchese family, 171
Luntz, Frank, 239, 319
Lupica, Mike, 225
Lynch, Bill, 23, 39–40, 50, 52, 83,
  239, 297, 317

Macchiarola, Frank, 62
Machiavelli, Niccolò, xii, xiii, xiv,
  121, 159–60, 218
MacLaine, Shirley, 71
MacMahon, Lloyd, 71, 108
Maddox, Alton, 22–23
Maier, Henry, 57
Main, Tom, 160
Malcolm X, 105
Maloney, Andrew, 171
Mandela, Nelson, 53
Mandery, Evan, 203, 208
Manhattan Institute for Policy
  Research, 60–65, 283
Manton, Tom, 71
Maple, Jack, 146, 147, 148, 150n
Marlin, George, 82–83, 175
Marshall, Helen, 246
Marshall, Will, 58
Mason, C. Vernon, 22–23, 106
Mason, Jackie, 32
Massing, Michael, 150n
Mastro, Randy, 168–70, 172, 173,
  184, 224, 252, 253
Matthews, Jolena, 195
mayoral campaigns, 25–33, 68–72,
  75–84, 201–11; Democrat pri-
  maries, 70–71, 203–4, 291–97,
  309–10, 312–15; Green vs.

Bloomberg, 316–21; race issues,
  78–81, 83–84, 134–35, 293,
  297, 316n
Mayoral Committee on the Status
  of Women, 114
Mayronne, Richard, 192
McCabe, Kevin, 127
McCain, John, 328, 329
McCall, Carl, 316n
McCarthy, Andrew, 89, 227
McGoldrick, Joseph, 4
McGovern, George, 27
McKnight, John, 155n
McLaughlin, Megan, 158
McManus, Jimmy, 205
McNickel, Chris, 12
McPhail, Sharon, 86
Mean, Larry, 62
Medicaid, 91, 110, 116, 130, 205,
  296
Meese, Ed, 25
Menino, Thomas, 87, 141
Merrill Lynch, 29, 39
Messinger, Ruth, 21–22, 25, 53–54,
  66, 202–6; and Citizens Budget
  Commission, 206, 219; mayoral
  campaign, 21–22, 202–11; and
  Sharpton, 221–22, 293; wealth,
  204
Metropolitan Transportation
  Authority, 73, 126, 174,
  176–78, 219, 271
Meyers, Michael, 223, 283
Michael, Philip, 38, 47
Midnight Cowboy, 192
Milken, Michael, 25, 27
Miller, John, 183–84, 226n, 339
Million Man March, 198
Milwaukee, 51, 57–58, 87; school
  vouchers, 270
Miranda, Louis, 119
Mirrer, Louise, 246–47
Missionaries of Charity, 189
mob. *See* Cosa Nostra
Molinari, Guy, 69, 89, 137
Mollen, Milton, 145
Mollenkopf, John, 38

Mone, Larry, 61
Moran, Richard, 141
Morgan, J.P., 2, 4
Morgenthau, Robert, 165–66, 168, 171–72
Morris, Dick, 204, 210, 294, 319
Moses, Robert, 2, 8, 112
Muslim Brotherhood, 337–38
Moss, Mitchell, 61, 270
Moynihan, Daniel Patrick, x, xii, 49, 55, 74–75, 76, 103, 129–30, 150, 152, 203n, 231; on family breakdown, 155; leaves Senate, 249; and Sharpton, 134–35; welfare reform, 157, 159, 160
Muhammed, Vergie, 185
Mumia Abu Jamal, 237
Municipal Assistance Corporation (MAC), 10, 45–46, 78, 101, 117, 120, 122, 136
municipal employees, 38, 45–46, 78, 102; downsizing, 64, 102, 117, 120–22; strikes, 46; unionizing, 6–7; see also civil service system; public-sector unions
murder rate, 44, 45, 99, 143, 149, 215, 276, 279, 283, 284
Murphy, Patrick, 105, 143
Murray, Charles, 60, 63

NAACP, 51
Nadler, Gerald, 305
Napoli, Louie, 340
Nasser, Gamel Abdel, 338
Nathan, Judith, 274–75
Nation, The, 84
Nation of Islam, 105–6, 223
National Action Network, 198–99, 293
National Association of Social Workers, 288
National Guard, 262–63
National Journal, 17
National League of Cities, 39
National Security Council, 226
National Urban Summit, 48
Navarete, Presley, 150

neighborhood renewal, 267–70
Neighborhood Youth Corps, 8
Nelson, Lars-Erik, xiii
New Alliance Party, 320
New Amsterdam Theater, 192
New Deal, 2, 3–4, 5, 58, 59, 63, 80; and interest group politics, 132
New Paradigm Society, 59
New York Bar Association, 83
New York Board of Trade, 5
New York City Council, 63, 169, 180; Black and Latino Minority Caucus, 113–14; charter changes, 35–36, 83, 85, 89, 101, 160, 252–55; Committee on Higher Education, 245–46; cooperation by, 89, 116, 125–28; and welfare reform, 160–61
New York City Partnership, 91, 101, 290
New York City Police Department (NYPD), xii, 42, 84, 92, 143–50, 279–85; "broken windows" policy, 62, 72, 94–95, 147–48, 187, 192, 237, 284–85, 294, 319; "civilianization," 122; community policing, 144–45, 237–38, 319; community relations, 282–83; corruption, 143, 145, 146; Diallo incident, 233–39, 282; and Dinkins, 144–45; Dorismond killing, 273–74, 293; federal funds, 130; Ferguson shooting, 273; Harlem mosque incidents, 104–7; information sharing (CompStat), 147–49, 216, 238, 294, 340; Kerik tenure, 280–85; Louima assault, 206–8; merger, 122, 177–78; Operation Pressure Point, 144; race issues, 19, 43, 106, 207–8, 233–37, 272, 283, 293, 294; "reengineering" of, 146–49; Street Crime Unit, 233–36; Tactical Narcotics

Teams, 149; terror investigation, 226, 227–28, 340; Y2K plans, 262

New York Civil Liberties Union, 43, 102, 142, 174, 207, 235

New York Civil Rights Coalition, 223

New York Daily News, xiii, 52, 78, 82, 179, 218, 225, 280, 328; on CUNY, 244; on Diallo case, 237; on jaywalking, 220, 221

New York Fire Department (FDNY), 228, 260; on September 11, 302, 304–5, 307–8

New York Housing Authority, 73

New York Magazine, 67, 75, 104, 138, 149, 200, 210, 219, 232

New York Observer, 210

New York Post, 26–27, 40–41, 45, 280; criticism of Giuliani, 180, 184; on Diallo case, 238–39; pro-Giuliani, 80; on Vallone, 295

New York State Power Authority, 109

New York Stock Exchange, 258

New York Times, xi, xii, 17, 40, 53, 64, 73, 122, 136, 162, 324; on community policing, 144–45; on Diallo case, 236; on Kummerfeld Report, 90, 91, 92; on "Mayberry" mores, 276; pro-Dinkins, 79–80; on Rahman case, 227n

New York Yankees, 90, 184, 224–25, 249, 251, 319–20

New Yorker, 80, 184, 274, 307; on Diallo case, 237; on West Nile virus, 259

Newark International Airport, 175

Newfield, Jack, 155

Newsday, 18, 46, 47, 53, 54, 64, 65, 68, 75, 91, 136, 167, 185, 276–77, 280

Newsweek, 18, 197

9/11 Commission, 304, 305–6n

Nixon, Richard, 48n

Nitzburg, Arthur, 314

Nolan, Catherine, 177

Norman, Clarence, 119

Norquist, John, 51, 57–58, 87, 270

Norris, Eddie, 226n

Nosair, El Sayyid, 226n, 338–40; Giuliani comments on, 339

Noville, Virginia, 167

Obermaier, Otto, 339

O'Brien, John P., 2

O'Dwyer, William, 5–6

Office of Emergency Management, 227–28, 301; anticipating attacks, 257–58; West Nile virus, 259; Y2K preparations, 257, 259–63

Office of Management and Budget, 88

Office of Operations, 88

Off-Track Betting Corporation, 72

Ofili, Chris, 250–51

Ognibene, Tom, 179

O'Hare, Joseph, 90n

O'Keefe, Michael, 51–52, 79

100 Black Men in Law Enforcement, 79

O'Neill, Paul, 261

Operation Pressure Point, 144

Oppenheimer, Robert J., 337

oratory: farewell, 323–24; inaugural, 99–101; "Quality of Life" speech, 75–76; State of the City, 116–17, 152–53, 216–18, 265–66

organized crime. *See* Cosa Nostra

Osborne, David, 58–60, 63, 65–66, 108, 146

Owens, Major, 18

Pagones, Stephen, 222n

panhandlers, 42, 43

Parking Violations Bureau, 65, 73

Parks, Rosa, 41

Parsons, Richard, 93, 108, 109

Pasha, Imam, 196–97

Pataki, George, xv, 131, 216, 222,

231, 232, 310, 312, 319;
budget, 153–54; and CUNY,
244; gubernatorial campaign,
134–38; and Harlem, 197, 198;
on mob influence, 173–74; on
Port Authority, 176; re-election
campaign, 224, 225, 228; on
rent control, 204; tax-reduction,
152, 153
Paterson, Basil, 21, 41
Paterson, David, 41, 223
Patterson, Belknap and Webb, 90
Peace Dividend Network, 39
pedestrian dangers, 219–21
Perez, Rosie, 123
Perine, Jerilyn, 192
Perkins, Bill, 245–46, 286
Perl, Jed, 251
Perry, Carry Saxon, 87
Peruggi, Regina, 31
Peters, Mike, 87
Philadelphia, 158, 206; crime rate,
279; Rendell reforms, 63, 108,
195
Pinkerton, Jim, 59
Podell, Bert, 26
Podhoretz, John, 319
police. *See* New York City Police
Department
Police Benevolent Association, 320
polls: on Bloomberg, 315; Giuliani
approval ratings, 119, 180–81,
186, 233, 237, 253–54, 274, 277,
291; presidential prospects, 329
Pooley, Eric, 104
Port Authority of New York and
New Jersey, 174–78; and air-
ports, 175, 177; origins, 174–75;
and Port Elizabeth, 175; on September 11, 304; successes, 175;
and World Trade Center, 175–76
Powell, Colin, 241
Powell, Michael, 75, 174, 179
Powell, Morris, 196, 197, 198–99
Powers, Peter, 118, 125, 127, 215,
252
presidential campaigns, 52–55,

201–2, 271–72, 328–30; Giuliani prospects, 215, 219, 329,
330–31
Pressman, Gabe, 27
Preston, Richard, 259
Primus, Wendell, 289
Prince, The (Machiavelli), xii, 121
Prince George's County, 235
Prince of the City, The (film), 25
privatization, 64, 65–66, 113, 205;
and corruption, 65; of Harlem
housing, 189; in Philadelphia, 63
Procurement Policy Board, 92
Proscio, Tony, xi, 290
Public Advocate office, 253–54
public-sector unions, x, 6–7, 9,
120–22, 296, 313n; AFSCME,
47, 72, 116, 121; and competi-
tive bids, 113; corrections officer
strike, 46; in Detroit, 86; politi-
cal power, 156–57; and
privatization, 161; severance
package, 120–22, 127, 136; and
Taylor Law, 24, 46, 173, 295;
Working Families Party, 254
Puerto Rican parade, 276
Purdum, Todd, 15, 80
Purnick, Joyce, 162–63, 183

quality-of-life issues, 72, 75–77,
220–21; in presidential campaign, 277n
Qutb, Mohammed, 338
Qutb, Sayyid, 337–38

Raab, Jennifer, 26, 28, 29, 71–72
race issues, x, 8, 10, 18–19, 93,
103–7, 124, 195–200, 221–24,
293; Arabs, 123; and crime,
43–44, 72, 143, 237–38; at
CUNY, 242–44; Diallo incident,
233–39; and Dinkins, 15–16,
22–23, 32, 68, 78; in governor's
campaign, 134–35; Harlem
mosque incidents, 104–6;
Hawkins funeral & protest,
24–25; and Koch, 18–19;

Korean grocery boycott, 40–42;
Louima incident, 207–8; in mayoral campaigns, 32–33, 78–81,
83–84, 293, 297, 316n; and
police, 19, 43, 106, 207–8,
233–37, 272, 283, 293, 294;
and polls, 180; and schools, 186,
271
Rahim, Rayman, 165–66
Rahman, Omar Abdel ("Blind
Sheik"), 226n, 227, 257, 338
Rangel, Charles, 19, 21, 33, 39, 40,
79, 105, 313; Apollo Theater
scandal, 232, 272; and
Bloomberg, 317; and Harlem
machine, 197–200, 245; on
House Ways and Means Com-
mittee, 197–98; on Khalid
Muhammad, 223; sniping at
Giuliani, 104, 106–7, 196; on
welfare reform, 160
Raske, Kenneth, 154–55
Ravitch, Richard, 23n
Reagan, Ronald, 13, 15, 17, 31;
Giuliani likened to, 119–20, 202
Real Estate Board of New York,
170–72
Red Apple Grocery, 40–41
Red Cross, 262
Reengineering the Corporation
(Hammer/Champy), 147
regulations: building permits, 166;
and extortion, 165–66; zoning
codes, 188–89
Reinventing Government
(Osborne), 59, 64–66, 108,
146–47
Reiter, Fran, 109, 138
Rendell, Ed, 63, 108, 130, 131,
195, 277n
rent control, 6, 91, 93, 189, 204
Reppetto, Thomas, 44, 237
Republican Party, 26–29, 61,
201–2, 215n, 216, 249; and
Bloomberg, 317, 319; in city
council, 180; and Clinton crime
bill, 131; Giuliani's status, 231,

327, 328; governor races, 133,
134–38; House control, 151;
and media, 182; national con-
vention, 328–29; presidential
prospects (2008). 329, 330–31;
religious right, 329
Ressam, Ahmed, 261–62
Reynolds, Ann, 241
Rice, Norman, 15–16
Richman, Richard, 268
Rikers Island prison, 123, 280–82;
parolees, 284; strike, 46
Rinfret, Pierre, 133, 319
Riordan, Richard, 86, 131, 210,
277n
riots, 18, 273; Crown Heights, 76,
81–82; Los Angeles, 50, 197;
Rikers Island, 123, 280; threats
of, 103–4, 105; Washington
Heights, 51–52, 76, 79
Rivera, Dennis, 232, 316–17, 320
Rivera, Louis, 273
Riverside Church, 104
Robb, Chuck, 59
Robbins, Harvey, 52, 88
Roberts, Sam, xi, 72, 101
Robertson, Pat, 135
Robinson, James, 30
Robles, Victor, 127
Rockefeller, David, 12, 175–76
Rockefeller, Nelson, 110, 132,
175–76, 325
Rockefeller Foundation, 61
Rohatyn, Felix, 29, 30, 45–47, 78,
122, 311
Roosevelt, Franklin D., 3–4, 5, 54,
58, 63, 157, 335
Roosevelt, Theodore, 3, 58, 334
Rose, Jeffrey, 67
Rose, Joe, 188
Rosenbaum, Marc, 269
Rosenberg, Jan, 238, 285
Rosenfield, Rob, 173
Rothmyer, Karen, 68
Rowland, John, 153
Royal Academy, 250
Royster, John ("Zodiac killer"), 187

"Rudycrats," 81, 316
Russert, Tim, 275
Ruth, Heather, 78

Saatchi, Charles, 250
Sacco & Vanzetti, 333n
Sachar, Emily, 43
Safe Streets/Safe City, 84
Safir, Howard, 187, 193, 224, 228,
    260, 282; on Diallo incident,
    235; public relations, 238–39;
    resignation, 279; Street Crime
    Unit expansion, 233
Salama, Jerry, 191–92
Salk, Jonas, 241
sanctuary policy, 340
Sand, Leonard, 43
Sandler, Ross, 88–89
Santiago, Isaura Santiago, 244
Sarandon, Susan, 236
Saunders, Lee, 313n
Schanberg, Sidney, 44
Schell, Paul, 261n
Schembri, Anthony, 123
Schlesinger, Alvin, 339
Schmidt, Benno, 245–47
Schmoke, Kurt, 51
Schneider, William, 17
Schoen, Doug, 319
schools, ix, x; 184–86, 206,
    235–36; administrative bloat,
    185; Beacon Schools, 129; bilin-
    gual education, 217–18; budgets,
    110–11, 113, 114–16, 117, 124,
    154, 167, 185–86; corruption in,
    115n, 166–67, 271; CUNY, 218;
    lawlessness, 43; local autonomy,
    114–15; merit pay, 270; "pro-
    gressive" curriculum, 325–26;
    Rainbow Curriculum, 82, 114;
    security, 217; social promotion,
    218; teacher quality, 243–44;
    tenure, 270; vouchers, 270, 271;
    see also City University of New
    York
Schrader, Richard, 171–72, 254,
    320

Schulman, Claire, 89, 209, 218
Schumer, Charles, 130, 157, 222;
    Senate race, 224, 228–29, 231;
    and Sharpton, 232
Schundler, Bret, 39, 87
Schwartz, Fritz, 36n
Schwartz, Richard, 66, 155, 161,
    191
Schwartz, Thomas, 90n
Seabrook, Larry, 120
Seabury, Samuel, 36n
Seattle: Space Needle plot, 261;
    WTO riots, 261n
Secret Service, 226
Segal, Lydia, 115n
Segara, Ninfa, 101
Seifman, David, 184
Seigel, Norman, 102
Selver, Paul, 188
"Sensation" exhibit, 250–51, 253
September 11. *See* World Trade
    Center attack (2000)
Serpico, 25
Shange, Sikhulu, 199
Shapiro, Ettie, 67
Sharpton, Al, xi, 8, 19, 24, 41, 196,
    221–24, 313–15, 321; Brawley
    episode, 22–23; and Crew, 271;
    Crown Heights riot, 81n; on
    Diallo case, 235–37, 239; and
    Freddy's massacre, 203–4; on
    Garcia shooting, 52; and Green,
    316–17; and Hevesi, 293; and
    Koch, 232; and Louima, 207–8;
    mayoral campaign, 203–4,
    207–8, 222; National Action
    Network, 198–99, 293; power
    of, 231–32; presidential debates,
    272; revenge plans, 211; Senate
    campaign, 134–35
Shaw, Marc, 111
Shefter, Martin, 2
Sheinkopf, Hank, 223n, 293–94,
    297, 316
Sheirer, Richard, 301–2
Ship Without a Captain, A, 92
Shipp, E.R., 196

Siegel, Al, viii
Siegel, Fred, 62, 63
Siegel, Norman, 142, 174
Silicon Alley, 188, 215, 268, 269
Silver, Sheldon, 101, 110–11, 120, 174
Silver, Shelly, 271
Silverman, Eli, 148, 149
Silverstein, Larry, 176n
Sinatra, Frank, 71
Skurnick, Jerry, 154
Sleeper, Jim, 78
Smith, Al, 5, 168
Smith, Roland, 199
social services, 13, 62, 91, 156–57, 206; Dinkins on, 45, 84; vs. police force, 84; *see also* welfare
Sohmer, Bernard, 243
SoHo, 188
Speer, Albert, 335
Spiegelman, Art, 237
Spigner, Archie, 127
squeegee arrests, 102–3
Stancik, Edward, 167, 271
Standard & Poor's, 91, 101, 102
Starr, Roger, 62
State of the City address, 116–17, 216–18, 265–66
Staten Island secession movement, 83
Steed, Herbert, 151
Stein, Andrew, 22, 46, 61, 63, 65–66, 68, 103; as mayoral candidate, 69–71
Steinbrenner, George, 225
Steinfels, Margaret O'Brien, 251
Steisel, Norman, 101n
Stelzer, Irwin, 180
Stephney, Bill, 238
Stern, Sol, 61–62, 65, 70, 206
Stone, Michael, 226n
St. Paul's Church, 323
Stuyvesant, Peter, 42, 220n
subways, 43, 94, 95, 130; strike threat, 259–60
Summer of Sam (film), 258
Sunshine, Ken, 239
Sutton, Percy, 21, 31

Tammany Hall, ix, 1, 2, 4–7, 156–57
taxes, 4, 5, 7, 88n, 91, 152, 153, 180; Clinton hikes, 54–55; cuts, 72, 112–13, 266; Dinkins, 38–39, 46, 57
Taylor Law, 24, 46, 173, 295
Teamsters, 38, 47, 65
Teele, Arthur, Jr., 141
terrorism, 227, 333–40; anthrax, 315, 319; Confederate attack, 333–34; drills, 301–2; German WWI attack (Black Tom), 334–35; Kenya embassy bombing, 301; in Middle East, 328; Puerto Rican bombings, 333n; Space Needle plot, 261; Tokyo subway attack, 227, 261; Wall Street attack (1920), 333n; Y2K drills, 260–63, 303; *see also* World Trade Center attack (1993); World Trade Center attack (2000)
Terrorist Threat Integration Center, 227n
Third Street Men's Shelter, viii
Thompson, Bill, 315n
Tierney, John, 181
Time, 149, 265; Bratton cover, 187
Times Square, 192–93, 215, 269–70; New Year's Eve (Y2K) celebration, 262–63, 265
Timoney, John, 146
Tokyo subway attack, 227, 261
Tomasky, Michael, 77, 84, 200, 210, 232
Torres, Jose, 80
Towns, Ed, 209, 211
Trade Waste Commission, 172
Transit Police, 122, 148, 177
trash hauling, 170–72
Travis, Jeremy, 144
triangulation, 205–6
Tugwell, Rexford, 3, 5
Turner, Jason, 284–88, 289n, 292

United Federation of Teachers, 23, 271

United Pentecostal House of Prayer, 198–99
United Seafood Workers, Smoked Fish and Cannery Union, 169–70
U.S. Civil Rights Commission, 236
U.S. Conference of Mayors, 13, 39, 54
U.S. Department of Justice, 90, 236, 339; Giuliani in, 25–26, 28–29
U.S. News and World Report, 200
U.S. Tennis Center, 90

Vallone, Peter, xv, 45, 46, 63, 74, 109, 216, 222, 287; as ally, 89, 116, 123, 125–27, 169, 266, 309; on budget, 224–25; on charter reform effort, 251–54, on emergency command center, 226; gubernatorial race, 224–25, 228; mayoral race, 291–92, 295, 297, 309–10; on MTA, 176; on Port Authority, 174–75; on teacher merit pay, 270
Verizon, 262
Viacom, 192
Vigilante, Richard, 62
Village Voice, 26, 67, 77, 106
Vitullo-Martin, Julia, 282
Von Essen, Thomas, 260n, 302–3, 305
von Mantey, Eberhard, 334
Voting Rights Act, 36

Wachner, Linda, 108
Wagner, Bobby, 62, 80
Wagner, Robert, Jr., 6–7, 37, 72
Walentas, David, 269
Walker, Jimmy, 1–2, 36, 74, 154
Walker, Wyatt T., 106
Wall Street Journal, 17, 27
Wallace, George, 18, 32, 119
Wallach, E. Robert, 25
Ward, Ben, 18–19, 105, 143–44, 148
Washington, D.C., 84, 180; police in, 235

Washington, Harold, 84, 207
Washington, Rudy, 106, 169–70, 196; on September 11, 303
Washington Heights riot, 51–52, 70, 76, 79, 105, 144, 258, 283
Washington Post, 103, 129
Watkins, Brian, 44
Wealth and Poverty (Gilder), 60
Webb, Wellington, 277n
Weisbrod, Carl, 268
Weiss, Murray, 238–39
welfare, xiii, 8, 9, 11, 74, 87, 92, 99, 103; administration jobs, 155–56; alternatives to, 286; under Bloomberg, 324; and budgets, 153–56; and Clinton, 162, 201, 289; eligibility reviews, 162; expansion, 153, 157; and family breakdown, 155–56; fraud, 151, 154, 162; for immigrants, 201; Job Centers, 285–86; labor force participation rates, 158, 159; reform, 60, 62, 66, 113, 151–63, 201, 217, 241, 285–90; roll reduction, 216, 284, 285; Safety Net program, 287; in Wisconsin, 158, 285, 289n; Work Experience Program, 161; work requirements, 62, 116, 157–58, 159, 160, 161–62, 285–88
Wells, H.G., 336
West Nile virus, 259
White, E.B., 337
White, Mike, 48, 86–87
White, Otis, ix
Whitman, Christine, 112, 153
Whitman, Walt, 75
Whyte, William H., 72
Wicks Law, 91
Wigton, Richard, 69
Wilder, Douglas, 14
Wilhelm, Kaiser, 334
Will, George, 103
Wilson, James Q., 62
Wilson, Woodrow, 58
Winfrey, Oprah, 327
Wolfe, Tom, 8, 42, 269

Wolmer, Bruce, 250
Women for Giuliani, 92
Woo, Mike, 86
Wooten, Priscilla A., 115n
Wooten, Queenie, 115n
Work Experience Program, 161
workfare, 62, 116, 157–58, 159,
    160, 161–62, 285–88; oppo-
    nents of, 286–88
Working Families Party, 254
World Trade Center: emergency
    command center, 225–28, 303;
    engineering of, 303n; Port
    Authority control, 175–76; secu-
    rity, 257–58; vacancy rate, 176
World Trade Center attack (1993),
    100, 123, 225, 226–27, 260,
    302, 323, 338, 340; NYPD on,
    226, 340
World Trade Center attack (2000),
    vii–viii, 297, 301–8; economic
    impact, 310–12; evacuations,

304; firefighter losses, 303,
    304–5, 307–8; memorializing,
    324; reconstruction, 311–12,
    319
World Trade Organization, 261n
World War I, 334–35
World War II, 335–36, 337
Wright, Deborah, 92–94, 190–92,
    199–200
Wulf, Mel, 20
Wylde, Kathryn, 11n, 190, 197

Yankee Stadium, 90, 224–25, 228,
    326
Yankees, 184, 224–25, 249, 251,
    319–20
Yassin, Abdul, 101n
Year 2000 Project Office, 260
Young, Coleman, 86
Young, Dennis, 88, 90, 301
Youssef, Ramzi, 100–1n